criterion confuses the *successful culmination* of scientific effort with *science* itself, and is an unnecessarily harsh criterion that would exclude management, and conceivably all social sciences, from being designated sciences.

Focusing on science as a *process* seems more reasonable. Braithwaite notes:

> the function of science . . . is to establish general laws covering the behaviors of empirical events or objects with which the science in question is concerned, and thereby to enable us to connect together our knowledge of the separately known events, and to make reliable predictions of events as yet unknown (5).

In this broader view, science has as its main purpose the discovery of laws and theories to explain and predict phenomena. The result of this effort is an aspect of science, but not science in its entirety.

This point has implications for management in particular because there is disagreement concerning whether or not management will ever produce a general, unifying theory (2, 13, 14, 20, 24, 33). Consider the "approaches to" or "schools of" management theory listed by Koontz (20). The various "schools" are: management process, empirical, human behavior, social system, decision theory, and mathematical. Can these schools be joined together in a unified theory of management or are they fundamentally irreconcilable?

Many writers are openly pessimistic. Behling typifies their views by asserting:

> that fundamental and inescapable substantive differences do exist among the various approaches to the study of management, that these differences are practically unresolvable, and thus, that a unified theory of management is an impossibility (2).

Others, like Laufer (23) and Suojanen (33), adopt a more optimistic perspective. Laufer draws a striking parallel between the *present* problems of management and the *past* problems of biology. Biologists were able to resolve their discipline-definitional problems only after they successfully reached general agreement on a taxonomy for biological phenomena. *That is, biologists reached a consensus on the nature of their discipline by first reaching a consensus on its scope.* Perhaps the same process would succeed in management.

Laufer further suggests that management theory is amenable to rigorous classification, although the results are likely to be a polythetic arrangement (32). With polythetic classifications, the phenomena in any given class will share many characteristics in any given class will share many characteristics in common, but no individual phenomenon need possess *all* characteristics of the class. Laufer's own taxonomical effort utilizes the pattern followed in the Periodic Table with the functions of management (planning, organization, directing, staffing, control) as a basis. The result is a first step, open to further elaboration and refinement. While the actual taxonomy proposed may be questionable, the proposed procedure remains reasonable and we are well advised to heed his final point: "One purpose of a science is to synthesize the parts . . . into an organized conception of its field of study" (23).

Granting that the *pursuit* of empirically testable laws and theories constitutes scientific activity, three other observations should help clarify the nature of science. First, for a discipline to be characterized as a science in its own right, separate from other sciences, it must have a distinct subject matter drawn from the real world serving as the focal point of investigation. "Distinct" does not imply that other disciplines have no interest in the subject matter. Rather, each science has its own *point of focus*. For example, the science of chemistry focuses on *substances* and attempts to understand and predict phenomena related to them. Physics is also interested in substances but does not *focus* on them. Hence, chemistry and physics (though related) are appropriately referred to as separate sciences.

Consider the following recent definitions of management. Management is:

the process by which the elements of a group are integrated, coordinated, and/or utilized so as to effectively and efficiently achieve organizational objectives (9).

a process or form of work that involves the guidance or direction of a group of people toward organizational goals or objectives (30).

the work of creating and maintaining environments in which people can accomplish goals efficiently and effectively (1).

Distilling these definitions, one finds the *primary* subject matter to be *coordination for goal accomplishment*. Some may limit management to coordination within a distinct organization while others may expand the domain to include coordination activities across organizations and/or cultures, but all recognize coordination of the interdependent parts of organizational systems as essential to management. Other disciplines will overlap with the subject matter of management, for example, psychology, social psychology, organizational behavior, and sociology. But only in management is *coordination* the focal point. The first distinguishing characteristic of a science is that it has its own subject matter (some more distinct than others). With coordination activity as its primary focus, management would seem to fulfill this requirement.

The second characteristic of science rests in the attempt to develop "general laws" which govern the behavior of empirical events. A major assumption of any scientific endeavor is that there are underlying uniformities or regularities interrelating the subject matter. These regularities may not be initially evident, but their eventual discovery produces empirical regularities, lawlike generalizations, and laws. The underlying regularities are necessary because (a) the primary goal of science is to find general explanations of empirical events, and (b) regularities are a necessary component for theory development, since "theories are systematically related sets of statements, including some lawlike generalizations, that are empirically testable". (29).

The question becomes: are there underlying uniformities or regularities interrelating the phenomena comprising the subject matter of management? The answer can be affirmatively based on the following arguments. First, the coordination of activities is one small part of human behavior. Since numerous uniformities and regularities have been observed in other sciences involving human behavior (3), there is no *a priori* reason to believe the same will not be found in behavior focusing on coordination for the purpose of goal accomplishment. The second argument rests in a review of any journal reporting scholarly research in management. While the literature makes one aware of how much has yet to be done, progress has been made in identifying some uniformities. Leadership, motivation, and organizational design are but three of the areas in which significant progress has been made in the last decade.

The final characteristic of science is its method. Management may have a distinct subject matter and there may exist underlying regularities, but we still must decide if the scientific method (the activities and *process* of science) is applicable to management, for as Bunge (somewhat tautologically) suggests, "No scientific method, no science" (7).

Detailed explication of the scientific method is beyond the scope of this note (18), but the cornerstone requirement of the method of science must be mentioned. The word science has its origins in the Latin verb *scire*, meaning "to know." There are many ways *to know* things. The methods of tenacity, authority, faith, intuition and science are often cited (10). The characteristic which separates scientific knowledge from other ways to "know" things is the notion of *intersubjective certification*.

Scientific knowledge, in which theories, laws, and explanations are primal, must be objective in the sense that its truth content must be empirically testable. This ensures that its theories, laws, and explanation will be intersubjectively certifiable since different (but competent) investigators with differing attitudes, opinions, and beliefs will be able to make observations and conduct experiments to ascertain their truth content. As Pierce notes:

> To satisfy our doubts . . . therefore, it is necessary that a method should be found by which our beliefs may be determined by nothing human, but by some external permanency—by something upon which our thinking has no effect. . . . The method must be such that the ultimate conclusion of every man shall be the same. Such is the method of science (6).

Berelson and Steiner (3) have also discussed the scientific method. They propose six distinguishing characteristics:

1. The procedures are public,
2. The definitions are precise,
3. The data-collecting is objective,
4. The findings must be replicable,
5. The approach is systematic and cumulative,
6. The purposes are explanation, understanding, and prediction.

The first five of their characteristics are all subsumable under the *intersubjectively certifiable* criterion.

Can the scientific method by applied to management phenomena? One approach is to suggest that there is no reason to presume that it cannot. Another approach is to recognize that the practice of management is embedded in observable behavior, that this behavior is measurable through public and replicable procedures, and that one can proceed in a systematic fashion for the purpose of understanding and predicting managerial behavior. This is not to say that in every instance the method is appropriately applied. The quality of application depends on the research scholars applying the method. While difficulties abound (measurement being a prime example), it is heartening to note the scientific quality of much recent scholarship in the area.

One further point deserves consideration. We are not suggesting that science lacks any artistic characteristics. Kuhn (21) speaks of the development of scientific knowledge through revolution. While a vast amount of scientific endeavor is considered "normal science," there comes a time when the old "paradigm" no longer suffices and revolutions occur. Rudner (29) labels this process the "logic of discovery." In either case, the process or procedure which generated the new insight may have substantial artistic content. But the testing of whether or not an insight is correct remains in the realm of "science."

To summarize, each science: (a) has a distinct subject matter drawn from the real world; (b) presumes underlying uniformities or regularities that specify relationships among the phenomena studied; and (c) applies inter-subjectively certifiable methods to the study of the subject matter. This perspective can be described as a consensus summation of views on science. For example, Wartofsky suggests that a science is:

> an organized or systematic body of knowledge, using general laws or principles, that it is knowledge about the world; and that it is that kind of knowledge concerning which universal agreement can be reached by scientists sharing a common language (or languages) and common criteria for the justification of knowledge claims and beliefs (36).

CONCLUSION

It is our conclusion that management is a science. Some may disagree. For example, Carlisle (9) asserts that for a discipline to be a science, it must have a systematized body of knowledge and that management presently lacks a generally accepted knowledge base. Without this, management remains an art and experience continues to be the best teacher. Implicit in this argument is the process-product ambiguity noted earlier. Carlisle assumes a narrow definition of science while we argue for a broader view that includes process activities.

Having analyzed three other dimensions of science (existence of a distinct subject matter, presumption of underlying regularities, and application of the scientific method), in each instance we conclude that the discipline of management satisfies these criteria and can therefore appropriately be labeled a science. If disagreement is to continue, this paper provides criteria for focusing the debate. These dimensions will lead to more effective discussion and resolution of the issue.

REFERENCES

1. Albanese, Robert. *Management: Toward Accountability for Performance* (Homewood, Ill.: Richard D. Irwin, 1975).
2. Behling, Orlando, "Unification of Management Theory: A Pessimistic View," *Business Perspectives*, Vol. 3, No. 4 (Summer 1967), 4–9.

3. Berelson, Bernard, and Gary A. Steiner, *Human Behavior: An Inventory of Scientific Findings* (New York: Harcourt, Brace and World, 1964), 16–64.

4. Boettinger, Henry. "Is Management Really an Art"? *Harvard Business Review* (January-February 1975), 54–64.

5. Braithwaite, R. *Scientific Explanation* (Cambridge: Cambridge University Press, 1955), 1.

6. Buchler, J. (Ed.). *Philosophical Writings of Pierce* (New York: Dover, 1955).

7. Bunge, Mario. *Scientific Research I: The Search for System* (New York: Springer-Verlag, 1967).

8. Buzzell, Robert. "Is Marketing a Science," *Harvard Business Review*, Vol. 41 (January-February 1963), 32+.

9. Carlisle, Howard M. *Management: Concepts and Situations* (Chicago: Science Research Associates, 1976).

10. Cohen, Morris R., and Ernest Nagel. *Logic and the Scientific Method* (New York: Harcourt, Brace and World, 1934).

11. Drucker, Peter. *The Practice of Management* (New York: Harper & Row, 1954).

12. Dubin, Robert. *Theory Building* (New York: Free Press, 1969).

13. Frederick, William C. "The Next Development for Management Science: A General Theory," *Journal of the Academy of Management*, Vol. 6, No. 3 (September 1963), 212–219.

14. Greenwood, William T. "Future Management Theory: A Comparative Evolution to a General Theory," *Academy of Management Journal*, Vol. 17, No. 3 (September 1974), 503–513.

15. Gulick, Luther. "Management Is a Science," *Academy of Management Journal*, Vol. 8, No. 1 (March 1965), 7–13.

16. Haimann, Theo, and William G. Scott, *Management in the Modern Organization*, 2nd ed. (Boston: Houghton Mifflin, 1974).

17. Hempel, Carl G. "The Theoretician's Dilemma," in *Aspects of Scientific Explanation* (New York: The Free Press, 1965).

18. Hunt, Shelby D. *Marketing Theory: Conceptual Foundation of Research in Marketing* (Columbus, Ohio: Grid Publishing Co., 1976).

19. Kerlinger, Fred N. *Foundations of Behavioral Research* (New York: Holt, Rinehart and Winston, 1964).

20. Koontz, Harold. "The Management Theory Jungle," *Journal of the Academy of Management*, Vol. 4, No. 3 (December 1961), 174–188.

21. Kuhn, Thomas S. *The Structure of Scientific Revolutions*, 2nd ed. (Chicago: University of Chicago Press, 1970).

22. Kyburg, Henry E. *Philosophy of Science* (New York: Macmillan, 1968).

23. Laufer, Arthur C. "A Taxonomy of Management Theory: A Preliminary Framework," *Academy of Management Journal*, Vol. 11, No. 4 (December 1968), 435–442.

24. Litchfield, Edward H. "Notes on a General Theory of Administration," *Administrative Science Quarterly*, Vol. 1, No. 1 (June 1956), 3–29.

25. Luthans, Fred. "The Contingency Theory of Management," *Business Horizons*, Vol. 16, No. 3 (June 1973), 67–72.

26. Nagel, Ernest. *The Structure of Science* (New York: Harcourt, Brace and World, 1961).
27. Popper, Karl R. *The Logic of Scientific Discovery* (New York: Harper & Row, 1959).
28. Rescher, Nicholas,. *Scientific Explanation* (New York: The Free Press, 1970).
29. Rudner, Richard S. *The Philosophy of Social Science* (Englewood Cliffs, N.J.: Prentice-Hall, 1966).
30. Rue, Leslie W., and Lloyd L. Byars. *Management: Theory and Application* (Homewood, Ill.: Richard D. Irwin, 1977).
31. Simonds, Rollin. "Toward a Science of Business Administration," *Journal of the Academy of Management*, Vol. 2, No. 2 (August 1959), 135–138.
32. Sokal, Robert R., and Peter H. A. Sneath. *Principles of Numerical Taxonomy* (San Francisco: W. H. Freeman, 1963).
33. Suojanen, Waino. "Management Theory: Functional and Evolutionary," *Academy of Management Journal*, Vol. 6, No. 1 (March 1963), 7–17.
34. Urwick, Lyndall F. "Papers in the Science of Administration," *Academy of Management Journal'* Vol. 13, No. 4 (December 1970), 361–371.
35. Walker, J. M. "Paper on the Science of Administration: Comment," *Academy of Management Journal*, Vol. 14, No. 2 (June 1971), 259–265.
36. Wartofsky, Marx W. *Conceptual Foundations of Scientific Thought* (New York: Macmillan, 1968).

SYSTEMS AND ENVIRONMENT

During the last two decades, the advent of the systems approach (systems thinking, systems concepts, or simply systems) has provided a new way of understanding and managing organizations. The systems approach portrays an organization as an open system that depends for survival on a continuous interaction with its external enivronment. The organization as a system "imports" from its external enivronment human and physical resources, transforms them into useful and usable products and services that it "exports" into the environment for consumption and usage. A portion of the end result of the transformation process is used by other systems that assist people in their struggle for survival. Another portion of this output goes into the physical environment to be consumed by other, nonhuman, systems. It is management's overall role and responsibility to maximize the former output while minimizing the latter.

The articles in this section have been selected for the purpose of further amplifying, clarifying, and enhancing understanding of this new and very useful approach.

In the first selection, "Towards a System of Systems Concepts," Russell L. Ackoff atttempts to clarify certain key concepts and terms used in explaining the concept of systems and the systems approach. Ackoff, a pioneer of the systems approach, has provided excellent explanations and definitions of the main concepts of systems in general and of the organization in particular. This much-needed and painstaking process of defining and clarifying concepts is, in Ackoff's words, "frequently treated by scientists as an annoying necessity to be completed as quickly and thoughtlessly

31

as possible." Yet, many a problem in the daily life of managers could be avoided if a careful and thoughtful explanation and definition of the major concepts—a system of concepts—had preceded each proposal for a new plan.

The second selection represents Ian H. Wilson's current thinking on the changes in the organization's external environment and their impact on business management. Wilson, who heads General Electric's corporate strategic planning department, is among the small group of people who pioneered the concept of corporate "monitoring" of the external business environment and the designing of "early warning systems," to alert line executives of impending problems, threats, and opportunities. In this article, Wilson describes how new developments in the external environment are "shaking the seven pillars of business, namely, growth, technology, profit and the market system, private property, management authority, hard work, and company loyalty." His advice to the young manager is, "Think as men of action; act as men of thought."

Social responsibility has been, is, and will continue to be, one of those concepts that seems to have been invented for the purpose of confusing managers. In our third selection for this section, Patrick E. Murphy attempts to set the record straight by tracing the origin and developments of social responsibility literature and organizing it into four early eras of social responsibility (philanthropic, awareness, issue, and responsiveness). He asserts that the term used today (and that should be used in the future) to describe an organization's sensitivity to society is responsiveness because "many organizations appear to be continuously responding, as opposed to reacting, to their social constituencies."

In the last selection, Donald R. Welsh and Robert W. Lee, from the New York office of Peat, Marwick and Mitchell, a large management and accounting consulting firm, demonstrate how conventional planning systems (annual budget systems, capital budget systems, and strategic planning systems) must change to incorporate and accommodate external environmental factors, which affect the design and functioning of these systems. In this article the reader will find an elegant and sophisticated meshing of the rather academic and idealistic demands for increasing the sensitivity of an organization's management to external forces with a sober approach for a better application of systems thinking.

All in all, the articles in this section provide a mixture of academic and practitioner views on the complex and increasingly important issue of the interactions between a system and its environment. It is our contention that managers of the future will be utilizing the systems approach to deal with the way in which their organization interfaces with the external environment.

Russell L. Ackoff

University of Pennsylvania

TOWARDS A SYSTEM
OF SYSTEMS CONCEPTS

INTRODUCTION

The concept *system* has come to play a critical role in contemporary science.[1,2,3] (Churchman, Emery.) This preoccupation of scientists in general is reflected among management scientists in particular for whom the *systems approach* to problems is fundamental and for whom *organizations*, a special type of system, are the principal subject of study.

The systems approach to problems focuses on systems taken as a whole, not on their parts taken separately. Such an approach is concerned with total-system performance even when a change in only one or a few of its parts is contemplated because there are some properties of systems that can only be treated adequately from a holistic point of view. These properties derive from th *relationships* between parts of systems: how the parts interact and fit together. In an imperfectly organized system even if every part performs as well as possible relative to its own objectives, the total system will often not perform as well as possible relative to its objectives.

Despite the importance of systems concepts and the attention that they have received and are receiving, we do not yet have a unified or integrated

Russell Ackoff, "Towards a System of Systems Concepts," *Management Science*, July 1971, pp. 661–671.

set (i.e., a system) of such concepts. Different terms are used to refer to the same thing and the same term is used to refer to different things. This state is aggravated by the fact that the literature of systems research is widely dispersed and is therefore difficult to track. Researchers in a wide variety of disciplines and interdisciplines are contributing to the conceptual development of the systems sciences but these contributions are not as interactive and additive as they might be. Fred Emery[3] has warned against too hasty an effort to remedy this situation:

> It is almost as if the pioneers [of systems thinking], while respectfully noting each other's existence, have felt it incumbent upon themselves to work out their intuitions in their own language, for fear of what might be lost in trying to work through the language of another. Whatever the reason, the results seem to justify the standoffishness. In a short space of time there has been a considerable accumulation of insights into system dynamics that are readily translatable into different languages and with, as yet, little sign of divisive schools of thought that for instance marred psychology during the 1920s and 1930s. Perhaps this might happen if some influential group of scholars prematurely decide that the time has come for a common conceptual framework.

Although I sympathize with Emery's fear, a fear that is rooted in a research perspective, as a teacher I feel a great need to provide my students with a conceptual framework that will assist them in absorbing and synthesizing this large accumulation of insights to which Emery refers. My intent is not to preclude further conceptual exploration, but rather to encourage it and make it more interactive and additive. Despite Emery's warning I feel benefits will accrue to systems research from an evolutionary convergence of concepts into a generally accepted framework. At any rate, little harm is likely to come from my effort to provide the beginnings of such a framework since I can hardly claim to be, or to speak for, "an influential group of scholars."

The framework that follows does not include all concepts relevant to the systems sciences. I have made an effort, however, to include enough of the key concepts so that building on this framework will not be as difficult as construction of the framework itself has been.

One final word of introduction. I have not tried to identify the origin or trace the history of each conceptual idea that is presented in what follows. Hence few credits are provided. I can only compensate for this lack of bibliographic bird-dogging by claiming no credit for any of the elements in what follows, only for the resulting system into which they have been organized. I must, of course, accept responsibility for deficiencies in either the parts or the whole.

SYSTEMS_____

1. A *system* is a set of interrelated elements. Thus a system is an entity which is composed of at least two elements and a relation that holds between each of its elements and at least one other element in the set. Each of a system's elements is connected to every other element, directly or indirectly. Furthermore, no subset of elements is unrelated to any other subset.

2. An *abstract system* is one all of whose elements are concepts. Languages, philosophic systems, and number systems are examples. *Numbers* are concepts but the symbols that represent them, *numerals*, are physical things. Numerals, however, are not the elements of a number system. The use of different numerals to represent the same numbers does not change the nature of the system.

In an abstract system the elements are created by defining and the relationships between them are created by assumptions (e.g., axioms and postulates). Such systems, therefore, are the subject of the so-called "formal sciences."

3. A *concrete system* is one at least two of whose elements are objects. It is only with such systems that we are concerned here. Unless otherwise noted, "system" will always be used to mean "concrete system."

In concrete systems establishment of the existence and properties of elements and the nature of the relationships between them requires research with an empirical component in it. Such systems, therefore, are the subject of study of the so-called "non-formal sciences."

4. The *state of a system* at a moment of time is the set of relevant properties which that system has at that time. Any system has an unlimited number of properties. Only some of these are relevant to any particular research. Hence those which are relevant may change with changes in the purpose of the research. The values of the relevant properties constitute the state of the system. In some cases we may be interested in only two possible states (e.g., off and on, or awake and asleep). In other cases we may be interested in a large or unlimited number of possible states (e.g., a system's velocity or weight).

5. The *environment of a system* is a set of elements and their relevant properties, which elements are not part of the system but a change in any of which can produce* a change in the state of the system. Thus a system's

---

* One thing (x) can be said to produce another (y) in a specified environment and time interval if x is a necessary but not a sufficient condition for y in that environment and time period. Thus a producer is a "probabilistic cause" of its product. Every producer, since it is not sufficient for its product, has a coproducer of that product (e.g., the producer's environment).

environment consists of all variables which can affect its state. External elements which affect irrelevant properties of a system are not part of its environment.

6. The *state of a system's environment* at a moment of time is the set of its relevant properties at that time. The state of an element or subset of elements of a system or its environment may be similarly defined.

Although concrete systems and their environments are *objective* things, they are also *subjective* insofar as the particular configuration of elements that form both is dictated by the interests of the researcher. Different observers of the same phenomena may conceptualize them into different systems and environments. For example, an architect may consider a house together with its electrical, heating, and water systems as one large system. But a mechanical engineer may consider the heating system as a system and the house as its environment. To a social psychologist a house may be an environment of a family, the system with which he is concerned. To him the relationship between the heating and electrical systems may be irrelevant, but to the architect it may be very relevant.

The elements that form the environment of a system and the environment itself may be conceptualized as systems when they become the focus of attention. Every system can be conceptualized as part of another and larger system.

Even an abstract system can have an environment. For example, the metalanguage in which we describe a formal system is the environment of that formal system. Therefore logic is the environment of mathematics.

7. A *closed system* is one that has no environment. An *open system* is one that does. Thus a closed system is one which is conceptualized so that it has no interaction with any element not contained within it; it is completely self-contained. Because systems researchers have found such conceptualizations of relatively restricted use, their attention has increasingly focused on more complex and "realistic" open systems. "Openness" and "closedness" are simultaneously properties of systems and our conceptualizations of them.

Systems may or may not change over time.

8. A system (or environmental) *event* is a change in one or more structural properties of the system (or its environment) over a period of time of specified duration; that is, a change in the structural state of the system (or environment). For example, an event occurs to a house's lighting system when a fuse blows, and to its environment when night falls.

9. A *static (one-state) system* is one to which no events occur. A table, for example, can be conceptualized as a static concrete system consisting of four legs, top, screws, glue, and so on. Relative to most research purposes it displays no change of structural properties, no change of state. A compass

may also be conceptualized as a static system because it virtually always points to the Magnetic North Pole.

10. A *dynamic (multi-state) system* is one to which events occur, whose state changes over time. An automobile which can move forward or backward and at different speeds is such a system, or a motor which can be either off or on. Such systems can be conceptualized as either open or closed; closed it its elements react or respond only to each other.

11. A *homeostatic system* is a static system whose elements and environment are dynamic. Thus a homeostatic system is one that retains its state in a changing environment by internal adjustments. A house that maintains a constant temperature during changing external temperatures is homeostatic. The behavior of its heating subsystem makes this possible.

Note that the same object may be conceptualized as either a static or dynamic system. For most of us a building would be thought of as static, but it might be taken as dynamic by a civil engineer who is interested in structural deformation.

System Changes

12. A *reaction* of a system is a system event for which another event that occurs to the same system or its environment is sufficient. Thus a reaction is a system event that is deterministically caused by another event. For example, if an operator's moving a motor's switch is sufficient to turn that motor off or on, then the change of state of the motor is a reaction to the movement of its switch. In this case, the turning of the switch may be necessary as well as sufficient for the state of the motor. But an event that is sufficient to bring about a change in a system's state may not be necessary for it. For example, sleep may be brought about by drugs administered to a person or it may be self-induced. Thus sleep may be determined by drugs but need not be.

13. A *response* of a system is a system event for which another event that occurs to the same system or to its environment is necessary but not sufficient; that is, a system event produced by another system or environmental event (the *stimulus*). Thus a response is an event of which the system itself is a coproducer. A system does not have to respond to a stimulus, but it does have to react to its cause. Therefore, a person's turning on a light when it gets dark is a response to darkness, but the light's going on when the switch is turned is a reaction.

14. An *act* of a system is a system event for the occurrence of which no change in the system's environment is either necessary or sufficient. Acts,

therefore, are self-determined events, autonomous changes. Internal changes—in the states of the system's elements—are both necessary and sufficient to bring about action. Much of the behavior of human beings is of this type, but such behavior is not restricted to humans. A computer, for example, may have its state changed or change the state of its environment because of its own program.

Systems all of whose changes are reactive, responsive, or autonomous (active) can be called reactive, responsive, or autonomous (active), respectively. Most systems, however, display some combination of these types of change.

The classification of systems into reactive, responsive, and autonomous is based on consideration of what brings about changes in them. Now let us consider systems with respect to what kind of changes in themselves and their environment their reactions, responses, and actions bring about.

15. A system's *behavior* is a system event(s) which is either necessary or sufficient for another event in that system or its environment. Thus behavior is a system change which initiates other events. Note that reactions, responses, and actions may themselves constitute behavior. Reactions, responses, and actions are system events *whose antecedents are of interest*. Behavior consists of system events *whose consequences are of interest*. We may, of course, be interested in both the antecedents and consequences of system events.

Behavioral Classification of Systems

Understanding the nature of the classification that follows may be aided by Table 1 in which the basis for the classification is revealed.

16. A *state-maintaining system* is one that (1) can react in only one way to any one external or internal event but (2) it reacts differently to different

TABLE 1
Behavioral Classification of systems

Type of System	Behavior of System	Outcome of Behavior
State-Maintaining	Variable but determined	Fixed
Goal-Seeking	(reactive)	Fixed
Multi-Goal-Seeking and Purposive	Variable and chosen (responsive)	Variable but determined
Purposeful	Variable and chosen	Variable and chosen
	Variable and chosen	

external or internal events, and (3) these different reactions produce the same external or internal state (outcome). Such a system only reacts to changes; it cannot respond because what it does is completely determined by the causing event. Nevertheless it can be said to have the *function* of maintaining the state it produces because it can produce this state in different ways under different conditions.

Thus a heating system whose internal controller turns it on when the room temperature is below a desired level, and turns it off when the temperature is above this level, is state-maintaining. The state it maintains is a room temperature that falls within a small range around its setting. Note that the temperature of the room which affects the system's behavior can be conceptualized as either part of the system or part of its environment. Hence a state-maintaining system may react to either internal or external changes.

In general, most systems with "stats" (e.g. thermostats and humidistats) are state-maintaining. Any system with a regulated output (e.g., the voltage of the output of a generator) is also state maintaining.

A compass is also state-maintaining because in many different environments it points to the Magnetic North Pole.

A state-maintaining system must be able to *discriminate* between different internal or external states to changes in which it reacts. Furthermore, as we shall see below, such systems are necessarily *adaptive*, but unlike goal-seeking systems they are not capable of learning because they cannot choose their behaviour. They cannot improve with experience.

17. A *goal-seeking system* is one that can respond differently to one or more different external or internal events in one or more different external or internal states and that can respond differently to a particular event in an unchanging environment until it produces a particular state (outcome). Production of this state is its goal. Thus such a system has a *choice* of behavior. A goal-seeking system's behavior is responsive, but not reactive. A state which is sufficient and thus deterministically causes a reaction cannot cause different reactions in the same environment.

Under constant conditions a goal-seeking system may be able to accomplish the same thing in different ways and it may be able to do so under different conditions. If it has *memory*, it can increase its efficiency over time in producing the outcome that is its goal.

For example, an electronic maze-solving rat is a goal-seeking system which, when it runs into a wall of a maze, turns right and if stopped again, goes in the opposite direction, and if stopped again, returns in the direction from which it came. In this way it can eventually solve any solvable maze. If, in addition, it has memory, it can take a "solution path" on subsequent trials in a familiar maze.

Systems with automatic "pilots" are goal-seeking. These and other goal-seeking systems may, of course, fail to attain their goals in some situations.

The sequence of behavior which a goal-seeking system carries out in quest of its goal is an example of a process.

18. A *process* is a sequence of behavior that constitutes a system and has a goal-producing function. In some well-definable sense each unit of behavior in the process brings the actor closer to the goal which it seeks. The sequence of behavior that is performed by the electronic rat constitutes a maze-solving process. After each move the rat is closer (i.e., has reduced the number of moves required) to solve the maze. The metabolic process in living things is a similar type of sequence the goal of which is acquisition of energy or, more generally, survival. Production processes are a similar type of sequence whose goal is a particular type of product.

Process behavior displayed by a system may be either reactive, responsive, or active.

19. A *multi-goal-seeking* system is one that is goal-seeking in each of two or more different (initial) external or internal states, and which seeks different goals in at least two different states, the goal being determined by the initial state.

20. A *purposive system* is a multi-goal-seeking system the different goals of which have a common property. Production of that common property is the system's purpose. These types of system can pursue different goals but they do not select the goal to be pursued. The goal is determined by the initiating event. But such a system does choose the means by which to pursue its goals.

A computer which is programmed to play more than one game (e.g., tic-tac-toe and checkers) is multi-goal-seeking. What game it plays is not a matter of its choice, however; it is usually determined by an instruction from an external source. Such a system is also purposive because 'game winning' is a common property of the different goals it seeks.

21. A *purposeful system* is one which can produce the same outcome in different ways in the same (internal or external) state and can produce different outcomes in the same and different states. Thus a purposeful system is one which can change its goals under constant conditions; it selects ends as well as means and thus displays *will*. Human beings are the most familiar examples of such systems.

Ideal-seeking systems form an important subclass of purposeful systems. Before making their nature explicit we must consider the differences between goals, objectives, and ideals and some concepts related to them. The differences to be considered have relevance only to purposeful systems because only they can choose ends.

A system which can choose between different outcomes can place different values on different outcomes.

22. The *relative value of an outcome* that is a member of an exclusive and exhaustive set of outcomes, to a purposeful system, is the probability that the system will produce that outcome when each of the set of outcomes can be obtained with certainty. The relative value of an outcome can range from 0 to 1.0. That outcome with the highest relative value in a set can be said to be *preferred*.

23. The *goal* of a purposeful system in a particular situation is a preferred outcome that can be obtained within a specified time period.

24. The *objective* of a purposeful system in a particular situation is a preferred outcome that cannot be obtained within a specified period but which can be obtained over a longer time period. Consider a set of possible outcomes ordered along one or more scales (e.g., increasing speeds of travel). Then each outcome is closer to the final one than those which precede it. Each of these outcomes can be a goal in some time period after the "preceding" goal has been obtained, leading eventually to attainment of the last outcome, the objective. For example, a high-school freshman's goal in his first year is to be promoted to his second (sophomore) year. Passing his second year is a subsequent goal. And so on to graduation, which is his objective.

Pursuit of an objective requires an ability to change goals once a goal has been obtained. This is why such pursuit is possible only for a purposeful system.

25. An *ideal* is an objective which cannot be obtained in any time period but which can be approached without limit. Just as goals can be ordered with respect to objectives, objectives can be ordered with respect to ideals. But an ideal is an outcome which is unobtainable in practice, if not in principle. For example, an ideal of science is errorless observations. The amount of observer error can be reduced without limit but can never be reduced to zero. Omniscience in another such ideal.

26. An *ideal-seeking system* is a purposeful system which, on attainment of any of its goals or objectives, then seeks another goal and objective which more closely approximates its ideal. An ideal-seeking system is thus one which has a concept of "perfection" or the "ultimately desirable" and pursues it systematically; that is, in interrelated steps.

From the point of view of their output, six types of system have been identified: state-maintaining; goal seeking, multi-goal-seeking, purposive, purposeful, and ideal-seeking. The elements of systems can be similarly classified. The relationship between (1) the behavior and type of a system and (2) the behavior and type of its elements is not apparent. We consider it next.

RELATIONSHIPS BETWEEN
SYSTEMS AND THEIR ELEMENTS_____

Some systems can display a greater variety and higher level of behavior than can any of their elements. These can be called *variety increasing*. For example, consider two state-maintaining elements, A and B. Say A reacts to a decrease in room temperature by closing any open windows. If a short time after A has reacted the room temperature is still below a specified level, B reacts to this by turning on the furnace. Then the system consisting of A and B is goal-seeking.

Clearly, by combining two or more goal-seeking elements we can construct a multi-goal-seeking (and hence a purposive) system. It is less apparent that such elements can also be combined to form a purposeful system. Suppose one element A can pursue goal G_1 in environment E_1 and goal G_2 in another environment E_2; and the other element B can pursue G_2 in E_1 and G_1 in E_2. Then the system would be capable of pursuing G_1 and G_2 in both E_1 and E_2 if it could select between the elements of these environments. Suppose we add a third (controlling) element which responds to E_1 by "Turning on" either A or B, but not both. Suppose further that it turns on A with probability P_A where $0 < P_A < 1.0$ and turns on B with probability P_B where $0 < P_B < 1.0$. (The controller could be a computer that employs random numbers for this purpose.) The resulting system could choose both ends and means in two environments and hence would be purposeful.

A system can also show less variety of behavior and operate at a lower level than at least some of its elements. Such a system is *variety reducing*. For example, consider a simple system with two elements one of which turns lights on in a room whenever the illumination in that room drops below a certain level. The other element turns the lights off whenever the illumination exceeds a level that is lower than that provided by the lights in the room. Then the lights will go off and on continuously. The system would not be state-maintaining even though its elements are.

A more familiar example of a variety-reducing system can be found in those groups of purposeful people (e.g., committees) which are incapable of reaching agreement and hence of taking any collective action.

A system must be either variety-increasing or variety-decreasing. A set of elements which collectively neither increase nor decrease variety would have to consist of identical elements either only one of which can act at a time or in which similar action by multiple units is equivalent to action by only one. In the latter case the behavior is nonadditive and the behavior is redundant. The relationships between the elements would therefore be irrelevant. For example, a set of similar automobiles owned by one person do not constitute a system because he can drive only one at a time and which he drives makes no difference. On the other hand a radio with two speakers can provide stereo sound; the speakers each do a different thing and together they do something that neither can do alone.

ADAPTATION AND LEARNING_____

In order to deal with the concepts "adaptation" and "learning" it is necessary first to consider the concepts "function" and "efficiency."

27. The *function(s)* of a system is production of the outcomes that define its goal(s) and objective(s). Put another way, suppose a system can display at least two structurally different types of behavior in the same or different environments and that these types of behavior produce the same kind of outcome. Then the system can be said to have the function of producing that outcome. To function, therefore, is to be able to produce the same outcome in different ways.

Let C_i ($1 \le i \le m$) represent the different actions available to a system in a specific environment. Let P_i represent the probabilities that the system will select these courses of action in that environment. If the courses of action are exclusive and exhaustive, then $\sum_{i=1}^{m} P_i = 1.0$. Let E_{ij} represent the probability that course of action C_i will produce a particular outcome O_j in that environment. Then:

28. The efficiency of the system with respect to an outcome O_j which it has the function of producing is $\sum_{i=1}^{m} P_i E_{ij}$.

Now we can turn to "adaptation."

29. A system is *adaptive* if, when there is a change in its environment and/or internal state which reduces its efficiency in pursuing one or more of its goals which define its function(s), it reacts or responds by changing its own state and/or that of its environment so as to increase its efficiency with respect to that goal or goals. Thus adaptiveness is the ability of a system to modify itself or its environment when either has changed to the system's disadvantage so as to regain at least some of its lost efficiency.

The definition of "adaptive" implies four types of adaptation:

29.1. *Other-other adaptation:* A system's reacting or responding to an external change by modifying the environment (e.g., when a person turns on an air conditioner in a room that has become too warm for him to continue to work in).

29.2. *Other-self adaptation:* A system's reacting or responding to an external change by modifying itself (e.g., when the person moves to another and cooler room).

29.3. *Self-other adaptation:* A system's reacting or responding to an internal change by modifying the environment (e.g., when a person who has chills due to a cold turns up the heat).

29.4. *Self-self adaptation:* A system's reacting or responding to an internal change by modifying itself (e.g., when that person takes medication to suppress the chills). Other-self adaptation is most commonly considered because it was this type with which Darwin was concerned in his studies of biological species as systems.

It should now be apparent why state-maintaining and higher systems are necessarily adaptive. Now let us consider why nothing lower than a goal-seeking system is capable of learning.

30. To *learn* is to increase one's efficiency in the pursuit of a goal under unchanging conditions. Thus if a person increases his ability to hit a target (his goal) with repeated shooting at it, he learns how to shoot better. Note that to do so requires an ability to modify one's behavior (i.e., to display choice) and memory.

Since learning can take place only when a system has a choice among alternative courses of action, only systems that are goal-seeking or higher can learn.

If a system is repeatedly subjected to the same environmental or internal change and increases its ability to maintain its efficiency under this type of change, then it *learns how to adapt.* Thus adaptation itself can be learned.

ORGANIZATIONS

Management Scientists are most concerned with that type of system called "organizations." Cyberneticians, on the other hand, are more concerned with that type of system called "organisms," but they frequently treat organizations as though they were organisms. Although these two types of system have much in common, there is an important difference between them. This difference can be identified once "organization" has been defined. I will work up to its definition by considering separately each of what I consider to be its four essential characteristics.

(1) An organization is a purposeful system that contains at least two purposeful elements which have a common purpose.

We sometimes characterize a purely mechanical system as being well organized, but we would not refer to it as an "organization." This results from the fact that we use "organize" to mean, "to make a system of," or, as one dictionary puts it, "to get into proper working order," and "to arrange or dispose systematically." Wires, poles, transformers, switchboards, and telephones may constitute a communication system, but they do not constitute an organization. The employees of a telephone company make up the organization that operates the telephone system. Organization of a system is an activity that can be carried out only by purposeful entities; to be an organization a system must contain such entities.

An aggregation of purposeful entities does not constitute an organization unless they have at least one common purpose; that is, unless there is some one or more things that they all want. An organization is always organized around this common purpose. It is the relationships between what the purposeful elements do and the pursuit of their common purpose that give unity and identity to their organization.

Without a common purpose the elements would not work together unless compelled to do so. A group of unwilling prisoners or slaves can be organized and forced to do something that they do not want to do, but if so they do not constitute an organization even though they may form a system. An organization consists of elements that have and can exercise their own wills.

(2) An organization has a functional division of labor in pursuit of the common purpose(s) of it elements that define it.

Each of two or more subsets of elements, each containing one or more purposeful elements, is responsible for choosing from among different courses of action. A choice from each subset is necessary for obtaining the common purpose. For example, if an automobile carrying two people stalls on a highway and one gets out and pushes while the other sits in the driver's seat trying to start it when it is in motion, then there is a functional division of labor and they constitute an organization. The car cannot be started (their common purpose) unless both functions are performed.

The classes of courses of action and (hence) the subsets of elements may be differentiated by a variety of types of characteristics; for example:

(a) by *function* (e.g., production, marketing, research, finance, and personnel, in the industrial context),
(b) by *space* (e.g., geography, as territories of sales offices),
(c) by *time* (e.g., waves of an invading force).

The classes of action may, of course, also be defined by combinations of these and other characteristics.

It should be noted that individuals or groups in an organization that *make* choices need not *take* them: that is, carry them out. The actions may be carried out by other persons, groups, or even machines that are controlled by the decision makers.

(3) The functionally distinct subsets (parts of the system) can respond to each other's behavior through observation or communication.*

In some laboratory experiments subjects are given interrelated tasks to perform but they are not permitted to observe or communicate with each other even though they are rewarded on the basis of an outcome determined by their collective choices. In such cases the subjects are *unorganized*. If they were allowed to observe each other or to communicate with each other they could become an organization. The choices made by elements or subsets of an organization must be capable of influencing each other, otherwise they would not even constitute a system.

(4) At least one subset of the system has a system-control function.

This subset (or subsystem) compares achieved outcomes with desired outcomes and makes adjustments in the behavior of the system which are directed toward reducing the observed deficiencies. It also determines what the desired outcomes are. The control function is normally exercised by an executive body which operates on a feed-back principle. "Control" requires elucidation.

31. An element or a system *controls* another element or system (or itself) if its behavior is either necessary or sufficient for subsequent behavior of the other element or system (or itself), and the subsequent behavior is necessary or sufficient for the attainment of one or more of its goals. Summarizing, then, an "organization" can be defined as follows:

32. An *organization* is a purposeful system that contains at least two purposeful elements which have a common purpose relative to which the system has a functional division of labor; its functionally distinct subsets can respond to each other's behavior through observation or communication; and at least one subset has a system-control function.

Now the critical difference between organisms and organizations can be made explicit. Whereas both are purposeful systems, organisms do not contain purposeful elements. The elements of an organism may be state-maintaining, goal-seeking, multi-goal-seeking, or purposive; but not purposeful. Thus an organism must be variety increasing. An organization, on the other hand, may be either variety increasing or decreasing (e.g., the

---

* In another place, Ackoff [1], I have given operational definitions of "observation" and "communication" that fit this conceptual system. Reproduction of these treatments would require more space than is available here.

ineffective committee). In an organism only the whole can display will; none of the parts can.

Because an organism is a system that has a functional division of labor it is also said to be "organized." Its functionally distinct parts are called "organs." Their functioning is necessary but not sufficient for accomplishment of the organism's purpose(s).

CONCLUSION

Defining concepts is frequently treated by scientists as an annoying necessity to be completed as quickly and thoughtlessly as possible. A consequence of this disinclination to define is often research carried out like surgery performed with dull instruments. The surgeon has to work harder, the patient has to suffer more, and the chances for success are decreased.

Like surgical instruments, definitions become dull with use and require frequent sharpening and, eventually, replacement. Those I have offered here are not exceptions.

Research can seldom be played with a single concept; a matched set is usually required. Matching different researches requires matching the sets of concepts used in them. A scientific field can arise only on the base of a system of concepts. Systems science is not an exception. Systems thinking, if anything, should be carried out systematically.

REFERENCES

1. Ackoff, R. L. (1967) *Choice, Communication, and Conflict*, a report to the National Science Foundation under Grant GN-389, Management Science Center, University of Pennsylvania, Philadelphia.
2. Churchman, C. W. (1968) *The Systems Approach*, Delacorte Press, New York.
3. Emery, F. E. (1969) *Systems Thinking*, Penguin Books Ltd., Harmondsworth, Middlesex, England.

Reprinted from Ackoff, R. L. (1971) "Towards a system of systems concepts", *Management Science*, **17**, 11.

Ian H. Wilson

The General Electric Company

BUSINESS MANAGEMENT AND THE WINDS OF CHANGE

Fifteen years ago we started to hear, in the management rhetoric of the times, pronouncements about "winds of change." Looking back at those times from our present vantage point, we must think of those winds as gentle breezes compared with the gales that have subsequently ripped through our society. When we spoke of change, we did not have in mind such divisive and disruptive trends and events as campus and urban riots, Vietnam and Watergate, double-digit inflation and nearly comparable unemployment, the energy crisis, and changing values. The past fifteen years also spawned a plethora of movements—the minority movement, the youth movement, the women's movement, the consumer movement, and the environmental movement. We now find ourselves bruised and breathless, wary, even distrustful, bracing for the next blow, and with our confidence shaken in our leadership, in our institutions, and in ourselves.

The Changing Character of Management

In this crucible of change the essential character of management has been transformed: it has changed from administering continuity to managing

Ian H. Wilson, "Business Management and the Winds of Change," *Journal of Contemporary Business*, Winter 1978, pp. 45–54.

uncertainty. We seem to be able to take fewer and fewer things for granted—the area of normalcy in our business lives seems to be progressively decreasing, while the area of discontinuity and risk is progressively increasing. This is assuredly the case with top general management; but, I suggest, it also applies to functional management—including the function of public relations and public affairs.

Despite these changes in the character of management and in the character of change itself, we are neither helpless nor hopeless. We should still be able to say, with William Ernest Henley's "Invictus":

Under the bludgeonings of chance
My head is bloody, but unbowed

Indeed, if we have learned the lesson of the past 15 years well, we can still be the masters of our fate.

The lesson of this "future" shock is this: To manage uncertainty successfully, we must be anticipatory, flexible and enterprising. We should learn to identify and deal with issues before they become crises.

We can define an issue, in the corporate context, as "a major strategy or policy question posed by the impact of environmental trends on the business." In using the term environmental, I am thinking not just of the physical environment, but rather of the overall social, political, economic, and technological environment in which the corporation lives and moves. Thus an issue can be triggered with respect to any element of the corporation's purpose, scope, relations or operations. I will focus this article on policy issues that seem to me to be emerging as items on the corporate agenda over the next ten years.

DEVELOPING AN ENVIRONMENTAL EARLY WARNING SYSTEM_____

The first prerequisite for anticipatory action is the development of an early warning system to monitor and interpret the ever-changing kaleidoscope of developing trends. The purpose of such a system is to buy time to identify emerging issues in sufficient time for adaptive, noncrisis action to be taken. While it may be absorbing and analyzing current data, the system must never lose its future focus.

In 1967 we established our business environment studies component at General Electric, to analyze long-term social and political trends in the

United States and their implications for the corporation. Eight years ago we announced the introduction of our strategic planning system, of which the long-term environmental forecast is a key element. In looking at our experience with these ventures, I derive the following characteristics for a successful environmental early warning system:

THE EARLY WARNING SYSTEM: PIECE, NOT PIECEMEAL_____

1. It must be holistic in its approach to the future business environment. For example, it should view trends—social, political, economic, technological— as a piece, not piecemeal. Ecology and general systems theory both point to the maxim that "everything is related to everything else"—a corporation, a city or a society—with its dynamic, interacting parts and constantly operating feedback loops cannot operate as a closed system. The early warning system should be comprehensive in scope and integrative in its approach.

Cybernetic Pulsing Through the Future

2. It must also be continuous, iterative in its operation. In a fast-changing world, it makes little sense to rely on one-shot, or even periodic, analyses of the environment. Only constant monitoring, feedback, and modification of forecasts can be truly useful. Carrying on the radar analogy, I call this a "cybernetic pulsing through the future."

Future Alternatives

3. The system must be designed to deal with alternative futures. In an uncertain environment we can never truly know the future, no matter how much we may perfect our forecasting techniques. It is highly misleading to claim that an early warning system can predict the future. If well designed, it can help us clarify our assumptions about the future, speculate systematically about alternative outcomes, assess probabilities, and make more rational choices.

Contingency Planning

4. It should lay heavy stress on the need for contingency planning. There is a strong logical connection in our thinking among uncertainty, alternatives,

and contingencies—the three concepts are strongly bound together. In the final analysis, after considering alternatives, we have to commit to a plan of action based on our assessment of the most probable future. But lesser probabilities should not be neglected, for they represent the contingencies for which we should also plan. A committment to contingency planning is the essence of a flexible strategy.

Early Warning in Decision Making

5. Most important, the early warning system should be an integral part of the decision-making system of the corporation. Speculation about alternative futures makes no real contribution to corporate success if it results merely in interesting studies. To contribute, it must be issue oriented and help make today's decisions with a better sense of futurity. But it can do this only if the planning and decision-making system is designed to include the requirement of such monitoring and early warning.

These are five principles that an early warning system should follow in its approach to issue identification: It should be *holistic, iterative, concerned with alternative futures and contingency planning,* and *integrated into the mainstream of corporate decision making.*

Identifying Issues

The early warning system is merely the first step on the road to anticipatory action. It identifies and analyzes the developing trends. These must then be analyzed and interpreted for their significance to the business.

If one accepts my definition of an issue as "a major strategy or policy question posed by the impact of environmental trends on the business," it is easy to see that the most obvious approach to issue identification is by means of a matrix. It lists major trends on one axis and principal sectors or functions of the business on the other. Each cell of the matrix would be completed with a listing of the key strategy or policy questions posed by the impact of that trend on that sector or function. The trend toward increasing quality-of-life expectations raises questions for the marketing function about consumers' expectations of product and service quality and their relative emphasis on experiences rather than things as the way to status and self-expression. It poses questions for the personnel function about employees' future demands for purpose, participation, and educational opportunity in their work; and for the manufacturing function, about environmental impact in plant siting and operating processes.

The phrasing I have suggested for such questions is generic and indicative only. In actuality it would be much more precise. For instance, the marketing question might be: "How can XYZ Department retain market share and increase profitability in a market of slowing growth but rising quality expectations, with a product line oriented to a mass middle market and increasingly vulnerable to commoditization?"And the personnel question might be: "Granted the need for continuous operations in Plant A, how can we use redesign work schedules to meet employees' growing desire for flexibility in work hours?"

The matrix approach at least has the advantages of comprehensiveness and of enforcing a disciplined attention to detail. It may, however, have the pitfall of focusing on the parts to the neglect of the whole. That is why, in addition to sectoral and functional columns, one should be added dealing with the corporation's overall scope, structure, and governance. Incidentally, I hope I have made it clear that, in identifying and classifying issues, I make no distinction between operational issues and those referred to as social responsibility issues. I am convinced that such a distinction is invalid and misleading. It also tends to separate social issues from what is considered really important, and to relegate them automatically to a lower order of significance.

EMERGING POLICY ISSUES

I would like to discuss another approach to identifying emerging policy issues. Calling an issue a policy issue does not diminish its significance. I would argue that, in aggregate, these issues represent the central challenge of the future to corporate growth and profitability.

My starting point for this listing is changing value systems, the New Reformation as I have termed it—a re-formation, or reordering, of individual and societal values. I have summarized these changes, not in terms of the greening of America nor as the triumph of the counterculture, but as rather more subtle, but nonetheless pronounced, shifts in the emphasis of our thinking:

Some Shifts in Thinking

- From considerations of quantity, toward considerations of quality.
- From the concept of independence, toward the concept of interdependence (of nations, institutions, individuals, all natural species).

- From mastery over nature, toward living in harmony with it.
- From the primacy of technical efficiency, toward considerations of social justice and equity.
- From the dictates of organizational convenience, toward the aspirations of self-development in an organization's members.
- From authoritarianism and dogmatism, toward participation.
- From uniformity and centralization, toward diversity and pluralism.
- From the concept of work as hard, unavoidable, and a duty, toward work as purposive and self-fulfilling, and toward a recogniton of leisure as a valid activity in its own right.
- From the satisfaction of private material needs, toward awareness of the need to attend to social wants.

The business impact of these shifts shows up in a shaking of the seven pillars of business, those basic values that undergird our economic and business system—growth; technology; profit and the market system; private property; managerial authority; hard work; and company loyalty. As with the broader societal shifts, so with these basic business values it is more of a reassessment and redefinition than an outright rejection of them that is taking place.

SHAKING THE SEVEN PILLARS OF BUSINESS

The concept of growth as an unqualified good is being seriously modified, both in our thinking and in public and private decisions, by considerations of quality and balance. There is little dispositon to accept the need for imposing immediate and absolute limits to growth, but a very great willingness to aim our policies toward balanced growth, quantity with quality.

Technology, which has been a major dynamic of our economic growth, is now subjected to challenge on the grounds of our need for environmental protection, safety, and social stability. Like growth, technology is not destined for the junk heap of societal thinking. Even so strong a critic of the negative by-products of unrestrained technology as Barry Commoner subscribes to the theory that "the answer to bad technology is not no technology, but good technology." There can be little doubt that the parameters within which technology will be permitted to develop in the future will be more circumscribed by considerations of its potential negative externalities and its longer-term second- and third-order consequences.

Profit is being questioned as a statement of the purpose of business. Debate will continue about the extent to which the profit motive can be squared with the need for business to assume additional social responsibility. It is probable profit will remain a motivator to the entrepreneurial spirit and a measure of social and business success. However, business in general, and individual companies in particular, will have to develop a more socially oriented statement of purpose and mission.

The concept of private property is already being modified, both philosophically and practically. Donald S. MacNaughton, chairman of Prudential Insurance Company, has exposed the myth of the typical corporation being considered a private property institution. It is incongruous to seek in the notion of private property the basis for the legitimacy and rights of management of corporations. New restrictions are also being placed on untrammeled property rights as land-use planning grows in state and community application.

The legitimacy of managerial authority is being called into question, with demands for *greater participation by employees* and other corporate constituencies in the decision-making process. There has been a strong reaction to the authoritarian exercise of power. There is also a widespread feeling among the public that they want more say in, and control over, corporate decisions that affect their lives and work.

The notion of hard work is being put aside in favor of developing meaningful work, responsive to an individual's interests and self-development needs. This is not the place to discuss the so-called erosion of the Puritan ethic, but work values are changing as a better-educated, more affluent workforce takes over. It is unrealistic to expect that traditional methods of organizing work and motivating people can long continue to go unchanged.

Finally, *the concept of company loyalty* is being narrowed more and more, both by the realities of career mobility and by the belief that any employee caught in conflict between loyalty to his company and the public interest should always resolve the conflict in favor of the public.

CHANGING BUSINESS VALUES
AND EMERGING ISSUES

I acknowledge that issues are caused by multiple factors. Nevertheless, I believe there is a clear association between changes in basic business values

and a range of emerging issues that will engage corporate attention over the next ten years. For instance:

A New Role for Growth

It is our re-examination of the role and nature of growth that lends impetus to a rethinking of the trade-offs we are prepared to make between quantity and quality. The issues of job creation versus environmental nondegradation and increasing energy supply versus energy conservation are just two examples of a broader phenomenon. At some point, increasing affluence has a feedback that tends to moderate its own growth, at least in material terms. From this same root spring the second-generation environmental issues of resource conservation, waste management and recycling, and land–use planning. One might even argue that growth-management ideas are at least a contributory factor in the onset of the national economic planning debate.

TECHNOLOGY UNDER SCRUTINY_____

Redefining the parameters of technology makes it a safe bet that technology assessment—and the relative roles of the public and private sectors in that process—will be a rising issue of the 1980s. Of major concern in the technology area will be the issues of health and safety as they relate to corporate products, equipment, and manufacturing processes, and questions as to the appropriateness of scale in technological projects.

Profit: Not the Only Business Purpose

The questioning of profit—as a statement of business purpose—has already brought the issue of corporate social responsibility to the fore. There is a growing convergence between ethical expectations and business performance. We should anticipate that corporations will be increasingly judged against moral criteria by the public, as well as against financial criteria by investors. We have seen this already on arms sales, kickbacks, South Africa, and the Arab boycott. There is no reason to doubt the growing pervasiveness of this issue of explicit ethics into advertising, treatment of employees, customers and suppliers, product testing and so on.

Private Property and Corporate Disclosure

Doubts about the appropriateness of private property as a legitimizing concept for corporate management bring forward the issue of the governance of the corporation. If the corporation is not truly private property, then maybe it should be publicly accountable—and governed. From this reasoning the issues of corporate disclosure and of the proper role and composition of the board of directors emerge and lead, in turn, to the overall question of federal chartering, part of whose thrust is directed toward the divestiture issue. If there is some question about the validity of the market and private property concepts, the notion of determining market and corporate size and structure by means of some publicly determined criteria becomes more plausible.

Managerial Authority

Debate about the nature and extent of managerial authority turns on issues of employee and community participation in corporate decisions. The employee participation issue is much broader—and much deeper—than the Western European question of union representation on boards of directors. It is more a reflection of higher education than of greater unionization, and so affects a much larger segment of the work force. It is not merely a matter of co-determination at the policy level, but also a more pervasive diffusion of decison-making authority on work-related matters. Beyond this lies the issue of public participation, active intervention in the decision-making process by a variety of corporate constituency or interest groups.

A Redefinition of Work and Loyalty

Beyond employee participation, there is a range of issues arising from the redefinition of work and loyalty concepts—the sixth and seventh pillars. In a generic sense, these issues might be said to be concerned with the quality of the work environment and to include such elements as:

- The meaningfulness (or sense of purpose) in work.
- The structure and scheduling of work.
- An employees' "Bill of Rights".
- Privacy (although this is, of course, much broader than an employee issue).
- Whistle-blowing on corporate activities.
- Productivity, with particular emphasis on motivation as a major lever for improving the quality and quantity of output.

PRIORITIES AND CORPORATE STRATEGIES_____

Two aspects of issues management—establishing priorities and developing corporate strategies—are also important.

The Timetable

The range of emerging issues is too great for all of them to be treated equally, with the same level of effort, at the same time by any one corporation. Even in my listing, there are 24 to 30 issues, so priorities for action have to be established.

A priorities study that we conducted for the public issues committee of General Electric's board of directors illustrates one way of going about this. To get a fix on which issues may develop more rapidly than others, we assessed each of the societal pressures on the corporation (97 in all) in terms of:

1. Its convergence with major environmental trends.
2. The intensity and diffusion of interest groups' pressure.

From this ranking we did some initial sorting of priorities that were refined by injecting a third criterion—degree of impact on the company. As a result of this process we were able to suggest to the committee a list of six major public issues for their future agenda.

Strategies

From priorities, we will now turn to strategies. Buying lead time with a good early warning system is pointless if the time is not used. In issues management we need to develop the same spirit of initiative that we associate with entrepreneurial activity. Strategy should become as much a part of our vocabulary as it is of marketing.

Active, Not Reactive Approach

A proactive strategy beats a reactive posture every time. Our company dictum is "Without a proper business response, societal expectations of today become the political issues of tomorrow, legislated requirements the next day, and litigated penalties the day after that." At each stage in that sequence, there is a progressive narrowing of the opportunities and maneuvering space for business and an intensification of constraints and problems. This is the antithesis of entrepreneurial action, which seeks to maximize opportunities and minimize problems. It also hastens the translation of an issue into a public policy issue.

There are just five guidelines for strategy development that I would like to mention here:

1. Assess long-term trends in terms of the opportunities they offer as well as the problems they present.
2. Develop a constructive rationale for action, matching your options to the long-term trends. If developed early enough, the action can be both internal in shaping the corporation and external in helping shape the trends.
3. Build flexibility into your strategy.
4. Search out opportunities for alliances—with other companies, with labor, with interest groups, with government. This guideline applies mainly, but not exclusively, at the public policy stage, when political realities dictate a course of cooperative action. The business Roundtable and the labor–management group provide us with models of what is possible here.
5. Apply the normal managerial tools, goals, objectives, schedules, and measurements to this activity: The task requires, and deserves, no less than the best in professional management.

Finally, on a more philosophical note, I still like the advice that the French philosopher Henri Bergson gave to his peers: "Think as men of action; act as men of thought."

Patrick E. Murphy

Marquette University

AN EVOLUTION: CORPORATE SOCIAL RESPONSIVENESS

The concept of corporate "social responsibility" has been defined, debated, studied, and prescribed by many thoughtful writers in recent years. However, it remains a nebulous term to many individuals. One reason for this lack of understanding may be its evolutionary nature. In other words, what is considered to be socially responsible today is not synonymous with what it was ten years ago. Several chronological "eras" of social responsibility are identified and discussed in this paper.

Before examining the earlier stages of this concept, the rationale for labeling the current one needs clarification. The term "responsiveness" seems to capture the contemporary stance of many corporations to their social role. In other words, social responsiveness is a more positive and accurate term than social responsibility. Ackerman and Bauer carefully distinguished between the use of the words responsibility and responsiveness. They felt that responsibility connotes the process of assuming an obligation and places the emphasis on motivation, whereas responsiveness can be described as a strategy emphasizing social and economic performance.[1]

A further reason for calling this the responsiveness era is that many

Patrick E. Murphy, "An Evolution: Corporate Social Responsiveness," *University of Michigan Business Review*, November 1978, pp. 19–25.

corporations have already recognized their responsibility (i.e., obligation) to society and now are reacting to these demands in diverse ways. For instance, some companies were quick to respond to the ozone controversy by voluntarily discontinuing the use of fluorocarbons in their aerosal containers. Furthermore, "consumer affairs" departments have been established by many manufacturers and retailers. Although this practice originally arose because of consumerism problems, these departments now deal with community as well as consumer issues. The role of the consumer affairs executive and the successful programs of Whirlpool, Giant Foods, and Polaroid are well documented.[2] As a result of these and other factors, the label "responsiveness" is being accepted in the literature.[3]

By analyzing the social responsibility in an historical context, a conceptual structure can be developed to replace the usual disjointed discussion. Although Hay and Gray identified three phases of social responsibility and corresponding managerial styles, they did not make a distinction between the more subtle social changes in this concept over the last two decades.[4] Specifically, the posture of corporations toward the notion of social responsibility has undergone significant modification in the past few years. Therefore, the eras in the evolution of corporate social responsibility warrant attention. To properly understand these contemporary stages, a brief examination of the initial eras is necessary.

EARLY ERAS OF SOCIAL RESPONSIBILITY

The Philanthrophic Era

Table 1 depicts the four eras of social responsibility along with their corresponding time periods and primary characteristics. The philanthropic era began early this century and continued until the early fifties. During this period corporate responsibility to society was limited to charitable contributions. Some of the more significant occurrences of this stage was the relief support to victims of the 1906 San Francisco earthquake by Standard Oil of California, gifts to the YMCA by U.S. Steel and Standard Oil of New Jersey, the Community Chest movement of the 1930s and business's contributions to education, the arts, and politics during the forties and early fifties.[5] The historical events of this period—two world wars and the Depression—were factors which perpetuated this limited view of social responsibility.

TABLE 1
Corporate Social Responsibility Eras

Era	Dates	Primary Characteristics
Social Responsibility		
Philanthropic	To early 1950s	Concentration on charitable donations
Awareness	1953–1967	Recognition of overall responsibility Involvement in community affairs
Issue	1968–1973	Concern about urban decay Correction of racial discrimination Alleviation of pollution problems Assessment of the social impact of technology
Corporate Social Responsibility		
Responsiveness	1974–present	Alteration of boards of directors Examination of ethics and corporate behavior Utilization of social performance disclosures

The Awareness Era

The second era shown in Table 1 is labeled the "awareness" stage which expanded the scope of social responsibility. In the 1950s, Bowen posited that voluntary assumption of moral and social duties would lead to the realization of economic goals. Precisely, he stated that businessmen "are servants of society and that management merely in the interests [narrowly defined] of stockholders is not the sole end of their duties."[6] Bowen's treatise was the first attempt to suggest a comprehensive approach to this area.

Later in that decade, Richard Eells articulated the challenge to business regarding social responsibility. He explained the decision on whether to accept these societal responsibilities in terms of a dilemma. The following excerpt captures his thinking:

I have observed a growing acceptance of the thesis that corporations must assume many extralegal obligations, as well as their obvious ones, in order to survive and prosper. Certainly, many leading corporate executives have responded—at times at considerable risk to their own positions—with increased concern for the local community, the needs of education, and the imperatives of research, to mention but a few areas.[7]

It should be noted that during this era opposition to the social responsibility notion surfaced. The most adamant spokesmen of this alternative view were Theodore Levitt and Milton Friedman. Levitt argued that the goal of business is to generate profits, and social responsibility is the concern of government. Therefore, business should fight any effort to delimit its major objective of profit maximization.[8] Friedman echoed these sentiments at that time and has continued to persuasively contend that "the business of business is to increase profits."[9]

Specifically, Friedman believes that in a free enterprise system the manager is an employee of the owners and consequently is directly responsible to them. If the manager spends stockholder money on social problems, without their approval, he is not acting as a proper employee. Also, Buchholz reiterated this argument by pointing out allocation of resources and accountability problems related to business assumption of their social responsibility.[10] Most recently, Carson stated that the corporation is an inappropriate institution for the achievement of socioeconomic reform.[11]

During the early and mid-sixties corporations focused largely on their community involvement (see Table 1). Firms were recognized as being important, if not leading, community citizens. Therefore, they were expected to contribute both in financing and planning for the housing and recreational needs of their immediate geographic area. Since one or a few firms often employed the majority of persons in a given city, their responsibility to the social, political, educational, and recreational needs, as well as economic well-being, were widely acknowledged.[12]

At the end of this awareness era, Professor Keith Davis advanced the "power–responsibility equation" concept. He stated that the more economic power a corporation wields, the more responsibility it has to society.[13] This idea signaled a change in thinking which meant that social responsibility went beyond the community involvement. Consequently, a new phase was about to begin.

The "Issue" Era

Although shorter in terms of years, the issue era which began in the late sixties was a tumultuous one. Corporations were perceived as being closely associated with the social ills that plagued society at that time. Several significant catalysts—riots in major cities, unrest on college campuses precipitated by the escalation of the war in Vietnam, and mass recognition of the declining quality of the natural environment—caused firms to reevaluate their position in society.

Angry inner-city leaders pressured companies that they felt were racially prejudiced and unresponsive to consumer needs. College students questioned the authority of all major institutions (i.e., government, big business, religion and higher education, itself) and believed that, for the most part, they were insensitive to social needs. It might be added that this skepticism gradually expanded to other parts of the population. Pollution of all types caused by the manufacture, use or disposal of many firms' products was also recognized as a serious problem. Since major corporations were associated with these catalysts, the belief emerged that companies should play a major role in alleviating society's problems.

As a result, the specific social issues of urban decay, racial discrimination, pollution, and technology received substantial attention from many corporate leaders. To combat the further decline in urban areas, companies constructed office buildings, plants and retail stores in many deteriorating central cities.[14] In addition, programs were initiated to hire, train and ultimately promote members of minority groups.[15] Corporate responses to the ecological crisis ranged from platitudes, to product reformulations, to the installation of various pollution control devices.[16] The consequences of technological advancement which traditionally went unquestioned were also critically assessed by managers and government leaders.[17] Other problems, such as consumerism and zero economic growth, surfaced during this era, but the issues examined above were representative of the period.

Although corporations were responding to specific social issues confronting them, a plethora of publications by academicians and corporate executives appeared on the general nature of social responsibility. For instance, a new journal entitled *Business and Society Review* was launched in 1972. Writers expressed differing views on the concept but the general tenor seemed to be that corporations did have a general responsibility to society.[18] This may seem like an extension of the awareness era discussed previously, but the creation of new programs and positions and expenditures of substantial time and money on solving these issues suggest that social responsibility became institutionalized in many firms.[19]

THE ERA OF CORPORATE SOCIAL RESPONSIVENESS___

As shown in Table 1, the current era of social responsibility began approximately in 1974. At this time corporate concern seemed to shift from the specific issues of the previous few years to more pervasive factors affecting their role in society. These areas concern (1) boards of directors, (2) ethics and (3) social performance disclosures. Once again, what distinguishes this era from the previous ones is that many corporations appear to be consciously responding, as opposed to reacting, to their social constituencies.

Boards of Directors

The makeup of boards of directors has been undergoing change for many years. Years ago, only corporate officers and major stockholders were seated on most boards. Today, membership of "outsiders" on the board is commonly accepted as a way to insure better economic and social performance by the company.[20] In recent years, blacks, women and academicians have been actively recruited to represent outside viewpoints.

The mere presence of outside directors, however, does not assure more socially responsible management. Some companies (i.e., Armco Steel, Chrysler, Dow Chemical, General Mills, etc.) have instituted "public responsibility" standing committees which advise the board on social issues.[21] These committees can be described as the audit committee in the societal arena. To be effective, these public responsibility committees must receive adequate staff and technical support.

A more radical proposal for altering boards of directors has been suggested. The idea of "public directors" was proposed by Arthur Goldberg (former Supreme Court Justice), Robert Townsend (former president of Avis) and Christopher Stone (law professor).[22] They believe that the public must have representation on boards so that society's needs can be served. One outside director, Dr. Clifton Wharton, who is a college president and black, stated that "[he views his] role as primarily that of a public director" on the boards on which he serves.[23]

Ethics

Just as the events of the sixties precipitated many of the corporate actions in the same era, Watergate probably was the underlying cause for a more open discussion of ethics during this period. Several corporations (i.e., American Airlines, Phillips Petroleum, and others) were linked directly to the scandal because of illegal political contributions, while many others were scarred because of their strong support for the Nixon administration.[24] These happenings have led to several responses by corporations to the "ethics crisis."

Initially, the leading periodicals aimed at the business community raised the consciousness of corporate executives to the ethics controversy. Max Ways, former *Fortune* editor, wrote that: "Hard thinking about business ethics is a task long overdue." He further argued that new rules need to be developed that take into account both the selfish and altruistic sides of reality.[25] Other articles proclaimed that stiffer rules for ethical conduct were now in effect and that executives have a moral obligation not only for personal behavior but also for the behavior of the entire corporation.[26] In addition, several empirical studies were conducted to gauge the ethical conduct of business practitioners. Carroll asked respondents, in a survey of 238 executives, to react to propositions about business ethics reported in the news media. He concluded

that managers, particularly those below the top level, feel pressures to conform to what they perceive to be their superior's expectations of them, even though it may require the managers to compromise their personal values and standards[27]

In another study of 121 managers, Newstrom and Ruch reported that ethics remain largely a personal concept, employees express similar perceptions of ethics as top management, and that managers often feel others to be less ethical than they profess to be. Actions that management might take, they suggest, are to determine the state of ethical behavior within their organization, to set up a corporate model of ethics, and to recognize that altering personal ethics is a long-term goal.[28] Most recently, surveys of Pitney-Bowes and Uniroyal managers revealed that they too felt pressure to compromise personal ethics to achieve corporate goals.[29]

From the results of these studies it cannot necessarily be argued that business executives are becoming more ethical. However, this exposure and more open discussion of corporate ethics may contribute to a greater overall ethical sensitivity in the long run. To cope with the short-term problem, many firms have instituted "codes of ethics."[30] In fact, two companies which received great criticism a few years ago, Lockheed and Gulf Oil Company, have developed strict ethical codes. Furthermore, Steiner suggested that "ethical advisors" might be appropriate for some firms.[31] Cummins Engine and Monsanto are two companies currently utilizing a person in this capacity.

Social Performance Disclosures

The third distinguishing feature of the corporate responsiveness era is the use of various social performance disclosures by many companies. There are basically two avenues used to document activities undertaken in this area. First, the annual report is sometimes employed as a forum for discussing social programs, or secondly, a "social audit" may be performed.

In recent years many corporations have begun to include social responsibility information in their annual reports. Dilley classified these disclosures into several categories: itemized within financial statements, footnotes to financial statements, letter to shareholders, and separate reports on social performance. Among the companies he noted were DuPont, Bethlehem Steel and Standard Oil of California.[32] In an examination of firms in the food business, Bowman and Haire found that medium activity (in terms of attention devoted to corporate responsibility in the annual report) was more closely associated with high profitability than was either little or much activity. Consequently, they argue that a balance between internal and external activity must be struck.[33] The status of social disclosures is summed up well by the following statement.

> In the early 1970's, when "corporate social responsibility" became a management buzzword, most companies felt obligated at least to pay lip service to the idea in their annual reports. In recent years fewer corporations have been playing up this theme. But those that do are getting away from the more general "God, mother, and country" approach and are making far more factual analyses. Norton, for example, issued a separate eight-page special report this year, detailing its corporate social philosophy and progress. Ford, Celanese, Merck, and Shell Oil all gave detailed employment data on women and minority groups.[34]

Although one source indicated that the social audit was first formulated in the 1940s, only in recent years has it received serious consideration by corporations.[35] The audit provides another mechanism for firms to measure and report upon their social activities. The measurement of social programs' costs and benefits is thought to be the logical end to social responsibility. Table 2 lists several different conceptualizations of the audit and briefly describes the various methodologies which have been suggested for operationalizing the notion.

Despite the significant attention that has been devoted to social reporting and auditing, its use is in the embryonic state of development. The quantification of social responsibility will continue to be difficult, but not impossible. One attempt to disclose social information which does not fall in either of the above categories warrants notice. Last year 186 life and health insurance companies cooperated in a joint social reporting program which covered six areas including community projects, contributions, women and minority employment, environment and energy, individual involvement, and investments. The resulting publication provided a status report on this industry.[36]

CONCLUSION_____

From the foregoing discussion, it is evident that corporate social responsibility is not a static concept. It has evolved through the various eras from a narrow interpretation including only philanthropic activity to the current "responsiveness" era. The characteristics of this present era—changing boards of directors, more open discussion of ethics and utilization of social

TABLE 2
Different Conceptualizations of the Social Audit

Author	Year	Label	Description
T. J. Kreps[1]	1940	Social performance measurement	Studied three companies' efforts in six areas (such as employment, production, consumer effort)
H. R. Bowen[2]	1953	Social audit	Proposed that independent outside experts appraise a firm's policies toward eight areas (prices, wages, human and community relations)
F. H. Blum[3]	1958	Social audit	Conducted attitude survey of managers on meaning of their work in terms of their need for unity and integrity
D. F. Linowes[4]	1968	Socio-economic operating statement (SEOS)	Computed in dollar figures a company's social contributions against social costs
C. C. Abt[5]	1972	Social operations and income statement	Measured in dollar terms his firm's position with respect to social benefits, quality of life other than fringes, career advancement, and social cost
R. A. Bauer and D. H. Fenn, Jr.[6]	1972	Corporate social audit	Proposed a "process audit" as an initial step in measuring social responsibility
B. L. Butcher[7]	1973	Social audit	Discussed the "program management approach" utilized by Bank of America
F. D. Sturdivant[8]	1974	Social assessment system (SAS)	Examined five indicators of social performance (human investment, ecology, consumer welfare, openness of the system, and responsiveness to social issues)

[1] "Measurement of the Social Performance of Business," Monograph No. 7, Temporary National Economic Committee.

[2] *Social Responsibilities of the Businessman* (New York: Harper and Brothers, 1953), pp. 155–156.

[3] "Social Audit of the Enterprise," *Harvard Business Review*, March–April 1958, pp. 77–86.

[4] "Socio-Economic Accounting," *The Journal of Accountancy*, November 1968, pp. 37–42; and "Let's Get on With the Social Audit," *Business and Society Review*, Winter 1972–73, pp. 39–49.

[5] "Managing to Save Money While Doing Good," *Innovation*, January 1972, pp. 38–47; and Abt Associates Annual Report and Social Audit 1971–1974.

[6] *The Corporate Social Audit* (New York: Russell Sage Foundation, 1972); and "What is a Corporate Social Audit?" *Harvard Business Review*, January–February 1973, pp. 37–48.

[7] "The Program Management Approach to the Corporate Social Audit," *California Management Review*, Fall 1973, pp. 11–16.

[8] "The Social Assessment System: A Framework for Analyzing Corporate Social Responsibility," in *Changing Values and Social Trends: How Do Organizations React?* (Chicago: American Marketing Association, 1976), pp. 135–142.

TABLE 2 (continued)
Different Conceptualizations of the Social Audit

Author	Year	Label	Description
S. K. Cooper and M. H. Raiborn[9]	1974	Accounting for social responsibility	Argued that current accounting structure must be revised to deal with social problems
N. C. Churchill[10]	1974	Social accounting	Contended that a theory of social accounting is necessary
E. J. Burton, Jr.[11]	1976	Statement of social responsiveness	Proposed the utilization of several scaling techniques to measure social performance
D. H. Blake W. C. Frederick and M. S. Myers[12]	1976	Social auditing	Provided a comprehensive framework for conducting a social process audit
J. E. Post and M. J. Epstein[13]	1977	Social reporting	Called for scanning as a methodology for developing criteria for social reporting
AICPA[14]	1977	Corporate social performance measurement	Posited an ideal system of social measurement, but developed an initial system which generates information about indicators of performance for the environment, human resources, the community, etc.

[9] "Accounting for Corporate Social Responsibility," *MSU Business Topics*, Spring 1974, pp. 19–26.
[10] "Toward a Theory for Social Accounting," *Sloan Management Review*, Spring 1974, pp. 1–7.
[11] "Statement of Social Responsiveness: A Proposal," *The Government Accountants Journal*, Winter 1976, pp. 12–19.
[12] *Social Auditing: Evaluating the Impact of Corporate Programs* (New York: Praeger Publishers, 1976).
[13] "Information Systems for Social Reporting," *Academy of Management Review*, January 1977, pp. 81–87.
[14] *The Measurement of Corporate Social Performance* (New York: American Institute of Certified Public Accountants, 1977).

performance disclosures—indicate the most pervasive corporate acceptance of social responsibility to date. Although no end is in sight for this stage, the concept will undoubtedly take on new meaning in the future.

REFERENCES

1. Robert Ackerman and Raymond Bauer, *Corporate Social Responsiveness: The Modern Dilemma* (Reston: Reston Publishing Company, 1976), pp. 6–13.
2. Milton L. Blum, John B. Stewart and Edward W. Wheatley, "Consumer Affairs: Viability of the Corporate Response," *Journal of Marketing*, April 1974, pp. 13–

19; "Corporate Clout for Consumers," *Business Week*, 12 September 1977, pp. 144 & 148.

3. Frederick D. Sturdivant and James L. Ginter, "Corporate Social Responsiveness: Management Attitudes and Economic Performance," *California Management Review*, Spring 1977, pp. 30–39; Donald S. McNaughton, "Managing Social Responsiveness," *Business Horizons*, December 1976, pp. 19–24.

4. Robert D. Hay and Ed Gray, "Social Responsibilities of Business Managers," *Academy of Management Journal*, March 1974.

5. Morrell Heald, *The Social Responsibilities of Business* (Cleveland: Case Western Reserve University Press, 1970).

6. Howard R. Bowen, *Social Responsibilities of the Businessman* (New York: Harper and Brothers, 1953), p. 44.

7. Richard Eells, "Social Responsibility: Can Business Survive the Challenge?" *Business Horizons*, Winter 1959, pp. 33–41.

8. Theodore Levitt, "The Dangers of Social Responsiblity," *Harvard Business Review*, September-October 1958, pp. 41–50.

9. See Milton Friedman, "The Social Responsibility of Business is to Increase Its Profits," *New York Times Magazine*, 13 September 1970, pp. 32–33+.

10. Rogene A. Buchholz, "An Alternative to Social Responsibility," *MSU Business Topics*, Summer 1977, pp. 12–16.

11. Deane Carson, "Companies as Heroes? Bah! Humbug!!" *The New York Times*, 25 December 1977, editorial page.

12. See Keith Davis and Robert L. Blomstrom, "Business Involvement in Community Activities," Chapter 16 in *Business, Society, and Environment* (New York: McGraw Hill, second edition, 1971), pp. 265–282.

13. Keith Davis, "Understanding the Social Responsibility Puzzle," *Business Horizons*, Winter 1967, pp. 45–50. For a recent discussion of this concept applied to small business, see C. Ray Gullet and James D. Powell, "The Power-Responsibility Equation: A Second Look for the Small Business," *University of Michigan Business Review*, January 1977, pp. 7–10.

14. See Robert C. Albrook, "Business Wrestles With Its Social Conscience," *Fortune*, August 1968, pp. 88–90+; Seymour Lusterman, "Socially-Motivated Ghetto Ventures," *The Conference Board Record*, March 1971, pp. 21–24; "Corporations and the Problems of the City," *Journal of Contemporary Business*, July 1974, entire issue.

15. James L. Koch, "Employing the Disadvantaged: Lessons From the Past Decade," *California Management Review*, Fall 1974, pp. 68–77.

16. See A. Charnes, W. W. Cooper and G. Kozmetsky, "Management Science, Ecology and the Quality of Life," *Management Science: Application*, June 1973, entire issue; James Brian Quinn, "Next Big Industry: Environmental Improvement," *Harvard Business Review*, September-October 1971, pp. 120–131; Etienne Cracco and Jacques Rostenne, "The Socio-Ecological Product," *MSU Business Topics*, Summer 1971, pp. 27–34.

17. Henry M. Boettinger, "Technology in the Manager's Future," *Harvard Business Review* November-December 1970, pp. 4–14+; Walter Hahn, "Technology Assessment and Corporate Planning," *Planning Review*, June 1973.

18. Keith Davis, "The Case For and Against Business Assumption of Social Responsibilities," *Academy of Management Journal*, June 1973. pp. 312–322.
19. "How Social Responsibility Became Institutionalized," *Business Week*, 30 June 1973, pp. 74–82.
20. Ralph F. Lewis, "Choosing and Using Outside Directors," *Harvard Business Review*, July-August 1974, pp. 70–78: "The Changing Fashion in Company Directors," *Business Week*, 14 March 1977, p. 32.
21. Michael L. Lovdal, Raymond A. Bauer and Nancy H. Treverton, "Public Responsibility Committees of the Board," *Harvard Business Review*, May-June 1977, pp. 40–46+.
22. "Arthur Goldberg on Public Directors: A Business and Society Review Interview," *Business and Society Review/Innovation*, Spring 1973, pp. 35–39; Robert Townsend, "Let's Install Public Directors," *Business and Society Review*, Sping 1972, pp. 69–70; Christopher D. Stone, "Public Directors Merit A Try," *Harvard Business Review*, March-April 1976, pp. 20–34+.
23. Clifton R. Wharton, Jr., "Going Public," *Newsweek*, 29 April 1974, pp. 16–17.
24. "How Clean is Business?" *Newsweek*, 1 September 1975, pp. 50–54.
25. Max Ways, "Business Faces Growing Pressures to Behave Better," *Fortune*, May 1974, pp. 193–195+.
26. "Stiffer Rules for Business Ethics," *Business Week*, 30 March 1974, pp. 87–92; Irving Kristol, "Ethics and the Corporation," *The Wall Street Journal*, 16 April 1975, p. 18
27. Archie B. Carroll, "Managerial Ethics: A Post-Watergate View," *Business Horizons*, April 1975, pp. 75–80.
28. John W. Newstrom and William A. Ruch, "The Ethics of Management and the Management of Ethics," *MSU Business Topics*, Winter 1975, pp. 29–37.
29. "The Pressure to Compromise Personal Ethics," *Business Week*, 31 January 1977, p. 107.
30. E. Morgenthaler and B. E. Calame, "More Concerns Issue Guidelines on Ethics In Payoffs Aftermath," *The Wall Street Journal*, 16 March 1976, p. 1+; "How Companies React to the Ethics Crisis," *Business Week* 9 February 1976, pp. 78–79.
31. John F. Steiner, "The Prospect of Ethical Advisers for Business Corporations," *Business and Society*, Spring 1976, pp. 5–10.
32. Steven C. Dilley, "External Reporting of Social Responsibility," *MSU Business Topics*, Autumn 1975, pp. 13–25.
33. Edward H. Bowman and Mason Haire, "A Strategic Posture Toward Corporate Social Responsibility," *California Management Review*, Winter 1975, pp. 49–58.
34. "More Meat in Annual Reports," *Business Week*, April 1976, pp. 78–79.
35. Archie B. Carroll and George W. Beiler, "Landmarks in the Evolution of the Social Audit, *Academy of Management Journal*, September 1975, pp. 589–599.
36. Stanley G. Karson, *1976 Social Reporting Program of the Life and Health Insurance Business* (New York: Clearinghouse on Corporate Social Responsibility, 1976).

Donald R. Welsh
Robert W. Lee

Peat, Marwick and Mitchell, New York

ADAPTING SYSTEMS TO COPE WITH MULTIPLE FUTURES

The corporate long-range planning approaches developed during the relative stability of the 1950s and 1960s are fast becoming inadequate to cope with today's turbulent climate. Planning was, for the most part, based on future assumptions that could be trusted to endure for five years or more. But the rapid-fire "major dislocations of the early 1970s made planning an anxiety-provoking exercise," says *Planning Under Uncertainty*, a report published last year by The Conference Board, a New York-based research organization.

After an in-depth study of planning, its methodologies, its shortcomings, and efforts to improve it, the report concludes that many corporate planning systems must be redesigned to adapt to a broad spectrum of present and future uncertainties.

A majority of other experts attempting to diagnose the future is in general agreement with The Conference Board's outlook. They recognize that seldom, if ever, have U.S. businessmen confronted such a bewildering variety of rapid changes, few of which are predictable over a span of more than several months. The only certainty seems to be that the future may take a number of paths, each with a separate probability of occurrence.

Donald R. Welsh and Robert W. Lee, "Adapting Systems to Cope With Multiple Futures," *Management Focus*, January/February 1979, pp. 6–17.

GOOD PLANS DEMAND BROAD VIEWS

Nevertheless, fresh approaches promise to enable planners to seize advantages from an uncertain future, provided that their planning systems are sensitive and flexible enough to adapt to abrupt changes. Planners can no longer safely consider only a single future. Instead, they must allow for many possible outcomes—some more likely than others, but all deserving examination and evaluation.

No longer can planners assume that they work in a world that is friendly or, at worst, neutral. They must take into account the numerous changing dimensions of society: the external factors that may greatly affect their planning process. Some of the many crucial factors and their manifold influences are shown in the left-hand column of Table 1.

Readers will be able to add to the table many more details relevant to their own experiences and also to judge how vulnerable their own plans and operations may be to the multiple alternative estimates of the future that lies ahead.

In addition to responding to these uncertain external influences, corporate planners must also be prepared to react effectively to new requirements of their own management. In most corporations, these goals and objectives are changing in reaction to the changing business and social environment. These corporate changes are creating new organizational forms which must be accounted for in planning systems.

The key factors affecting corporate organization and goals are listed on page 73. The speed with which change occurs requires closer attention to the relationship between short term budgets and longer term capital evaluations and strategic plans. Good planning must be disciplined by strict attention to the relationship between time horizons, which are suggested by the three groups of columns shown: Annual budgets, which encompass no more than one year or, alternatively, a single production cycle; capital budgets, which extend as far out as three years for evaluating proposed business expansion; and strategic plans which reach out from three to five years (sometimes longer) and focus on determining future directions for the company, must all be coordinated and adapted to changing external conditions with the logical interactions examined. The second and third categories overlap somewhat, since capital budgets have strategic elements.

Whatever the nature and lifespan of the plan, it must be compared frequently against actual performance, then changed if it has become unrealistic. Otherwise, a company may find itself wandering through a future that no longer exists.

A WISTFUL GLANCE AT A SIMPLER WORLD

It is difficult for many planners and corporate managers to realize how drastically their worlds have changed in only a few years. The relative economic and social stability of the early 1960s has given way to the uncertainty of the 1970s. Controllable or predictable environments can no longer be relied upon. The firm and reassuring planning system of the 1960s has been transmuted into systems used for identifying uncertainty and minimizing risk. The targeted trend forecast is now blurred into a spectrum of alternative scenarios, and focus on prediction has shifted to awareness of a multiplicity of possible outcomes. The single strategic plan that served as a long-term guide has become a sometimes bewildering set of contingency plans.

Why have the rules of the planning game changed so swiftly and drastically? Here are the major trends to be faced in the 1980s which represent a shift in the allocation of human and natural resources:

- from manufactured goods to professional and personal services
- from growing monetary income to the uses of affluence to achieve a more gratifying quality of life
- from centalized management and control to local or regional influence over the decisions affecting our lives
- from the development of capital and physical capabilities to the improvement of human resources
- from production of physical products to the creation and dissemination of information and knowledge
- from transformation of resources for production and economic growth to the conservation of those resources for future generations
- from the free market economic decision process to increasing accountability for the social and environmental impact of corporate decisions

Throughout these trends the one common thread of concern to planners is that response times in business decision making have shrunk at an alarming rate. Communications are virtually instantaneous. Accounting and operating information pours out at a much faster rate from modern computer systems. Product life cycles are shorter. Economic and policy analyses are generated at astounding rates. Social and economic policies are changing faster and more frequently.

Similarly, the dimensions of society are undergoing changes that were scarcely contemplated as late as the mid-1960s. Life-style preferences are

Factors affecting systems	Marketing	Production
Domestic economic	• 1979 slowdowns likely • Consumer indebtedness at an alltime high • Pre-inflation buying patterns for consumer durables	• Availability and price of raw material continue to fluctuate with growing reliance on foreign resources
International economic	• Growing dollar incomes of foreigners due to strong foreign economies and weak U.S. dollar encourage foreign investment in United States	• More efficient plants abroad encourage foreign competition • Lower wage scales from LDC producers increase price competition • Restrictions on availability of materials purchased abroad
Technological	• Computer systems reducing normal inventory cushions in regional warehouses	• Use of energy saving equipment vs increasing labor productivity • Expanding the work force vs more overtime work
Social and demographic	• Greater diversity of taste and demand within similar demographic market segments requires better marketing policy • Two breadwinner family changes demand for traditional products • Growing senior citizens population creates new marketing opportunities • Awareness of new balance between work/education/leisure alters consumption patterns	• More women in work force • Demand for more flexible work schedule • Labor union attitudes toward productivity and technology • Alternative life styles for white collar workers mixing work and education
Political and regulatory		• FTC and FDA require more restrictive product safety standards • More rigid safety standards in the work place (OSHA)
Professional		
Ecological and environmental	• Product design/marketing affected by ecological perceptions of the dangers of technology	• Urban vs suburban plant location decision • Introduction of new production methods requires lengthy study of environmental impact
Corporate objectives	• Deeper penetration of existing markets vs expanding into new markets	• Vertical vs horizontal integration of production
Corporate organization	• Marketing organization designed to serve domestic, regional or international customer base	• Worker participation in management decisions • Competitive position of technology used in production

| Annual budget systems | Capital budget systems | Strategic planning systems |
Financial		
• Credit crunch occurs in capital markets causing higher interest rates and limited funds for investment	• Period of slow economic growth with 3% annual growth in GNP • Innovations in financial instruments which are tied to current interest rates • Service and knowledge oriented industries dominan	• Changing consumer attitudes towards inflation and durable goods purchases • Capital markets and government may provide capital f : small innovative companies
• Government policies such as commodity politics and foreign trade restrictions that prohibit orderly planning • Inflow of capital from OPEC and Third World Sources	• Increasing protection of local markets . by government policy • Development of resources for local consumption by government policy • Attractive nature of U.S. economy for foreign investors as a source of stable investment opportunities	• More efficient international exchange of production, capital, and information • Entry of Third World and OPEC wealth into transnational business community
• Efficient transfer of funds will alter fund utilization patterns • Efficient transfer of funds will alter fund utilization patterns — EFTS	• Availability of computer-driven capital equipment for production • Service industry technology not meeting social demands in government sector and non-profit groups	• Availability of alternative energy sources • Reduced availability of petroleum energy • Increasing analysis and control of climate and weather
• Social welfare contributions for employees continue to grow	• Demands for community development activities where plants are located • Slowing rate of population growth	• Need for constant retraining of knowledge for industry workers • Rapid obsolescence of work force under changing production technology • Workers with higher education skills than required • Increased speed of communication and information exchange
• Demands for disclosure of information other than historical financial performance	• Tax policy to encourage capital investment by business • Equal employment and fringe benefit policies raise cost of labor	• No recognized economic theory underlying policy decisions • Awareness of corporate and professional responsibility to consumers through increasing malpractice suits and product liability actions
• SEC encouraging soft information disclosure • Data base accounting systems which provide no historical detail	• AICPA procedures to review non-financial and soft information	• Decentralized record keeping and control require new control and review procedures
• Demands for disclosure of non-financial information by companies — human resources, social responsibility and environmental impact	• Requirements for non-polluting production facilities • Use and preparation of recycled raw materials	
• Centralized vs decentralized management structure • Financial structure and capitalization • Working capital requirements	• Growth through merger/acquisition activity vs plant and equipment expansion	
• Relationship between planning/ operations/executive functions in decision making • Limits of corporate information system to provide planning information • Nature of production cycle and accounting periods • Position of major products in product life cycle	• Greater demands on corporate officials for ethical conduct • Finance at the division or parent level • Local or international financial markets used to raise capital	• Top Down theory of management or Bottom-up theory • Attitude of management toward risk taking • Adaptive planning for expansion vs integrative for consolidation

FIGURE 1 Overview of a Planning System in Context

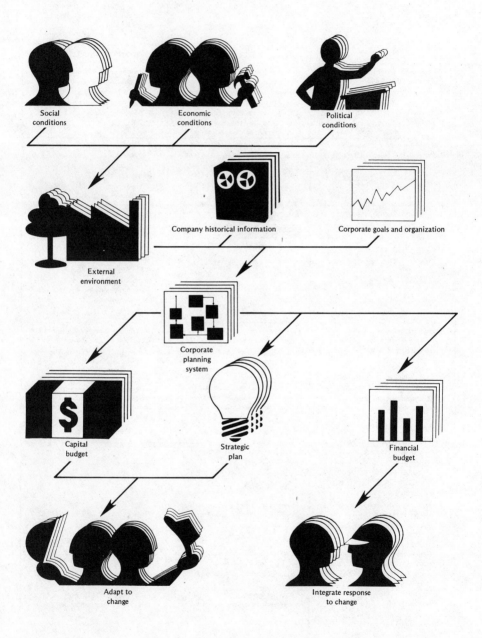

different, not just for teenagers and young adults, but also for many of their elders. Demographics have changed in many ways. The workforce is now dominated by people born during the baby boom, who are now in their late twenties or early thirties. Many of these young adults are jobless or cannot find work commensurate with their education. Large numbers of women of all ages have entered the labor force, well educated, ambitious, seeking meaningful careers as well as fair compensation.

One provocative view of social change is expressed by Robert Theobald, an economist who is the editor of *Futures Conditional*. He writes: "The key issue of our time is our view of people. If people are incapable of understanding themselves and their society, then we are indeed caught in the dilemmas advanced by those who debate growth limiting policies. If, on the other hand, people are willing and able to make decisions about their own lives and help run society, then we need to provide them with more opportunity to be involved in effective decision making." This statement, in short, suggests a coming decentralization of knowledge and authority never before envisioned—still another challenge for tomorrow's planners.

Government intervention in many areas has changed its character. The shift, in part, results from our leaders' frustrations with the pace of change and their inability to grasp the entire scope of the problems. Protection of the natural environment, consumer interests, and preservation of resources are now almost universal concerns. They are causing federal and local government to undertake new initiatives in these areas. Industries facing maturing and less profitable life cycles, such as transportation and utilities, are beginning to shift responsibility to government. Meanwhile, federal regulators are beginning to assume more passive roles in areas such as commercial aviation where they believe the market mechanism may be more effective.

The increase in the number and speed of factors affecting business indicates why planning grows continually more elaborate, though less certain. Some of the major elements and their interrelationships are shown in Figure 1. We can see from this simple diagram that the comprehensive planning system today must anticipate a multitude of external environmental influences, adjust to the changing historical information created by the company's accounting system, and react to new corporate objectives, goals, and forms of organization. The modern planning system must combine all these inputs into multiple scenarios for different time horizons. Strategic plans and capital spending evaluation must contribute to the company's ability to adapt to change. The annual budget must aid the company in integrating its response to the environment so as to improve corporate performance in the short term.

THE YEARNING FOR CERTAINTY IS UNABATED

The replacement of best-estimate forecasts by assortments of scenarios that describe possible futures in some detail has been forced upon planners. Yet in most corporate settings, decision makers still feel uncomfortable when presented with a stack of scenarios. They tend to tell the planner: "If you can't tell me what is going to happen, at least narrow your predictions down to the one that is most likely." As a result, many organizations fail to take full advantage of a range of contingency plans, especially those designed to cope with unlikely combinations of events. The importance of this advantage can be recognized when one considers the implication of emerging trends, such as California's Proposition 13 and the business tax reforms.

Many in the business world have, however, reconciled themselves to meeting uncertainty head-on. The response to the questionnaire discussed in the previous article came from persons who are willing to accept risk and uncertainty when they are expressed in such terms as: "very likely" or "somewhat unlikely." Quite possibly the next generation of decision makers will think and talk in the numerical terms of probability. One participant in The Conference Board study (a bank executive) stated flatly: "Forecasts are meaningless unless they are accompanied by probabilities."

It is likely that a larger proportion of decision makers find comfort in the predictive reliability of business cycles. Many short term fluctuations represent changes that are no more than random occurrences and therefore barely more meaningful than radio static. Nevertheless, certain well-established cycles have been studied and may have an important role in long-range corporate planning.

One well-known analyst has formalized the study of various cycles into a computer simulation model that may or may not comfort today's corporate planners. Jay W. Forrester of MIT's Sloan School of Management has constructed a model that projects the responses of the U.S. economy to a variety of events. The reason for having and trusting such a cycle-driven model, he explains, is that "intuition and political debate are proving inadequate tools for managing economic change."

In a recent article in *Technology Review* he writes at length on three economic cycles that seem to have worldwide significance. They are the familiar three-to-seven-year business cycle first proposed by Arthur Burns and Wesley C. Mitchell; the 15-to-25-year investment (or Kuznetz) cycle; and the 45-to-60-year Kondratieff cycle. The two longer cycles seem to be closely related to capital investment in such ways that they are potentially important considerations for corporate planners. Forrester states: "I am coming to believe that the long cycle is more important in explaining economic behavior than either the business or Kuznets cycles." He believes that the effects of this long wave may explain why simple extrapolation of economic trends no longer serves as a reliable guide to the future. Pointing out that the Kondratieff cycle seems to account for the depressions of the 1830s, 1890s, and 1930s, Forrester says that it may be of critical importance in explaining our current economic situation.

He concludes: "The challenge of the 1980s will be to cope with change. I believe we are at the top of a long-wave peak. If so, we are nearing the end of a technological era . . . We are in a hiatus between the ending of our present technological wave and the vigorous development of the next. . . . A pause occurs while we shift gears."

Although Professor Forrester represents perhaps the most conspicious user of business cycles in futures planning, many noted economic consultants are influenced by the realities of business cycles in their forecasting work. Dr. Otto Eckstein and his Data Resources, Inc. consulting firm prepare various ten-year economic projection alternatives based on the likelihood that cyclical factors will dominate the U.S. economy. In the near-future DRI projections, careful watch is kept on the underlying factors that may cause the economy to reach a cyclical peak or trough. The Wharton School forecasters, headed by Professor Lawrence Klein, and the Chase Econometrics projections, prepared under the direction of Dr. Michael K. Evans, also reflect the underlying flows of economic and financial activity caused by cyclical influences.

PLANNERS ARE SWAMPED WITH INFORMATION_____

The current output of economists, psychologists, environmentalists, soothsayers, lawmakers, scholars, and spouses makes it easy for a planner to identify factors that may affect corporate performance. The difficult problem is to organize, rank, and evaluate the all-too-abundant information. Then comes the still harder task of integrating this knowledge into planning systems that can lead to effective decision making.

In the development of a planning system, two kinds of factors should be considered in broad terms. Those that do not affect the chances of achieving the plan's objectives can be ignored for the time being, although they should be reviewed periodically as conditions change. Factors that appear likely to alter the risk that the resulting plan will or will not succeed warrant painstaking analysis. A broadbrush view of important factors and their interrelationships is shown in Figure 2.

This simplified diagram attempts to portray the complex linkages among the major dimension of our society. The dangers faced by our natural environment and the changing character of the U.S. and world populations contribute to the basic thrust of our social attitudes and institutions. As people become more educated, they react more quickly to the threats to our natural surroundings. The dangers perceived are translated into calls for political action and economic response.

Advanced technology has some sweeping negative effects that disturb environmentalists, government regulators, and other influential groups. Some of the best drugs have had side effects. Common chemicals, such as Red Dye #2, are suspected of causing cancer. Radiation and the disposal of nuclear wastes complicate plans for increasing energy output. The public has been sensitized to production methods that may endanger the health or lives of workers—black lung disease in the coal mines. Some management reorganizations result in severe personal dislocation that may lead to divorce or alienation from families.

The reactions to our environment and technology evoke our social moods and values. The state of technology and the depth of our knowledge profoundly affect our economic organization. Industrial technology determines the efficient scale of operation for various economic organizations. The accumulation of scientific and other human knowledge in our economic systems contributes to what and how we produce or provide.

A critical encounter for the business planner is the impact of the social environment on the economy. This dialogue reflects the difference between the values and needs of society and the current implementation of these goals. In the midst is a political system that reacts to and affects the outcome of our social system.

REDUCING THE RISKS OF MANAGEMENT

An article in *Harvard Business Review*, by George A. W. Boehm, editor of *Management Focus*, observed in the autumn of 1976: Managing is more of a gamble than ever, but systematically organized and analyzed information helps executives to hedge their bets. "The uncertainties of these times have

FIGURE 2 **Dimensions of Society**

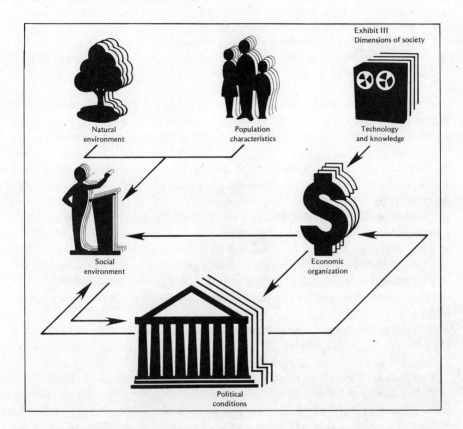

Political
conditions

forced a shotgun marriage between the executive decision maker and the systems analyst. . . . With enough ingenuity, it is possible to cope with an unsure future at least cleverly enough to minimize the chance of outright disaster."

To an even greater extent today, wrestling with uncertainty is the corporate planner's main task. The areas of uncertainty are difficult to identify and even more difficult to manage rationally. Here are a few specifics that most planners must contemplate and evaluate:

- What are likely impacts of the changing social environment?
- Will corporate and professional responsiblities to the consumer continue to grow as rapidly as they have in recent years?

- What will be the behavior of an aging population as the baby-boom bulge moves more people into their forties and fifties?
- How will steadily increasing participation by women affect the economy?
- Will the fear of technological advance grow?
- Can the nation sustain its historic optimistic view that somehow the future will work out well?

These kinds of domestic questions affect the planning process across many time horizons.

When consumer markets and attitudes change, does the planner:

1. Change his annual revenue budget, recompute his expected return on a capital expenditure project getting under way, or consider altering his company's competitive position in that market? Or perhaps, should he do all three?

When the price or availability of an essential production raw material changes significantly, does the planner:

2. Change his annual cost-of-goods-sold budget, reconsider the kind of technology built into a capital expenditure project, or review changing the mix of products sold by the company? Should he not do all three?

When the cost of borrowing in the capital markets rises sharply, does the planner:

3. Change his annual inventory and accounts receivable financing policy, recalculate the required rate of return on a pending project, or consider merging with or acquiring a similar competitor?

Probably all three.

These kinds of questions and the need for complex, dynamic answers require that modern corporate planning systems be sensitive to external factors. The advantages of having externally sensitive systems are many in the uncertain environment that prevails today. Plans can be quickly adjusted to mesh with external change. The outcomes of various scenarios can be tested in advance with the aid of computers. The outcomes of management policies can be tested against different external scenarios. Internal performance can be measured against external conditions and modified if necessary. Finally, the implications of any mix of external changes can be coordinated from the annual budget through the five-year strategic plan.

PLANNING FOR THE INDIVIDUAL IN A COMPLEX SOCIETY_____

E. H. Erikson, well-known student of human growth and behavior, describes the passage of a person's psychosocial life between the early and middle stages of adulthood. This period corresponds roughly to the present stage of the baby-boom generation, the dominant U.S. social force.

Although the characteristics of an entire society or era cannot be compared strictly to those of an indivdual, some interesting parallels include:

- The reexamination of life goals and objectives.
- Awareness of the complexity of life and the need to manage one's small piece of it.
- Evidence of one's vulnerablity and helplessness to change or divert major social forces.
- Struggle between the desire to participate in society or to withdraw from it.
- Loss of optimism about the automatic success of events of the future.
- Movement toward more basic values of family, career, and community.

If the parallel with Erickson is accurate, American society is approaching a middle stage of maturity. The realities of the natural environment have forced us to reexamine our priorities. The outlook for stable population growth has helped to bring expectations in line with the realities of our potential. These and many other reevalutions have become possible because our economic system has helped to create an affluence never before known in history.

THE PLANNER'S ROLE AS TOMORROW'S PHILOSOPHER_____

Social analyses like that of Erickson may not be in the mainstream of day-to-day corporate planning. Nevertheless, factors and events triggered by the changing outlooks of people play a major role in most planning phases. Planners who hope to squeeze the most assurance from a basically uncertain future can profit by reflecting upon the observations of philosophically minded psychologists and economists.

This is a worrisome—even frantic—era for those who must make plans and base decisions on them. But they can be heartened by the fact that even the economic and social turmoil of today was foreseen in broad terms as long as 20 years ago by humanistic thinkers such as Harvard economist Robert L. Heilbroner. In his book, *The Future as History*, he wrote:

> *Optimism as a philosphy of historic expectations can no longer be considered a national virtue. It has become a dangerous national delusion. . . . We limit our idea of what is possible by excluding from our control the forces of history themselves. . . . To rid oneself of this comforting notion is not to lessen one's ardor to resolve the difficulties of the present, but to arm oneself realistically for the continuation of the human struggle in the future.*

And that, in capsule form, expounds the role of today's corporate planner.

PROCESS

Management can be viewed as a process of planning, controlling, organizing, and decision making in order to achieve the organization's objectives. Each of these functions or processes has specific characteristics, but they combine together to describe what management does in the ongoing operation of making organizations perform.

Because planning and controlling are perhaps the most significant of these processes, we have included five articles in this section, each of which addresses various planning and controlling issues. First, Harold Koontz discusses strategic planning. In this article he defines strategy and supplies guidelines for the effective implementation of strategic planning. In the second article George S. Odiorne takes an historical look at management by objectives (MBO). He argues that MBO is alive and well and its future looks promising. In the third article, Heinz Weihrich continues the examination of MBO. He suggests that the process may fail if it is superimposed on the organization without understanding the existing climate or "culture." Mark L. McConkie, in the fourth article, examines the writings of leading MBO experts and identifies those elements that are common to successful practice. Archie B. Carroll closes out the planning articles with a unique piece that applies MBO goal-setting guidelines to the often ambiguous domain of social responsibility performance.

Three articles are included on the subject of the organizing function of the management process. First, Michael B. McCaskey presents an introduction to organizational design. In this article he presents various definitions and reviews research which has been conducted on organizational design. In the second article, Jay R. Galbraith presents an overview of matrix organization designs. He discusses how matrix design is basically an effort to combine functional and project structures into a matrix form. Finally, Stanley M. Davis and Paul R. Lawrence address problems of matrix organizations. They identify the problems created by matrix structures, diagnose why and how they arise, and then prescribe prevention and treatment measures that matrix managers can use.

Decision making is the subject of three articles that close out this part of the book. In the first article, John M. Roach presents an interview with 1978 Nobel laureate, Herbert A. Simon. Dr. Simon won his Nobel prize for landmark work on decision-making processes. In the article, Simon's view of decision making as a "satisficing" experience is presented. In the second article, Clarence W. Von Bergen and Raymond J. Kirk discuss the issue of "groupthink." Their thesis is that group decision making often yields a less than adequate answer because group psychological pressures tend to cloud the basic issues. In the final article in this section, Roy Rowan discusses the role of business hunches in decision making. He discusses how managers often must use their intuition rather than scientific methodologies in reaching decisions.

Taken together, the articles combine to provide interesting insights and helpful guidelines on the process aspect of making organizations perform. Managers and prospective managers should find the articles quite stimulating.

Harold Koontz

University of Southern California

MAKING STRATEGIC PLANNING WORK

It is widely agreed that the development and communication of strategy is the most important single activity of top managers. Joel Ross and Michael Kami, in their insightful book on the lack of success of many large U.S. companies, said, "Without a strategy the organization is like a ship without a rudder, going around in circles. It's like a tramp; it has no place to go."[1] They conclude from their study that without an appropriate strategy effectively implemented, failure is only a matter of time.

Although strategies are important, their development and implementation have posed many problems. The term strategy is often valueless and meaningless, even though it may be mouthed constantly by academics and executives. As one prominent consultant declared with respect to strategic planning, "In the large majority of companies, corporate planning tends to be an academic, ill-defined activity with little or no bottom-line impact."[2]

Many corporate chief executive officers have brushed strategic planning aside with such statements as "Strategic planning is basically just a plaything of staff men," or "Strategic planning? A staggering waste of time."[3] A number of companies and even some government agencies that have tried strategic planning have been observed wallowing around in generalities,

Harold Koontz, "Making Strategic Planning Work," *Business Horizons*, April 1976, pp. 37–47.

[1] Joel E. Ross and Michael J. Kami, *Corporations in Crisis: Why the Mighty Fall* (Englewood Cliffs, N.J.: Prentice-Hall, Inc., 1973), p. 132.

[2] Louis V. Gerstner, "Can Strategic Planning Pay Off?" *Business Horizons* (December 1972), pp. 5-16.

[3] *Ibid.*, p. 5.

unproductive studies, and programs that do not get into practical operation. In one large company, a far too patient president watched a succession of top planning officers and their staffs flounder for 12 years, until his patience was finally exhausted and he insisted on practical action.

The basic cause of disillusionment with strategic planning is the lack of knowledge in four areas: (1) what strategies are and why they are important; (2) how strategies fit into the entire planning process; (3) how to develop strategies; and (4) how to implement strategies by bringing them to bear on current decisions.

WHAT STRATEGIES ARE

Strategies are general programs of action with an implied commitment of emphasis and resources to achieve a basic mission. They are patterns of major objectives, and major policies for achieving these objectives, conceived and stated in such a way as to give the organization a unified direction.

For years, strategies were used by the military to mean grand plans made in view of what it was believed an adversary might or might not do. Tactics were regarded as action plans necessary to implement strategies. While the term strategy still has a competitive implication, it is increasingly used to denote a general program that indicates a direction to be taken and where emphasis is to be placed. Strategies do not attempt to outline exactly how the enterprise is to accomplish its major objectives. This is the task of a multitude of major and minor supporting programs.

Failure of strategic planning is really one aspect of the difficulties encountered in making all kinds of planning effective. Although the sophistication with which planning is done has risen remarkably in the past three decades, and despite the fact that planning is considered the foundation of management, it is still too often the poorest performed task of the managerial job. As every executive knows, it is easy to fail in all aspects of effective planning without really trying.

WHY PLANNING FAILS

What are some of the major reasons why effective planning is so difficult to accomplish? By summarizing some of the principal reasons in practice in both business and nonbusiness enterprises, some light may be cast on the reasons for disillusionment and ineffectiveness in many strategic planning programs.

One of the major reasons for failure is managers' lack of commitment to planning. Most people allow today's problems and crises to push aside planning for tomorrow. Instead of planning, most would rather "fight fires" and meet crises, for the simple reason that doing so is more interesting, more fun, and gives a greater feeling of accomplishment. This means, of course, that an environment must be created that forces people to plan.

Another cause of failure is confusing planning studies with plans. Many are the companies and government agencies that have stacks of planning studies. But for a planning study to become a plan, a decision must be made that will commit resources or direction; until then it is only a study.

Problems also arise when major decisions on various matters are made without having a clear strategy, or without making sure that decisions, such as one to develop and market a new product, fit a company's strategy.

Another reason for failure is the lack of clear, actionable, attainable, and verifiable objectives or goals. It is impossible to do any effective planning without knowing precisely what end results are sought. Objectives must be verifiable in the sense that, at some target date in the future, a person can know whether they have been accomplished. This can, of course, be done best in quantitative terms, such as dollars of sales or profits. But since many worthwhile objectives cannot be put in numbers, goals can also be verified in qualitative terms, such as a marketing program with specified character-istics to be launched by a certain date.

Perhaps the most important cause of failure in planning is neglecting or underestimating the importance of planning premises or assumptions. These are the expected environment of a decision, the stage on which a certain program will be played. They not only include economic and market forecasts, but also the expectation of important changes in the technological, political, social, or ethical environment. They may also include decisions or commitments made, basic policies, and major limitations. One thing is sure; unless people know and follow consistent planning premises, their planning decisions will not be coordinated.

Another problem area is the failure to place strategies within the total scope of plans. Anything that involves selecting a course of action for the future may be thought of as a plan. These include missions or purposes, objectives, strategies, policies, rules, procedures, programs, and budgets. Unless strategies are seen as one of the major types of plans, it is easy to regard them as isolated directional decisions unrelated to other kinds of plans.

Ineffective planning may also be the result of failure to develop clear policies. Policies are guides to thinking in decision making. Their essence is defined discretion. They give structure and direction to decisions, mark out an area where discretion can be used, and thereby give guidelines for plans. Without clear policies, plans tend to be random and inconsistent.

Planning often suffers, too, from not keeping in mind the time span which should be involved. Long-range planning is not planning for future decisions, but planning the future impact of present decisions. In other words, planning is planning. Some plans involve commitments that can be fulfilled in short periods, such as a production plan, and others can only be discharged over longer periods, as in the case of a new product development or capital facilities program. Obviously, unless a decision maker does not try to foresee, as best as can be done, the fulfillment of commitments involved in today's decisions, he is not doing the job that good planning requires.

Another danger of planning lies in the tendency of people, especially those with considerable experience, to base their decisions on that experience—on what did or did not work in the past. Since decisions must operate for the future, they should be based on *expectations* for the future, not on experience and facts of the past.

Finally, a major cause of deficient planning is the inability of some people to diagnose a situation in the light of critical or limiting factors. In every problem (opportunity) situation, there are many variables that may affect the outcome of a course of action. But in every problem area there are certain variables that make the most difference. Thus in a new product development program, the critical factors may be whether a proposed product will fit a company's marketing channels and competence, or whether its efficient production might require capital facilities beyond a company's financial ability. Clearly, the adept decision maker will search for, identify and solve critical factors.

MAJOR TYPES OF STRATEGIES

For a business enterprise at least, the major strategies which give it an overall direction are likely to be in the following seven areas.

New or Changed Products and Services. A business exists to furnish products or services of an economic nature. In a very real sense, profits are merely a measure—albeit an important one—of how well a company serves its customers.

Marketing. Marketing strategies are designed to guide planning in getting products or services to reach customers, and getting customers to buy.

Growth. Growth strategies give direction to such questions as: How much growth and how fast? Where?

Financial. Every business, and for that matter every nonbusiness, enterprise must have a clear strategy for financing its operations. There are various ways of doing this and usually many serious limitations.

Organizational. This kind of strategy has to do with the type of organizational pattern an enterprise will follow. It answers such practical questions as how centralized or decentralized decision-making authority should be, what kind of departmental patterns are most suitable, whether to develop integrated profit-responsible divisions, what kind of matrix organization structures are used, and how to design and utilize staffs effectively. Naturally, organization structures furnish the system of roles and role relationships to help people perform in the accomplishment of objectives.

Personnel. Major strategies in the area of human resources and relationships may be of a wide variety. They deal with union relations, compensation, selection, recruitment, training and appraisal, as well as strategy in such matters as job enrichment.

Public Relations. Strategies in this area can hardly be independent but must support other major strategies and efforts. They must also be designed in the light of the company's type of business, its closeness to the public, its susceptibility to regulation by government agencies and similar factors.

STRATEGY REQUISITES

For developing major strategies of any kind, there are a number of key requirements. If a company fails to meet them, its strategic planning program is likely to be meaningless or even incorrect.

Corporate Self-Appraisal

This requirement involves asking the questions: What is our business? What kind of business are we in? These simple questions, as many businesses have discovered, are not always easy to answer. The classic case is the railroad industry that too long overlooked the fact that its companies were in the transportation business, and not just the railroad business. Glass bottle manufacturers in the United States almost missed their opportunities by seeing themselves for too long as glass bottle makers rather than as liquid container manufacturers, as plastic and metal containers came to be used in many applications in place of glass. Likewise, many believe that the steel companies over the world have stayed too long with the belief that they are steel makers, rather than in the structural materials business, which includes many materials not made of steel.

On answering this question, a company should be regarded as a total entity, its strengths and weaknesses analyzed in each functional area—marketing, product development, production and other operations areas, finance, and public relations. It must focus attention on its customers and what they want and can buy, its technological capabilities, and financial resources. In addition, note must be made of the values, aspirations, and prejudices of top executives.

In assessing strengths, weaknesses, and limitations, an enterprise must, of course, be realistic. In doing so, however, there is a danger in overstressing weaknesses and underestimating strengths. History is replete with examples of companies that have spent so much effort in shoring up weaknesses that they did not capitalize on their strengths. To be sure, weaknesses should be corrected to the extent possible. But taking advantage of identified strengths in formulating strategies offers the most promise.

Assessing the Future Environment

Strategies, like any other type of plan, are intended to operate in the future; thus, the best possible estimate of the future environment in which a company is to operate is necessary. If a company can match its strengths with the environment in which it plans to operate, opportunities can be detected and taken advantage of.

A prerequisite of the assessment of the future environment is forecasting. In general, modern businesses do a fairly good job of forecasting economic developments and markets, although, of course, there can be many errors and uncertainties. Few would have forecast the price impact of the oil-producing nation's cartel and the extent of inflation in recent years. A few companies have found rewarding results in forecasting technological changes and predicting technological developments. Some companies in highly regulated industries have even forecast political environments, particularly governmental actions that would affect their company. But only recently have companies, research institutes, and government agencies even started the task of attempting to forecast social attitudes and pressures.

Clearly, the better an enterprise can see its total environment, the better it can establish strategies and support plans to take advantage of its capabilities in preparation for the future. However, experience to date indicates that, except for economic and market forecasts, it is difficult to get the forecast and assessment of other environmental factors into practical use. This can be done through an active and effective program that would use planning premises as the background for decision making, but this is one of the areas of planning that has especially not been performed well.

An important element of the future environment, of course, is the probable actions of competition. Too often, planning is based on what competition has been doing and not on what competitors may be expected to do. No one can plan on the assumption that his competitors are asleep.

Organization Structure Assuring Planning

If strategies are to be developed and implemented, an organizational structure which assures effective planning is needed. Staff assistance is important for forecasting, establishing premises and making analyses. But there is the danger of establishing a planning staff and thinking planning exists when all that really exists is planning studies, rather than decisions based on them.

To avoid ivory-towered and useless staff efforts, several things are needed. A planning staff should be given the tasks of developing major objectives, strategies and planning premises, and submitting them to top management for review and approval. They should also be responsible for disseminating approved premises and strategies, and they should help operating people to understand them. Before major decisions of a long-range or strategic impact are made, the staff group should be given the task of reviewing them and making recommendations. These few tasks can be advantageous in that they force decision makers to consider environmental factors, and also prevent the staff from becoming a detached and impractical group.

Another major organizational device is the regular, formal and rigorous review of planning programs and performance, preferably by an appropriate committee. This has long been done in well-managed divisionalized companies where division general managers are called in before a top executive committee. Perhaps it should be done at lower levels, too. Doing so has the advantage of forcing people to plan, of making sure that strategies are being followed by programs, and where strategies do not exist or are unclear, making this deficiency apparent.

Assuring Consistent Strategies

One of the important requirements of effective strategic planning is to make sure that strategies are consistent, that they "fit" each other. For example, one medium-sized company had a successful sales record as the result of a strategy of putting out quality products at lower prices than its larger competitors, who did their selling through heavy and expensive advertising. Pleased with this success, and after adding to its product line through acquisitions, the company then embarked on an additional strategy of trying to sell through heavy advertising, with disastrous effects on profits.

The Need for Contingency Strategies

Because every strategy must operate in the future, and because the future is always subject to uncertainty, the need for contingency strategies cannot be overlooked. If a regulated telephone company, for example, has had some of its services opened to competition (as has happened recently in the United States when other companies were allowed to furnish facilities that were once the monopoly of the telephone companies), and adopts a strategy of aggressive competition on the assumption that regulatory commissions will allow competitive pricing, the strategy would become inoperative if the commissions do not actually allow such pricing. Or if a company develops a strategy based on a certain state of technology, and a new discovery changes materially the technological environment, it is faced with a major need for a contingency strategy.

Where events occur which make a strategy obsolete (and they often can without warning), it is wise to have developed a contingent strategy based on a different set of premises. These "what if" kinds of strategies can be put into effect quickly to avoid much of the "crisis management" that is seen so often.

PRODUCTS OR SERVICES STRATEGIES_____

To develop strategies in any area, certain questions must be asked in each major strategy area. Given the right questions, the answers should help any company to formulate its strategies. Some key questions in two strategic areas will be examined—new products and services, and marketing. A little thought can result in devising key questions for other major strategic areas.

One of the most important areas is strategy involving new products or services, since these, more than any other single factor, will determine what a company is or will be. The key questions in this area may be summarized as follows.

What is our business? This classic question might also be phrased in terms of what is *not* our business. It is also necessary to raise the question:

What is our industry? Are we a single product or product-line industry, such as shoes or furniture? Or are we a process industry, such as chemicals or electronic components? Or are we an end-use industry, such as transportation or retailing?

Who are our customers? Peter Drucker has long said that the purpose of a business is to "create a customer," although he could hardly have meant to create customers without regard to profits. In answering this question, it is important to avoid too great an attachment to *present* customers and products. The motion picture industry failed to avoid this when home television first appeared on the market and was considered a threat to movie theaters. They fought television for years until they realized that their business was entertainment and their customers wanted both motion pictures in theaters and on television. They then found one of their most lucrative markets in renting old movies to television and in using their studios and other facilities for producing television shows.

What do our customers want? Do they want price, value, quality, availability, service? The success of the Hughes Tool Company, for example, has been based largely on a shrewd analysis of what oil and gas well drillers wanted, and furnishing them with the exact drill bit, of a high quality, in the place the bit was needed, and with adequate service to support the product. Likewise, IBM's leadership in business computers has been due in large part to its knowledge of what customers wanted and needed; maintaining advancement of product design; having a family of computers; and developing a strong service organization.

How much will our customers buy and at what price? This is a matter that involves what customers think they are buying. What they consider value and what they will pay for it will determine what a business is, what it should produce, and whether it will prosper. The answer to this question will be a key to product or service strategy.

Do we wish to be a product leader? It may seem that the answer to this question would be obvious, but it is not. Some companies owe their success to being a close second in product leadership. The product leader will often have an advantage in reaching a market first, but such a company may incur heavy costs of developing and attempting to market products which do not become commercial successes, as well as those which do. One of the major airlines, for example, prided itself on being the leader in acquiring and putting into service new aircraft. But after suffering financial losses as a result of their extensive debugging of several new planes, they adopted the strategy of letting someone else be the leader, and becoming a close second.

Do we wish to develop our own new products? Here again, a company must decide whether it should develop its own new products, whether it should rely on innovations by competitors to lead the way, or whether it should lean heavily on product development by materials suppliers. In the chemicals field, such innovative raw materials producers as Du Pont and Dow Chemical discover new chemical compositions and then cast about to ascertain where they can be used in new products. Companies without adequate resources to mount a strong product research program can often find a gold mine of product ideas in the developments of such suppliers.

What advantages do we have in serving customer needs? Most companies like to have a unique product or service that is difficult for a competitor to duplicate. Some larger companies look only for products that require a high capital investment in tooling and machinery, heavy advertising, strong engineering, expensive service organizations, and similar characteristics that tend to discourage the entry of smaller competitors into a market. Many larger companies also purposefully keep out of products with small volume markets—products that can be manufactured and marketed by small companies—feeling that the small operators can offer a personalized service and incur lower overhead costs than the larger company.

What of existing and potential competition? In deciding on a product strategy, it is important to assess realistically the nature and strength of existing competition. If a competitor in a field has tremendous strength in new products, marketing and service, as IBM has had in the computer field, a company should consider carefully its chances to enter the field. Even the large RCA Corporation found it had to swallow a loss of some $450 million after attempting unsuccessfully to complete with IBM with a head-on strategy.

How far can we go in serving customer needs? There are often important limitations. One is, of course, financial: a company must consider whether it has the financial resources to support necessary product research, manufacturing facilities, inventory and receivables, advertising and marketing, and a requisite service competence.

Legal limitations may also be important, as Procter and Gamble found when it was forced by the antitrust laws to divest itself of the Clorox Company (household bleach), or as certain pharmaceutical companies have found when their introduction of new products is held up by the Pure Food and Drug Administration.

Other important limitations may be found in the availability of suitably competent managers and other personnel. Thus, Ford, a well-managed automobile company, had difficulties in managing Philco. Litton Industries apparently found that running its shipbuilding subsidiary was beyond its managerial abilities.

What profit margins can we expect? A company naturally wants to be in a business where it can make an attractive profit. One of the keys is the gross profit margin, that profit above operating expenses which will carry overhead and administrative expenses and yield a desired profit before taxes.

What basic form should our strategy take? In formulating a product or service strategy, a company should determine the direction it wishes to go in terms of intensive or extensive product diversification. If it follows an intensive strategy, it might move in the direction of market penetration—going further in present product markets. Or it might decide on one of market development—going into markets it has not been in before. Thus, Reynolds Aluminum years ago expanded into such consumer products as aluminum kitchen wrappings. Or a company might concentrate on developing, improving, or changing products it already has.

If a company follows an extensive product strategy, it can go in three basic directions. First, it might concentrate on vertical integration. If it is a retailing company it might, as Sears Roebuck and Company has done so often, go into making products it sells. Or if it is a manufacturing company, it might go into retailing, as Sinclair Paints has done. Second, a company might diversify extensively by line diversification, going into products utilizing existing skills, capacities, and strengths. Lever Brothers has done this for many years by expanding their operations to a large number of products marketed through grocery stores. A third kind of extensive strategy is conglomerate diversification, going into not necessarily related products with the hope of getting synergistic advantages from combining such skills and strengths as marketing, new product development, management and financial resources. The difficulty with this strategy, as many conglomerates have found, is that too rapid and too varied a program of acquisition can lead to situations that cannot be managed effectively and profitably.

MARKETING STRATEGIES_____

Marketing strategies are closely connected to product strategies, and must be supportive and interrelated. As a matter of fact, Drucker regards the two basic business functions as innovation and marketing. It is true that a business can hardly survive without these. But while a company can succeed by copying products, it can hardly succeed without effective marketing.

In this area, as in products and services, there are certain questions which can be used as guides for establishing a marketing strategy.

Where are our customers and why do they buy? This question is really asking whether customers are large or small buyers, whether they are end users or manufacturers, where they are geographically, where they are in the production–ultimate user spectrum, and why they buy. Xerox answered some of these questions cleverly and effectively when it saw customers not as copy machine buyers but rather as purchasers of low-cost copies. As a result of their leasing program and charging on a per-copy basis, this company has had phenomenal success. Likewise, the Farr Company, one of the nation's most innovative and successful air filter companies, has effectively marketed its engine air filters for locomotives and trucks by the strategy of considering its real customers to be the buyers and users of such transport vehicles rather than the equipment manufacturers. Thus, by getting large railroads and trucking companies to specify Farr filters on new equipment, they in effect forced the use of their filters on equipment manufacturers.

How do customers buy? Some customers buy largely through specialized distributing organizations, as is the case with medical and hospital supplies. Some buy through dealer organizations, as with automobiles. Others are accustomed to buying directly from manufacturers, as in the case of major defense procurement, large equipment buyers, and most raw material users in such fields as chemicals, electronic components, and steel products; but even in these cases, specialized distributors and processors may be important for certain buyers and at certain times.

How is it best for us to sell? There are a number of approaches to selling. Some companies rely heavily on preselling through advertising and sales promotion. Procter and Gamble owes much of its success to a strategy of preselling customers through heavy advertising and sales promotion expenditures (said to average 20% of every sales dollar). At the same time, a much smaller company in the soap and detergents field, the Purex Corporation, had great success in selling its liquid and dry detergents through the appeal of lower consumer prices and higher margins for retailers. Other companies may find their best strategy is to sell on the basis of technical superiority and direct engineering contacts with customers.

Do we have something to offer that competitors do not? The purpose of product differentiation is, of course, to make buyers believe a company's products are different and better than similar products offered by competitors, whether in fact they are or not. It is often possible to build a marketing strategy on some feature in a product or service that is different, regardless of the significance of the difference. This many be an attractive innovation in product design or quality, as in the case of Sylvania's push-button television sets. Or it might be an innovation in service, such as American Motors' all-inclusive automobile warranty. Obviously, what every marketer wants is a claim of product or service uniqueness in order to obtain a proprietary position.

Do we wish to take steps, legally, to discourage competition? There are many things a company can do to discourage competition, other than to run afoul of the antitrust or fair trade laws. Mere size and the ability to finance expensive specialized machinery and tools, or a geographically spread sales and service organization are among these. The success of the Hughes Tool Company in oil drilling bits and that of IBM in the computer field fall into this category. But even medium-sized companies can discourage the very small would-be competitors in the same way. Or a company's marketing strategy might be helped by innovative advertising and product image, which will entrench the company in a market and discourage competition.

Do we need, and can we supply, supporting services? A company's effectiveness in marketing can be greatly influenced by the degree of need for supporting services such as maintenance, and the ability to supply them. Often, certain foreign-made automobiles were slow in getting a position in the American market because of the lack of availability of dealer repair services. Mercedes Benz, for example, had difficulty in making much of a dent in the automobile market until it was able to establish service capabilities in at least the larger cities of the United States. Packard Bell enjoyed a strong position in television in the western states some years ago because of its strong service organization in this area; and for years because of this, limited sales to that area. The major telephone companies, the Bell System and General Telephone, have recently developed a marketing strategy for their industrial and commercial switchboard systems against the rising competition of special equipment manufacturers by emphasizing their prompt and competent maintenance service capabilities.

What is the best pricing strategy and policy for our operation? There are many strategies that can be used. Suggested list prices, quantity and other discounts, delivered or F.O.B. sellers' place of business prices, firm prices, or prices with escalation, and the extent of down payments with orders or prices that vary with labor and material costs are among the wide number of variations. How goods or services are priced may be a matter of custom in a market, a marketing tool of a supplier, a matter of achieving price stability versus price cutting; or may reflect the understandable desire of a producer to guard against losses from uncertainty, as in the case of "time and material" contracts.

IMPLEMENTING STRATEGIES

Thus far, much of the emphasis has been on the development of clear and meaningful strategies. If strategic planning is to be operational, certain steps must be taken to implement it.

Strategies should be communicated to all key decision-making managers. It naturally does little good to formulate meaningful strategies unless they are communicated to all managers in the position to make decisions on plans designed to implement them. Strategies may be clear to the executive committee and the chief executive who participate in making them, but nothing is communicated unless they are also clear to the receiver. Strategies should be in writing, and meetings of top executives and their subordinates should be held to make sure that strategies are understood by everyone involved.

Planning premises must be developed and communicated. The importance of planning premises has been emphasized earlier. Steps must be taken so that those premises critical to plans and decisions are developed and disseminated to all managers in the decision-making chain, with instructions to generate programs and make decisions in line with them. Too few companies and other organizations do this. But if it is not done and if premises do not include key assumptions for the entire spectrum of the environment in which plans will operate, decisions are likely to be based on personal assumptions and predilections. The result is almost certain to be a collection of uncoordinated plans.

Action plans must contribute to and reflect major objectives and strategies. Action plans are tactical or operational programs and decisions, whether major or minor, that take place in various parts of an organization. If they do not reflect desired objectives and strategies, vacuous hopes or useless statements of strategic intent result. If care is not taken in this area, then certainly strategic planning is not likely to have a bottom-line impact.

There are various ways of ensuring that action plans do contribute to strategies. If every manager understands strategies, he can certainly review the program recommendations of his staff advisers and his line subordinates to see that they contribute and are consistent. It might even be advisable, at least in major decisions, to have them reviewed by an appropriate small committee, such as one including a subordinate's superior, the superior's superior, and a staff specialist. This would lend an aura of formality to the program decisions, and important influences on implementation of strategies might become clear. Budgets likewise should be reviewed with objectives and strategies in mind.

Strategies should be reviewed regularly. Even carefully developed strategies might cease to be suitable if events change, knowledge becomes more clear, or it appears that the program environment will not be as originally thought. Strategies should be reviewed from time to time, certainly not less than once a year, and perhaps more often.

Consider developing contingency strategies and programs. Where considerable change in competitive factors or other elements in the environment might occur and it is impractical to develop strategies that would cover the changes, contingency strategies should be formulated. No one, of course, can wait until the future is certain to make plans. Even where there is considerable uncertainty, there is no choice but to proceed on the most credible set of premises. But this does not mean that a company need find itself totally unprepared if certain possible contingencies do occur.

Make organization structure fit planning needs. The organization structure should be designed to support the accomplishment of goals and the making of decisions to implement strategies. If possible, it is best to have one position (or person) responsible for the accomplishment of each goal and for implementing strategies in achieving this goal. In other words, end result areas and key tasks should be identified and assigned to a single position as far down the organization structure as is feasible. Since this sometimes cannot be done, there may be no alternative but to utilize a form of grid organization. Where this is done, the responsibilities of the various positions in the grid should be clearly spelled out.

In an organizational structure, the roles of staff analysts and advisers should be defined and used so that staff studies and recommendations enter the decision system at the various points where decisions are actually made. Unless this is done, independent staff work of no value to planning is the result.

Continue to teach planning and strategy implementation. Even where a workable system of objectives and strategies and their implementation exists, it is easy for it to fail unless responsible managers continue to teach the nature and importance of planning. This may seem like a tedious process and unnecessary repetition, but learning can be assured in no other way. Teaching does not have to be done at formal meetings or seminars. Rather, much of the instruction can take place in the day-to-day consideration and review of planning proposals and in the review of performance as superiors undertake their normal control functions.

Create a company climate that forces planning. As mentioned earlier, people tend to allow today's problems and crises to postpone effective planning for tomorrow. Therefore, the only way to assure that planning of all kinds will be done, and that strategies will be implemented, is to utilize devices and techniques that force planning.

There are many ways that an environment compulsive of planning can be created. Managing by objectives is one way; verifiable and actionable objectives cannot be set without some thought on how they are to be achieved. The rigorous and formal review of objectives, programs and performance will help create a planning environment. Similarly, review of budgets will force people to plan, especially if managers are required to explain their total budget needs and are not permitted to concentrate only on changes from a previous period. As pointed out earlier, a clear results-oriented organization structure and staff assistance in the actual decision process will help force planning. Goals, strategies, policies, and premises, if communicated effectively, can also aid the planning process, especially since most people prefer to make decisions that are consistent with them.

Also, since strategies normally involve a fairly long-term commitment, care must be taken to insure that long-range and short-range plans are integrated. There are few day-to-day decisions that do not have an impact on longer-range commitments. In reviewing program proposals, even those that appear to be minor, superiors should make sure that they fit long-range strategies and programs. This is easy to do if managers know what they are and are required to think in these terms.

Strategic planning can be made to have a bottom-line impact. Effective top managers can assure this if they have carefully developed strategies and taken pains for their implementation. In fact, if a company or any other kind of organization is to be successful over a period of time, it really has no other alternative.

George S. Odiorne

University of Massachusetts, Amherst

MBO:
A BACKWARD GLANCE

In the world of the academic and the industrial manager, few people are neutral about management by objectives (MBO). In the United States and abroad, popular and scholarly management periodicals are replete with articles by both university-based researchers and operating managers about this managerial technique. An abundance of doctoral dissertations, trade books by consultants and professors, and case studies for use in academic classrooms deals with various facets of MBO as a modern management technique. New applications and adaptations, sometimes matched by critical and satirical comments, keep coming forth.

Recently, a Canadian scholar prepared a list of books and articles in the area of MBO, consisting of some 55 pages with more than 700 books, articles, monographs, dissertations, and theses listed.[1] In addition to these, it would be possible to identify more than 300 readings, foreign journal articles, and audio and video cassette training packages on MBO. Hundreds of company-prepared manuals and documents are designed for internal company training and guidance in applying MBO. At least one regular monthly journal and several newsletters on MBO are currently in existence. Keeping track of new developments in the growth and modification of MBO is, therefore, a prodigious task.

George S. Odiorne, "MBO: A Backward Glance," *Business Horizons*, October 1978, pp. 14–24.

[1] Richard Mansell, *A Management by Objectives Bibliography*, mimeographed (Waterloo, Ontario: University of Waterloo, 1977).

Writers, consultants, practitioners, and researchers who deal with MBO can be classified into three major categories. *of individuals who deal with MBO*

1. The *constructors* are those managers, writers, and researchers who have shaped the form and direction of MBO.
2. The *devotees* are those who advocate it, cite its successes in their own organization, improve upon it, and espouse it for others' use.
3. The *haters* are those who find in MBO a seriously defective management system and are strong in their condemnation. Although this group is surprisingly small in numbers, it has existed and made loud, objectionable sounds since MBO's inception.

THE CONSTRUCTORS_____

Origins

One of the more popular pastimes among academics is uncovering the origins of MBO. A plethora of originators has been proposed. Old Testament quotations and examples, including Abraham's covenant with God and Moses' search for the Promised Land, have been cited. The Koran is quoted: "If you don't know where you are going, any road will get you there." Several ancient Greeks, including Aristotle, noted the importance of a definite purpose to ultimate success. Disraeli proposed that "success is a product of unremitting attention to purpose." C. West Churchman, trained as a philosopher and recognized as a leading figure in the systems approach, has also noted that the earliest constructions of that approach are found in the writings of Plato, Aristotle, St. Thomas Aquinas, Nietzsche, Descartes, Hobbes, Leibniz, Bentham, Kant, and Marx, among others.[2]

The definition of goals as a preliminary step to action seems to have permeated most management theory. It would be easy to construct an underlying management theory of goals and results-centered management from the histories of organizers of great corporations, such as Andrew Carnegie or Pierre Du Pont.

When young Pierre Du Pont, at the turn of the century, joined his family business, he came under the tutelage of Arthur Moxham, who taught him the virtues of cost accounting. But even more, "he came away profoundly

[2] C. West Churchman, *The Systems Approach* (New York: Dell, 1977): 239–240.

impressed with analytical management."[3] Moxham's balance sheets told, at a glance, which parts of the company made money and which did not, thus making it possible to have a rational basis for investment decisions. This attention to accounting and its development through statistical analysis was in its formative stage at the turn of the century, and offered a set of lessons that Du Pont was to carry successfully to other places and times. Upon moving to the presidency of General Motors in 1920, one of Pierre Du Pont's first acts was to reorganize GM into divisions and to initiate the development of impersonal statistical and financial controls. When Du Pont resigned as president of General Motors in 1923, he left in place a management system with clear targets in such areas as inventory, ROI, sales, and output.

Starting in 1925, General Motors adopted a concept created by Donaldson Brown that related "a definite long-term return on investment objective to average or standard volume expectations over a number of years."[4] Goals were set for volume, costs, prices, and rates of return on capital. Standard cost hours, amounts paid for each purchased part, and the hours of labor required for each function were determined. These breakdowns were, at least in part, accounting techniques, for they included statistical data, ratios, rates, and amounts for every business purpose. As Alfred P. Sloan has written, "The guiding principle was to make our standards difficult to achieve, but possible to attain, which I believe is the most effective way of capitalizing on the initiative, resourcefulness, and capabilities of operating personnel."[5]

This concept, Sloan points out, makes profit residual for most managers and makes it possible to estimate very closely what profit would be at various volumes. Tied to the executive bonus plan, based on rewarding performance as it related to standards, the development of this concept would suggest that Sloan, with his associates Donaldson Brown and Albert Bradley, perfected the major elements of modern MBO. Indeed, Peter Drucker, who many years later conducted a study of GM's management system, reported to John Tarrant, his biographer, that he first heard the term "management by objectives" used by Alfred P. Sloan.

In the marketing field, it was neither Du Pont nor Sloan who evidenced the first rudimentary examples of MBO, but John Henry Patterson of National Cash Register. Patterson had acquired the sagging National Manufacturing Company and changed its name. After overhauling the design of the cash register so that it could be manufactured economically, he turned

---

[3] Alfred D. Chandler and Stephen Salsbury, *Pierre S. Du Pont and the Making of the Modern Corporation* (New York: Harper & Row, 1971): 499.

[4] Alfred P. Sloan, *My Years with General Motors* (New York: Doubleday, 1963): 144.

[5] Sloan: 147.

his attention to launching a selling and sales training program of unmatched effectiveness. As one business historian has noted, "He established a quota system and guaranteed territory, altering a competitive concept which, in the past, had pitted one salesman against another in the same circumscribed area."[6] This quota system ran contrary to all selling concepts prior to Patterson's time and led NCR to market domination in the field with 94 percent of the market.

It was this system under which Thomas Watson, Sr., learned his trade as a marketer; he was later to transfer it to his own firm, the International Business Machines Corporation, in 1914. By 1924, Watson had made it clear that his style of management was unique and astonishingly successful. The creation of the One Hundred Percent Clubs, open to those who had achieved their quota, was supplemented with an evangelical enthusiasm for success. Part of the new IBM spirit was that no man was to think of himself as a boss; "the farther we keep away from the boss proposition, the more successful we are going to be," Watson said in 1925.[7] On the other hand, one could be a leader on a one-to-one basis, with one man giving guidance to another, not telling him what to do but helping him to do it. Thus the supportive aspect of management—setting tough goals and showing great enthusiasm, then helping the subordinate to get there—so highly regarded in modern MBO, was commonplace in IBM under Watson.

In 1927, he told members of the Hundred Percent Club, "It is a shame for any man, if he is in good health, to put in twelve months in a territory in our business and not come through with 100 percent of quota."[8] Watson demonstrated with unremitting energy that he would set high goals and exhorted everyone toward attainment of those goals. If top management support, as is so often said, is an essential ingredient of MBO, then Watson was living proof of its effectiveness. By 1930, goals-centered management was spreading.

Quite independently, at Standard Oil of New Jersey, President Walter Teagle faced up to growing administrative problems in that giant worldwide firm. He issued a memorandum in 1933 that effected a basic MBO program, even though that label was not attached to it. In effect, that memorandum brought to an end the era of the "entrepreneurial genius" method of management. It provided for a complete delegation of operating authority to independent operating units, making each unit responsible for its operations in a given territory. A coordinating committee at the corporate level

6 William Rodgers, *Think, A Biography of Watson and IBM* (New York: New American Library, 1970): 37.

7 Rodgers: 89.

8 Rodgers: 90.

defined goals and policies, approved operating and capital budgets, and approved operating indicators proposed by the units. At annual meetings, previously secret information was widely shared, along with a strong program of training for younger managers.[9] By 1940, this model of decentralized operating authority was recognized as a necessary form of organization in most major corporations. Reduced control over means of operation was being coupled with growing attention to outputs and results.[10]

Peter Drucker, Theoretician — *founded concept of MBO*

In the late 1930s, Peter Drucker, an Austrian by birth and an immigrant to this country, was invited to consult with the management of General Motors. As an economist and an outsider, he brought to his study of the corporate giant the observational skills of a Tocqueville or a Darwin. Without questionnaires or statistical techniques, Drucker walked about, conducting informal interviews, making notes, and drawing conclusions from common sense and systematic observations. He later wrote perceptively of his observations in *The Concept of the Corporation* (1946).

Drucker's discovery of the significance of decentralization and divisional forms of corporate organization seemed to be his major focus. His distinction between "federal" and "functional" decentralization was widely copied. The fact that he only saw goals and objectives as a natural product of that key concept is often missed. In his lectures at New York University in later years, he impressed upon his students the importance of decentralization as a route to greater industrial democracy, the personalization of large bureaucratic corporations, and the pushing down, or delegation, of decisions.

The major drawback of MBO as a means of making divisionalization work is its tendency to draw up only financial goals. Yet it becomes apparent that no other viable concept of management will work with divisional organization. General Foods, with some seventeen divisions, General Electric with seventy divisions, or ITT with 300 divisions could not be run by the most capable individual except by control of outputs and resources. The variety and sheer volume of activity in the large corporation makes the idea of close control unthinkable.

It is not surprising, therefore, that General Mills in 1954 changed from a functional to a divisional form prior to adopting MBO as its management style. The Drucker refinement of organizational planning defined also by

[9] H. M. Larson, E. H. Knowlton, and C. S. Popple, *History of Standard Oil: New Horizons 1927–1950* (New York: Harper & Row, 1971): 22.

[10] See Alfred D. Chandler, *Strategy and Structure* (Cambridge, Mass.: MIT Press, 1962).

Louis A. Allen's NICB study supplanted the previous "principles of organizations" approach.[11]

Public concern over the size of corporations was widespread during the 1930s. In his charge to the Temporary National Economic Committee (TNEC) in 1937, President Roosevelt requested that Congress address the question of whether or not the concentration of great power in private hands was in the public interest. It is reasonable to speculate that without decentralization/divisionalization, more severe antitrust legislation or other laws to break up large corporations might have been enacted. Certainly, without divisionalization and the management processes to make it viable, no conglomerates could exist.

Drucker was undoubtedly forced into paying attention to MBO as a natural product of decentralization by the response of his audience in lectures and books. The fact that Drucker is a political scientist at heart, and a management scientist by request only, is often overlooked. For him, MBO was a simple technique brought about and made necessary and logical by the need for political reform inside the modern corporation. His structures for management behavior did not grow out of any efficiency-engineer motivation. Underlying his thinking was the strong belief that the preservation of the capitalist system required some basic structural changes in the corporate system, and preferably from within. He was probably closer to his fellow Austrians Frederick Hayek and Ludwig Von Mises than he was to Douglas McGregor, Abraham Maslow, or Rensis Likert.

In *The Concept of the Corporation*, Drucker described his concept of General Motors' plan of decentralization, which Sloan had firmly put in place and skillfully operated. Drucker characterized this decentralization as a kind of "federalism." He noted that the relationship between central management and the respective divisions was achieved "through the power of the central management to set the goals for each division," and through setting limits on authority, checking progress, offering help, and relieving divisions of all work not related to their goal attainment.[12]

In his 1954 book, *The Practice of Management*, Drucker first used the expression "management by objectives and self-control" that struck such a popular chord. In part, the expression "MBO" caught on as a concept to be copied and applied by other large firms because of Drucker's extensive speaking schedule before management groups. In the years following the publication of *The Practice of Management*, Drucker moved the concept to the center of his thinking, rather than keeping it as a sideline to the major theme of decentralization.

[11] Lewis A. Allen, *Management and Organization* (New York: McGraw-Hill, 1958).
[12] Peter F. Drucker, *The Concept of the Corporation* (New York: John Day, 1946): 41–79.

The Systems Approach

If a theoretical basis for MBO is absolutely necessary, then it perhaps might be found in the evolution of management science, operations research, and the "systems approach." Originating in the operations research movement during World War II, the systems approach emerged when physical scientists were drafted into duty to help solve complex strategic problems for the British Navy. By applying mathematical programming and modeling, they brought new, rigorous methods of analysis to dealing with both military and social problems. This approach is commonly expressed in an almost universally accepted definition by C. West Churchman: "A system is a set of parts coordinated to accomplish a set of goals."[13] The techniques of the systems approach were mathematical and more sophisticated than most managers are accustomed to employing, but the stages are simply stated as identification of

1. Total system objectives.
2. The system's environment and fixed constraints.
3. The resources of the system.
4. The activities of each component of the system.
5. A method of managing to attain the goals.

The most common elements in the systems approach are inputs, activities (processes), and outputs. The first step is to define the objectives in terms of hoped-for outputs. The choice of objectives is, of course, the first step in all variations of the systems approach, and without objectives, operations research is pointless. In the years since 1946, this field has become variously known as management science, operations research, and, in colleges and university curricula, as quantitative methods. In decision making, the definition of objectives (sometimes called the "objectives function") dominates the theoretical work that follows. Operations research is thus the scientific approach to managing by objectives.

MBO has directed attention to the systems approach, and the training of thousands of managers and technical specialists in management science has perhaps had a more important effect upon decision making than is ordinarily appreciated by traditional management and MBO's devotees. The increasing use of the systems approach in the many management decisions that affect marketing, plant location, inventory control, cash management, and investment decisions has, in fact, altered substantially the ways in which more complex management decisions are made.

[13] Churchman: Chapter 3.

Recent Developments

In more modern times, such management theoreticians as Herbert Simon, Russell Ackoff, and Martin Starr have made contributions to a goals-centered cybernetic system to solve managerial problems.

My book, *Management by Objectives*, published in 1965, is subtitled *A System of Managerial Leadership*, which implied not just operations research but rather an extension of previous theories that made MBO a kind of think-piece formulation or a behavioral device for producing participative management. Walter Mahler, a New York-based consultant, has developed a package of consulting services that draw heavily on the systems approach to describe and apply MBO to his clients.[14]

It has not been the systems aproach to MBO that has drawn the most attention, however, but rather MBO's behavioral and human resource development aspects. The majority of the literature directly dealing with MBO has, in fact, centered on the management problems of managing mangers, managing professionals, setting standards of performance for managerial appraisal, doing a better job of salary administration and merit increases in pay, and handling the related psychological problems of motivation, achievement, and incentives.

Standards-of-Performance Movement

Before MBO as a philosophhy could gain acceptance in the halls of corporate headquarters or in the administrative office, some deeply held attachments had to be supplanted. For one thing, performance appraisal was strongly tied to personality assessment and trait-rating systems. The early human relations movement had made amateur psychologists of many managers. Appraisal systems were often comprised of lists of such personality traits as initiative, drive, integrity, and loyalty. Managers were required to rate subordinates against these traits, and their amateur clinical judgments became a part of the subordinates' permanent personnel file.

By the 1950s, a series of widespread attacks upon personality-based management had been made by both business and academic groups. William H. Whyte wrote a widely read book, *The Organizational Man*, which proposed that such personality assessment methods were an invasion of privacy and were false scientism. Meanwhile, in industrial psychology an increasing body of evidence showed that the concept of the occupational personality was not be found, no matter how hard people searched.

[14] Walter R. Mahler, "A Systems Approach to Managing by Objectives," *Systems and Procedures Journal*, April 1972: 12–19.

The American Management Associations, which became the leader in adult education of executives, came down hard in favor of more objective standards of managerial performance based upon agreed goals and targets. Hundreds of thousands of managers from leading firms attended seminars, conferences, and courses where they were admonished to avoid personality-based assessments and were urged to define, in their place, standards of managerial performance.[15]

While the standards-of-performance movement of the 1950s can be credited with our turning away from personality-based assessment systems, it often faltered and fell by the wayside because of two obstacles. Group appraisal required an inordinate amount of time, as well as reams of paper. Furthermore, evaluations were almost wholly oriented to activities and duties rather than to outputs.

The standards-of-performance movement changed our way of thinking about managerial performance, but it was unsystematic. It did, however, pave the way for the MBO movement that was to emerge in the late 1950s and to blossom fully in the 1960s.

MBO's Original Adopters

Following the publication of *The Practice of Management*, and a book and several articles by another consultant, Edward Schleh, a number of companies began to consider how to apply the basic concept to their own business[16] These were not companies already following the basic MBO idea without calling it MBO, such as General Motors, but rather companies turning away from decentralization or seeking an improved managerial appraisal plan.

Among the earliest of these was General Mills, in 1955. A year earlier, it had divisionalized under its president, Charles Bell. Durward Balch, vice-president of personnel, conducted an extensive study of the MBO idea. Professor Earl Brooks of Cornell, an early pioneer in designing and installing MBO programs, became a major consultant in implementation at General Mills. Not only did the creation of 12 new divisions in 1954 call for the selection, development, and appraisal of new division general managers. This change also required that new group vice-presidents, with profit responsibility, have some clear-cut ideas of what they expected and how executive bonuses would be administered.[17]

[15] See Virgil Rowland, *Standards of Managerial Performance* (New York: Harper, 1959).
[16] See Edward Schleh, *Successful Executive Action* (Englewood Cliffs, N.J.: Prentice-Hall, 1955). This was probably the first book-length exposition of MBO. Schleh also wrote on MBO in *Personnel*, May 1953.
[17] See "How Am I Doing?," pamphlet issued by General Mills, Inc. Minneapolis, in 1955.

During this period, Howard Johnson, later director of the Sloan Program, dean, and then president of MIT, was employed at General Mills as Balch's assistant. His influence was undoubtedly great, and perhaps it was he who was one of the earliest to note the important behavioral aspects of MBO in addition to its functional, profitable aspects. When he left General Mills to join MIT, it was he who told Douglas McGregor of General Mills' unique appraisal system. This was the basis for McGregor's classic article, "An Uneasy Look at Performance Appraisal," which appeared in the *Harvard Business Review* in 1959. McGregor was unabashedly a humanist, strongly advocated participative management, and supported MBO as a participative management vehicle.

At this time General Mills was instrumental in organizing an executive development course, owned jointly by four Minneapolis companies: General Mills, Honeywell, Dayton's and the Northwest Bancorporation. Through this course, in the ensuing years, all top managers in the four companies were trained in management with a strong results-centered style. From this emerged a generation of managers whose basic management style was clearly labeled MBO. This four-company course (now the multicompany course) started with the chairmen and chief executives of the four companies, and went through the officers' ranks. It became the first example of formal implementation of what others had crept into in a more tentative fashion following decentralization.[18]

By 1960, if you didn't have an MBO system, it was assumed that you could acquire it by training your managers, starting at the top and working down through the organization. In 1959, the University of Michigan initiated the first monthly seminar to train managers in MBO. This led the way for a rash of other university and association programs of seminars, conferences, and courses on MBO.

THE DEVOTEES

It was during the 1960s that the flood tide of MBO plans got under way. Surprisingly, there were few, if any, books on the subject. The first book with the title *Management by Objectives* was written by me in 1962 and was published in 1965, after considerable testing in the Michigan seminar. Following that time, however, the literature grew rapidly.

[18] Walter Wikstrom, *Managing with and by Objectives*, Studies in Personnel Policy, No. 212 (New York: National Industrial Conference Board, 1968).

One of the more important researchers in the field was Edwin A. Locke of the University of Maryland. His research was crucial to the acceptance of MBO on a widespread basis inside corporations that were professionally staffed with sophisticated human resources personnel. His first rigorous research probed such basic questions as "Does MBO change behavior?" and found that having goals improves performance results; it motivates people to work, and when people set goals and achieve them, they enjoy their work more. Locke produced an astonishing 21 articles, mainly in psychological journals, that probed and defined the effects of MBO. It was Locke who demonstrated in his research that MBO really works. Without his research, there might not have followed a host of other scholarly research studies that, in effect, shape the conditions under which MBO must live to succeed in practice.[19]

This spate of rigorous study, in turn, generated further studies refining Locke's ideas. Henry Tosi and Stephen Carroll determined the kinds of people with whom goal setting would work, and more generally defined predictable responses from MBO programs when varying implementation techniques were tried.[20] The journals in which this literature appeared spanned the field of psychology, management, education, and public and hospital administration. Locke, Gary Latham, Anthony Raia, Tosi, William Reddin, Heinz Weihrich, William Reif, and Bruce Kirchoff produced a great volume of research about the psychological aspects of MBO. In addition, at least ten doctoral dissertations in MBO—its extent of use, condition for success, and special applications—were produced during this period.

In management literature, my thiry-five books, articles, and publications led the field, with John Humble, Dale McConkey, George Morrissey, Charles Hughes, and Glen Varney among the major writers. A division of labor existed that was most productive. The management journal writers were advocates and refiners, and wrote about MBO based upon field experience and "by construction." Major developments in the field took place, and the management writers, often fresh from successes or failures with client companies, described new areas of application and new techniques in design and implementation. The application of MBO to such chronic management problems as selection, discipline, collective bargaining, compensation, marketing, and purchasing were described in case study

---

[19] Most of Locke's twenty-one articles were published between 1965 and 1970 when MBO was becoming widespread. They appeared in numerous publications, including the *Journal of Applied Psychology*.

[20] Tosi's first research report was published in *Personnel Management* in 1965; Tosi's and Carroll's work subsequently appeared in the *Academy of Management Journal, MSU Business Topics, Management Review,* and the *California Management Review.*

form and prescriptive articles. At every step, the academic researcher probed and tested, drawing up lines of reservation and constraint, questioning assumptions, pricking bubbles, and refining techniques. The management professors and consultants initiated, designed, constructed, theorized, and speculated; the behavioral researchers follwed closely, deflating overly ambitious claims and clarifying the requirements of MBO in theory. Without doubt, MBO as a management technique is one of the best tested, most thoroughly researched methods in recent times.

THE HATERS

While the ranks of those who detest the entire system of MBO are actually small, their vehemence has been real and their motives understandable. In one category are those who must be defined as journalistic needlers. The editor who casts about and assigns writers to "find a very popular idea and stick a pin in it" belongs in this category. An issue of *Purchasing* a few years back had a drawing of a tombstone on its front cover, with "MBO—R.I.P." etched into the stone. The story inside began with a series of provocative leads suggesting that MBO had indeed expired and proposed that the following article would comprise its obituary. The content of the article, based upon interviews with leading corporate purchasing directors, seemed to have a hedging character, for most of the stories stated conditions that could cause MBO to falter and then proceeded to describe how purchasing departments had overcome these defects. MBO was not really dead, it seemed, but it was certainly capable of failure.

Professor Ed Wrapp of the University of Chicago attracted considerable attention in the business press with an article in the magazine, *Steel*, with the provocative title "Management by Objectives—or Wheel and Deal?" He proposed that top management doesn't really set objectives, but actually wheels and deals without much attention to goals, strategies, or performance measures.[21]

Dr. Harry Levinson's article, "Management by Whose Objectives?" in the *Harvard Business Review* was a more fundamental attack upon the idea of MBO, however. Levinson, a former staff psychologist at the Menninger Clinic and long interested in the mental health of managers, expressed deep

[21] H. E. Wrapp, "Management by Objectives—or Wheel and Deal?," *Steel*, May 29, 1967: 46–47.

concern over the suppressive and top-down effects of MBO programs. These effects were to produce barriers for people seeking their ego ideal at work, a matter of considerable importance in Levinson's mind. While the article did not bar MBO in all of its forms, it did propose serious limitations on its top-down character.[22]

Many other critical articles about MBO cannot be included in the "hater" category, for they were written in a research vein. Such articles were more apt to describe the kinds of MBO practices that would cause its ultimate failure. Tosi, Carroll, Raia, John Ivancevich, Kirchoff, and Locke certainly were not blind in their acceptance of the idea of MBO, but defined the kinds of conditions that were necessary to its effectiveness.

The National Education Association (NEA) strongly opposed to MBO's use in appraising teaching performance, expressed strong distaste for the whole idea. Teachers' unions, it suggested, should come down strongly against MBO-based rating systems by which the school board and superintendent might crack down on teachers and bust their unions. The article did concede, however, that such schemes as MBO might be satisfactory for administrators and principals rating one another, but for the classroom teacher (the "learning locale") it should be avoided like the plague.[23]

One suspects that this attitude grew more out of a basic mistrust of any kind of administrative overture relating to teachers than to the unique character of MBO, however. Indeed, teacher evaluation has been the exact use for which some school systems have employed MBO, and perhaps the position of the unions, considering their actual experience, is justified. One school superintendent in the West announced the introduction of MBO in a city-wide policy as follows: "We have adopted a new and modern management system known as MBO this fall. Every teacher will be required to submit their MBOs in September. If they are failing to achieve these MBOs by January, in detail, they will be warned. If they are still failing to achieve their MBOs at the year's end, their employment will be terminated for cause." It is not surprising that in a single memo he had created a most ample complement of fearful MBO haters.

Similar applications in firms and government agencies have likewise produced coteries of mistrustful and angry MBO haters. The use of MBO has grown rapidly in federal, state, and local government and has generated several types of opposition.

The antiplanners are a common type of manager in both business and

---

[22] Harry Levinson, "Management by Whose Objectives?," *Harvard Business Review*, July-August 1970: 125–134.
[23] See "Should Teachers Say No to MBO?," *Briefing News* (Washington, D.C.: National Education Association, 1976).

government. Churchman has identified several types of antiplanners.[24] One is the adherent to "practical approaches" growing out of experience coupled with sound intuition, solid leadership, and a brilliant mind. A second kind of antiplanner is the skeptic, who believes that life and the world are so complicated that nobody could possible understand it well enough to control it or even predict it. Therefore, he is considerably reluctant to try, and is hostile to those who insist that he should do so. His objectives, he believes, are grounded in "It all depends" and "We do things informally." Wrapp falls into this category, and he has ample company.

A more serious kind of antiplanner is the determinist, who believes that human choices are not in the hands of responsible people but instead are controlled by immutable social or physical forces that will produce outcomes without human intervention. Evidence and analysis are pointless, for "What will be, will be."

Government administrators who favor political maneuvering and incremental budgeting are often violently opposed to program planning and MBO. They believe that the determinism of changing political tastes and trends will determine goals. These goals will, in turn, determine budgets, which will inevitably rise. Religious determinists reject the idea of defining human plans, for the Almighty has already chosen what will be.

In another category of antiplanners are those concerned almost wholly with the integrity of the self and with individual differences. The major purposes of life, they propose, are to know oneself, to be oneself, and to like oneself; any formal system that would diminish these is banned. This perhaps best expresses the rationale behind Levinson's opposition. While it might also be characteristic of other behavioral scientists, it would not include the "third force" group of psychologists such as McGregor, Maslow, or Frederick Herzberg, for they place work and its fruits high in the scheme of things by which individuals find their self-expression and identity.

A final category of anti-MBO groups is that of the existentialist. Members adhere to a philosophical system that detests systems. Camus expressed it: "If you lack character, you need a system." The world and human personality are rooted in existence and determined by luck, guilt, situations, and death; all else is futile. Existence precedes essence, and man makes himself by his own choice. Yet a close study reveals that purposes even comprise an important part of the existentialist's scheme of things.

It is apparent, from its history, that MBO is much more than a set of procedural rules for managing a business. As a philosophy it is consistent

[24] See Churchman: Chapter 13.

with the temper of our times. It responds to the restlessness which people feel toward the bureaucracy—the sense of powerlessness and alienation from the remote leadership of the large organization. It is at once functional in terms of what top management demands and developmental in terms of the people at work. It calls for human commitment rather than simply assuming that orders from the top will be self-executing. It compels forward planning and living life in an anticipatory mode rather than responding to events. It isn't based upon the prediction of the future but rather upon the creation of that future.

As a technique MBO has an air of logic about it that is compelling to logical people. It is easily proven to be job-related rather than related to caste, class, or personality. MBO makes achievement easier to distinguish when it occurs and helps solve some chronic areas of concern in management, such as rewarding performance, appraising performance, training to increase performance levels, and coaching people to do better.

Finally, it comprises a style of management which permits individual differences, is mainly democratic in operation, and allows previously left-behind populations such as women and minorities to demonstrate their competence in readily tested terms. MBO's future impact on personnel training and governmental budgeting and its potential behavioral applica-

Heinz Weihrich

Arizona State University

MBO IN FOUR MANAGEMENT SYSTEMS

Many of the largest companies in the United States now use management by objectives (MBO), yet only a few have realized its full potential. As currently practiced, MBO frequently is superimposed on the existing organization without sufficient effort to evaluate the organizational climate and make changes so that the managerial system is congruent with the MBO philosophy. For most organizations, MBO requires a change in managerial style—a new way of managing. Rensis Likert and his associates have developed a model of four systems of management which facilitates the assessment of the existing organizational environment.[1] The purpose of this article is to approximate the relationships between these four managerial systems and the steps in the MBO process.

The practice of MBO not only differs widely among companies, but the MBO concept itself has changed and evolved over the years. In the early stages of its development, MBO was viewed primarily as an appraisal tool to overcome the weaknesses of the traditional appraisal approaches that focused on personality traits rather than performance.

The motivating power of MBO soon became evident. Participation facilitates the integration of personal and organizational objectives. The individual derives satisfaction by contributing to the aims of the organization. In addition, individuals are encouraged to set personal development objectives.

Heinz Weihrich, "MBO in Four Management Systems," *MSU Business Topics*, Autumn 1976, pp. 51–56.

Consequently, managers—and also nonmanagers—recognize that MBO facilitates professional growth and self-development.

In the earlier stages of the development of the MBO concept, emphasis primarily was on short-term objectives, which seldom included aims that went beyond one year. (The terms *aims*, *goals*, and *objectives* are used interchangeably.) This, of course, can have negative consequences because the short-term focus may result in undesirable managerial behavior. In an effort to meet this year's objectives, long-term opportunities may be ignored. Recognizing these limitations, some firms have included long-range and strategic planing in their approach. This certainly is a step in the right direction, but it should not be the end in the development of MBO. To be fully effective, MBO must become a comprehensive system of managing that integrates MBO in the total managerial process. This does not mean generating a lot of paperwork; rather, MBO must become a way of managing.[2]

The focus here will be on the essentials of the MBO process. Simply stated, MBO involves the steps of (1) setting objectives, (2) developing action plans, (3) implementation, and (4) controlling of organizational performance and appraising individual results. These steps will serve as a framework for this discourse.

FOUR SYSTEMS OF MANAGEMENT_____

Likert and his associates thoroughly studied many organizations and their effectiveness. Managerial styles and their related organizational factors were identified and grouped into four systems. Likert named System 1 *exploitative-authoritative;* System 2, *benevolent-authoritative;* System 3, *consultative;* and System 4, *participative group*.

System 1 is highly autocratic with little trust and confidence. Motivation is through fear, threat, and punishment. Communication is downward and decisions are made almost entirely at the top of the organization.

System 2 is marked by a condescending approach to management. Motivation is through rewards and some punishment. Communication is still mostly downward. Although there is some delegation, policy control is at the top.

System 3 management is characterized by substantial, bot not complete, confidence in subordinates. Motivation is through rewards and involvement; but there is also some punishment. Communication flows down and up, and subordinates are generally consulted in decisions related to their jobs.

System 4 management is highly participative, with a great deal of confidence and trust in subordinates. This system is marked by effective teamwork and individuals feel motivated to achieve the goals of the organization. Communication is downward and upward, as well as with peers. Decision making is well integrated at all levels of the organization. Goals are set primarily by the group, with little or no resistance to the aims.

It is evident that these different systems of management will have an impact on the steps in the MBO process; this is the focal point of the following conjectural discussion.

MBO IN THE FOUR SYSTEMS

Management by objectives is a process that requires interaction among superior, subordinate, and peers. It involves managerial leadership, effective motivation, open communication, decision making, and measuring of performance.

MBO in System 1: Exploitative–Authoritative

In this system, management has no trust in subordinates, uses mainly threats and punishment, has very little real communication, makes decisions basically at the top, issues orders to lower levels, and concentrates control at the top. This environment leaves a distinct mark on the way the steps of MBO are carried out.

Step 1: Setting Objectives. In this kind of organization, objectives are set at the top, or by the superior in an autocratic manner. Subordinates, therefore, have little or no opportunity to set their own objectives. Nor do they provide any inputs to the departmental aims. In general, top management determines objectives, which may or may not be communicated down the organization structure. The set of objectives is rather limited and only a few alternative aims are considered. If some objectives are set by organizational units, they seldom are coordinated with other departments.

The set of individual objectives usually pertains to performance only and does not include personal development objectives. Because managers do not see how they personally benefit from MBO, there is a great deal of resistance to writing down objectives and making commitments.

Step 2: Action Planning.   As in the goal-setting process, superiors are very directive. They determine the tasks and develop action plans for their subordinates. There is little awareness that in most situations there are alternative courses of action that can be taken to achieve objectives. Also, the superior establishes the time-frame for the tasks with little input from those who have to carry out the activities. Consequently, there are often severe problems in coordinating and timing the tasks of the various organizational units, especially when the activities are interdependent. And even if extensive action plans are developed, they are not communicated to all who contribute to them or who will be affected by them.

Step 3: Implementation.   Top management and superiors determine the implementation of plans. Subordinates are simply required to follow orders. Thus, subordinates may be indifferent to MBO or they may even boycott the efforts of upper management. The program is mechanistic and rigid, with heavy emphasis on filling out forms and meeting the bureaucratic requirements. There is an emphasis on activities and on busy work, rather than on results. Individuals overtly or covertly resist MBO and take little initiative to utilize the potential benefits of the system. It is evident that such an organization does not manage in a way that is congruent with the MBO philosophy, which places responsibility on the subordinate and encourages initiative.

Step 4: Controlling and Appraising.   Organizational control is rigid and concentrated at the top. Moreover, control standards are externally imposed on departments and individuals. Consequently, inappropriate standards—that is, those that measure the wrong things—may be set and pursued.

Performance appraisal provides little opportunity for self-control or self-development. Instead, the superior is viewed as a judge who acts in a punitive manner. Subordinates, of course, have a low degree of trust in their superiors. In the appraisal meeting, attention is given only to past performance, although the past cannot be changed. Feed-forward control, which is designed to prevent undesirable deviations from occurring in the future, is completely ignored. Yet, it is the future that provides opportunities for individual as well as organizational growth and development.

MBO in System 2: Benevolent–Authoritative

In a System 2 environment, management has a condescending confidence in subordinates. Rewards and some punishment are used to motivate individuals. The flow of information is still primarily downward. Although there is some delegation, policy decisions are made at the top. Comments are invited when establishing objectives. Control is exercised to a great extent at the top.

Step 1: Setting Objectives.   There is a condescending use of authority. Objectives are usually set by the superior, but some inputs from subordinates are invited. There may even be some participation in setting objectives. But objectives are still communicated from the top of the organization downward with only limited upward information flow. There are some alternative objectives considered and some effort is made to coordinate the objectives of different organizational units. If personal development objectives are considered, they are set mostly by superiors.

Step 2: Developing Action Plans.   Tasks and responsibilities are determined mainly by the superior, although subordinates provide some inputs to the plans to achieve the objectives. But the information flow is mostly downward, and some problems in the coordination of plans may develop. In such an organization there may even be some plans for contingencies.

Step 3: Implementation.   The implementation of MBO is characterized by a benevolent attitude on the part of the superiors. Subordinates, then, largely follow direction without a real commitment to the MBO program. Because of the limited amount of upward and horizontal communication, some difficulties may develop in the coordination of activities within the organizational unit as well as among departments. Some covert resistance to MBO also may be encountered. If MBO is accepted, it is only with superficial commitment.

Step 4: Controlling and Appraising.   Control is still primarily at the top and upper management, with insufficient responsibility placed on subordinates. Inappropriate standards for control may be set and pursued. During appraisal, the superior plays an active part, using rewards and punishment. There is little participation by subordinates in the evaluation of their own performance. In such an environment, self-appraisal is usually not feasible.

MBO in System 3: Consultative

System 3 is characterized by considerable trust, rewards, and occasional punishment, an up and down information flow, and a moderate amount of teamwork. Although top management makes general decisions, more specific ones are made at lower levels. The control function is moderately delegated to lower levels.

Step 1: Setting Objectives. Subordinates are consulted on important matters, and there is considerable participation in setting goals. Also, objectives are fairly well communicated, both vertically and horizontally. Consequently, there is usually a good coordination of objectives. Goals are set in several crucial areas. Besides performance goals, personal development objectives are set by subordinates in consultation with their superiors, who may, however, reserve the right to make changes.

Step 2: Developing Action Plans. Subordinates are consulted in developing the action plans. Moreover, there is considerable participation in deciding on the course of action. Plans are quite well communicated to those who need to know. Consequently, there is a fairly good coordination of tasks as well as responsibilities. Plans for contingencies are developed in consultation with subordinates.

Step 3: Implementation. In the implementation phase, subordinates are consulted and there is a moderate commitment to MBO in most parts of the organization. The information flows reasonably well, both vertically and horizontally. In operational decision making, inputs from peers as well as subordinates are given serious consideration.

Step 4: Controlling and Appraising. Controls are installed at different points in order to measure performance. The standards give a moderately accurate picture of organizational accomplishments. There is considerable participation by subordinates in the evaluation of their own performance, and some problem solving occurs during the appraisal meeting. Although the focus is on past performance, some attention is given to preventing undesirable deviations of performance in the future.

MBO in System 4: Participative Group

In System 4 there is extensive trust and confidence in subordinates. Moreover, people at all levels feel responsible for results and share the control function. With a great deal of teamwork and free flow of information, decisions at various levels are well integrated.

Step 1: Setting Objectives. The supportive environment is conducive to real participation in setting objectives. This results not only in an integration of personal objectives and organizational demands, but it also elicits commitment toward the achievement of aims. Before the set of objectives is finalized, many alternatives are considered. Also, objectives ar not set in isolation, rather they are communicated to all who have a need to know. The effect is a well-coordinated network of goals throughout the organization, resulting in a synergistic effect. The organizational climate encourages individuals to set high performance standards that are congruent with the aims of the team.

Step 2: Developing Action Plans. In almost all situations, alternative courses of action can be taken to achieve the objectives. System 4 fosters creativity and is conducive to identifying, evaluating, and deciding on the tasks and activities necessary to achieve results. Individual and organizational plans are integrated; system optimization is accomplished through the team effort of individuals whose tasks are seen as being interrelated.

Step 3: Implementation. Managers—and even nonmanagers—at all organizational levels are committed to the achievement of common goals. With the goals set, individuals can use their creativity in finding better ways of doing things. Consequently, there are many opportunities for personal and professional growth. The organization is seen as an interlocking system. If conflicts occur—and they do in any organization—they are effectively resolved through open communication based on trust and confidence. Rather than individuals pursuing their own—sometimes conflicting—goals, it is a true team approach that results in synergistic effects.

Step 4: Controlling and Appraising. In the System 4 environment, control of performance is at critical points in the organization. Deviations from standards are analyzed and steps are taken to prevent undesirable ones from re-occurring in the future. In fact, the focus in on forward-looking controls that attempt to prevent deviations rather than to correct them.

During appraisal, the superior does not sit in judgment over his subordinates. Instead of acting as a judge, the superior is like a coach interested in helping subordinates to improve their performance. Appraisal, then, is primarily self-appraisal aimed at promoting professional development, and the free flow of communication results in a fair evaluation of individual performance.

Implications

While management by objectives is one of the most widely used approaches to managing, not all organizations have been successful in implementing it.

The MBO approach may fail when it is superimposed on the organization without proper understanding of the existing climate. It is, for example, unrealistic to expect that managers who have operated for many years under System 1 can suddenly become participative team members (System 4). In fact, forcing these drastic changes without coaching may disturb the organizational equilibrium in a way that results in undesirable consequences.

To effectly implement MBO, it must be understood that MBO is a process as well as a philosophy of managing. If this philosophy is completely incongruent with the organizational climate, problems will occur. What is needed is a systems approach to organizational development that focuses on both the organizational climate and the MBO steps of setting objectives, action planning, implementation, as well as controlling and appraising.

An alternative to the traditional "try and hope for the best" approach to implementing MBO is *data based organizational development*. This involves the measurement of critical organizational characteristics such as suggested by Likert. The data derived by using his questionnaire facilitate the grouping of organizational factors into System 1 (exploitative–authoritative), System 2 (benevolent–authoritative), System 3 (consultative), and System 4 (participative group). Likert and his colleagues found that over a period of time organizations that moved *toward* System 4 also became more effective. Similarly, the author suggests, most organizations will become more effective when the steps in the MBO process are carried out in ways approximating those described in System 4. But this change will have to come gradually and must be accompanied by changes in the organizational environment. The framework of the four systems and the relationships to the steps in MBO as discussed in this article can facilitate this change process.

The practicing manager, of course, is interested in operationalizing this new approach to the implementation of MBO. Although there are different ways, the focus here is on the *action research model* that may involve: (1) Collection of data and diagnosis of the organization. Based on this information, a profile of organizational characteristics can be developed and grouped into Systems 1 to 4. (2) Discussion of these findings within the organization and a comparison with the characteristics of the four steps in the MBO process. (3) Joint planning of actions to change the organization and the MBO process in the direction of System 4. This also requires the teaching of the MBO concepts as well as MBO philosophy. (4) A repetition of these three processes is then repeated until MBO becomes an integral part of dynamic organizational development.

The approach suggested here differs substantially from traditional ones that often superimpose MBO on the organization. There are several advantages of this new approach for implementing MBO. First, it is a systems approach that recognizes many critical organizational variables. Second, it is data-based, starting with the existing organization and moving toward an ideal one in a planned manner. Third, it is dynamic, flexible, and tailored for a particular organization. Fourth, the emphasis is on collaborative management, with a great deal of team effort. Fifth, it is an ongoing process that continuously aims at improving the organization.

In conclusion, to be effective, MBO must be congruent with organizational characteristics. It is suggested that the manner in which the steps in the MBO process are carried out will differ for the four management systems. The wise administrator will collect data on the existing managerial system and developed a change strategy that takes into account both MBO and the organizational environment. Effective implementation of MBO requires time and effort, but the results can be rewarding.

REFERENCES

1. Rensis Likert. *New Patterns of Management* (New York: McGraw-Hill Book Company, 1961); also, Rensis Likert, *The Human Organization* (New York: McGraw-Hill Book Company, 1967).
2. Heinz Weihrich. "A Study of the Integration of Management by Objectives with Key Managerial Activities and the Relationship to Selected Effectiveness Measures (Ph.D. diss., University of California, Los Angeles, 1973

Mark L. McConkie

University of Colorado—Colorado Springs

A CLARIFICATION OF THE GOAL-SETTING AND APPRAISAL PROCESSES IN MBO

While goal setting and performance appraisal clearly constitute the heart and flow of Management by Objectives (MBO), a great deal of confusion still exists as to what actually constitutes "goal setting" and "performance appraisal." Consequently, much confusion surrounds the meaning of MBO, causing Kirchoff (34, p. 17) to complain that "... there is probably no other term in the vocabulary of contemporary management that is so inadequately defined." Earlier, Wikstrom (103, p. 1) registered the same frustration, saying MBO has become an "all purpose term, meaning almost anything one chooses to have it mean," a fact which Schuster (86, p. 18) says gives rise to "radically different and sometimes contradictory meanings."

To help clarify much of the confusion surrounding MBO, this article synthesizes from the works of leading MBO experts the common elements of their respective descriptions and definitions of how goals should be set and how performance appraisals should be conducted under the MBO rubric. In this review of the MBO literature, authors were judged to be experts or authorities if they have published a book dealing specifically with

Mark L. McConkie, "A Clarification of the Goal Setting and Appraisal Processes in MBO," *Academy of Management Review*, January 1979, pp. 29–40.

TABLE 1
How the Authorities View the MBO Goal-Setting Process

KEY: ● indicates that the author(s) at the top of the column agree(s) that MBO should include the feature described in the rows at the left.[a]

	Drucker (13,14)	Schleh (82,83)	McGregor (56,57)	Likert (47)	Schaffer (80)	Huse (28,29)	Hughes (23,24)	Odiorne (64,65)	McConkey (53,54,55)	Valentine (95,96)	Miller (59,60,61)	Wikstrom (102,103)	Howell (21,22)	Scanlan (77,78,79)	Tosi & Carroll (8,9,91,94)	Ivancevich (30,31,32)
THE GOAL-SETTING PROCESS																
Top management sets goals, subordinates agree							●									
Subordinates set goals, subordinates agree	●		●	●				●				●				●
Superiors and subordinates jointly set goals					●					●	●			●	●	
MBO is adaptable: degree of goal-setting participation varies with each organization			●					●		●			●		●	
Some combination of the above as a joint goal-setting venture		●				●			●				●		●	
No description of goal setting procedure given																
GOALS & OBJECTIVES SHOULD . . .																
Be defined in terms of measurable results	●	●	●	●	●	●	●	●	●	●	●	●	●	●	●	●
Be specific	●	●	●	●	●	●	●	●	●	●	●	●	●	●	●	●
Always be "verifiable" and quantifiable whenever possible	●	●		●		●	●	●		●	●	●	●	●		
Include target date for completion	●	●	●	●		●			●	●	●	●		●	●	●
Be in writing		●			●			●			●					
Be reviewed 2 to 4 times per year			●													
Be reviewed "periodically"			●	●	●	●		●	●	●	●	●	●	●	●	●
Have priority weightings	●	●				●	●		●	●	●		●		●	
Have an accompanying action plan			●	●	●	●	●		●	●		●			●	
Set maximum cost/resource factors						●	●		●	●						●
Be flexible; change as needed		●	●			●			●	●			●	●	●	
Integrate individual and organizational goals	●	●	●	●	●	●	●	●	●	●	●	●	●	●	●	●

[a] While Kirchoff (34) qualifies as an expert in terms of the criteria used here, his work is not referred to in this table because it makes no attempt to define or describe MBO.

Sloan & Schrieber (84,89)	Levinson (44,45,46)	Morrisey (62)	Reddin (70,72,73,74)	Lasagna (43)	Chartrand (11,12)	Koontz (37,38)	Lahti (41,42)	Schuster (85,86)	Varney (27,48,97,98,99)	Carvalho (10)	Humble (25)	Mali (50)	Mahler (2,49)	Kleber (35,36)	Knezevich (39,40)	Beck & Hillmar (4,5,19)	Brady (6)	White (100,101)	Raia (69)	Shetty & Carlisle (87,88)	McConkie (55)	Total Number of Responses	Percentage of Authorities in Agreement
						●	●	●		●	●								●			2	5%
●	●	●							●					●	●								
			●		●					●			●	●		●	●					11	29%
			●	●	●								●	●			●			●		13	34%
																		●				1	3%
●	●	●	●	●	●	●	●	●	●	●		●	●		●	●	●	●	●	●	●	37	97%
●	●	●	●	●	●	●	●	●	●	●		●	●		●	●	●	●	●	●	●	37	97%
●		●	●	●		●		●	●	●		●	●		●			●	●	●	●	26	68%
●		●	●	●	●	●	●					●	●	●	●			●	●	●	●	27	71%
●		●	●				●	●				●						●	●	●	●	14	37%
●		●					●	●													●	5	14%
●	●	●	●		●	●	●	●	●	●		●	●	●			●		●	●	●	31	82%
		●	●		●				●			●			●	●	●		●		●	19	50%
●		●	●		●			●	●	●			●			●	●		●		●	21	55%
		●	●	●						●			●			●	●		●		●	15	40%
			●	●	●	●	●	●	●		●	●	●	●	●	●	●		●	●	●	25	66%
●	●	●	●	●	●	●	●	●	●		●	●	●	●	●	●		●	●	●	●	36	94%

MBO and at least three other articles or books quote from or cite the book; and/or they have published at least two journal articles which are either cited or quoted from in three or more articles or books. Authors who quoted themselves were not included. A total of 39 authorities emerged. Table 1 contains a representative sampling of their writings, from which the conclusions in this article regarding MBO goal setting and performance appraisal are drawn.

GOAL SETTING UNDER MBO

Table 1 shows how the different authorities have responded to different goal-setting issues, and Table 2 presents, in aggregate form, their modal responses.

TABLE 2
The Goal-Setting Process as Seen by Leading Authorities

	Total Number of Responses[a]	Percentage of Authorities in Agreement
1. Goals and objectives should be specific	37	97
2. Goals and objectives should be defined in terms of measurable results	37	97
3. Individual goals should be linked to overall organization goals	37	97
4. Objectives should be reviewed "periodically"	31	82
5. The time period for goal accomplishment should be specified	27	71
6. Wherever possible, the indicator of the results should be quantifiable; otherwise, it should be at least verifiable	26	68
7. Objectives should be flexible; changed as conditions warrant	26	68
8. Objectives should include a plan of action for accomplishing the results	21	55
9. Objectives should be assigned priorities of weights	19	50

[a]In this table, the total number of responses actually represents the total number of authorities responding; thus, the percentages also represent the percent of authorities in agreement with the statements made.

As Table 2 indicates, experts agree substantially on at least nine features of the complete goal-setting process. Nearly universal agreement exists on three items: (a) that goals and objectives should be specific; (b) that they should be defined in terms of measurable results; and (c) that individual and organizational goals should be linked one to another.

While some of the leading early works recommend that objectives and goals should be reviewed every six months (13,57), there has been a recent shift toward more flexibility. Some (41) suggest appraising progress every six months and resetting goals every year. The current consensus seems to be that managers review (and if they choose, reset) their goals periodically—i.e., according to managerial discretion. More than 80 percent of the authorities agree that periodic goal reviews most helpfully facilitate effective MBO (see Table 2).

Table 2 highlights several other important goal setting items. Over 70 percent of the authorities concur, for example, that a specified time period for goal accomplishment should be included as a part of the goal. While not all goals can be expressed quantitatively (14) a total of 68 percent of the authorities agree that they should at least be written in verifiable terms—meaning that they are clear enough to eliminate any uncertainty over their attainment. Because not all goals are easily quantifiable, Drucker (13,14) has urged that goals be made flexible—and 68 percent of the authorities agree. Authorities also largely agree about the need for an action plan in the goal-setting schema and for prioritized goals.

Subordinate Involvement in Goal Setting

As Table 3 indicates, the authorities largely agree on heavy subordinate involvement in the goal setting process. Only two of 40 authorities suggest anything other than involving subordinates in goal setting from the initial stages. Twenty-nine percent specify the path goal setting should follow—from subordinates to superiors; an equal number make no clarification of the process, but simply say goals should be jointly set. The highest percentage in any one category is 34, representing those favoring some combination of different goal-setting techniques as a form of mutual goal setting. This category includes those, like Schleh (82), who believe that under different circumstances goal setting procedures change, but that nonetheless, the most effective goal setting is a joint venture.

Goal Setting and Planning

The overall sense of the empirical literature cautiously supports the notion that MBO improves managerial goal setting. Three studies (1,29,91) found that MBO led to increased specificity in goals and plans. Moreover, the act of setting clear goals generally results in better task performance (7,15,17,90). Three studies (69,87,90) found that MBO helped improve overall planning. Elsewhere, Meyer, Kay, and French (59) relate that MBO adoption increased the overall ability of the manager to plan. Related studies, dealing with specific aspects of planning, also conclude that MBO improves planning. For example, Tosi and Carroll (91) discovered that the adoption of MBO led to increased capacity to pinpoint problem areas. Resource allocation (100) and career planning as it related to organization task accomplishment (8) also improved after the implementation of MBO, two authors claim.

Elsewhere (56), in classifying the level of empirical rigor with which these MBO/goal setting studies were conducted, several studies (1,29,58,68, 86,90,107) were classified as "low in empirical rigor," and therefore the conclusion that MBO "improves goal setting" is only "cautiously" suggested.

To summarize, then, where the goal setting phase of MBO is concerned, several features stand out. *First*, nine items seem to constitute the backbone of MBO goal setting. These are summarized in Table 2. *Second*, the authorities also agree on high levels of subordinate involvement in the goal setting process, although differences exist as to the form that the involvement should assume. *Third*, there is empirical evidence which, although of a low level of empirical rigor, suggests that MBO leads to increased goal specificity and that it helps improve overall planning.

TABLE 3
The Goal-Setting Process and Subordinate Involvement

	Total Number of Responses	Percentage of Authorities in Agreement
1. Top management sets goals, subordinates agree	2	5%
2. Subordinates set goals, present them to top management for review, critique and approval	11	29%
3. Superiors and subordinates jointly set goals	11	29%
4. Some combination of the above as a joint goal-setting venture (e.g., numbers 1 and 3, or 2 and 3)	13	34%
5. No description of goal-setting process	1	3%
Totals	38	100%

THE APPRAISAL PROCESS

Perhaps no facet of the MBO process has been considered as important as performance appraisal. Indeed, some studies (37,80,92,95) identify the appraisal function as the most important part of MBO. Occasionally MBO modifications have received such titles as "appraisal by results" (18,102,103) and "work progress and review" (28,59,68,69). The consensus of MBO experts seems to be that "where performance is measured, performance improves." In this section we review the literature which ties performance appraisal to MBO and then draw conclusions as to how appraisals should be conducted and as to appropriate definitional guidelines.

Objective Performance Standards

A representative sense of the appraisal literature is contained in Table 4, in which the experts agree that the day of objective performance measures must come. Eighty-seven percent state that objective criteria and performance standards must be clearly defined as a part of the MBO process; the remaining 13 percent make no specific mention of objective criteria but apparently assume that it should be a part of the MBO structure.

The most frequent complaint registered against the traditional approach to appraisal is that the manager must, in McGregor's words, "play God" in judging the personalities of subordinates. Kindal and Gatza (33) not only agree with the McGregor analysis, but add that such appraisals generally become one-way conversations in which the subordinate is told what to do and what is expected. The problems of these "beauty contests" are sometimes thought to be solved by introducing quantitative measures against which goal achievement can be monitored. Rigid mathematical formulas have frequently proven disappointing, because too many managers tend to assume that since the mathematical standard has been set, they need not insert their own judgments and opinions into the management process. In so behaving, they remove themselves from their management responsibilities. These mathematical formulas, the argument goes, make no allowance for the difficulty of the goals being pursued. All of these problems occur, says one, because of the "lack of performance criteria that are related to job responsibilities" (67,p. 64). To overcome these negative features of the performance appraisal, McGregor and others recommend the use of objective measures.

The degree of subordinate participation in the establishment of performance standards varies with different authors, but the basic concept remains:

many of the negative features of the traditional performance appraisals can be overcome by joining managers and subordinates in some fashion and establishing objectives against which performance is measured. While the names vary, most of these programs represent different shades of management by objectives.

The empirical evidence in this connection is consistent and compelling, for the impact of MBO on appraisal systems has been amazingly positive. Eight studies (28,29,59,68,69,75,87,91) have, in one fashion or another, determined that the introduction of management by objectives has led to more objective-centered and less trait-centered appraisals. In four of these studies (28,29,59,68), significant and favorable changes in the attitudes of personnel about performance appraisal followed the MBO application. In two of these studies (29,59), subordinates knew, as a result of the MBO type

TABLE 4
How the Authorities View the Appraisal Process

	Number of Authorities in Agreement	Percentage of Authorities
Objective criteria and performance standards must be clearly included in MBO	33	87%
Did not mention "objective criteria," but appear to assume it as a part of MBO	5	13%
Total	38	100%

	Number of Authorities in Agreement	Percentage of Authorities in Agreement
No explanation of the appraisal process given	14	21%
Superior appraises subordinates goal-attainment process in a one-on-one situation	17	25%
Some combination of the above are employed	23	34%
Subordinate self-appraisal of goal-attainment progress	7	10%
A team or group appraises progress of individuals	2	3%
Team appraisal—without clarifying what team appraisal means	4	6%
Total	67	99%[a]

[a]Differences from 100% due to rounding error.

appraisals, of specific improvements expected of them in areas where traditional performance appraisals had never before helped. In these same two studies, the perceived value of the performance appraisals also increased, as did the perceived fairness of the appraisals. MBO appraisals have also been perceived by subordinates as providing better data against which to conduct self-evaluation (87,88,104).

Motivation and Goal Clarity

Raia found that the performance review itself has a motivational impact. Specifically, "nine out of ten managers interviewed indicated that the desire to 'look good' at the reviews motivated them to perform well" (68, p. 45). Raia reports that, according to one manager, "in the past, emphasis was on what you were *not* doing. Now it's on what you *are* doing." Another manager said there was a strong motivation to "raise goals, be competitive, and get recognition. It's a good feeling to set a high goal and then reach it." The feelings of these managers represent fairly most of what has been written about MBO. The same is true of the conclusion drawn by Raia: "Many such statements made during the interviews indicated that the periodic performance reviews provided participants with strong motivation to improve their performance."(68, p. 43).

Just as Raia saw the appraisal process as having a motivational impact, he also saw it as a means of helping subordinates clarify their goal orientations and increase their sense of control over their own goal attainment. Huse (28) also found the appraisal process significantly affected superior-subordinate relationships. In his study, subordinates began to see superiors more as helpers than as judges. In addition, others (32,91) have found that these benefits may be extended over time if there is constant review and periodic appraisal.

APPRAISAL FORMAT AND ORGANIZATIONAL CULTURE_____

While not all of the effects of performance appraisals under the MBO schemata have been positive, the overwhelming tone of the literature is very positive with regard to objectives-centered appraisals. Still, some confusion exists, for many who have written about MBO either neglect or pay little attention to the appraisal issue. In fact, 37 percent of the authorities make no attempt at explaining the appraisal process; of those who do, nearly half opt for the format suggested by McGregor. In the format's one-on-one situations, the superior appraises the subordinate's goal attainment progress. Some recommend an MBO system in which subordinate self-appraisals of progress are central, but in more recent years, largely on the wake of the OD thrust, team and group appraisal have received increased attention.

The kind of appraisal—one-on-one or group—which is most appropriate is moderated by several significant variables, such as psychological perspectives of those involved and habit patterns of the past. French, Kay, and Meyer (15) found, for instance, that where performance appraisals were involved.

> The usual level of participation was significantly associated with manager relations as measured before the appraisal interview. Both mutual understanding and the acceptance of job goals were higher for those subjects accustomed to a high level of participation. These high usual participation subjects also expressed more favorable attitudes toward the appraisal system (15, p. 18).

The habit patterns of the past were quite influential in determining how people responded to the performance appraisal. A subject's willingness to participate in performance appraisal was largely influenced by his/her perception of any new level of participation in relation to past experiences.

Just as the culture of the organization or the past experience of appraisal programs influence how people respond to MBO appraisal, so do past performance levels. Illustratively, Meyer, Kay, and French found that "subordinates who received a high participation level in the performance interview reacted more favorably than did those who received a low participation level" (59, p. 121). Those with a high participation level also achieved greater percentage of their goals, and they manifest more favorable feelings toward the appraisal system with greater self-realization on the job. Those employees who traditionally participated less in their daily relationships with the manager "did not necessarily perform better under the high participation treatment" of MBO. Indeed, those employees who received greater amounts of criticism in their appraisal interviews actually performed better when their managers set goals for them than when they set their own goals.

What do these findings indicate? Meyer, Kay, and French interpret these data to mean that the person "who usually does not participate in work planning decisions considers job goals set by the manager to be more important than goals (he/she) sets for him/herself)." If their conclusion is correct, it illustrates that there are those who would prefer being told what to do and could be expected to be happy with a one-on-one appraisal where the manager tells the subordinate what is expected. Humphrey (26) argues that one of the flaws of most MBO systems is that they do not allow for the fact that there are many who would prefer to be told what to do and who dread the added responsibility which participative forms of MBO carry. For these people, one-on-one appraisal may be the most effective.

There are other circumstances, however, where group appraisals appear more beneficial. Major proponents of this position include French and Hollmann (16), Reddin (72), and others. Their arguments are generally similar to those of Novit (64) who reasons that group appraisals provide opportunity to focus attention on the incompatible expectations of those doing the appraising, enabling differences to more readily surface and be dealth with. He also sees a more subtle factor at work: the group appraisal "helps insure the manager's having at least one or more persons participating in (his/her) appraisal with whom (he/she) feels the greatest rapport. This offers some protection against those with whom (he/she) does not have this bond" (64, p. 7). In addition, Novit discovered that the group pressures exerted upon managers during the appraisal process frequently led them to conform to the agreed upon terms of the appraisal conference.

One of the most respected critics of one-on-one MBO is Harry Levinson, a proponent of group appraisals. Levinson fears that MBO has a built in reward-punishment psychology which is largely a part of the one-on-one relationships of goal setting and appraisals (45). He suggests that group appraisals will introduce a cooperative psychology of motivation. He had earlier (44) argued that group appraisals would diminish the feeling of the superior that appraisals were hostile and destructive. While subordinates would still have to be judged on their performance, this judgment could occur in the context of continuing consideration for personal needs and reappraisal of organizational and environmental realities. He contends that problems would more likely be solved spontaneously at the lowest possible levels and thus free superiors simultaneously from the burden of the passed buck and the onus of being the purveyors of hostility.

The Performance Appraisal: A Recapitulation

It is hard to argue with an objectives-centered performance appraisal, and few do; it represents one of the features in the entire MBO schema upon which there is the most universal agreement. The particular shape which the performance appraisal assumes, however, is something that most properly should be determined on an individual basis, with judgments made, preferably, after some data-based diagnosis.

This seems important because there are many factors—psychological forces, past work experiences, present working climate, and scores of others—which so forcefully impact upon the individuals in the organization that their behaviors may be difficult to mold into the MBO appraisal format.

The urgency of appropriate appraisal formats is heightened by the cautious but increasingly impressive weight of empirical evidence indicating that MBO does a great deal to create the objective performance appraisal which McGregor (58) sought. That evidence is cautious because, like the goal selling literature, some of the research is not rigorously empirical; it is increasingly impressive in that it is growing. In addition, there is considerable empirical evidence that if the value of objective centered appraisals is to be realized, the appraisal must be both periodic and constant.

In addition, it seems wise to ensure that the appraisal process penetrate the entire organization—not just the level of the chief executive. This will inevitably mean the establishment of what McConkey (51) calls "multiple levels of accountability", whereby all management levels are appraised. This total systemic appraisal might appropriately include a provision by which subordinates also evaluate and appraise the progress of their superiors (44).

CONCLUSION

This review of the literature largely confirms Hodgson's observation that "MBO, like ice cream, comes in twenty-nine flavors" (20, p. 423); it also isolates a number of elements which are common to the central issues of goal setting and performance appraisal. These commonalities have been outlined and represent a solid notion of what MBO is generally thought to be.

With regard to goal setting, we observe that the goal and objective setting processes generally adopt objectives which are specific, measurable, placed in a time framework, prioritized, and joined to an action plan. A high degree of subordinate involvement during goal setting is generally seen as facilitative of the integration of individual and organizational goals, and most experts urge sufficient goal flexibility to enable changes as goals and circumstances warrant.

Moreover, the appraisal process becomes a part of the next planning phase, for in it goals and objectives are reviewed and reset. Thus it is important that appraisals be held at least periodically—meaning as often as is needed. Perhaps the point most frequently emphasized in the literature is the need to have appraisals conducted on the basis of objective performance standards which are mutually agreed upon by both superiors and subordinates.

While MBO is more easily described than defined, and perhaps more appropriately placed into a model, a review of the relevant literature suggests that MBO can be properly defined as:

> *A managerial process whereby organizational purposes are diagnosed and met by joining superiors and subordinates in the pursuit of mutually agreed upon goals and objectives, which are specific, measurable, time bounded, and joined to an action plan; progress and goal attainment are measured and monitored in appraisal sessions which center on mutually determined objective standards of performance.*

REFERENCES

1. Altergott, B. H. *Management by Objectives for the Public Schools* (Ph.D. Dissertation, University of Indiana, 1970).
2. Beach, D. N., and Mahler, W. "Management by Objectives," in A. J. Marrow (Ed.), *The Failure of Success* (New York: The American Management Association, 1972), pp. 231–240.
3. Beck, A. C., and E. D. Hillmar. *A Practical Approach to Organization Development Through MBO—Selected Readings* (Reading, Mass.: Addison-Wesley, 1972).
4. Beck, A. C., and E. D. Hillmar. "OD to MBO or MBO to OD: Does it Make a Difference?" *Personal Journal*, Vol. 51 (1972), 827–834.
5. Beck, A. C., and E. D. Hillmar. *Making MBO/R Work* (Reading, Mass.: Addison-Wesley, 1976).
6. Brady, R. M. "MBO Goes to Work in the Public Sector," *Harvard Business Review*, Vol. 51, No. 2 (1973), 65–74.
7. Bryan, J. F., and E. A. Locke. "Goal Setting as a Means of Increasing Motivation," *Journal of Applied Psychology*, Vol. 51 (1967), 274–277.
8. Carroll, S. J., Jr., and H. L. Tosi. "The Relation of Characteristics of the Review Process as Moderated by Personality and Situational Factors to the Success of the 'Management by Objectives' Approach," in R. G. Scott and P. P. LeBreton (Eds.), *Academy of Management Proceedings* (1969), pp. 139–143.
9. Carroll, S. J., Jr., and H. L. Tosi. *Management by Objectives: Application and Research* (New York: The MacMillan Company, 1973).
10. Carvalho, G. F. "Installing Management by Objectives: A New Perspective on Organization Change," *Human Resource Management*, Vol. 2 (Spring 1972), 23–30.

11. Chartrand, P. J. "From MBO to Business Planning," *Canadian Personnel and Industrial Relations Journal*, Vol. 28 (Sept., 1971), 15–22.
12. Chartrand, P. J. "Business Planning in the Canadian Post Office," *Canadian Personnel and Industrial Relations Journal*, Vol. 28 (Oct., 1971), 17–22.
13. Drucker, P. F. *The Practice of Management* (New York: Harper and Row, 1954).
14. Drucker, P. F. "What Results Should You Expect? A User's Guide to MBO," *Public Administration Review*, Vol. 36, No. 1 (1976), 12–19.
15. French, J. R. P., Jr., E. Kay, and H. H. Meyer. "Participation and the Appraisal System," *Human Relations*, Vol. 19, No. 1 (1966), 3–20.
16. French, W., and R. W. Hollmann. "Management by Objectives: The Team Approach," *California Management Review*, Vol. 17, No. 1 (1975), 13–22.
17. Fryer, F. W. *An Evaluation of the Level of Aspiration as a Training Procedure* (Englewood Cliffs, New Jersey: Prentice Hall, 1964.
18. Heier, H. D. "Implementing an Appraisal-by-Results Program," *Personnel*, Vol. 47, No. 6 (1970), 24–32.
19. Hillmar, E. D. "Where OD and MBO Meet: Implementing Both to be Truly Successful," *Training and Development Journal*, Vol. 29 (April 1975), 34–38.
20. Hodgson, J. S. "Management by Objectives: The Experience of a Federal Government Department," *Canadian Public Administration*, Vol. 16, No. 4 (1973), 422–431.
21. Howell, R. A. "A Fresh Look at Management by Objectives," *Business Horizons*, Vol. 10, No. 4 (1967), 51–58.
22. Howell, R. A. "Managing by Objectives—A Three Stage System," *Business Horizons*, Vol. 13, No. 1 (1970), 41–45.
23. Hughes, C. L. *Goal Setting: Key to Individual and Organizational Effectiveness* (New York: American Management Association, 1965).
24. Hughes, C. L. "Assessing the Performance of Key Managers," *Personnel*, Vol. 45, No. 1 (1968), 38–43.
25. Humble, J. W. *How to Manage by Objectives* (New York: American Management Association, 1972).
26. Humphrey, A. S. "MBO Turned Upside Down," *Management Review*, Vol. 63, (August 1974), 4–8.
27. Hunaday, R. J., and G. H. Varney. "Salary Administration: A Reason for MBO!" *Training and Development Journal*, Vol. 28 (Sept. 1974), 24–28.
28. Huse, E. "Putting in a Management Development Program that Works," *California Management Review*, Vol. 9, No. 4 (1966), 73–80.
29. Huse, E. F., and E. Kay. "Improving Employee Productivity Through Work Planning," in J. W. Blood (Ed.), *The Personnel Job in a Changing World* (New York: The American Management Associations, 1964), pp. 289–315.
30. Ivancevich, J. M. "The Theory and Practice of Management by Objectives," *Michigan Business Review*, Vol. 21 (March 1969), 13–16.
31. Ivancevich, J. M. "A Longitudinal Assessment of Management by Objectives," *Administrative Science Quarterly*, Vol. 17, No. 2 (1972), 126–138.
32. Ivancevich, J. M., J. H. Donnelly, and H. Lyon. "A Study of the Impact of

Management by Objectives on Perceived Need Satisfaction," *Personnel Psychology*, Vol. 23, No. 2 (1970), 139–151.

33. Kindall, A. F., and J. Gatza. "Positive Program for Performance Appraisal," *Harvard Business Review*, Vol. 41, No. 6 (1963), 153–166.

34. Kirchoff, B. A. "Understanding What the Experts are Saying," *MSU Business Topics*, Vol. 22, No. 2 (1974), 17–22.

35. Kleber, T. "The Six Hardest Areas to Manage by Objectives," *Personnel Journal*, Vol. 51 (August 1972), 571–575.

36. Kleber, T. "Forty Common Goal-Setting Errors," *Human Resource Management*, Vol. 2, No. 3 (1972), 10–13.

37. Koontz, H. *Appraising Managers as Managers* (New York: McGraw-Hill, 1971).

38. Koontz, H. "Making Managerial Appraisal Effective," *California Management Review*, Vol. 20, No. 4 (1972), 46–55.

39. Knezevich, S. J. "MBO: Its Meaning and Application to Educational Administration," *Education*, Vol. 93 (Sept.-Oct., 1972), 12–21.

40. Knezevich, S. J. *Management by Objectives and Results—A Guidebook for Today's School Executive* (Arlington, Virginia: American Association of School Administrators, 1973).

41. Lahti, R. E. "Management by Objectives," *College and University Bulletin*, Vol. 51 (July 1971), 31–33.

42. Lahti, R. E. "Implementing the Systems Means Learning to Manage Your Objectives," *College and University Business*, Vol. 52 (February 1972), 43–46.

43. Lasagna, J. B. "Make Your MBO Pragmatic," *Harvard Business Review*, Vol. 49, No. 6 (1971), 64–69.

44. Levinson, H. "Management by Whose Objectives?" *Harvard Business Review*, Vol. 48, No. 4 (1970), 125–134.

45. Levinson, H. "Management by Objectives: A Critique," *Training and Development Journal*, Vol. 26 (April 1972), 3–8.

46. Levinson, H. "Appraisal of *What* Performance?" *Harvard Business Review*, Vol. 54, No. 4 (1976), 30–40, 44–46, 160.

47. Likert, R. "Motivational Approach to Management Development, *Harvard Business Review*, Vol. 37, No. 4 (1959), 75–82.

48. MacKenzie, R. A., and G. H. Varney, "The Missing Link in MBO," *The Business Quarterly*, Vol. 38 (Autumn 1973, 72–80.

49. Mahler, W. R. "Management by Objectives: A Consultant's Viewpoint," *Training and Development Journal*, Vol. 27 (April 1972), 16–19.

50. Mali, P. *Managing by Objectives: A Systems Approach* (New York: John Wiley and Sons, 1972).

51. McConkey, D. D. "Judging Managerial Performance: Single vs. Multiple Levels of Accountability," *Business Horizons*, Vol. 7, No. 3 (1964), 47–54.

52. McConkey, D. D. *How to Manage by Results* (New York: American Management Associations, 1965).

53. McConkey, D. D. "Taking the Buck out of Measuring Managers," *S.A.M. Advanced Management Journal*, Vol. 33 (October 1968), 35–40.

54. McConkey, D. D. "Twenty Ways to Kill Management by Objectives," *Management Review*, Vol. 41 (October 1972), 4–13.
55. McConkie, M. L. *Management by Objectives: A Corrections Perspective.* (Washington, D.C.: U.S. Government Printing Office, 1975).
56. McConkie, M. L. *Management by Objectives in the Public Sector: Defining the Concept and Testing Its Application* (Ph.D. Dissertation, University of Georgia, 1977).
57. McGregor, D. M. "An Uneasy Look at Performance Appraisal," *Harvard Business Review*, Vol. 35, No. 3 (1957), 89–94.
58. McGregor, D. M. "The Human Side of Enterprise," *The Management Review*, Vol. 46, No. 11 (1957), 22–28, 88–92.
59. Meyer, H. H., E. Kay, and J. R. P. French, Jr., "Split Roles in Performance Appraisal," *Harvard Business Review*, Vol. 43, No. 1 (1965), 123–129.
60. Miller, E. C. *MBO and the Use of Performance Standards* (New York: The American Management Associations, 1965).
61. Miller, E. C. *Objectives and Standards of Performance in Marketing Management* (New York: The American Management Association, 1967).
62. Miller, E. C. *Objectives and Standards: An Approac!: to Planning and Control* (New York: American Management Association, 1968).
63. Morrisey, G. L. *Management by Objectives and Results* (Reading, Mass.: Addison-Wesley, 1970).
64. Novit, M. "Performance Evaluation and Dual Authority: A Look at Group Appraisal," *Management of Personnel Quarterly*, Vol. 8, No. 1 (1969), 3–8.
65. Odiorne, G. S. *Management by Objectives: A System of Managerial Leadership* (New York: Pitman Publishing Co., 1965).
66. Odiorne, G. S. "Management by Objectives and the Phenomenon of Goals Displacement," *Human Resource Management*, Vol. 13, No. 1 (1974), 2–7.
67. Patton, A. "How to Appraise Executive Performance," *Harvard Business Review*, Vol. 38, No. 1 (1960), 63–70.
68. Raia, A. P. "Goal Setting and Self-Control," *The Journal of Management Studies*, Vol. 2 (February 1965), 34–53.
69. Raia, A.P. "A Second Look at Management Goals and Controls," *California Management Review*, Vol. 13, No. 1 (1966), 49–58.
70. Raia, A. P. *Managing by Objectives* (Glenview, Illinois: Scott, Foresman and Co., 1974).
71. Reddin, W. J. Managerial Effectiveness (Toronto: McGraw-Hill, 1970).
72. Reddin, W. J. *Effective Management by Objectives* (New York: McGraw-Hill, 1971).
73. Reddin, W. J. "MBO and the Behavioral Sciences," *Optimum*, Vol. 3, No. 2 (1972), 5–13.
74. Reddin, W. J. "Do MBO Systems Differ?" *Optimum*, Vol. 4, No. 1 (1973), 42–50.
75. Reddin, W. J. "Reddin Speaks on MBO," *Management*, Vol. 20 (September 1973), 22–23.
76. Rossano, M. *A Study of Management by Objectives as Perceived and Practiced*

by *Junior College Administrators* (Ph.D. Dissertation, University of Texas at Austin, 1975).

77. Scanlan, B. K. "Quantifying the Quantifiable, or Can Results Management be Applied to the Staff Man's Job?" *Personnel Journal*, Vol. 47 (March 1968), 162ff.

78. Scanlan, B. K. "Participation in Objective Setting," *The Personnel Administrator*, Vol. 14, No. 2 (1969), 1–12.

79. Scanlan, B. K. *Principles of Management and Organizational Behavior* (New York: Wiley and Sons, 1973).

80. Schaffer, R. H. *Managing by Total Objectives* (New York: American Management Association, 1964).

81. Schleh, E. C. "The 'Results' Approach to Salaries," *Personnel*, Vol. 31, (1955), 393–405.

82. Schleh, E. C. "Management by Objectives: Some Principles for Making it Work," *The Management Review*, Vol. 48 (November 1959), 26–33.

83. Schleh, E. C. *Management by Results* (New York: McGraw-Hill, 1961).

84. Schrieber, D. E., and S. Sloan. "Management by Objectives," *The Personnel Administrator*, Vol. 15, No. 3 (1970), 20–26.

85. Schuster, F. E. "A Systems Approach to Managing Resources," *The Personnel Administrator*, Vol. 16, No. 2 (1971), 27–37.

86. Schuster, F. E. "Management by Objectives—What and Why," *The Personnel Administrator*, Vol. 17, No. 2 (1972), 27–32.

87. Shetty, Y. K., and H. Carlisle. "Application of Management by Objectives in a University Setting: An Exploratory Study in Faculty Reactions," *Educational Administration Quarterly*, Vol. 10, No. 1 (1974), 65–81.

88. Shetty, K., and H. Carlisle. "Organizational Correlates of a Management by Objectives Program," *Academy of Management Journal*, Vol. 17, No. 1 (1974), 155–160.

89. Sloan, S., and D. E. Schrieber. "What We Need to Know About Management by Objectives," *Personnel Journal*, Vol. 49 (March 1970, 206–208, 249.

90. Stedry, A. C., and E. Kay. "The Effects of Goal Difficulty on Performance: A Field Experiment," *Behavioral Science*, Vol. 11 (1966), 459–470.

91. Tosi, H. L., and S. J. Carroll. "Managerial Reaction to Management by Objectives," *Academy of Management Journal*, Vol. 13, No. 4 (1968), 415–426.

92. Tosi, H. L., and S. J. Carroll. "Some Factors Affecting the Success of 'Management by Objectives'," *Journal of Management Studies*, Vol. 7 (May 1970), 209–223.

93. Tosi, H. L., and S. J. Carroll. "Improving Management by Objectives: A Diagnostic Change Program," *California Management Review*, Vol. 16, No. 3 (1973), 57–66.

94. Tosi, H. L., J. R. Rizzo, and S. J. Carroll. "Setting Goals in Management by Objectives," *California Management Review*, Vol. 7, No. 2 (1970), 70–78.

95. Valentine, R. F. "Laying the Groundwork for Goal Setting," *Personnel*, Vol. 48, No. 1 (1966), 34–41.

96. Valentine, R. F. *Performance Objectives for Managers* (New York: The American Management Association, 1966).

97. Varney, G. H. *Management by Objectives*. (Chicago: Dartnell Corporation, 1971).

98. Varney, G. H. *Management by Objectives*. (Chicago: Dartnell Corporation, 1971).

99. Varney, G. H. "Management by Objectives: Making it Work," *Supervisory Management*, Vol. 17, No. 1 (1972), 24–30.

100. White, D. D. "Factors Affecting Employee Attitudes Toward the Installation of a New Management System," *Academy of Management Journal of Business Research*, Vol. 2 (July, 1974), 289–302.

102. Wikstrom, W. S. "Management by Objectives or Appraisal by Results," *The Conference Board Record*, Vol. 3 (July 1966), 27–31.

103. Wikstrom, W. S. *Managing by—and with—Objectives* (New York: The Conference Board, 1968).

104. Williams, E. "MBO for the Management Professor," in W. F. Glueck (Ed.), *Academy of Management Proceedings* (1974), p. 29.

Archie B. Carroll

University of Georgia

SETTING OPERATIONAL GOALS FOR CORPORATE SOCIAL RESPONSIBILITY

Goal setting is an integral part of the planning process and consequently deserves substantial attention from management. Too frequently in the past, however, goal setting has been forced into second class status relative to the action-oriented task of implementing managerial decisions. In addition, goal setting as it pertains to the social domain of the organization has even received less attention.

Research, literature, and acclamations by business practitioners have suggested in recent years that the social dimension of management has not been adequately considered from a managerial decision-making perspective. Considerable debate has concluded that business organizations do have social responsibilities, but the extent and nature of these responsibilities are not clear.

Though the debate is ongoing, the typical business organization has demonstrated by its actions that it does, indeed, perceive a social responsibility to society. That being the case, and managers being the uncertainty-reducing beings that they are, efforts logically turn to the subject of applying

Archie B. Carroll, "Setting Operational Goals for Corporate Social Responsibility," *Long Range Planning Journal*, April 1978, pp. 35–38.

145

known concepts of management to the relatively unknown or still ambiguous domain of social responsibility performance.

It is the intent of this discussion to suggest that just as goal setting has come to assume an indispensable role in the more traditional phases of management (e.g., production, finance, and marketing), it should also assume an important role in the arena of social performance decision making. Social performance decision making is defined here as encompassing those managerial decisions as to the organization's performance in such areas as equal employment opportunity, consumer product safety, occupational safety and health, corporate philanthropy, environmental protection, consumerism issues, and other such categories that are today typically defined as being under the purview of an organization's social responsibilities.

All too frequently managers assume that the management technology they have developed and learned to use cannot—or should not—be applied in the area of the company's social responsibility performance. There are many valid reasons why this is so; however, our intent is not to debate that issue here.

Our concern in this article is to identify one general problem that has frequently bogged down efforts to improve businesses' social performance, and to propose an approach for helping solve that problem. In addition, illustrations will be provided showing how the proposed approach might work in practice.

THE PROBLEM: AESTHETIC SOCIAL OBJECTIVES

The problem to which reference is being made is the problem of business and managers not going beyond the *aesthetic level* in the setting of their social objectives. By aesthetic level, reference is made to the widespread practice of setting broad, general, pleasing-to-the-eye type objectives. This practice has been widespread over the years in areas such as finance ("make the *highest* possible profit"), marketing ("to sell the most we can"), production ("to achieve the lowest possible costs") and other traditional business functions.

To some degree, managers have moved beyond the aesthetic level in these traditional business areas, but have chosen not to in many instances in the area of the firm's social performance. It is not all together clear why management has chosen to remain at the level of aesthetics in the area of social performance but it is anticipated that the reasons might be: "Social responsibility is such a nebulous thing," or "Social issues are not our bread-and-butter concern."

In any event the problem is basically the unwillingness—or inability—of management to go beyond the level of aesthetic social objectives—those objectives which are of the window dressing variety with such platitudinous generalities as "to be a good corporate citizen," "to improve the level of ethics in our company," "to serve the community as best we can," and "to always operate with the public interest in mind." To be sure, these types of general statements are necessary for public relations purposes and to convey management's social responsibility philosophy; however, if *goal accomplishment* is the objective then management must move beyond aesthetic objectives.

THE SOLUTION: OPERATIONAL SOCIAL GOALS

It is proposed here that management decision makers can learn much from the literature and practice of MBO (Management By Objectives) which has evolved and become more sophisticated in recent years. A large number of guidelines on operationalizing goals have been set forth in areas where MBO may be applicable. Carroll and Tosi, for example, suggest that "one purpose of MBO is to facilitate the derivation of specific objectives from general ones. . . ."[1] And, indeed, this is what operationalizing goals or objectives means. It means converting general (aesthetic) objectives into specific ones for which goal *attainment* is readily accomplishable and identifiable.

A number of guidelines for the operationalization of objectives are available in management writing, and it is suggested that these guidelines be used to develop specific statements of social goals for the business firm. In terms of these guidelines to objective writing, Carroll and Tosi suggest that the objective statement be as follows.

(1) Clear, concise, and unambiguous.
(2) Accurate in terms of the true end state or condition sought.[2]

Dale McConkey, writing on this same subject, suggests that objectives should be "specific," "specify results to be achieved" (as opposed to activities in which one may engage), and should be "realistic and attainable."[3] One way of making an objective realistic and attainable, asserts McConkey, is to make sure it contains "stretch."

This means that the objective "should be set at a level of difficulty and achievement that requires managers to exert more than normal effort or a business-as-usual approach."[4]

Further guidelines for operationalizing objectives are recommended by George Morrisey. Morrisey argues that a well-written objective should:

(1) Start with the word *to*, followed by an action verb.
(2) Specify a *single key result* to be accomplished.
(3) Specify a *target date* by which the accomplishment is expected.
(4) Specify *maximum cost* factors involved.
(5) Be as *specific* and *quantitative* (and hence measurable and verifiable) as possible.[5] [emphasis added].

In effect, then, it is suggested that the aesthetic social objectives that so frequently characterize social goal setting in business organizations be fashioned after the guidelines that have emerged over the last 5–7 years in the experience of MBO. Though MBO objectives typically are written *by* individual managers *for* individual managers, there is no valid reason why this same procedure cannot be used in operationalizing social goals.

OPERATIONAL SOCIAL GOALS: ILLUSTRATIONS

Illustrations from a number of different areas of how aesthetic objectives may be converted to specific objectives are set forth demonstrating the method by which social goals can be operationalized according to the guidelines discussed above. Though the objectives may not in every case conform to every guideline, they generally conform to the guidelines set forth.

(1) *Aesthetic Objective*: To be a good community citizen by supporting community projects.

Operational Objectives: (a) To begin a program on improved race relations by holding the first community meeting at company headquarters on June 15, 1977, with an initial dollar support of whatever costs are necessary to fund the meeting, up to $1,000.

(b) To provide 10 hours a week released time for each of two executives to serve on the community's Committee on Crime Prevention for 2 years at a cost of $18,000 to the company.

(c) To underwrite the costs of the annual Christmas concert put on by the Boy's Club of Athens for the 1977 year at a cost of $5,000.

(d) To participate in the YWCO-sponsored daycare program by permitting their officials to disseminate promotional literature through the company's internal mail system during the months of August and February each year for the next 3 years.

(2) *Aesthetic Objective*: To support the employment and promotion of women and members of minority groups.

Operational Objectives: (a) To employ minorities at a rate equal to the percentage of minorities in the local community for the next 5 years.

(b) To assure that women and minorities are represented in the work force by appointing a fair employment ombudsman to advocate their fair and equitable treatment by July 25, 1978.

(c) To hire and promote women and minorities to positions in the job categories of manager, technician, and professional on the basis of equal employment opportunity guidelines laid out by the EEOC.

(3) *Aesthetic Objective*: To protect the environment and promote energy conservation.

Operational Objectives: (a) To require that all new machinery purchased after January 1, 1978 meet all requirements laid down by the Environmental Protection Act (EPA) for antipollution standards and energy useage.

(b) To develop a formal company policy on environmental protection and energy conservation by July 15, 1978.

(4) *Aesthetic Objective*: To support worthwhile organizations by contributing money to their causes.

Operational Objectives: (a) To increase our pledge to the Urban League by 15 percent over last year's contribution.

(b) To donate to education, including both higher and secondary education, 1 per cent of the company's net profits for fiscal year 1976–1977.

(c) To match with company funds all donations of company employees to such federated drives as the United Fund and Community Chest during the 1977 calendar year.

Managerial Implications

If a planning process such as the one described above is effectively implemented, a number of positive consequences may likely follow.

1. Integrity of planning process is established. One of the major criticisms set forth against planning efforts is that they are frequently vacuous; that is, they represent considerable "planning for planning's sake" and do not result in visible or tangible outcomes for the organization. To create integrity in the planning process means to make it meaningful and functional, with specific, identifiable end results. Once it is established that planning for social performance is not just "wheel spinning," a more favorable attitude on the part of management and involved personnel will result. This favorable attitude and meaningfulness of the planning effort will enhance goal setting and accomplishment through successive cycles (or years) using the approach.

2. Improved social responsibility programs. The planning process as described will result in improved quality social performance programs. This is a logical end result of the operational goal setting process but should be emphasized since considerable criticism and, indeed, skepticism, has resulted from recent years' efforts on the part of some organizations. Tangible accomplishments over a period of time can be documented as a consequence of operational goal setting.

3. Success will reinforce future efforts in the social arena. The adage "success breeds success" is pertinent here. One of the primary reasons social responsibility programs have been impotent in the past is failure to achieve visible results which can then be pointed to as consideration is given to social responsibility programs in future planning efforts. Specific, tangible results provide sound rationale for next year's planning when social programs have to compete—as they inevitably do—for scarce organizational resources.

4. Specific goal attainment facilitates appraisal of managerial personnel. One reason top level executives have not been highly successful in effectively integrating social concerns into their organizations is traceable to an inability on their part to measure performance on the social dimension. As many managers would likely attest, behaviors that are not easily factored into the performance appraisal equation have a tendency to be considered less important, if not dropped completely. Without question social performance is not as crucial as economic performance; however, in this changing world of environmental impact statements, class action suits, discrimination charges, and product liability indictments, the social side of the organization's performance is assuming a significance heretofore unparalleled in society's history.

5. Enhanced credibility with the organization's multiple publics will follow. In this day and age of justifying corporate accomplishments to pressure groups, social critics, regulatory bodies, and increasingly vocal

shareholders and employees, the organization able to document its social accomplishments with a factual record rather than with vacuous platitudes, will have the edge when charges of irresponsibility arise. Such charges can be deflated rapidly with specific results of social programs emanating out of an operational goal setting system. Furthermore, an approach of this type provides prima facie evidence that management is sincerely interested in providing a *social response* rather than debating endlessly whether it has a social responsibility or simply assuaging its conscience.

CONCLUSION

More formality in social responsibility planning efforts is a concept which is extremely pertinent in today's conditions. Rewards will accrue to the organization that can move beyond aesthetic objectives and achieve operationality in social responsibility goal setting. This requires, basically, the application of techniques that have proved to be successful in MBO programs. By translating broadly stated social objectives into goals that are clear, concise, time related, and cost related, management will inject an increased measure of integrity into its planning process, improve social responsibility programs, assure future successes in the social performance arena, facilitate the appraisal of management personnel, and enhance the organization's credibility with its multiple publics. Positive benefits will flow to the organization, its immediate publics, and to the society at large as a consequence of operational planning methods as described herein.

REFERENCES

1. S. J. Carroll, Jr. and H. L. Tosi, Jr., *Management By Objectives: Applications and Research*, pp. 69–70, Macmillan, New York (1973).
2. *Ibid.*, p. 72.
3. Dale D. McConkey, *MBO for Nonprofit Organizations*, pp. 56–57, ANACOM, New York (1975).
4. *Ibid.*, p. 57.
5. George L. Morrisey, *Management By Objectives and Results*, pp. 52–54, Addison-Wesley, Reading, Massachusetts (1970).

Michael B. McCaskey

Harvard Business School

AN INTRODUCTION TO ORGANIZATIONAL DESIGN

How does a manager choose among organizational design alternatives? How does he, for example, decide how precisely to define duties and roles? Should decision-making be centralized or decentralized? What type of people should he recruit to work on a particular task force? Organization design tries to identify the organizational structures and processes that appropriately "fit" the type of people in the organization and the type of task the organization faces.

Organizational design determines what the structures and processes of an organization will be. The features of an organization that can be designed include: division into sections and units, number of levels, location of decision-making authority, distribution of and access to information, physical layout of buildings, types of people recruited, what behaviors are rewarded, and so on. In the process of designing an organization, managers invent, develop, and analyze alternative forms for combining these elements. And the form must reflect the limits and capabilities of humans and the characteristics and nature of the task environment.[1]

Designing a human social organization is extremely complicated. An organization is a system of interrelated parts to that the design of one subsystem or of one procedure has ramifications for other parts of the

Michael B. McCaskey, "An Introduction to Organizational Design," *California Management Review*, Winter 1974, pp. 13–21.

system. Furthermore, the criteria by which a system design is to be evaluated (economic performance, survival capability, social responsibility, and the personal growth of organizational members) cannot be maximized simultaneously—the design of a human social organization can never be perfect or final. In short, the design of organizational arrangements is intended to devise a complex set of trade-offs in a field of changing people, environment, and values.

Minor adjustments in organizational design are always being made during the life of an organization, but the times for major concentration on organizational design are:

- Early in the life of an organization, most likely after the basic identity and strategy have been largely worked out;
- When significantly expanding or changing the organization's mission; or
- When reorganizing.

Who designs the organization, organizational units, and task forces? Since organizational design concerns the arrangement of people and the division of tasks, a designer or planner has to have some influence or control over these variables. This task is most often handled by middle-level managers and up. However, the charter to design could be broadened to give organizational members at all levels more of a say in organizational design matters.

KEY CONCEPTS AND QUESTIONS_____

In approaching an organization design problem, some of the important questions to be answered are:

1. How uncertain is the task environment in which the organization operates?
2. In what ways should the organization be mechanistic and in what ways organic?
3. How should the sub-tasks be divided and how should the organization be differentiated? Should subsystems be organized by the *functions* people perform, by the *products* or services the company provides, or should some other form, such as a matrix organization, be used?

4. What kind of people are (or can be recruited to become) members of the organization? Under what conditions do they work and learn best?
5. How are activities to be coordinated and integrated? What mechanisms will be used, involving what costs?

Research and theory provide some findings that can be used as design guidelines, and we turn to consider them now.

Mechanistic Patterns of Organizing

Tom Burns and G. M. Stalker's 1961 study[2] of electronics firms and firms contemplating entering the electronics industry in Scotland and England contributed the important design principle of distinguishing between mechanistic and organic patterns of organizing.

Mechanistic organizational units are the traditional pyramidal pattern of organizing. In a mechanistic organizational unit, roles and procedures are precisely defined. Communication is channelized, and time spans and goal orientations are similar within the unit. The objective is to work toward machine-like efficiency. To that end the task is broken into parts that are joined together at the end of the work process. Authority, influence, and information are arranged by levels, each higher level having successively more authority, more influence, and more information. Decision-making is centralized at the top and it is the top levels that make appreciative judgments[3] to determine what is important in the environment. Top levels also determine the channels whereby the lower echelons will gather and process information.

Thus the social organization is designed as a likeness of a machine. People are conceived of as parts performing specific tasks. As employees leave, other parts can be slipped into their places. Someone at the top is the designer, defining what the parts will be and how they will all fit together.

Under what conditions is this pattern of organization appropriate? When the organizational unit is performing a task that is stable, well-defined, and likely to be programmable, or when members of the organization prefer well-defined situations, feel more secure when the day has a routine to it, and tend to want others to supply direction, the mechanistic pattern is applicable. Organization design findings show that, to the extent these conditions hold, a mechanistic form of organizing is more likely to result in high performance.

The mechanistic form is efficient and predictable. For people with a low tolerance for ambiguity it provides a stable and secure work setting. However, the mechanistic form is less flexible—once a direction and procedures have been set, it is hard to change them. Furthermore, mechanistic forms also entail the danger of stultifying their members with jobs that are too simple, with little responsibility, and no sense of worthwhile accomplishment.

Organic Patterns of Organizing

In contrast to mechanistic units, organic organizational units are based on a more biological metaphor for constructing social organizations. The objective in designing an organic unit is to leave the system maximally open to the environment in order to make the most of new opportunities. The demands of the task environment are ambiguously defined and changing, so people have multiple roles which are continually redefined in interaction with others. All levels make appreciations and there are few predetermined information channels. Decision-making is more decentralized, with authority and influence flowing to the person who has the greatest expertise to deal with the problem at hand. An organic organizational unit is relatively heterogeneous, containing a wider variety of time spans, goal orientations, and ways of thinking. The boundaries between the system and the environment are deliberately permeable, and the environment exerts more influence over the activities of the system than is true for the mechanistic unit.

An organic form is useful in the face of an uncertain task or one that is not well enough understood to be programmed. The organic form is also appropriate for people who like the disorder of an ambiguous setting, for people who prefer variety, change, and adventure and who grow restless when they fall into the same routine day after day. The organic form is flexible and responds quickly to unexpected opportunities. However, the organic form is often wasteful of resources. Not having precisely defined authority, control, and information hierarchies, time can be wasted in search activities that duplicate the efforts of other members. Furthermore, the stress of uncertainty and the continual threat of power struggles can be exhausting.

Making the Choice

The choice of the most suitable form of organization is *contingent* upon the task and the people involved. There is no one form of organization that will work best in all situations, in all cultures, with every type of person. Organization design scholars using a contingency theory approach emphasize the need to specify the particular conditions under which a given form is most appropriate.

Note, too, that the same organizational unit can change its position on the organic/mechanistic continuum over time. The unit might start out being very mechanistically organized. But as the environment or staff change, the unit might move toward the organic end of the continuum. In fact, if the unit does not change its structures and processes to meet changed conditions, it is likely to suffer low performance.

Even more important, one organization is likely to contain both organic units and mechanistic units at the same time. Burns and Stalker[4] characterized whole organizations as mechanistic or organic, but Paul Lawrence and Jay Lorsch[5] found that these descriptions more accurately described units of an organization. They researched and elaborated on a major contribution to organization design in the concepts of differentiation and integration (D&I).

DIFFERENTIATION

Differentiation, the creation or emergence of differences in the organization, can take place in several ways:

- Vertically—into levels;
- Horizontally—into sections, department, divisions, and so on;
- Division of labor—into occupational roles; and
- Patterns of thinking—differences between units in members' goals, time, and interpersonal orientations.

By differentiating, the organization gains the advantages of both economies of scale and people becoming experts in particular areas like production, accounting, contracting, and so on.

Lawrence and Lorsch found horizontal differentiation and the differentiation of patterns of thinking to be the most important types of differentiation for organizational design. The organization segments the environment into parts so that organizational units interact with different subenvironments. While marketing interacts with the media, ad agencies, legal departments, competitors' advertising, and the other elements that make up the marketing sub-environment, production is dealing with the machines, labor market, scheduling, cost consciousness, and safety regulations that pertain to their subenvironment. Furthermore, the structure and setting for each unit must supply the appropriate training and support for different job demands. Scientists, for example, need a milieu that will supply specialized information as well as support in projects that may take years to complete.

An important question in organization design, therefore, is how differentiated should the organization be? How should the environment be segmented and what activities should be grouped together? To what extent should the units differ in structures and procedures, types of people, and patterns of thinking?

Research indicates that business organizations in newer and more uncertain industries, like aerospace and electronics, need to be more highly differentiated because they face a greater range of subenvironments. As James Thompson[6] argues, organizations try to shield their technical core from the uncertainties of the environment. The subenvironment of the core technology unit, then, will be relatively stable and call for more mechanistic patterns of organizing. The units having uncertain subenvironments (often the R&D subenvironment) will need to be more organically organized. Looking at the organization as a whole, the differences between the units will be significant because the range of unit organizational patterns extends from the mechanistic end to the organic end of the continuum.

Conversely, research indicates that organizations in older, more established and more certain industries need to be less differentiated. They face a narrow range of subenvironments near the certainty end of the spectrum, and will probably pursue the efficiency given by more mechanistic patterns of organizing. An organization in a relatively stable and certain environment benefits from having uniform rules and procedures, vocabularly, and patterns of thinking throughout the organization. The problem of integration for these organizations, therefore, is less demanding.

INTEGRATION _____

At the same time the organization is differentiated to work more effectively on tasks, some activities of organizational units must be coordinated and brought together, or integrated. The manager/designer must resist differentiating the organization too radically—the greater the differences between the units, the harder it is for them to coordinate activities with each other. If all the units have similar goals, values, and time horizons, messages and meanings are more likely to be clear. But when an organization is highly differentiated, people have to spend more effort translating and appreciating the frameworks of people in different units. Most people habitually think in their own terms and it takes increased effort to move into another's frame of reference. The chances for misunderstandings increase in a highly differentiated organization.

The greater the differentiation, the heavier the burden on information processing and upon decision making in the organization. This shows up in the array of techniques for coordinating the activities of a firm:

1. The use of rules and procedures along with the hierarchy of authority;
2. If two units are crucial and have trouble integrating, the appointment of a liaison;[7]
3. The building of a new unit into the work flow to serve as an integrating department.

This list of coordinating mechanisms shows progressively more elaborate ways to achieve integration. With greater differentiation, an organization has to spend more effort integrating and use the more expensive devices.

So in addition to asking how much the organization should differentiate to meet environment and people requirements, another question must simultaneously be raised. How much differentiation, at that cost, can the organization successfully integrate? How should people be grouped to provide the best working conditions for individuals *and* to secure the most advantageous work flow for the whole organization? A manager/designer works for the best practical answer to these questions. Many times he may decide to stop short of differentiating to perfectly meet task environment demands because his staff would find it too great a strain or because it would be too costly. Research findings show that in uncertain environments, the most successful organizations are the most highly differentiated and the most integrated. The difficult design decision of how to differentiate and how to integrate is often framed as the choice between product or functional organization,[8] or some newer form like a matrix organization.[9]

THE RESEARCH STUDIES

Table I summarizes a selection of research findings important for organization design theory. The studies were conducted mainly, although not entirely, with business firms. A wide range of methodologies has been used including historical study methods, an intensive case study of one division, a questionnaire survey of managers in different organizations, surveying and interviewing the top managers of all the business organizations in a given georgraphical area, and so on. All of these studies support a contingency approach to organizational design. Researchers found that explaining their data required them to specify the conditions upon which the rest of a particular organization form was contingent.

In spite of different methods and vocabularies, certain patterns and continuities run through the findings. The design principle of distinguishing between mechanistic and organic forms is supported by the studies. Peter

TABLE I
Empirical Research Findings on Organizational Design

Researchers	Types of Organizations Studied	Selected Findings
Burns and Stalker (1961)	20 firms in U.K., including a rayon manufacturer, an engineering firm, several companies in electronics and others contemplating entry into electronics.	"Mechanistic" management system suited to an enterprise operating under relatively stable conditions; "organic" required for conditions of change.
Chandler (1962)	Historical studies of DuPont, General Motors, Standard Oil of New Jersey, and Sears Roebuck, supplemented by brief reviews of over 70 other large American business companies.	By trial and error a new structural form (decentralized, multidivisional form) developed to fit changed environmental conditions.
Woodward (1965)	100 English manufacturing firms.	Patterns in management practice associated with how complex and how predictable production technology is.
Lawrence and Lorsch (1967)	10 U.S. companies in plastics, consumer food, and standardized container industries.	1. High performing organizations are differentiated to meet environmental demands; diverse and uncertain environments require greater differentiation of the organization. 2. Differentiation and integration are antagonistic states; the more differentiated an organization is, the more elaborate the integrative devices must be. 3. Additional support for above findings.
Galbraith (1970)	Case study of the Boeing Aircraft Division.	Structural changes to deal with greater task environment uncertainty related to the need to process more information.

Blau and Richard Schoenherr's[10] findings based on all instances (53) of one type of government agency lends support to the Lawrence and Lorsch[11] findings based on a selected sample of ten business firms. Both studies found that environmental diversity is related to greater differentiation in the organization. Blau and Schoenherr[12] found that differentiation raises the requirements for managerial manpower, and this is similar to Lawrence and Lorsch's[13] finding that greater differentiation requires more elaborate integrative devices. Furthermore, Jay Galbraith's[14] research provides something of an explanatory picture. His findings suggest that the need for more managerial manpower and more elaborate integrative mechanisms is related to the need for the organization to process more information.

Robert Duncan's[15] findings that an organizational unit appears to change

TABLE I (continued)
Empirical Research Findings on Organizational Design

Researchers	Types of Organizations Studied	Selected Findings
Blau and Schoenherr (1971)	The 53 state employment security offices of the U.S. and territories.	1. Increasing size generates structural differentiation in organizations along various dimensions at decelerating rates. 2. Structural differentiation in organizations raises requirements for managerial manpower. 3. Horizontal, vertical, and occupational differentiation are positively related to environmental diversity.
Duncan (1971)	22 decision-making units in 3 manufacturing organizations and in 3 R&D organizations.	Structural profile used to make nonroutine decisions differs from that used to make routine decisions; suggests the same unit uses different organizing patterns over time.
Morse and Young (1973)	235 managers from 8 business organizations.	Individuals working on certain tasks preferred controlling authority relations and had a low tolerance for ambiguity; individuals working on uncertain tasks sought independence and autonomy and were high in tolerance for ambiguity.

its structure over time simply reinforces managers' feelings that organization charts are often incorrect and out-of-date. This is a promising area of research for developing a more accurate picture of how and when changes in organization structure occur.

As the studies indicate, substantial progress has been made. However, some important questions remain to be answered.

WORK YET TO BE DONE_____

Our knowledge of organizational design is still growing. Some of the important subjects which need further research are:

1. We need a better understanding of the *dynamics* of an organization developing a good fit to its environment and its members. The processes that span organization and environment, such as planning and selecting, recruiting and socializing new members, need to be researched. In addition to learning more about the enduring structural patterns, we also need to learn about the ways in which organization and environment adjust to one another.

2. We must consider the assertion of power in the interaction of organizations and their environments. How do organizations seek to make the environment more favorable to their operations? How does the environment coerce or influence the organization to meet its demands? What are the consequences of one element gaining sizeable amounts of control over the other? We need to learn about the processes which mediate this contest for control and influence.

3. Up until now researchers have mainly relied upon the criterion of economic performance to assess good fit. Clearly, using economic criteria alone is too limited. How can we judge goodness of fit in terms of people outcomes? Moreover, what about the people who are content to follow orders from the organization? Some argue that we cannot be normative on this value question. If a person is satisfied to be passive and dependent on the job, who can insist that he take more control over his own work life? My view is that a democracy can hardly afford a work system which mainly trains people to be docile, to follow orders, and above all to be loyal to the organization. But others emphasize that many prefer following orders, and this is where the issue is joined.

4. A related issue is the possible conflict between efficiency and human needs. Some elements of organization design concern social engineering to devise the most efficient organization to accomplish a task. Other elements

of organization design are concerned with the full growth and development of individuals. It is too optimistic to assume that efficiently designed organizations will always or even usually be conducive to human intercourse. Mammoth operations built to meet economies of scale considerations teach us that efficiently engineered operations can be inhumane. If we had better non-economic measures of outcomes, maybe we could more accurately assess the design tradeoffs. As it stands now, much of the organization design emphasizes an engineering approach, neglecting human growth aspects. Another challenge: How can we design organizations to meet both people and engineering concerns?

5. We also need to learn more about how facilities design supports or detracts from the intent of an organization design. How does the physical layout influence the pattern of social interaction? How does the visual display of information affect decision making? At what distance for what types of activities does physical separation of people or units greatly strain the organization's ability to integrate? How can facilities be designed so that physical spaces can be rearranged to fit changes in organizing patterns? Robert Propst,[16] Fritz Steele,[17] and Thomas Allen[18] have begun work on some of these questions.

SUMMARY _____

A convenient guideline for reviewing what we know about designing organizations is the continuum from mechanistic to organic patterns of organizing. Most suited to stable, certain environments and a staff that prefers stability, the mechanistic form is the traditional hierarchical pyramid that is controlled from the top and programs activities tightly. Most suited to an unstable, uncertain environment and people tolerant of ambiguity, the organic pattern of organizing is more collegial and stresses flexibility in rules, decision-making authority, procedures, and so on. Of course, there are more than these two types of organizing patterns. They should be considered the ends of a continuum of types of organizing patterns.

An organization is likely to contain both organically and mechanistically organized units. How widely the units should range on the mechanistic/organic continuum is part of the question of differentiation. How great should the differences be between units in terms of structures, types of people, and patterns of thinking? Overall, organizations in mature and stable industries contain units that face more or less well-defined and certain subenvironments. Therefore, to meet environmental demands, the units should generally be more mechanistically organized and the organization as a whole will be less differentiated.

On the other hand, organizations in dynamic new industries must have some units organically organized to deal with an uncertain subenvironment. At the same time it should devise more mechanistic units (for example, production and accounting) to face more stable subenvironments. To cover that range of subenvironments, the manager/organization designer creates or allows to develop greater differences between the units. In addition, the organization tends to create more job roles (occupational differentiation) and more levels (vertical differentiation) in response to environmental diversity. The organization, therefore, becomes more highly differentiated.

The opposite tendency from differentiation is the need to integrate, to coordinate the activities of different parts of the organization. The greater the differentiation, the harder it is to integrate. The choice of a particular integrating mechanism, such as a liaison in addition to rules, signals the manager/designer's decision to expend a certain amount of effort to coordinate activities. Concurrent with designing the extent of differentiation in an organization, a manager must consider what effort at what cost will be needed to integrate those differences. The greater the differentiation, the more elaborate and costly are the mechanisms needed for integration.

Organizational design choices are tradeoffs between good fit to the task environment and people characteristics, to monetary and human costs, and to short-term and long-term consequences. Such a design is never perfect or complete. Organizational design seeks to build knowledge about and provide guidelines for designing more efficient and more human organizations.

REFERENCES

1. Herbert A. Simon. *The New Science of Management Decision* (New York: Harper and Brothers, 1960), pp. 2, 43.
2. Tom Burns and G. M. Stalker, *The Management of Innovation* (London: Tavistock, 1961).
3. Geoffrey Vickers, *The Art of Judgment* (New York: Basic Books, 1965).
4. Burns and Stalker, *loc. cit.*
5. Paul R. Lawrence and Jay W. Lorsch, *Organization and Environment* (Boston: Graduate School of Business Administration, Harvard University, 1967).
6. James D. Thompson, *Organizations in Action* (New York: McGraw-Hill, 1967).
7. Paul R. Lawrence and Jay W. Lorsch, "New Management Job: The Integrator," *Harvard Business Review* (November-December 1967), pp. 142–151.
8. Arthur H. Walker and Jay W. Lorsch, "Organizational Choice: Product Versus

Function," *Harvard Business Review* (November-December 1968), pp. 129–138; and Jay R. Galbraith, *Designing Complex Organizations* (Reading, Mass.: Addison Wesley, 1973).

9. Donald Ralph Kingdon, *Matrix Organization: Managing Information Technologies* (London: Tavistock, 1973).

10. Peter M. Blau and Richard A. Schoenherr, *The Structure of Organizations* (New York: Basic Books, 1971).

11. Jay W. Lorsch and Paul R. Lawrence (eds.), *Studies in Organization Design* (Homewood, Ill.: Irwin-Dorsey, 1970).

12. Blau and Schoenherr, *loc. cit.*

13. Lawrence and Lorsch, *Studies in Organization Design, loc. cit.*

14. Galbraith, *loc. cit.*

15. Robert B. Duncan, *The Effects of Perceived Environmental Uncertainty on Organizational Decision Unit Structure: A Cybernetic Model*, Ph.D. dissertation, Yale University, 1971.

16. Robert Propst, *The Office: A Facility Based on Change* (New York: Taplinger Publishing Co., 1968).

17. Fred I. Steele, "Physical settings and organizational development," in H. Hornstein, *et al.* (eds.), *Social Intervention: A Behavioral Science Approach* (New York: The Free Press, 1971).

18. Thomas J. Allen, "Communication networks in R&D laboratories," *R&D Management*, 1, 1, (1970) Oxford, England, pp. 14–21.

Jay R. Galbraith

University of Pennsylvania

MATRIX ORGANIZATION DESIGNS: HOW TO COMBINE FUNCTIONAL AND PROJECT FORMS

Each era of management evolves new forms of organization as new problems are encountered. Earlier generations of managers invented the centralized functional form, the line–staff form, and the decentralized product division structure as a response to increasing size and complexity of tasks. The current generation of management has developed two new forms as a response to high technology. The first is the free-form conglomerate; the other is the matrix organization, which was developed primarily in the aerospace industry.

The matrix organization grows out of the organizational choice between project and functional forms, although it is not limited to those bases of the authority structure.[1] Research in the behavioral sciences now permits a detailing of the choices among the alternate intermediate forms between the project and functional extremes. Detailing such a choice is necessary since

Jay R. Galbraith, "Matrix Organization Designs: How to Combine Functional and Project Forms," *Business Horizons*, 1971.
[1] See John F. Mee, "Matrix Organization," *Business Horizons* (Summer, 1964), p. 70.

many businessmen see their organizations facing situations in the 1970's that are similar to those faced by aerospace firms in the 1960's. As a result, a great many unanswered questions arise concerning the use of the matrix organization. For example, what are the various kinds of matrix designs, what is the difference between the designs, how do they work, and how do I choose a design that is appropriate for my organization?

The problem of designing organizations arises from the choices available among alternative bases of the authority structure. The most common alternatives are to group together activities which bear on a common product, common customer, common geographic area, common business function (marketing, engineering, manufacturing, and so on), or common process (forging, stamping, machining, and so on). Each of these bases has various costs and economies associated with it. For example, the functional structure facilitates the acquisition of specialized inputs. It permits the hiring of an electromechanical and an electronics engineer rather than two electrical engineers. It minimizes the number necessary by pooling specialized resources and time sharing them across products or projects. It provides career paths for specialists. Therefore, the organization can hire, utilize, and retain specialists.

These capabilities are necessary if the organization is going to develop high technology products. However, the tasks that the organization must perform require varying amounts of the specialized resources applied in varying sequences. The problem of simultaneously completing all tasks on time, with appropriate quality and while fully utilizing all specialist resources, is all but impossible in the functional structure. It requires either fantastic amounts of information or long lead times for task completion.

The product or project form of organization has exactly the opposite set of benefits and costs. It facilitates coordination among specialties to achieve on-time completion and to meet budget targets. It allows a quick reaction capability to tackle problems that develop in one specialty, thereby reducing the impact on other specialties. However, if the organization has two projects, each requiring one half-time electronics engineer and one half-time electromechanical engineer, the pure project organization must either hire two electrical engineers—and reduce specialization—or hire four engineers (two electronics and two electromechanical)—and incur duplication costs. In addition, no one is responsible for long-run technical development of the specialties. Thus, each form of organization has its own set of advantages and disadvantages. A similar analysis could be applied to geographically or client-based structures.

The problem is that when one basis of organization is chosen, the benefits of the others are surrendered. If the functional structure is adopted, the technologies are developed but the projects fall behind schedule. If the project organization is chosen, there is better cost and schedule performance but the technologies are not developed as well. In the past, managers made a judgment as to whether technical development or schedule completion was more important and chose the appropriate form.

However, in the 1960's with a space race and missile gap, the aerospace firms were faced with a situation where both technical performance and coordination were important. The result was the matrix design, which attempts to achieve the benefits of both forms. However, the matrix carries some costs of its own. A study of the development of a matrix design is contained in the history of The Standard Products Co., a hypothetical company that has changed its form of organization from a functional structure to a matrix.

A COMPANY CHANGES FORMS_____

The Standard Products Co. has competed effectively for a number of years by offering a varied line of products that were sold to other organizations. Standard produced and sold its products through a functional organization like the one represented in Figure 1. A moderate number of changes in the product line and production processes were made each year. Therefore, a major management problem was to coordinate the flow of work from engineering through marketing. The coordination was achieved through several integrating mechanisms.

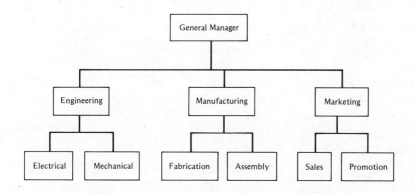

FIGURE 1   Standard's Functional Organization

Rules and procedures—*One of the ways to constrain behavior in order to achieve an integrated pattern is to specify rules and procedures. If all personnel follow the rules, the resultant behavior is integrated without having to maintain on-going communication. Rules are used for the most predictable and repetitive activities.*

Planning processes—*For less repetitive activities, Standard does not specify the procedure to be used but specifies a goal or target to be achieved, and lets the individual choose the procedure appropriate to the goal. Therefore, processes are undertaken to elaborate schedules and budgets. The usefulness of plans and rules is that they reduce the need for on-going communication between specialized subunits.*

Hierarchical referral—*When situations are encountered for which there are no rules or when problems cause the goals to be exceeded, these situations are referred upward in the hierarchy for resolution. This is the standard management-by-exception principle. This resolves the nonroutine and unpredictable events that all organizations encounter.*

Direct contact—*In order to prevent top executives from becoming overloaded with problems, as many problems as possible are resolved by the affected managers at low levels by informal contacts. These remove small problems from the upward referral process.*

Liaison departments—*In some cases, where there is a large volume of contacts between two departments, a liaison department evolves to handle the transactions. This typically occurs between engineering and manufacturing in order to handle engineering changes and design problems.*[2]

The Standard Products Co. utilized these mechanisms to integrate the functionally organized specialties. They were effective in the sense that Standard could respond to changes in the market with new products on a timely basis, the new products were completed on schedule and within budget, and the executives had sufficient time to devote to long-range planning.

Matrix Begins Evolution

A few years ago, a significant change occurred in the market for one of Standard's major product lines. A competitor came out with a new design utilizing an entirely new raw material. The initial success caused Standard to react by developing one of their own incorporating the new material. They hired some specialists in the area and began their normal new product introduction activities. However, this time the product began to fall behind schedule, and it appeared that the product would arrive on the market at a time later than planned. In response, the general manager called a meeting to analyze the situation.

---

[2] For a more detailed explanation, see Jay R. Galbraith, *Organization Design* (Reading, Mass.: Addison-Wesley Publishing Co., Inc., 1971).

Task Force.   After a briefing, it was obvious to the general manager and the directors of the three functions what was happening. Standard's lack of experience with the new material had caused them to underestimate the number and kinds of problems. The uncertainty led to a deterioration in usefulness of plans and schedules. The problems affected all functions, which meant that informal contacts and liaison processes were cumbersome; therefore, the majority of the problems were referred upward. This led to overloads on the directors of the functions and the general manager, which in turn added to the delays. Thus, the new situation required more decision making and more information processing than the current organization could provide.

The directors of engineering and manufacturing suggested that the cause of the problem was an overly ambitious schedule. More time should have been allowed for the new product; if realistic schedules were set, the current coordination processes would be adequate. They proposed that the schedules be adjusted by adding three to six months to the current due dates, which would allow more time to make the necessary decisions.

The director of marketing objected, reporting that the company would lose a good percentage of the market if the introduction was delayed. A number of big customers were waiting for Standard's version of the new product, and a delay would cost the company some of these customers. The general manager agreed with the marketing director. He proposed that they should not change the schedule to fit their current coordination processes, but that they should introduce some new coordination mechanisms to meet the scheduled due dates.

The group agreed with the general manager's position and began to search for alternative solutions. One of the solution requirements suggested was to reduce the distance between the sources of information and the points of decision. At this point the manufacturing director cautioned them about decentralizing decisions. He reminded them of previous experiences when decisions were made at low levels of the engineering organization. The data the decision makers had were current but they were also local in scope; severe problems in the manufacturing process resulted. When these decisions were centralized, the global perspective prevented these problems from developing. Therefore, they had to increase decision-making power at lower levels without losing the inputs of all affected units. The alternative that met both requirements was a group with representation from all the major departments to enter into joint decisions.

The group was appointed and named the "new product task force." It was to last as long as cross-functional problems occurred on the new product introduction. The group was to meet and solve joint problems within the budget limits set by the general manager and the directors; problems requiring more budget went to the top management group. The purpose was to make as many decisions as possible at low levels with the people most knowledgeable. This should reduce the delays and yet ensure that all the information inputs were considered.

The task force consisted of nine people—three, one from each function, were full-time and the others were part-time. They met at least every other day to discuss and resolve joint problems. Several difficulties caused them to shift membership. First, the engineering representatives were too high in the organization and, therefore, not knowledgeable about the technical alternatives and consequences. They were replaced with lower level people. The opposite occurred with respect to the manufacturing representatives. Quite often they did not have either information or the authority to commit the production organization to joint decisions made by the task force. They were replaced by higher level people. Eventually, the group had both the information and the authority to make good group decisions. The result was effective coordination: coordination = f (authority $\times$ information).

Creation of the task force was the correct solution. Decision delays were reduced, and collective action was achieved by the joint decisions. The product arrived on time, and the task force members returned to their regular duties.

Teams. No sooner had the product been introduced than salesmen began to bring back stories about new competitors. One was introducing a second-generation design based on improvements in the raw material. Since the customers were excited by its potential and the technical people thought it was feasible, Standard started a second-generation redesign across all its product lines. This time, they set up the task force structure in advance and committed themselves to an ambitious schedule.

Again the general manager became concerned. This time the product was not falling behind schedule, but in order to meet target dates the top management was drawn into day-to-day decisions on a continual basis. This was leaving very little time to think about the third-generation product line. Already Standard had to respond twice to changes initiated by others. It was time for a thorough strategy formulation. Indeed, the more rapid the change in technology and markets, the greater the amount of strategic decision making that is necessary. However, these are the same changes that pull top management into day-to-day decisions. The general manager again called a meeting to discuss and resolve the problem.

The solution requirements to the problem were the same as before. They had to find a way to push a greater number of decisions down to lower levels. At the same time, they had to guarantee that all interdependent subunits would be considered in the decision so that coordination would be maintained. The result was a more extensive use of joint decision making and shared responsibility.

The joint decision making was to take place through a team structure. The teams consisted of representatives of all functions and were formed around major product lines. There were two levels of teams, one at lower levels and another at the middle-management level. Each level had defined discretionary limits; problems that the lower level could not solve were referred to the middle-level team. If the middle level team could not solve the problem, it went to top management. A greater number of day-to-day operating problems were thereby solved at lower levels of the hierarchy, freeing top management for long-range decisions.

The teams, unlike the task force, were permanent. New products were regarded as a fact of life, and the teams met on a continual basis to solve recurring interfunctional problems. Task forces were still used to solve temporary problems. In fact, all the coordination mechanisms of rules, plans, upward referral, direct contact, liaison men, and task forces were used, in addition to the teams.

Product Managers.   The team structure achieved interfunctional coordination and permitted top management to step out of day-to-day decision making. However, the teams were not uniformly effective. Standard's strategy required the addition of highly skilled, highly educated technical people to continue to innovate and compete in the high technology industry. Sometimes these specialists would dominate a team because of their superior technical knowledge. That is, the team could not distinguish between providing technical information and supplying managerial judgment after all the facts were identified. In addition, the specialists' personalities were different from the personalities of the other team members, which made the problem of conflict resolution much more difficult.[3]

Reports of these problems began to reach the general manager, who realized that a great number of decisions of consequence were being made at lower and middle levels of management. He also knew that they should be made with a general manager's perspective. This depends on having the necessary information and a reasonable balance of power among the joint decision makers. Now the technical people were upsetting the power balance because others could not challenge them on technical matters. As a result,

[3] See Paul R. Lawrence and Jay Lorsch, "Differentiation and Integration in Complex Organizations," *Administrative Science Quarterly* (June, 1967).

the general manager chose three technically qualified men and made them product managers in charge of the three major product lines.[4] They were to act as chairmen of the product team meetings and generally facilitate the interfunctional decision making.

Since these men had no formal authority, they had to resort to their technical competence and their interpersonal skills in order to be effective. The fact that they reported to the general manager gave them some additional power. These men were successful in bringing the global, general manager perspective lower in the organization and to improve the joint decision-making process.

The need for this role was necessitated by the increasing differences in attitudes and goals among the technical, production, and marketing team participants. These differences are necessary for successful subtask performance but interfere with team collaboration. The product manager allows collaboration without reducing these necessary differences. The cost is the additional overhead for the product management salaries.

Product Management Departments. Standard Products was now successfully following a strategy of new product innovation and introduction. It was leading the industry in changes in technology and products. As the number of new products increased, so did the amount of decision making around product considerations. The frequent needs for trade-offs across engineering, production, and marketing lines increased the influence of the product managers. It was not that the functional managers lost influence; rather, it was the increase in decisions relating to products.

The increase in the influence of the product managers was revealed in several ways. First, their salaries became substantial. Second, they began to have a greater voice in the budgeting process, starting with approval of functional budgets relating to their products. The next change was an accumulation of staff around the products, which became product departments with considerable influence.

At Standard this came about with the increase in new product introductions. A lack of information developed concerning product costs and revenues for addition, deletion, modification, and pricing decisions. The general manager instituted a new information system that reported costs and revenues by product as well as by function. This gave product managers the need for a staff and a basis for more effective interfunctional collaboration.

[4] Paul R. Lawrence and Jay Lorsch, "New Management Job: the Integration," *Harvard Business Review* (November-December, 1967).

In establishing the product departments, the general manager resisted requests from the product managers to reorganize around product divisions. While he agreed with their analysis that better coordination was needed across functions and for more effective product decision making, he was unwilling to take the chance that this move might reduce specialization in the technical areas or perhaps lose the economies of scale in production. He felt that a modification of the information system to report on a product and a functional basis along with a product staff group would provide the means for more coordination. He still needed the effective technical group to drive the innovative process. The general manager also maintained a climate where collaboration across product lines and functions was encouraged and rewarded.

The Matrix Completed

By now Standard Products was a high technology company; its products were undergoing constant change. The uncertainty brought about by the new technology and the new products required an enormous amount of decision making to plan-replan all the schedules, budgets, designs, and so on. As a result, the number of decisions made at low levels increased considerably. This brought on two concerns for the general manager and top management.

The first was the old concern for the quality of decisions made at low levels of the organization. The product managers helped solve this at middle and top levels, but their influence did not reach low into the organization where a considerable number of decisions were made jointly. They were not always made in the best interest of the firm as a whole. The product managers again recommended a move to product divisions to give these low-level decisions the proper product orientation.

The director of engineering objected, using the second problem to back up his objection. He said the move to product divisions would reduce the influence of the technical people at a time when they were having morale and turnover problems with these employees. The increase in joint decisions at low levels meant that these technical people were spending a lot of time in meetings. Their technical input was not always needed, and they preferred to work on technical problems, not product problems. Their dissatisfaction would only be aggravated by a change to product divisions.

The top management group recognized both of these problems. They needed more product orientation at low levels, and they needed to improve the morale of the technical people whose inputs were needed for product innovations. Their solution involved the creation of a new role—that of subproduct manager.[5] The subproduct manager would be chosen from the functional organization and would represent the product line within the function. He would report to both the functional manager and the product manager, thereby creating a dual authority structure. The addition of a reporting relation on the product slide increases the amount of product influence at lower levels.

The addition of the subproduct manager was intended to solve the morale problem also. Because he would participate in the product team meetings, the technical people did not need to be present. The subproduct manager would participate on the teams but would call on the technical experts within his department as they were needed. This permitted the functional department to be represented by the subproduct manager, and the technical people to concentrate on strictly technical matters.

Standard Products has now moved to a pure matrix organization as indicated in Figure 2. The pure matrix organization is distinguished from the previous cross-functional forms by two features. *First*, the pure matrix

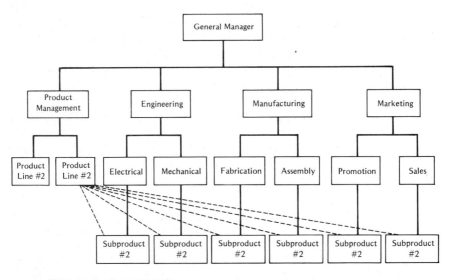

----- = Technical authority over the product.
——— = Formal authority over the product (in product organization, these relationships may be reversed).

FIGURE 2   Standard's Pure Matrix Organization

[5] Jay Lorsch, "Matrix Organization and Technical Innovations" in Jay Galbraith, ed., *Matrix Organizations: Organization Design for High Technology* (Cambridge, Mass.: The M.I.T. Press, 1971).

has a dual authority relationship somewhere in the organization. *Second*, there is a power balance between the product management and functional sides. While equal power is an unachievable razor's edge, a reasonable balance can be obtained through enforced collaboration on budgets, salaries, dual information and reporting systems, an dual authority relations. Such a balance is required because the problems that the organization faces are uncertain and must be solved on their own merits—not on any predetermined power structure.

Thus over a period of time, the Standard Products Co. has changed from a functional organization to a pure matrix organization using dual authority relationships, product management departments, product teams at several levels, and temporary task forces. These additional decision-making mechanisms were added to cope with the change in products and technologies. The changes caused a good deal of uncertainty concerning resource allocations, budgets, and schedules. In the process of task execution, more was learned about the problem causing a need for rescheduling and rebudgeting. This required the processing of information and the making of decisions.

In order to increase its capacity to make product relevant decisions, Standard lowered the level at which decisions were made. Coordination was achieved by making joint decisions across functions. Product managers and subproduct managers were added to bring a general manager's perspective to bear on the joint decision-making processes. In addition, the information and reporting system was changed in order to provide reports by function and by product. Combined, these measures allowed Standard to achieve the high levels of technical sophistication necessary to innovate products and simultaneously to get these products to the market quickly to maintain competitive position.

HOW DO I CHOOSE A DESIGN? _____

Not all organizations need a pure matrix organization with a dual authority relationship. Many, however, can benefit from some cross-functional forms to relieve top decision makers from day-to-day operations. If this is so, how does one choose the degree to which his organization should pursue these lateral forms? To begin to answer this question, let us first lay out the alternatives, then list the choice determining factors.

The choice, shown in Figure 3, is indicated by the wide range of alternatives between a pure functional organization and a pure product organization with the matrix being half-way between. The Standard Products Co.

could have evolved into a matrix from a product organization by adding functional teams and managers. Thus there is a continuum of organization designs between the functional and product forms. The design is specified by the choice among the authority structure; integrating mechanisms such as task forces, teams and so on; and by the formal information system. The way these are combined is illustrated in Figure 3. These design variables help regulate the relative distribution of influence between the product and functional considerations in the firm's operations.

The remaining factors determining influence are such things as roles in budget approvals, design changes, location and size of offices, salary, and so on. Thus there is a choice of integrating devices, authority structure, information system, and influence distribution. The factors that determine choice are diversity of the product line, the rate of change of the product line, interdependencies among subunits, level of technology, presence of economies of scale, and organization size.

Product Lines

The greater the diversity among product lines and the greater the rate of change of products in the line the greater the pressure to move toward

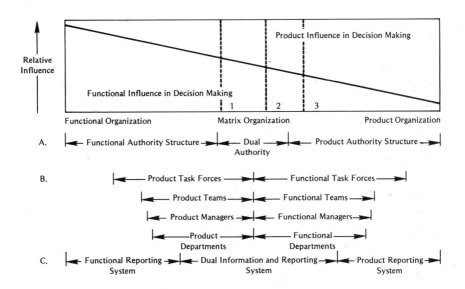

FIGURE 3 The Range of Alternatives

product structures.[6] When product lines become diverse, it becomes difficult for general managers and functional managers to maintain knowledge in all areas; the amount of information they must handle exceeds their capacity to absorb it. Similarly, the faster the rate of new product introduction, the more unfamiliar are the tasks being performed.

Managers are, therefore, less able to make precise estimates concerning resource allocations, schedules, and priorities. During the process of new product introduction, these same decisions are made repeatedly. The decisions concern trade-offs among engineering, manufacturing, and marketing. This means there must be greater product influence in the decision process. The effect of diversity and change is to create a force to locate the organization farther to the right in Figure 3.

Interdependence

The functional division of labor in organizations creates interdependencies among the specialized subunits. That is, a problem of action in one unit has a direct impact on the goal accomplishment of the other units. Organizations usually devise mechanisms that uncouple the subunits, such as in-process-inventory and order backlogs. The degree to which inventories and backlogs develop is a function of how tight the schedule is. If there is a little slack in the schedule, then the functional departments can resolve their own problems. However, if rapid response to market changes is a basis of competition, then schedules are squeezed and activities run in parallel rather than series.[7] This means that problems in one unit directly affect another. The effect is a greater number of joint decisions involving engineering, manufacturing, and production. A greater need for product influence in these decisions arises due to the tight schedule. Thus the tighter the schedule, the greater the force to move to the right in Figure 3.

Although the tightness of the schedule is the most obvious source of interdependence, tight couplings can arise from reliability requirements and other design specifications. If the specifications require a more precise fit and operation of parts, then the groups designing and manufacturing the parts must also "fit and operate" more closely. This requires more coordination in the form of communication and decision making.

[6] For product line diversity, see Alfred Chandler, *Strategy and Structure* (Cambridge, Mass.: The M.I.T. Press, 1962); for product change rate, see Tom Burns and G. M. Stalker, *Management and Innovation* (London: Tavistock Publications, 1958).

[7] For a case study of this effect, see Jay Galbraith, "Environmental and Technological Determinants of Organization Design" in Jay Lorsch and Paul R. Lawrence, eds., *Studies in Organization Design* (Homewood, Ill.: Richard D. Irwin, Inc., 1970).

Level of Technology

If tight schedules and new products were the only forces operating, every organization would be organized around product lines. The level of technology or degree to which new technology is being used is a counteracting force. The use of new technologies requires expertise in the technical specialties in engineering, in production engineering, in manufacturing, and market research in marketing. Some of the expertise may be purchased outside the organization.

However, if the expertise is critical to competitive effectiveness, the organization must acquire it internally. If the organization is to make effective use of the expertise, the functional form of organization is superior, as described earlier in the article. Therefore the greater the need for expertise, the greater the force to move to the left in Figure 3.

Economies of Scale and Size

The other factor favoring a functional form is the degree to which expensive equipment in manufacturing, text facilities in engineering, and warehousing facilities in marketing are used in producing and selling the product. (Warehousing introduces another dimension of organization structure, for example, geographical divisions. For our purposes, we will be concerned only with product and function dimensions.) It is usually more expensive to buy small facilities for product divisions than a few large ones for functional departments. The greater the economies of scale, the greater the force to move to the left in Figure 3. mixed structures are always possible. That is, the capital intensive fabrication operation can organize along functional process lines, and the labor intensive assembly operation can organize along product lines.

The size of the organization is important in that it modifies the effect of expertise and economies of scale. That is, the greater the size of the organization the smaller the costs of lost specialization and lost economies of scale when the product form is adopted. Thus while size by itself has little effect on organization structure, it does moderate the effects of the previously mentioned factors.

The Choice

While research on organizations has not achieved a sophistication that would allow us to compute the results of the above factors and locate a point in Figure 3, we can still make our subjective weightings. In addition, we can locate our present position and make changes in the appropriate directions as product lines, schedules, technologies, and size change during the normal course of business. The framework provides some basis for planning the organization along with planning the strategy and resource allocations.

If the organization's present structure is on the left side of the figure, many of the symptoms occurring in the Standard Products example signal a need for change. To what degree are communication overloads occurring? Are top executives being drawn into day-to-day decisions to the detriment of strategy development? How long does it take to get top level decisions made in order to continue work on new products? If the answers to these questions indicate an overload, then some movement toward a matrix is appropriate. Probably a sequence of moves until the bottlenecks disappear is the best strategy; this will allow for the proper attitudinal and behavioral changes to keep pace.

If the organization is product organized, then movements to the left toward a matrix are more subtle. They must be triggered by monitoring the respective technological environments.

An example from the aerospace industry may help. In the late fifties and early sixties the environment was characterized by the space race and missile gap. In this environment, technical performance and technology development were primary, and most firms adpoted organizations characterized by the dotted line at "1" in Figure 3. The functional departments had the greatest influence on the decision-making process. During the McNamara era, they moved to point "2." The environment shifted to incentive contracts, PERT-cost systems, and increased importance of cost and schedule considerations.

Currently, the shift has continued toward point "3." Now the environment is characterized by tight budgets, a cost overrun on the C–5 project, and Proxmire hearings in the Senate. The result is greater influence by the project managers. All these have taken place in response to the changing character of the market. A few firms recently moved back toward point "2" in response to the decreasing size of some firms. The reduction in defense spending has resulted in cutbacks in projects and employment. In order to maintain technical capabilities with reduced size, these firms have formed functional departments under functional managers with line responsibility. These changes show how changes in need for expertise, goals, and size affect the organization design choice.

Many organizations are experiencing pressures that force them to consider various forms of matrix designs. The most common pressure is increased volume of new products. Organizations facing this situation must either adopt some form of matrix organization, change to product forms of organization, or increase the time between start and introduction of the new product process.

For most organizations, the matrix design is the most effective alternative. Managers must be aware of the different kinds of matrix designs and develop some basis for choosing among them.

Stanley M. Davis

Columbia University

Paul R. Lawrence

Harvard University

PROBLEMS OF MATRIX ORGANIZATIONS

No organization design or method of management is perfect. And any form can suffer from a variety of problems that develop because of the design itself. This is particularly true when a company tries a new form. In this article we look at one relatively new organization form—the matrix—which has gained considerable popularity in recent years but which has some significant pathologies. Before discussing its ills, however, let us look for a moment at matrix management and organizations (see box on page 182) and at how widespread the matrix is in U.S. industry today.

The list of well-known companies that are using some form of a matrix is becoming long and impressive. Take, for example, a company that has annual sales of $14 billion and employs about 400,000 people in scores of diverse businesses—General Electric. For decades, despite the diversity of its businesses, GE used one basic structure throughout its organization—five functional managers reporting to one general manager. Employing the logic that a company must organize to meet the particular needs of each business,

Stanley M. Davis and Paul R. Lawrence, "Problems of Matrix Organizations," *Harvard Business Review*, May–June 1978, pp.. 131–142.

What is a matrix?

The identifying feature of a matrix organization is that some managers report to two bosses rather than to the traditional single boss; there is a dual rather than a single chain of command.

Companies tend to turn to matrix forms:

1. When it is absolutely essential that they be highly responsive to two sectors simultaneously, such as markets and technology;
2. When they face uncertainties that generate very high information processing requirements; and
3. When they must deal with strong constraints on financial and/or human resources.

Matrix structures can help provide both flexibility and balanced decision making, but at the price of complexity.

Matrix organization is more than a matrix structure. It must be reinforced by matrix systems such as dual control and evaluation systems, by leaders who operate comfortably with lateral decision making, and by a culture that can negotiate open conflict and a balance of power.

In most matrix organizations there are dual command responsibilities assigned to functional departments (marketing, production, engineering, and so forth) and to product or market departments. The former are oriented to specialized in-house resources while the latter focus on outputs. Other matrices are split between area-based departments and either products or functions.

Every matrix contains three unique and critical roles; the top manager who heads up and balances the dual chains of command, the matrix bosses (functional, product, or area) who share subordinates, and the managers who report to two different matrix bosses. Each of these roles has its special requirements.

Aerospace companies were the first to adopt the matrix form, but now companies in many industries (chemical, banking, insurance, packaged goods, electronics, computer, and so forth) and in different fields (hospitals, government agencies, and professional organizations) are adapting different forms of the matrix.

some GE groups, divisions, and departments, which have found the pyramid form cumbersome, have turned to the matrix as a fundamental alternative.

In projecting its organization over the next ten years, GE management states in its *Organization Planning Bulletin* (September 1976):

We've highlighted matrix organization . . . not because it's a bandwagon that we want you all to jump on, but rather that it's a complex, difficult, and sometimes frustraing form of organization to live with. It's also, however, a bellwether of things to come. But, when implemented well, it does offer much of the best of both worlds. And all of us are going to have to learn how to utilize organization to

prepare managers to increasingly deal with high levels of complexity and ambiguity in situations where they have to get results from people and components not under their direct control. . . .
Successful experience in operating under a matrix constitutes better preparation for an individual to run a hugh diversified institution like General Electric—where so many complex, conflicting interests must be balanced—than the product and functional modes which have been our hallmark over the past twenty years.

Other major corporations, in diverse activities, such as Bechtel, Citibank, Dow Chemical, Shell Oil, Texas Instruments, and TRW, to mention a few, have also turned to the matrix. Based on our studies of the matrix in these companies, we believe that while some of the matrix's popularity is simply a passing fad, most uses of it are founded on solid business reasons that will persist. The matrix's most basic advantage over the familiar functional or product structure is that it facilitates a rapid management response to changing market and technical requirements. Further, it helps middle managers make trade-off decisions from a general management perspective.

Because the matrix is a relatively new form, however, the companies that have adopted it have of necessity been learning on a trial and error basis. The mistakes as well as the successes of these pioneers can be very informative to companies that follow their lead. Here, we present some of the more common problems that occur when a company uses a matrix form. For the sake of easy reference, we diagnose each pathology first, then discuss its prevention and treatment. By using this format, however, we do not mean to suggest that simple first-aid treatment of pathologies will cure them.

ILLS OF THE MATRIX

Many of the ailments we discuss do arise in more conventional organizations, but the matrix seems somewhat more vulnerable to these particular ones. It is wise, therefore, for managers thinking of adopting a matrix to be familiar with the diagnoses, prevention, and treatment of nine particular pathologies: tendencies toward anarchy, power struggles, severe groupitis, collapse during economic crunch, excessive overhead, sinking to lower levels, uncontrolled layering, navel gazing, and decision strangulation.

Tendencies Toward Anarchy

A formless state of confusion where people do not recognize a "boss" to whom they feel responsible.

Diagnosis. Many managers who have had no firsthand familiarity with matrix organizations tend to have half-expressed fears that a matrix leads to anarchy. Are these concerns based on real hazards? Actually today, a considerable number of organizations are successfully using the matrix form, so we need not treat anarchy as a general hazard of the matrix. However, there are certain conditions or major misconceptions that could lead a company into the formless confusion that resembles anarchy.

Through firsthand experience we know of only one organization that, using a "latent" matrix form, quite literally came apart at the seams during a rather mild economic recession. Following a fast-growth strategy, this company used its high stock multiple to acquire, and then completely assimilate, smaller companies in the recreation equipment field. Within a period of about six months the company changed from an exciting success to a dramatic disaster. Its entire manufacturing, distribution, and financial systems went out of control leaving unfilled orders, closed factories, distressed inventories, and huge debts in their wake.

Of course, there are many possible reasons why this might have happened, but one perfectly reasonable explanation is that the organization design failed under stress. What was that design?

Essentially, the organization used a functional structure. As it acquired each small company, top management first encouraged the owners and general managers to leave, and then it attached the company's three basic functions of sales, production, and engineering to their counterparts in the parent organization. Within the parent marketing department, a young aggressive product manager would be assigned to develop for the acquired product line a comprehensive marketing plan that included making sales forecasts, promotion plans, pricing plans, projected earnings, and so forth. Once top managggement approved the plan, it told the selected product manager to hustle around and make his plan come true. This is where the latent matrix came in.

The product manager would find himself working across functional lines to try to coordinate production schedules, inventories, cash flow, and distribution patterns without any explicit and formal agreement about the nature of his relationships with the functional managers. Because he was locked into his approved marketing plan, when sales slipped behind schedule, his response was to exhort people to try harder rather than to cut back on production runs.

But once one or two things began to crumble, there was not enough reserve in the system to keep everything else from going wrong. As the product manager lost control, a power vacuum developed, into which the functional managers fell, each grabbing for total control. The result was that a mild recession triggered conditions approaching anarchy.

Prevention.   We believe the lesson of this experience is loud and clear. Organizations should not rely too much on an informal or latent matrix to coordinate critical tasks. Relationships between functional and product managers should be explicit so that people are in approximate agreement about who is to do what under various circumstances. Properly used, a matrix does not leave such matters in an indefinite status; it is a definite structure and not a "free form" organization.

A useful "anarchy index" is how many people in an organization do not recognize one boss to whom they feel responsible for a major part of their work. In a study of five medical schools, which are notoriously anarchichal, the one with the most explicit matrix structure was also the one with the least number of "bossless" people.[1]

Treatment.   Should the worst happen and a company plunge into anarchy, true crisis management would be the best response. The crisis response is really no mystery. The CEO must pull all key people and critical information into the center. He or she must personally make all important decisions on a round-the-clock schedule until the crisis is over. Then and only then can he undertake the work of reshaping the organization so that it can withstand any future shock, such as a minor recession.

Power Struggles

Managers jockey for power in many organizations, but a matrix design almost encourages them to do so.

Diagnosis.   The essence of a matrix is dual command. For such a form to survive there needs to be a balance of power, where its locus seems to shift constantly, each party always jockeying to gain an advantage. It is not enough simply to create the balance, but there must also be continual mechanisms for checking the imbalances that creep in.

In business organizations that operate with a balance of power form, there is a constant tendency toward imbalance. As long as each group or dimension in an organization tries to maximize its own advantage vis-à-vis others, there will be a continual balancing struggle for dominant power. A power struggle in a matrix is qualitatively different from that in a traditionally structured hierarchy because in the latter it is clearly illegitimate. In the

---

[1] From the forthcoming article by M. R. Weisbord, M. P. Charns, and P. R. Lawrence, "Organizational Dilemmas of Academic Medical Centers," *Journal of Applied Behavioral Science*, Vol. XIV, No. 3.

matrix, however, power struggles are inevitable; the boundaries of authority and responsibility overlap prompting people to maximize their own advantage.

Prevention. Most top managers will find it exceedingly difficult to forestall all power struggles. Equal strength on the part of the two parties, however, will prevent struggles from reaching destructive heights. Friendly competition should be encouraged, but all-out combat severely punished. Managers in a matrix should push for their advantages but never with the intention of eliminating those with whom they share power, and always with a perspective that encompasses both positions.

Treatment. The best way to ensure that power struggles do not undermine the matrix is to make managers on the power axes aware that to win power absolutely is to lose it ultimately. These managers need to see that the total victory of one dimension only ends the balance, finishes the duality of command, and destroys the matrix. They must see this sharing of power as an underlying principle, before and during all of the ensuing and inevitable power struggles.

Matrix managers have to recognize that they need worthy adversaries, counterparts who can match them, to turn the conflict to constructive ends. For this successful outcome three things are necessary.

First, matrix managers always have to maintain an institutional point of view, seeing their struggles from a larger, shared perspective. Second, they have to jointly agree to remove other matrix managers who, through weakness or whatever inability, are losing irretrievable ground. And, third, that they replace these weak managers with the strongest available people—even if to do so means placing very strong managers in weakened parts of the organization and reversing their power initiatives.

Another key element in stopping power struggles before they get out of hand and destroy the balance is the top level superior to whom the duelling managers report. Because of this element, the matrix is a paradox—a shared-power system that depends on a strong individual, one who does not share the authority that is delegated to him (say by the board), to arbitrate between his power-sharing subordinates.

The top manager has many vehicles for doing this: the amount of time he spends with one side of the matrix or the other, pay differentials, velocity of promotion, direct orders issued to one dimension and not to the other, and so forth. What he must do above all, however, is protect the weak dimension in the organization, not necessarily the weak manager in charge of that dimension.

Severe Groupitis

The mistaken belief that matrix management is the same as group decision making.

Diagnosis. The confusion of matrix behavior with group decision making probably arises from the fact that a matrix often evolves out of new project or business teams, which do suggest a group decision process. Under many circumstances, of course, it is perfectly sensible for managers to make decisions in groups. But managers should expect difficulties to arise if they believe group decision making to be the essence of matrix behavior.

We have seen one matrix organization that had a severe case of "groupitis." This multiproduct electronics company had a product manager and a product team, comprised of specialists drawn from the ranks of every functional department, assigned to every product. So far so good. But somehow the idea that the matrix structure requires that *all* business decisions be hammered out in group meetings became prevalent in the organization. To make decisions in other ways was considered illegitimate and not in the spirit of matrix operations.

Many of the decisions that had to be made about each product involved detailed matters with which only one or two people were regularly conversant. Yet all team members were constrained to listen to these issues being discussed until a decision was made, and were even expected to participate in the discussion and influence the choice. Some individuals seemed to enjoy the steady diet of meetings and the chance to practice being a generalist.

However, a larger number of people felt that their time was being wasted and would have preferred leaving the decisions to the most informed people. The engineers, in particular, complained that the time they were spending in meetings was robbing them of opportunities to strengthen their special competence and identities. As well as noting these personal reactions, senior managers reported a general disappointment with the speed and flexibility of organizational responses.

Prevention. Because the whole idea of a matrix organization is still unfamiliar to many managers, it is understandable that they confuse it with processes such as group decision making. The key to prevention is education. Top managers need to accompany their strategic choice to move toward a matrix with a serious educational effort to clarify to all participants what a matrix is and what it is not.

Treatment. In the case of the multiproducts electronics company, the problem came to light while we were researching the matrix approach. Once senior people had clearly diagnosed the problem, it was 90% cured. Top management emphatically stated that there was nothing sacred about group decisions and that it was not sensible to have all product team members involved all the time. Once the line between individual and group matters was drawn according to who had information really relevant to a decision, meetings became fewer and smaller and work proceeded on a more economical and responsive basis. The concept of teamwork was put in perspective; as often as necessary and as little as possible.

Collapse During Economic Crunch

When business declines, the matrix becomes the scapegoat for poor management and is discarded.

Diagnosis. Matrix organizations that blossom during periods of rapid growth and prosperity sometimes are cast away during periods of economic decline. On reflection, we can understand this. In prosperous times, companies often expand their business lines and the markets they serve. The ensuing complexity may turn them toward matrix management and organization.

However, if these companies follow the normal business cycle, there will be a period of two to five years before they experience another economic crunch which is more than enough time for the matrix concept to spread throughout a company. By that time the matrix occupies a central place in company conversations and is a familiar part of these organizations. Although there may still be some problems, the matrix seems there to stay.

When the down part of the economic cycle begins, senior management in these companies may become appreciably bothered by the conflict between subordinates as well as by the apparent slowness with which they respond to the situation. "We need decisive action" is their rallying cry.

In an authoritarian structure top management can act quickly because it need not consider the spectrum of opinion. Thinking there is no time for organizational toys and tinkering, the top level managers take command in an almost, but not quite, forgotten way, and ram their directives down the line. The matrix is "'done in."

Prevention. Top management can prevent this kind of collapse of the matrix by employing general managerial excellence, independent of the matrix, long before the crunch arrives. Good planning, for example, can often forecast downturns in the economic cycle. Corporate structures such as the matrix should not have to change because of standard changes in the business cycle. When management planning has been poor, however, the matrix is a readily available scapegoat.

Companies that experience severe economic crunches often make drastic changes in many directions at once: trimming product lines, closing offices, making massive personnel and budget cuts, and tightening managerial controls. The matrix is often done in during this period for several reasons: it represents too great a risk; "it never really worked properly" and giving it the coup de grace can disguise the failure of implementation; and the quality of decision making had not improved performance sufficiently to counterbalance the hard times. Measures management can take to prevent this pathology do not lie within the matrix itself, as much as with improvements in basic managerial skills and planning.

A real estate and construction company provides an example of how a company can anticipate and flexibly respond to an economic crunch that demonstrates the strength rather than the weakness of the matrix. The company has developed a structure as well as procedures that are especially well suited to the economic uncertainties of the business. These include a set of fully owned subsidiaries each the equivalent of a functional department in a manufacturing company and each the "home base" for varied specialists needed to execute all phases of a major building project. The heads of the subsidiaries act as chief salesmen for their various services, and often head up the bidding teams that put together sophisticated proposals.

As a proposal project proceeds, the selected project manager is drawn into the team in anticipation of securing the contract. This ensures an orderly transition to the project management phase. The project office is given first-line responsibility for control of costs, schedules, and quality of the project, but the top management team from the parent company reviews the project regularly as a backup.

The company has used the matrix to advantage in weathering major shifts in both the availability of business by market segment, for example, from schools to hospitals, and the level of construction activity. It maintains a cadre of professional specialists and project managers, who can be kept busy during the lows of the cycle, which it rapidly expands during the highs by subcontracting for temporary services.

Treatment. This is one pathology that requires preventive treatment; we do not know of any cure. When the matrix does collapse during an economic crunch, it is very unlikely that it can be resurrected. At best, the organization will go back to its pendulum days, alternating between the centralized management of the crunch period and the decentralized freedom of more prosperous times. Even if top management should try again, it is likely to get a negative response from lower level managers. "They said they were committed to the matrix, but at the first sign of hard times all the nice words about the advantages of the matrix turned out to be just that—nice words." If a company's conditioned response to hard times is to retrench, it should not attempt a matrix in the first place.

Excessive Overhead

The fear of high costs associated with a matrix.

Diagnosis.   On the face of it, a matrix organization would seem to double management costs because of its dual chain of command. This issue deserves thoughtful consideration.

The limited amount of research on matrix overhead costs indicates that in the initial phases overhead costs do in fact rise, but that, as a matrix matures, these extra costs disappear and are offset by productivity gains.[2] Our experience supports this finding. In a large electronics company we observed in some detail how initial overhead increases not only necessarily occur in a matrix but also how they can inflate unnecessarily. In this case, the company decided to employ the matrix design from the outset in setting up its new operating division at a new plant site.

This unique organizational experiment had a number of positive attributes, but one of its problems was with overhead costs. In staffing the new division, top management filled every functional office and every product manager's slot with one full-time person. This resulted in a relatively small division having top level managers as well as full-time functional group and full-time product managers. Within months, however, this top heavy division was pared down to more reasonable staffing levels; by assigning individuals to two or more slots, management got costs under control.

Prevention.   The division's problem was caused by top management's assumption that each managerial slot requires a full-time incumbent. Overstaffing is much less liable to occur when an organization evolves gradually from a conventional design into a matrix, and managers perform as both functional and product managers. While this technique can be justified as a transition strategy, it also has its hazards. A safer route is to assign managers

[2] C. J. Middleton, "How to Set Up a Project Organization," *Harvard Business Review*, March-April 1967, p. 73.

roles on the same side of the matrix (i.e., two functional jobs or two product management jobs).

As a final argument against the fear of overhead costs, consider that no well-run organization would adopt a matrix structure without the longer run expectation that, at a given level of output, the costs of operations would be lower than with other organizational forms. In what way can such economies be achieved?

The potential economies come from two general sources: fewer bad decisions and less featherbedding. First and most important, the matrix can improve quality of business decisions because it helps bring the needed information and emphasis to bear on critical decisions in a timely fashion. The second source, less featherbedding, is not so obvious, but potentially of greater significance. How can it work?

Treatment. Perhaps the clearest example of the matrix's potential to reduce redundancies in human resources is the way some consulting organizations employ it. These firms usually set up a matrix of functional specialists against client or account managers. The body of other consultants are grouped with their fellow specialists but are available for assignment to projects under the leadership of account or client managers.

From an accounting standpoint, therefore, consultants' time is directly billed to clients' accounts when they are working for an account or engagement manager. Otherwise, their time is charged against the budget of their function manager. The firm's nonbillable costs are, therefore, very conspicuous—both by department and by individual consultant. Of course, some time charged to functional departments, such as background study, research work, and time between assignments should by no means be thought of as wasted. But management can budget such time in advance so that it can scrutinize the variances from the budget.

As one senior manager in a consulting firm put it, "There is no place to hide in a matrix organization." This fact makes clear-cut demands on middle level people and consequently puts pressure on them to produce. For the long-term good of both the people involved and the organization, top managers need to keep such pressures from becoming too strong. Because it is perfectly possible to get too much as well as too little pressure, a creative tension is sought.

Sinking to Lower Levels

The matrix has some difficulty in staying alive at high levels of a corporation, and a corresponding tendency to sink to group and division levels where it thrives.

Diagnosis. Sinking may occur for two reasons. Either senior management has not understood or been able to implement the matrix concept as well as lower level managers, or the matrix has found its appropriate place. For example, if a company sets up a matrix between its basic functional and product groups, the product managers never truly relinquish their complete control, and the matrix fails to take hold at the corporate level.

But, say, one or two of the managers find the idea to be useful within their divisions. Their own functional specialists and project leaders can share the power they delegate and the design can survive within subunits of the corporation. For example, Dow Chemical's attempt to maintain the product/geography balance at the top failed, but the function/product balance held within the geographic areas for several years.

When sinking occurs because of top management misunderstanding, it is likely to occur in conjunction with other pathologies, particularly power struggles. For instance, if many senior executives consider adopting the matrix idea, but only one or a few really become convinced of its worth, there is a danger: those at the top who espouse a philosophy and method they did not employ themselves will be pitted against those who are able to show that it does work.

Prevention. If the corporate top management thinks through which dimensions of the company it must balance, and at what level of aggregation, it can keep the matrix from sinking. For example, top managers should ask themselves if all the business units need to be balanced by central functional departments. If the answer is no, then some business units should operate as product divisions with the traditional pyramid of command, while others share functional services in a partial matrix. However, sinking is not always bad and should be prevented only when it indicates that an appropriate design is disintegrating.

Treatment. Before matrix management can run smoothly, it must be in the proper location. As often as not, when a matrix sinks, it may simply be experiencing a healthy adjustment, and ought to be thought of as settling rather than as sinking. Settling is likely to occur during the early stages of a matrix's evolution and leads to manageable matrix units.

The question of size is a great concern for many managers who ask, in effect, "That sounds great for a $250-million company with a few thousand employees, but can it work for a $2-billion or $3-billion company with 50,000 employees? Its entire company is the size of one of our divisions." Our experience indicates that matrix management and organization seems to function better when no more than 500 managers are involved in matrix relationships. But that does not rule out the $2-billion to $3-billion company. In a company of 5,000 only about 50 managers are likely to be in the matrix; so in a company with 50,000 employees only about 500 may need to be involved in dual reporting lines. With that number, the people who need to coordinate regularly are able to do so through communication networks that are based on personal relations.

Whatever the size unit in which the matrix operates, the important thing is for management to have reasoned carefully from an analysis of the task to the design of the organization. Then, if settling occurs, it should be seen not as a pathology but as a self-adjustment that suggests the organization's capacity to evolve with growth.

Uncontrolled Layering

Matrices which lie within matrices which lie within matrices result frequently from the dynamics of power rather than from the logic of design.

Diagnosis. Sometimes matrices not only sink but also cascade down the organization and filter through several levels and across several divisions. This layering process may or may not be pathological. In fact, it may be a rational and logical development of the matrix, but we include it briefly here because it sometimes creates more problems than it solves. In terms of the metaphor we have used in this article, layering is a pathology only if the matrix begins to metastasize. When this occurs, organization charts begin to resemble blueprints for a complex electronic machine, relationships become unnecessarily complex, and the matrix form may become more of a burden than it is worth.

Prevention and Treatment. The best remedies for uncontrolled layering are careful task analysis and reduced power struggles. We have seen a few cases where one dimension of a matrix was clearly losing power to the other, so, adapting an "if you can't beat 'em, join 'em" philosophy, it created a matrix within its own dimension. A product unit, for example, developed its own functional *expertise* distinct from the functional *units* at the next level up. The best defense was a good offense, or so it seemed.

In two other cases, the international divisions of two large companies each created its own matrix by adding business managers as an overlay to its geographic format, without reconciling these with the managers who ran the domestic product/service groups. In each case, adequate conceptualization by top managers would probably have simplified the organization design and forestalled the layering, which occurred because of power maneuvers. Management can treat this unhealthy state best by rebalancing the matrix so that no manager of one dimension is either too threatened or pushed too hard toward a power goal.

Matrix design is complex enough without the addition of power struggles. A well-conceptualized matrix is bound to be less complex and easier to manage than one that is illogically organized.

Navel Gazing

Managers in a matrix can succumb to excessive internal preoccupation and lose touch with the marketplace.

Diagnosis. Because a matrix fosters considerable interdependence of people and tasks and demands negotiating skills on the part of its members, matrix managers sometimes tend to get absorbed in internal relations at the expense of paying attention to the world outside the organization, particularly to clients. When this happens, an organization spends more energy ironing out its own disputes than in serving its customers. The outward focus disappears because the short-term demands of daily working life have yet to be worked through.

The navel gazers are not at all lethargic; rather they are involved in a heated fraternal love/hate affair with each other. This inward preoccupation is more common in the early phases of a matrix, when the new behaviors are being learned, than in matrices that have been operating for a few years.

Prevention. Whatever other pathologies develop in a matrix, attention to their cure is bound to increase the internal focus of the members; so prevention of other pathologies will certainly reduce the likelihood of this one occurring. Awareness of the tendency will also help. Since the product dimension of the organization generally has a more external focus than the resource dimension, the responsibility for preventing an excessive introspection is not equally distributed. The product dimension people can help the others keep perspective, but a strong marketing orientation is the best preventative of all.

Treatment. If the managers in the matrix are navel gazing, the first step in the treatment is to make these managers aware of the effects. Are customers complaining a lot, or at least more than usual? Managers need to confront internal conflict, but also to recognize that confrontation is secondary to maintaining effective external relationships. Navel gazing generally occurs when the matrix has been fully initiated but not yet debugged. People acceept it, but they are engrossed in figuring out how to make it work.

The second step is to treat the inward focus as a symptom of the underlying issue: how to institutionalize matrix relationships so that they become familiar and comfortable routines, and so that people can work through them without becoming obsessed by them. Finally, it must always be remembered that any form of organization is only a means and should never become an end in itself.

Decision Strangulation

Too much democracy, not enough action?

Can moving into a matrix lead to the strangulation of the decision process, into endless delays for debate, for clearing with everybody in sight? Will decisions, no matter how well thought through, be made too late to be of use? Will too many people have power to water down all bold initiatives or veto them outright? Such conditons can arise in a matrix. We have in mind three situations—constant clearing, escalation of conflict, and unilateral style—each calling for slightly different preventive action and treatment.

Constant Clearing. In one company we know of various functional specialists who reported to a second boss, a product manager, picked up the idea that they had to clear all issues with their own functional bosses before agreeing to product decisions. This meant that every issue had to be discussed in at least two meetings, if not more. During the first meeting, the specialists and the product manager could only review the facts of the issue, which was then tabled until, at the second meeting, the specialists cleared the matter with their functional bosses—who by this process were each given a defacto veto over product decisions.

This impossible clearing procedure represented, in our view, a failure of delegation, not of the matrix. One needs to ask why the functional specialists could not be trusted to act on the spot in regard to most product decisions in ways that would be consistent with the general guidelines of their functional departments? Either the specialists were poorly selected, too inexperienced and badly informed, or their superiors were lacking in a workable degree of trust of one another. Regardless, this problem, and its prevention and treatment, needs to be addressed directly without making a scapegoat of the matrix.

Escalation of Conflict. Another source of decision strangulation in matrix organizations occurs when managers frequently or constantly refer decisions up the dual chain of command. Seeing that one advantage of the conventional single chain of command is that two disagreeing peers can go to their shared boss for a resolution, managers unfamiliar with the matrix worry about this problem almost more than any other. They look at a matrix and realize that the nearest shared boss might be the CEO, who could be five or six echelons up. They realize that not too many problems can be pushed up to the CEO for resolution without creating the ultimate in information overload. So, they think, will not the inevitable disagreement lead to a tremendous pileup of unresolved conflict?

Certainly, this can happen in a malfunctioning matrix. Whether it does happen depends primarily on the depth of understanding that exists about required matrix behavior on the part of managers in the dual structure. Let us envision the following scene: a manager with two bosses gets sharply conflicting instructions from his product and his functional bosses. When he tries to reconcile his instructions without success, he quite properly asks for a session with his two bosses to resolve the matter. The three people meet, but the discussion bogs down, no resolution is reached, and neither boss gives way.

The two bosses then appeal the problem up a level to their respective superiors in each of the two chains of command. This is the critical step. If the two superiors properly understand matrix behavior, they will first ascertain whether the dispute reflects an unresolved broader policy issue. If it does not, they know their proper step is to teach their subordinates to resolve the problem themselves—not to solve it for them. In short, they would not let the unresolved problem escalate, but would force it back to the proper level for solution, and insist that the solution be found promptly.

Often, conflict cannot be resolved; it can, however, be managed, which it must be if the matrix is to work. Any other course of action would represent management's failure to comprehend the essential nature of the design.

Unilateral Style.   A third possible reason for decision strangulation in a matrix system can arise from a very different source—personal style. Some managers have the feeling they are not truly managing if they are not in a position to make crisp, unilateral decisions. Identifying leadership with decisive action, they become very frustrated when they have to engage in carefully reasoned debates about the wisdom of what they want to do.

Such a manager is likely to feel frustrated even in regard to a business problem whose resolution will vitally affect functions other than his own, such as in a company that is experiencing critical dual pressure from the marketplace and from advancing technology. A matrix that deliberately induces simultaneous decision making between two or more perspectives is likely to frustrate such a person even further.

If managers start feeling emasculated by bilateral decision making, they are certain to be unhappy in a matrix organization. In such cases the strangulation is in the eye of the beholder. Such people must work on their personal decision-making style or look for employment in a nonmatrix organization.

AT LAST, LEGITIMACY

We do not recommend that every company adopt the matrix form. But where it is relevant, it can become an important part of an effective managerial process. Like any new method it may develop serious bugs, but the experiences that many companies are acquiring with this organization form can now help others realize its benefits and avoid its pitfalls.

The matrix seems to have spread despite itself and its pathologies: what was necessaary was made desirable. It is difficult and complex, and human flexibility is required to arrive at organizational flexibility.

But the reverse is also true; success has given the form legitimacy, and, as the concept spreads, familiarity seems to reduce the resistance and difficulties people experience in using the matrix. Managers are now beginning to say, "It isn't that new or different after all." This familiariiy is a sign of acceptance, more than of change or moderation of the design.

For generations, managers lived with the happy fiction of dotted lines, indicating that a second reporting line was necessary if not formal. The result had always been a sort of executive ménage à trois, a triangular arrangement where the manager had one legitimate relationship (the reporting line) and one that existed but was not granted equal privileges (the dotted line).

As executives develop greater confidence with the matrix form, they bring the dotted line relationship out of the closet, and grant it legitimacy. ·

Each time another organization turns to the matrix, it has a larger and more varied number of predecessors that have chartered the way. The examples of wider applicability suggest that the matrix is becoming less and less an experiment and more and more a mature formulation in organization design. As more organizations travel the learning curve, the curve itself becomes an easier one to climb. Similarly, as more managers gain experience operating in matrix organizations, they are bound to spread this experience as some of them move, as they inevitably will, into other organizations.

We believe that in the future matrix organizations will become almost commonplace and that managers will speak less of the difficulties and pathologies of the matrix than of its advantages and benefits.

John M. Roach

Editor of *Management Review*

SIMON SAYS... DECISION MAKING IS A "SATISFICING" EXPERIENCE

One day back in the mid-1950s, Dr. Herbert A. Simon was working in his study near the campus of Carnegie Institute of Technology (now Carnegie-Mellon University) trying to find an appropriate term for what he wanted to say. Eventually he plucked an obscure verb—*to satisfice*(satisfy)—from the Oxford English Dictionary. He used it to help explain a concept of economic decision making that, whether they realize it or not, business organizations and their managers use every day in both run-of-the-mill and complex problem situations. And last month, two decades later, Simon's concept of "satisficing" became a major factor in the Swedish Academy of Sciences' decision to award him the 1978 Nobel prize in economics for his "pioneering research into the decision-making process within economic organizations."

Simon had previously enunciated advanced views on the complexities of organized decision making in his now classic thesis, *Administrative Behavior*, published in 1947. And what he was trying to say that afternoon in Pittsburgh several years later—and did say in subsequent editions of his book—was that while Economic Man, that elusive "maximizer" of tradi-

John M. Roach, "Simon Says . . . Decision Making is a 'Satisficing' Experience," *Management Review*, January 1979, pp. 8–17.

199

tional economic doctrine, invariably "selects the best alternative from all those available to him," his cousin, Administrative Man (the real-life manager), "satisfices—looks for a course of action that is satisfactory or good enough."

Traditional economic doctrine holds that organizations always make key decisions on the basis of information that maximizes their results—that is, get the best possible price, the best possible share of market, and maximum profit. But in the "real world," this just doesn't happen, Simon explained in an interview with *Management Review* following announcement of his Nobel award—even with the help of today's sophisticated computer-based decision aids.

"Satisficing is intended to be used in contrast to the classical economist's idea that in making decisions in business or anywhere in real life, you somehow pick, or somebody gives you, a set of alternatives from which you select the best one—maximize," Simon said. "The satisficing idea is that first of all, you don't have the alternatives, you've got to go out and scratch for them—and that you have mighty shaky ways of evaluating them when you do find them. So you look for alternatives until you get one from which, in terms of your experience and in terms of what you have reason to expect, you will get a reasonable result."

But satisficing doesn't necessarily mean that managers have to be satisfied with what alternative pops up first in their minds or in their computers and let it go at that. The level of satisficing can be raised—by personal determination, setting higher individual or organizational standards and by use of an increasing range of sophisticated management science and computer-based decision-making and problem-solving techniques.

"As time goes on, you obtain more information about what's feasible and what you can aim at," Simon said. "Not only do you get more information, but in many, if not most, companies there are procedures for trying to raise individuals' aspiration levels. This is a major responsibility of top management."

The Carnegie-Mellon economist/scientist warns, however, that one organization doesn't necessarily become better than another just by setting higher aspiration levels for its managers and workers. Recalling the old saying that "If wishes were horses, beggars would ride," he stressed that the main problem is to get the organizatin to work "very hard and tight" against realistic objectives: "You can destroy morale and suffer a real boomerang effect . . . if you set objectives unrealistically high."

Simon, a member of the Carnegie faculty since 1949, is a multidiscipline scholar—social science, computer science, operations research, statistics, philosophy of science—and now holds the Richard King Mellon Chair in computer science and psychology. Virtually his entire academic career of some 40 years (he is now 62) has been focused on research into organizational and individual decision-making and problem-solving concepts and techniques—in effect, maintaining a lifelong effort in identifying and improving "how to decide what to do." And he is openly optimistic about prospects for improvement of our decision-making capabilities.

In citing Simon's work in organizational behavior and decision making, the Swedish Nobel award group took special note of his rejection of the "assumption made in the classic theory of the firm as an omniscient, rational, profit-maximizing entrepreneur." Modern business economics and administrative research "are largely based on Simon's ideas," the Swedish Academy said.

Author of a dozen books and hundreds of articles covering the full range of his academic interests, Simon wrote a lead article, "Management by Machine," that appeared in the November 1960 issue of *Management Review*. Reflecting his intense interest in the expanding capabilities of computer science, the article opened with these eye-catching predictions:

> *During the next 25 years, the job of manager will undergo some major changes as machines take over more and more of the activities that now seem too complex and "high level" ever to yield to automation. The chances are strong that, even before this decade is over, machines will be able to perform any function in the organization—and this includes the "thinking" and "deciding" tasks that are the basis of the manager's job.*
>
> *This doesn't mean that executives will become obsolete. But the business organization in 1985 will be a more highly automated man-machine system, and the nature of management will naturally be conditioned by the nature of the system being managed. . . .*

The timetable laid out in this forecast era of new decision-making capabilities appears to have slipped—but only slightly—from the schedule Simon envisioned on the pages of *Management Review* more than 18 years ago. He points out now, however, that machines already have taken over many of the "thinking and deciding" tasks of workers and managers. And he suggests that society in general and managers in particular can expect even more sophisticated advances in the decision-making capabilities of man-machine complexes.

Simon rejects suggestions that companies will actually be "managed" by computers. Nonetheless, he stresses that the decision-making powers of machines are advancing steadily with the development of ever more sophisticated computer and related software systems, further refinements in operations research and other management science techniques. He also cites expanding capabilities in the field of artificial intelligence and cognitive science–both activities concerned with programming computers to do humanoid things.

In spelling out his expectations of future advances in management decision-making processes in his discussion with *Management Review*, the Nobel laureate pointed to:

• Development of a second generation of management information systems that will be much more oriented toward decision-making activities. Managers, he said, really need systems "more oriented toward data that come into the organization from the environment rather than information generated inside the organization."

• The movement of large artificial intelligence programs out of the R&D phase into specific applications of professional-level tasks. As examples of what's ahead in this line, he cited INTERNEST, a computer-based medical diagnosis program, and DENDRAL, a Stanford University computer program that identifies molecules from mass spectogram data—formerly a month-long job for a single researcher.

• Increasing use of robotry in industry with the development of new sensing devices and related decision-making hardware.

Other highlights of the interview follow:

Under your concept of "satisficing" as a decision-making procedure, how do you know when you've assembled a sufficient range of alternatives from which to select a course of action? You have used the term "aspiration level" in connection with the satisficing process. Is a manager's aspiration level the ultimate criterion?

Simon: If you look at this concept from an evolutionary standpoint, you'll determine that any organism that's going to survive in a world that has its ups and downs is going to have to set targets that are realistically related to its environment. It must be prepared to lower those targets—at least, within limits—when the environment gets tougher, and it has to be prepared to raise those targets if the environment becomes more benign. That's what I mean by "aspiration level." And that, I believe, is the way targets get fixed in business decision making.

For example: How do we know what profit we're going to try to make this year and what sales we're going to shoot for. Well, we look at last year's profits and last year's sales, take a squint at the business situation as best we can—but through very clouded glasses—and then we add a little optimism or pessimism—which says something about us—and we set some targets. Some companies, of course, try to improve their accuracy with the aid of some sophisticated forecasting and other analytical techniques, but in general, businesses go through this routine every quarter and every year.

As time goes on, of course, you obtain more information about what's feasible and what you can aim at. Not only do you get some information, but in many, if not most companies, there are procedures for setting targets, which include procedures for trying to raise individuals' aspiration levels. This is a major responsibility of top management.

Furthermore, you have the whole question of what new alternatives we can discover that we haven't thought of before—what new opportunities we can find—and increasingly in our kind of world, we begin to institutionalize the process of looking for them. We don't leave them to chance; we say we're going to set up a particular part of the business, decide whose job it is to find new alternatives, and determine whether we are able to raise our aspiration levels. That's what research and development is all about. Also, there are many other business functions that look for new gaps that the organization can move into.

In an organization that's operating effectively, there is continual movement, a continual assessment of what's possible, and a continual attempt to try to widen what's possible.

In a sense, then, one of the ways to direct and improve the quality and evolution of an organization is by influencing the aspiration level against which satisficing is measured. Organization A can be better than Organization B if it has measured a higher satisfying criterion in its structure.

With an important qualification! You know the old saying: If wishes were horses beggars would ride. I can't just say that next year I'm going to make a million bucks and since I have that aspiration, I'm going to make it. The problem is how to get that organization to work very hard and tight against realistic operations. You can destroy morale and get a real boomerang effect with a collapse of aspirations if you set objectives unrealistically high. But it's a real-life matter for managers to decide what those levels ought to be.

When we discuss satisficing, aren't we really talking about a decision-making criterion that is more applicable at one organizational level than at another? That is, haven't we, in effect, defined a continuum of a decision-making criterion function that ranges from a kind of optimization or maybe even maximization at the bottom to a satisficing criterion at higher levels? Doesn't the actual decision-making format depend to some degree on the domain of the decision as well as the quality of the data?

Consider a linear programming situation where you have a very complex situation. One way you use optimizing techniques is to try to carve out a simplification of the situation or an approximation of it. Then you can take the simplified model of the situation, apply some sharp mathematical tools, and optimize within the model.

What I'm saying is, one way of satisficing is to simplify the situation as much as you need in order to be able to apply your optimizing tools; in effect, you're pretending that that's the real situation. As you suggest, you array decisions as a function of level and complexity, moving from very great difficulties in anything approaching maximization at top levels to more and more possibilities as you move down to concrete operations.

You have stated that many of the central issues of our time are "questions of how we use limited information and limited computational capacity to deal with enormous problems whose shape we barely grasp." But you also suggest that we live in a world where attention is a major scarce luxury—that "we cannot afford to attend to information simply because it is there." How do we cope with this problem?

You can discuss this problem at various levels of the organization—a person can do much to improve his system of setting priorities to improve his managerial style. But in terms of wider organizational issues, I believe this question focuses sharply these days on the kinds of information systems you deal with in a company.

After the first wave of enthusiasm for management information systems (MIS), a great deal of disappointment developed. Many of those systems were built on the idea that you could gather up all the important records that were lying around, stuff them all into a computer, and print out some papers, which you could then put on managers' desks—all good information that they didn't have before.

But if you start the other way around and ask what decisions have to be made, what issues an organization should be alerted to promptly, and what information you want to forget, then you start designing an information system, not just in terms of information you happen to have available, but in terms of need for information.

I think the next generation of information systems is likely to be much more realistic. In any event they will start with the concept of performing a decision-making job, planned with the realization that the aim of an information system is to conserve attention, not simply to flood people with data that, in some wild way, might have some potential use for them. It's a matter of directing the attention of people to important, priority matters but at the same time conserving attention.

What other changing dimensions in information technology do you foresee over the next decade?

The pacemaker here, of course, is the computer—the more bangs for a buck that we get out of it every year. Second, but coming much more slowly, I regret to say, is the software technology associated with computers.

As for the second generation of management information systems . . . in addition to the decision-making capabilities I mentioned previously, we also have a great need for a process much more oriented toward information that comes into the organization from the environment rather than information generated inside the organization. In any event, I think we're getting the software technology now to deal with that.

There is absolutely no excuse for a computer to have to learn how to scan print—although by now I think we know reasonably well how to do that. There is absolutely no reason why almost every piece of paper that's produced in our society shouldn't be produced in a machine-readable form at the same time it's produced in man-readable form. There's going to be a major shift, and you can see it beginning now. Take the securities industry—computers increasingly have available the same set of numbers and financial reports that the analysts have.

And in computer software, there's a growing sophistication in our ability to model various parts of the business environment—strategic planning made on the basis of being able to simulate various situations, to run off scenarios, to try alternatives, and to do that kind of thinking and planning that we increasingly need.

Twenty years ago you were forecasting that over the next 25 years, the job of the manager would undergo major changes, with machines taking over more and more of the activities that at the time seemed too complex and high level ever to yield to automation. You also foresaw changes in the general occupational profile, with organizations operating with a much higher ratio of machines to men than was characteristic of the late 1950s and early 1960s. As we all know, some of these forecast changes have occurred; others have been slower to take shape. What's ahead now?

The kinds of trends we've been seeing are very likely to continue.

First, there will be a continued increase in service occupations that have nothing much to do with automation. What happens there depends on consumption, on income, and on what things have greater elasticities of demand.

As for the clerical workforce, we're getting to the point where maybe an awful lot of things that can be squeezed out by, at least, our present forms of automation already have been squeezed out. Most of the office factories—the long lines of desks—that you used to see are gone. Now you see more of the secretarial and administrative types. Thus we are going to see more and more people in socalled service or face-to-face people kinds of occupations.

The question of skills is a tough one. But to illustrate a point, consider what percentage of people in our society drive automobiles well enough to get and maintain licenses. About 95 percent. Now run down the list of principal occupations and ask yourself what percentage of the workforce exercises skills on the job that are higher than the skills required to drive an automobile. My guess (and the personnel people I've tried it on haven't been outraged by it) is that 40 percent is a generous estimate. So 60 percent are using in their work today lower skills than they use in driving back and forth to their jobs. This doesn't sound to me like a world in which there's a major problem with the unskilled, especially since skills are rising in the population.

So when you look at the figures showing much higher unemployment among the unskilled than among the skilled, you should also look at two other things. One is minimum wages, which may make people unemployable in an economy at a given time at what happens to be a minimum wage in that economy. Secondly, you have to look at the whole employment process. I don't care what the skills are. Trot out a whole population full of Ph.D.s if you think that's a high skill—or expert billiard players—and in that society you have some percentage of people unemployed. You'll always find that the unemployed ones are the least skilled of that group, no matter what group it is, for all sorts of good reasons.

What I'm really saying is that although there certainly are problems of giving unskilled people an opportunity to make a contribution to society and to earn a reasonable standard of living in that society, I don't think that one should look at automation or technological change in general as a major factor in those problems. I don't see it as a major issue.

And the major issue is . . . ?

The major issue is, first, what we feel about degrees of equality or inequality in our society and how much we're willing to let differences in productive capacity reflect themselves in standards of living. That's a decision we make all the time in every society. And second, what really are the potentialities and capacities of the people who are the less productive members of our society? For example, there's an awful lot of useful, productive things that an illiterate person can do. We might have questions about whether the productivity of work he can do is high enough so that you would be willing to let him live on the income he can produce in that society. The minimum wage laws, for example, are arguments that we are not always willing to leave that test to the market. Welfare systems and guaranteed income schemes are ways of dealing with the fact that in our society, some people may be very much more productive than others, and we're not williing to let that be the sole determinant of income distribution.

In other words, increases in technology do not make it more and more of a villain in economic society.

It certainly does not make it a villain with respect to the viability of the unskilled. As a matter of fact, in my city, trash collectors, whom I don't want to call either skilled or unskilled, are in great demand, and I think probably come dearer than assistant professors . . . and you know, I don't see anything wrong with that.

On several occasions you have posed the question, "Will the corporation be managed by machines?" What is the shape of the future for managers?

Of course, the answer I gave (in *The New Science of Management Decision*, Prentice-Hall) was that the corporation wouldn't be managed by machine—although I predicted it *could* be in perhaps a shorter time span than I would right now. But the main argument of the book was based on a very classical proposition of economics—the doctrine of comparative advantage. I argued that you had to look at not merely what a machine could do, but at the things that machines are relatively good at—computers and factory automation—compared to people.

When computer development really got going after World War II, most people thought that computers could do the sorts of things that blue collar people do and perhaps some routine clerical duties, but that the higher things of the mind were beyond them. I think that our experience in the field of artificial intelligence over the last 20 years has been a little different from that—computers can and do perform far more complicated and even creative tasks.

The area in which the human being retains his largest comparative advantage, I believe, is in coordination of a pair of eyes, a mind, and a set of hands in dealing with an external environment. (For example, writing a computer program to simulate a college professor is a lot easier than writing programs to simulate a bulldozer driver.) Thus we've progressed much more rapidly with programming the kinds of things the central nervous system does than we have with the things the sensory organs do. So if you ask in what kinds of occupations in society is interaction with the environment crucial, you find, for example, a good many blue collar occupations that are slow to be automated and occupations that are largely concerned with the interactions of people with people. You can cite the salesman role, if you want, but even in instances like that you always have to think of the possibility of things being done in a different way than in the past.

My favorite example of this point is the old-fashioned family physician. What was his most needed skill and what did he spend the largest number of hours a week doing? The answer: driving a horse. But, as you know, that got automated pretty fast.

The conclusion I reached was that for the visible future—which is never really very long—the computer was going to reduce the number of people in white collar, well structured jobs and in factory and assembly-line operations. In management, I felt it probably was going to reduce somewhat the number of middle-management people who were making day-to-day management decisions. But beyond that, I didn't see that it was going to make drastic changes in the work force.

As it turned out, many changes have occured in the clerical area, and we have seen much change in the functions of middle management. But change has come more slowly with respect to factory automation, except in a few continuous process industries. Of course, we also have seen advances in the use of numerical control in activities such as machine tools and related operations, and now robotry is advancing very rapidly. In fact, for the next five or ten years robotry is probably going to be one of the areas of rather rapid change in factory operations of a more discrete kind where it has not been applicable previously because of the need for more sophisticated sensing and grasping devices.

For the past 20 years or so you have been concentrating on psychological studies designed to help understand how the human mind works. What specific tools in this area are available now and what's coming in the future that will help managers in their decision-making responsibilities?

Research on problem solving began as a natural continuation of the work we'd been doing on decision making. It became evident that there was a need to take a more fundamental and microscopic look at decision making, and problem solving is a good part of that.

First, by getting a better understanding of human problem solving, we developed some ideas about how to enlarge the range of operations research (OR) tools so that today we have not only some optimization techniques but also the so-called "heuristic search"—rule-of-thumb type—techniques.

Second, there is an increasing number of books and university courses on problem solving, and I believe that others outside the university setting—the Kepner-Tregoe organization is one example—are working well within this traditon. The people doing this work are drawing on some very old and classical ideas (we didn't invent the subject), but they are also drawing more and more on the psychological literature that's been turned out in the last couple of decades of research.

Third, we are seeing some large artificial intelligence programs that do professional-level tasks, though so far they are just getting out of the R&D phase into some specific applications—but mostly in fields other than management. For example, the University of Pittsburgh medical school has INTERNIST, a computer-based medical diagnosis program developed by Dr. Jack Meyers of the medical school and a computer scientist, Dr. Harry Pople. The system is used for diagnosing in the area of internal medicine, and it has reached the point at which physicians are beginning to consult it to check their own judgment and to see whether it thinks of something that they didn't.

Stanford University has a computer program called DENDRAL, that identifies molecules by analysis of mass spectogram data. Formerly, a chemist had to take a month out of his life to do one of these analyses.

In the management field there was some early movement in this direction in an artificial intelligence program that made investment decisions. It could take a trust agreement and make a set of decisions that simulated very closely the decisions that would be made by a bank trust officer. Now there is a wide range of computer aids in the investment field that, I believe, are partly a byproduct of that kind of research. The money manager now has at his computer console a lineup of analyses that represent the kinds of rules of thumb that one uses in decision making in that business. It would not be a difficult programming job to automate a large percentage of those decisions.

It sounds like INTERNIST *and* DENDRAL *are at the cutting edge of exciting developments in the artificial intelligence field. Is there anything like them on the horizon in the management area?*

INTERNIST and DENDRAL certainly illustrate the level that the technology has reached, but I can't cite clear-cut examples in the management area now because there hasn't been enough R&D in management fields. Moreover, it's astonishing to me how little R&D is going into these types of efforts over all—and especially management.

Who, for example, has mounted sizable efforts on this problem in business corporations—not counting the non-profit organizations that may have research projects? Xerox has a big R&D effort on this now, and I guess IBM is somewhat cranked up on some aspects of it. A number of Japanese companies have been concentrating mostly on the robotry and pattern recognition aspects. But the amount of commercial R&D in the whole area of artificial intelligence/decision making is very tiny, and most of the work that has been done has been supported by grants from the DARPA (Defense Advanced Research Projects Agency) unit in the Defense Department. Probably less that $20 million a year.

There's some reason for this situation, of course. Another old saying goes, "Be not the first by whom the new is tried. . . ." Also, corporations can't afford to do too much of the basic research, which then is appropriated by industry generally. For this reason then, one of the roles the government has to play in our economic society is a major one in developing new technology—as it has with nearly every major technology we have.

Are there any significant differences in the effectiveness of group vs individual decision making?

Sure, there are differences, but when I think about that aspect, I need a finer classification because there are many aspects of group decision making. Take, for example, the Japanese *ringi* system. When you talk about the so-called bottom-up decision-making process, in one very real sense, that's group decision making. Somebody has a notion that he thinks should be pushed. He develops a document or two on it, begins to circulate it around the organization, drinks tea with a lot of people, and after a while, a consensus begins to develop. I don't know how this is actually tested, but when the man feels that he has a consensus, he develops a formal document and sends it around, and everybody puts his stamp on it.

Is that group decision making? I don't know how many people are in the room.

On the other hand, you have the American system, operating in an organization that resembles a hierarchy. Somebody has an idea that he tries on a few people. After a while, maybe a document goes up the line, and at some point, the boss approves it. In many ways, it looks different, but at the same time, there's a lot of consultation—sometimes a meeting, a few people talking, somebody shipping a memo to somebody else who comments on it or takes a piece of it and works it out.

There's very little individual decision making in any organization I know about—that is, in the sense of one person going off by himself, kicking the idea around from ground level, finishing it, and then saying, "This is the way we're going to do it." But when you get down to the question of how you actually do group decision making, you run into issues like whether you get people around a table and what do you talk about. Another big point is who you get around the table.

Then the concept of satisficing applies to the group as it does to the individual?

I think so. If you just look at the flow of decisions, the flow of problem solving that takes place during the decision process, and take the names off the pieces of it so it's an abstract thing, I don't think the structure is terribly different from individual decision making.

When we're making a complex decision individually, we also divide it into pieces, work on one and then another, and then we've got to put them together again. Somewhere, at some point, you're a committee of the whole, yourself. So if you look at the problem abstractly, the similarities are much more visible than the differences for complex decisions.

In your discussions of the science of management decisions, you have expressed the view that the organizations will generally retain their traditional hierarchical structures. Does the matrix structure fit this pattern?

The matrix situation, if I understand it correctly, is not very different from the notion that Frederick Taylor had about functional foremanship and his general notion that unity of command was only an illusion. The matrix organization is a legitimization of the idea that decision premises have to come from several sources. It makes a task force idea workable by signaling that it's not an "illicit" way of doing business in an organization.

The matrix is a great step of progress, in which somebody invented a label (though it's more than that, of course) that made legitimate the fact we all knew before—but sort of felt ashamed of—that there is no unity of command, and can't be, in a complex organization and that because of the distribution of expertness, commands have to flow from a number of directions.

Aren't we saying then, in effect, that in those situations we do not have a pure hierarchical structure, that it is something different from what we heretofore assumed to be the preferred structure?

I think the change in our perceptions is greater than the change in reality. In a study of the controllership function back in 1953, we found that most of the problems in defining the role of the factory controller involved defining what his relative responsibilities were to the controller's department and to the factory manager. And that was difficult to do at the time because it was felt to be illegitimate for him to be responsible to both.

The matrix idea has helped us (1) to recognize the commonness of the situation by bringing it out into the open and (2) to develop a set of more or less common understandings of how you do deal with it and that people can live with multiple authority relations.

What we have then is a very dynamic hierarchical structure, in which the nature of the hierarchy shifts as the problem changes and the kind of expertness that is required for proper relationships also shifts.

It's fair to say then that if you look at almost all business organizations today there still is a fall-back hierarchy. When it comes to a clinch, the manager still knows who his boss is.

Perhaps some will tend to identify an organization structure as an administrative hierarchy for taking certain personnel oriented decisions and a functional hierarchy that is business-problem related. But what makes the former particularly important is that it's inevitable that a man looks at his career, more often than not, in terms of the administrative hierarchy.

You stated recently that it is "commonplace to observe that economics has traditionally been concerned with what decisions are made rather than how they are made." You have also argued that there is an urgent need to enlarge the established body of economic analysis to encompass the procedural aspects of decision making rather than adhering entirely to the concerns of substantive rationality. Can you then suggest what such economists or economic analysts should specifically utilize from other sciences that would be useful in providing greater assistance to the business community and its needs for work-a-day economic intelligence or know-how? Would we then have better economic forecasts—that is, more accurate predictions of business cycles and economic blips in the road ahead for business decision makers?

There are a number of answers to that. One is that there have been other fields whose concern has been to build actual decision procedures for solving problems, such as operations research. Actually, I think economics learned a great deal—for example, in linear programming—that has had a major impact on economic theory. But now we have the field of artificial intelligence coming along, which provides procedures for solving problems covering a wider range than you can handle with, say, OR techniques. I think economists need to learn something about AI. Also there is a subarea within computer science now called "computational complexity," where there have been efforts to apply some of these ideas to economic theory. Then, of course, over on the psychological side, having an understanding of how people do change their targets and do respond to environmental events is important in understanding things like the phenomenon of inflation.

As for getting better economic forecasts and analyses more useful to business, I guess the cautious way to put it is that if we are going to have any chance of getting better forecasts, we are going to have to look at what is known throughout the social sciences and about how people's expectations are formed and how they change. We can't do this in a vacuum without looking at those types of business and consumer behaviors. Likewise, we need to borrow some of the techniques of other social sciences for getting at these behaviors.

Take marketing as an example. I think there has been an increasing impact both of psychological theory and of techniques for getting data about people's marketing behavior. One shouldn't give the impression that none of these data has contributed to business cycle forecasting. But over all they have never had a very enthusiastic reception in economics.

In your writings on decision making, you have described yourself as a technical radical, an economic conservative, and a philosophic pragmatist. How do these terms shape your concept of the present and future process of management decision making?

By technological radical, I meant that from the beginning I've been unable to see what the ultimate limits of computers are in terms of the range of human functions that they will be able to perform. The early line about computers was that they were dumb beasts that did only what you programmed them to do. That's true, but sometimes you can program them to do surprising things. And that's where the technological radicalism comes in—a real belief that the computer is a powerful general purpose device that, as we learn how to use it, is going to be able to perform a wider and wider range of human functions.

By economic conservative, I meant that I believed that the real limiting factor on the rate at which the use of the computer in organizations would be extended was that you have to embody them in capital—steel, wires, glass, and what-not—and that for a long time to come, there might be a lot of fancy things you can do with a computer, but the question is: Which of these things will pay? After all, you can also hire people to perform many of these functions, and it isn't always clear how rapidly changeovers to computers will occur.

By philosophic pragmatist, I mean that I just can't get very excited about arguments about computers and "free will." I'd just like to see what we can do with computers; such philosophical questions will settle themselves in the long run.

Clarence W. von Bergen, Jr

Battle Creek, Michigan

Raymond J. Kirk

Army Research Institute

GROUPTHINK: WHEN TOO MANY HEADS SPOIL THE DECISION

Many of us have at one time or another lamented the results of groups, committees, or task forces in which we have participated or have been associated. Yet we continue to spend long hours in group decision making that might be handled on an individual basis.

Much of the research on group decision making questions the adequacy of groups for solving important problems. For example, separate researchers have found that for many kinds of tasks the pooled output of noninteracting individuals usually is better than that of interacting face-to-face groups. Indeed, Nietzsche is reported to have said that madness is the exception in individuals but the rule in groups.

One reason for continuing decision making in groups is that a group may be less likely to make bad decisions than will individuals. This appears to be particularly important when the cost of a wrong decision may be especially high. Although more person-hours may be employed to reach a collective decision, the resulting decision is more likely to be the correct one—which

Clarence W. Von Bergen, Jr. and Raymond J. Kirk, "Groupthink: When Too Many Heads Spoil the Decision," *Management Review*, March 1978, pp. 44–49.

may be one of the reasons why many high-level decisions made in business and governement are made in groups.

Also, rarely is a decision successful unless it is accepted by those who will implement it. Indeed, the proponents of participative decision making cite increased commitment to group-formulated decisions as one of the advantages of the participative approach. People are more inclined to accept and implement decisions that they or their representatives have helped develop.

There also has been an emphasis on group participation and decision making in organizational development (OD) activities. One survey of 45 companies engaged in OD-type activities indicated that 98 percent of the firms used participative methods in identifying and solving organizational problems.

OTHER GROUP BENEFITS_____

Group inputs are sought in these efforts because the quality of the contributions may be more in keeping with the values of authenticity and candor than if they came from an individual. This is particularly true for OD activities directed toward improvements in communication and resolution of conflicts.

Another reason for favoring group decision making deals with the diffusion of responsibility. Spreading of responsibility may appear very attractive when a good decision calls for actions that are unpopular, unpleasant, or risky. A single person may not be inclined to pursue a course of action because he or she alone will be held accountable for any negative consequences, whereas a group may decide to go on with an unpleasant, or risky, action because responsibility is shared among its members. The group may function, in effect, as a superindividual entity, in which members can achieve some degree of anonymity.

Group decision making also affords a relatively captive audience for those who like to hear themselves, a friendly club for those who seek sociability, satisfaction for those eager to deflate rivals, and a base for those who want power and status. For some individuals, satisfying those perosnal needs in a group is more important than the explicit goal of the group.

Finally, group decision making may be preferred because of the belief that "all of us know more than any one of us knows." Though it is not entirely supportable, this belief holds that the group's multiple perspectives, talents, and areas of expertise brought to bear in solving problems, setting goals, establishing policies, and carrying out projects or activities result in a superior product.

PITFALLS IN GROUPS

Unfortunately, many of us have been part of a group that did not function properly and whose conclusions were sometimes poorer than those an individual might have reached. The major barriers to effective group problem solving are those conditions that prevent the free expression of ideas in a group. Restraints can decrease the likelihood that the correct solution or the elements of such a solution will be made available to the group. Both obvious and subtle factors can work against the group's use of its resources.

Most of us know that obvious factors, such as embarrassment and fear of reprisal, tend to restrict free expression of ideas in groups. However, other more subtle restrictive factors, such as high regard for unanimity sought by members of groups, also are at work.

Groups tend to produce unanimous decisions, and their discussions tend to increase the uniformity of their members' individual judgements. One study reported that in groups ranging in size from two to five people, 64 percent of the groups gave unanimous answers despite instructions to members to disregard the group's discussion and that the final reports need not be unanimous.

Social-psychological studies have suggested that the more cohesive a group becomes, the less its members will deliberately censor what they say out of fear of being punished socially for antagonizing the leader or a fellow member. On the other hand, the more cohesive a group is, the more its members will unwittingly censor what they think because of their newly acquired motivation to preserve the unity of the group and to adhere to its norms. Thus, although the members of a highly cohesive group feel much freer to deviate from the majority, they also desire genuine concurrence on all important issues. A desire to match their opinions and conduct themselves in accordance with each other's wishes often inclines them not to use this freedom to dissent.

The danger is not that each will fail to reveal his strong objections to a proposal, but that each will think the proposal is a good one without even attempting to carry out a critical scrutiny that could reveal grounds for strong objections. The insecurity generated by possible rejection provides a strong incentive to agree with the other members. The more esprit de corps exhibited by a group of policymakers, the more likely independent, critical thinking will be replaced by "groupthink."

As a group becomes excessively close-knit, groupthink develops. The process is characterized by a marked decrease in the exchange of potentially conflicting data and by an unwillingness to conscientiously examine such data when they surface.

This type of group process emphasizes team play at all costs and often increases the probability that the collective membership will act in a spirit of seeking unanimity, overoptimism, and a lack of vigilance. It often formulates and implements a strategy that is ineffective and not in keeping with existing realities.

GROUPTHINK SYMPTOMS_____

Groupthink may be characterized as encompassing a number of symptoms, and one could argue that groupthink exists in a group to the degree that these eight symptoms are present.

1. Illusion of unanimity regarding the viewpoint held by the majority in the group and an emphasis on team play.
2. A view of the "opposition" as generally inept, incompetent, and incapable of countering effectively any action by the group, no matter how risky the decision or how high the odds are against the plan of action succeeding.
3. Self-censorship of group members in which overt disagreements are avoided, facts that might reduce support for the emerging majority view are suppressed, faulty assumptions are not questioned, and personal doubts are suppressed in the form of group harmony.
4. Collective rationalization to comfort one another in order to discount warnings that the agreed-upon plan is either unworkable or highly unlikely to succeed.
5. Self-appointed mindguards within the group that function to prevent anyone from undermining its apparent unanimity and to protect its members from unwelcome ideas and adverse information that may threaten consensus.
6. Reinforcement of consensus and direct pressure on any dissenting group member who expresses strong reservations or challenges or argues against the apparent unanimity of the group.

7. An expression of self-righteousness that leads members to believe their actions are moral and ethical, thus inclining them to disregard any ethical or moral objections to their behavior.
8. A shared feeling of unassailability marked by a high degree of esprit de corps, by implicit faith in the wisdom of the group, and by an inordinate optimism that disposes members to take excessive risks.

GROUPTHINK IN BUSINESS: A CASE STUDY

A company president, who wanted to implement a flexible work hours program, asked a committee of lower-level managers and professionals to investigate the feasibility of flexible work schedules in his firm. The committee was composed of nine salaried employees, most of whom were young and all of whom held staff positions.

For five of the individuals, membership on the committee was seen as unusual in that rarely had they been asked to consider corporatewide policies. It could be said that these group members felt honored to be a part of the group.

Two other members had initiated the idea of appointing the committee and were therefore committed to making it a success. Thus there existed a considerable degree of attraction to the group, with membership in it highly valued. Such circumstances are conducive to a high frequency of group-think symptoms which, in turn, can lead to a high frequency of decision-making defects.

The committee was aware of the president's favorable attitude toward flexible hours. However, several members exprssed skepticism about implementation of a flexible hour schedule.

Over the course of its meetings the committee critically appraised and reappraised the potential advantages and disadvantages of such a program. It solicited viewpoints and opinions from organizations that had experience with flexible-hour programs and interviewed representatives of five companies. Finally, it decided to give a positive recommendation and proceeded to deal with the details of implementation.

Following some initial disagreements, all of the procedural details were satisfactorily resolved, except how employees were to account for their work hours. Several options were open, each having precedent in the companies that were visited. One was an honor program in which the employees would simply indicate the number of hours worked each week on their time cards; a second required employees to sign in when they arrived for work and to sign out at the end of the day (also to sign in and out at lunch periods); the third required employees to operate an automatic time-accumulating device that would keep a cumulative record.

The matter of time accountability was discussed at several meetings, but the committee members tended to insulate themselves between meetings and did not discuss the issue with other managers. (Insulation of group members from outside input is typically encountered in groupthink situations). Moreover, most members were aware that the company president was quite receptive to the use of an automatic time accumulator (a factor that, in the end, facilitated concurrence).

The group's cohesiveness, insulation, and awareness of the president's desires increased the likelihood that independent, critical thinking was replaced by groupthink. The president's opinion, in particular, tended to focus the group's recommendation on the time-accumulator device, and five or six committee members initially expressed enthusiasm regarding it.

One of the sumptoms of groupthink, however, is illusion of unanimity, which, in the case of the flexible-hours committee, was apparent from the beginning of its discussions of time accountability. It was almost as if the decision had already been made and all that was needed was formal approval of the device. Although one of the more influential members of the group was unwilling to make up his mind about the time accumulator, he consistently refused to take a stand on the issue. Another member expressed some doubts that the accumulator was compatible with the objectives of flexible hours, but was almost apologetic in presenting her concerns. (In private conversations, however, this member was much more aggresive and opinionated,)

Such behavior typifies the self-censorship symptom of groupthink—that is, self-censorship on the part of individuals in raising objections to the apparent group consensus.

Another incident suggesting the operation of self-censorship involved a committee member who held strong reservations about the time device but expressed his feelings in the restroom rather than in the meeting room, where he sat quietly and did not raise questions or voice objections. Another group member who was aware of the other members' concerns also kept silent. Thus the group assumed that "silence gave consent."

Another groupthink symptom exhibited by this group was an expression of self-righteousness, which led members to regard their actions as ethical and just. (Flexible hours were viewed as a benefit designed to give employees more self-determination and freedom.)

Previously, only management and professional employees were permitted some degree of flexibility, although it was by no means as extensive as that envisioned in the proposed program. Thus the companywide proposal was seen as a noble cause; it had the president's support and was "right" for the employees involved. Even though the time-accumulator device might be seen by many employees and managers as a time clock and, thus, a regressive step, it would still be part of a "positive" program.

The committee had a sense of unlimited confidence and excessive optimism about flexible hours, and no time accumulator was about to ruin the program. Indeed, the committee exhibited a sense of invulnerability regarding the ability to successfully implement the program.

Three members of the group were aware of one outside manager's misgivings about the time accumulator, but were reluctant to voice his concerns. Thus there was a tendency to discount warnings that might have led the committee to reconsider its decisions.

At the last meeting before submitting the committee's recommendations to the president, the final details were discussed. At this late stage, it seemed taboo to bring up the issue of a time accumulator; nevertheless, an individual who had been sitting in on the meetings as an expert advisor asked what the final decision was regarding the time accumulator, saying there still appeared to be some unanswered questions.

The committee moderator seemed surprised at this intervention, saying that he thought the issue had been settled and that the accumulator would be recommended. Nonetheless, he proposed taking a quick poll, athough at that point he noted that the meeting had already gone past its scheduled period and that it was time for lunch.

The moderator started the poll by indicating why he favored the accumulator. As the voting went around the table, it became progressively more difficult for other group members to state divergent views. Such open voting puts considerable pressure on each group member to agree with the apparent consensus. Thus, the group leader's suggesting a certain approach and essentially acting as a mindguard, the public polling of the members, and the time pressures to make a decision before lunch all led to approval of the accumulators. Several days later the prsident received the recommendation and expressed general agreement with it.

It appeared, then, that the flexible-time program would be implemented using the time accumulator. But a manager who had earlier not felt free to voice his reservations quickly wrote a two-page letter to the moderator asking that the matter be reconsidered. Though not a group member, this manager had been invited to attend several sessions. In this letter he expressed concern that the accumulator would simply be a check on the employees and that its use was meaningless if the employees felt their rights were being violated.

This formalized reservation, together with some coffeebreak banter by several other managers, prompted the group moderator to get more detailed views from other corporate managers who would be obliged to introduce accumulators to their departments. When this survey of a few outside managers was completed, it was painfully clear that use of accumulators in conjunction with the flexible-hour program would be met with considerable resistance. Department managers would regard it as a threat to their autonomy in their departments.

On the basis of these developments, the group moderator proposed that the flexible-hours recommendation be modified so that, when the program was implemented, each department would determine how it would account for employees' time. The change was approved by the president, and a potentially disastrous problem was avoided.

PREVENTING GROUPTHINK_____

While most managers have probably experienced groupthink at one time or another, it is not inherent in all group decision-making activities and can be avoided. The following guidelines, while not all inclusive, are useful in preventing the appearance of groupthink.

Leader Encouragement. In most organizations group members need encouragement to feel free to disagree with the boss or group leader. The subordinates in the group must feel free to disagree if they are to contribute the best of their thinking.

The leader should encourage free expression of minority viewpoints. Since the majority viewpoint is more likely to be well known, it is easier to speak in its behalf. On the other hand, group members holding minority views are more likely to be on the defensive and more hesitant voicing their opinion. To introduce balance into the situation, the leader must do all he or she can to protect individuals who are attacked and to create opportunities for them to clarify their views. Such a process does not simply entail a challenge to the group with a quick "Does anyone object?" and, if no one raises a hand in two or three seconds, to proceed with "Let's go ahead then."

Diversity of Viewpoints. Attempt to structure the group so that there are different viewpoints. Diverse input will tend to point out nonobvious risks, drawbacks and advantages that might not have been considered by a more homogeneous group.

Legitimized Disagreement and Skepticism. Silence is usually interpreted as consent. It should be explained that questions, reservations, and objections should be brought before the group and that feelings of loyalty to the group should not be allowed to obstruct expression of doubts. Genuine, personal loyalty to the group that leads one to go along with a bad policy should be discouraged. Voicing objections and doubts should not be subordinated to fears about "rocking the boat" or reluctance to "blow the whistle." Each member should take on the additional role of a critical evaluator and should be encouraged by the leader and other members to air reservations.

Idea Generation vs. Idea Evaluation. A major barrier to effective decision making is the tendency to evaluate suggested solutions as they appear instead of waiting until all suggestions are in. Early evaluation may inhibit the expressing of opinions, and it tends to restrict freedom of thinking and prevents others from profiting from different ideas. Early evaluation can be particularly destructive to ideas that are different, new or lacking support. The group and the leader should encourage problem-mindedness at the expense of solution-mindedness.

Advantages and Disadvantages of Each Solution. The group should try to explore the merits and demerits of each alternative. This process of listing the sides of a question forces discussion to oscillate from one side of the issue to the other. As a result, the positive and negative aspects of each strategy are brought out into the open and may become the foundation for a new idea with all its merits and few of its weaknesses.

New Approaches and New People. In many cases, thinking about the problem by oneself or discussing it with an outside associate can result in refreshing new perspectives. Any belief that one should be able to generate correct answers to complex problems and issues the first time they are dealt with should be dispelled. Indeed, the norm should be "to think about it again, and think about it in a new way." This implies recording the answer derived by one approach, putting it aside for a while, then coming back to the problem afresh. Also, it may be helpful if, in the intervening time, each of the group participants consults a trusted colleague who is not a member of the group, to bounce off him or her the tentative decisions and feelings. Ideally, these colleagues should be someone different in expertise and orientation from the group members, so that they can offer critical, independent, and perhaps fresh ideas, which can be reported back to the group

Examination of Group Processes.   A group should periodically examine the processes it uses to assess how its members are working together. Perhaps after each decision has been made, the group should examine the process it used in generating the proposed solution. Such questions may include: Who talked to whom? Why didn't Joe say very much? Are all members participating? Is a majority pushing a decision through over other members' objections?

Although groupthink is a dysfunctional consequence of a group interaction, there is a strong reluctance by existing policy and decision-making groups to examine their own group processes and interpersonal behaviors.

First, through the years it has become customary not to be publicly explicit about the interpersonal process within the group, and this tradition or custom has become a determinant in its own right. How often do we hear something to the effect of "Let's be logical and keep personalities out of this"? In most cases the personality issue is synonomous with the group process issue, which, if not adequately addressed, can adversely affect the group product.

Second, the almost compulsive need to achieve specific goals is so prevalent that attention and time devoted to intermediary social process is often consciously neglected. Most organizations are geared to getting the product out the back door, and anything not directly associated with this task or entailing a short-run sacrifice is looked upon with suspicion, if not overt resistance. In many cases, the long-term investment in the constructive attention to group processes that may pay off in sound internal relations and increased performance is simply not recognized.

Third, bringing into the open the various roles, relationships, and group difficulties is almost inevitably anxiety-producing. Making differentiations among people creates tension. Publicly expressing one's observations, for example, who talks to whom, who talks the most, and so on, raises anxieties that many feel are better swept under the rug. Being aware of the symptoms of groupthink and recognizing it in their own group interactions may increase the willingness of decision-making groups to examine their own processes to minimize the adverse consequences of groupthink behavior.

Roy Rowan

THOSE BUSINESS HUNCHES ARE MORE THAN BLIND FAITH

The feasibility study is a beauty. The cost analysis looks right on the money. Even the sales projections, sometimes a little pie-in-the sky, seem pretty solid. All the ingredients needed for a sound decision say: "Go!" Yet this nagging voice from a mysterious echo chamber deep inside his brain keeps repeating: "No!"

"Let's hold off on this one," announces the chief executive officer (CEO) to his astonished subordinates. "We've got enough on our plates for now."

Lame excuses like that cannot disguise the fact that most of the chief executives who control the destinies of the biggest corporations are often guided by ill-defined gut feelings. The intuitive boss, of course, is a recurring figure in American business. J. P. Morgan (who was known to visit fortune-tellers) and Cornelius Vanderbilt (who consulted clairvoyants and believed in ghosts) took enormous pride in their enormously profitable hunches. So did their legendary contemporaries, without seeking the counsel of mediums. Even today, when the empirical world of business is practically paved over with M.B.A.'s who can figure the risk-reward ratio of any decision at the drop of a computer key, the old-fashioned hunch continues to be a managerial tool.

Roy Rowan, "Those Business Hunches Are More Than Blind Faith," *Fortune*, April 23, 1979, pp. 111–114.

224

WHEN BIOLOGY FEEDS BACK_____

Society's current addition to psychic advice is hardly what executives mean when they admit to following hunches. Biofeedback, for example, has proved helpful in the healing process, but most businessmen—and not businessmen only—would consider it just short of sorcery.

Yet a handful of scientists and academicians have come up with measurable proof that subconscious elements play a role in the decision-making process. They are convinced that heeding a strong hunch may be a wise move, and even see a correlation between the boss's precognitive ability and his company's profitability. In any case, they point out that it isn't realistic for executives to rely solely on logic to cope with the complexities of modern business.

Broach these thoughts to a board chairman or president, and you had better watch your language. To begin with, *hunch* is an odious word to the professional manager. It's a stock-market plunger's term, rife with imprecision and unpredictability. *Psychic* and *precognitive* are just as bad, since they smack of the occult. Self-proclaimed psychics pop up all over the place, insisting they can bend metal, project photographic images, or remove diseased organs by using nothing more than intense mental concentration. The business leader understandably shrinks from the thought of being associated with such kooks.

But suggest to this same executive that he might indeed possess certain intuitive powers, which could be of real assistance in generating ideas, choosing alternative courses of action, and picking people, and you'll elicit some interested responses:

• "The chief executive officer is not supposed to say, 'I feel.' He's supposed to say, 'I know,' " asserts David Mahoney, chairman of Norton Simon. "So we deify the word instinct by calling it judgment. But any attempt to deny instinct is to deny identity. It's the most current thing. It's me—in everything from picking a wife to picking a company for acquisition."

• "Intuition helps you read between the lines," says John Fetzer, owner of the Detroit Tigers and chairman of Fetzer Broadcasting Co. "Or walk through an office, and intuition tells you if things are going well." A staunch believer in mind over matter, Fetzer explains that he would never suggest to star pitcher Mark Fidrych that he stop talking aloud to the baseball and telling it where to go.

• "In a business that depends entirely on people and not machinery," says Robert Bernstein, chairman of Random House, "only intuition can protect you against the most dangerous individual of all—the articulate incompetent. That's what frightens me about business schools. They train their students to sound wonderful. But it's necessary to find out if there's judgment behind the language."

• "Physics is all hunches and intuition," admits Herman Kahn, a trained physicist-turned-futurist, and now director of the Hudson Institute. "My research is a combination of intuition and judgment. I don't know where it comes from. The mind simply puts things together."

Precisely how the mind puts things together has never been adequately charted. If only we knew how the human brain constantly delves into the subconscious to retrieve buried fragments of knowledge and experience, which it then instantaneously fuses with all the new information, we might better be able to define the hunch and assess its reliability.

ARE YOU FORTUNE'S DARLING?

Nevertheless, we do know certain characteristics of the hunch. It concerns relationships, involves simultaneous perception of a whole system, and can draw a conclusion (not necessarily correct) without proceeding through logical intermediary steps. As Max Gunther points out in *The Luck Factor*: "The facts on which the hunch is based are stored and processed on some level of awareness just below the conscious level. This is why the hunch comes with that peculiar feeling of almost-but-not-quite knowing." But Gunther, an author of books on human relations, also warns against disregarding those "odd little hunches that are trying to tell you what you don't want to hear. Never assume you are fortune's darling." Failure to maintain some degree of pessimism, he claims, is to be in a state of peril.

There are other caveats that the wily manager should heed: Never confuse hope with a hunch, and never regard a hunch as a substitute for first acquiring all known data (laziness usually produces lousy hunches). However, since judgment itself is an inexact science—frequently defined as the "art of making decisions with insufficient information"—even the most deliberate CEO may be forced to act prematurely on an inner impression.

Possibly, then, it is in matters of timing that the business hunch is most critical, as Robert P. Jensen, chairman of General Cable Corp., will testify. Last year, sensing the need for his company to diversify, he found himself faced with five major decisions that involved $300 million in sell-offs and acquisitions. "On each decision," says Jensen, "the mathematical analysis only got me to the point where my intuition had to take over"—as was the case with the $106-million cash purchase of Automation Industries. General Cable's strategic-planning department had come up with a purchase price based on Automation's future sales. "It's not that the numbers weren't accurate," Jensen recalls. "But were the underlying assumptions correct?"

An engineer not given to precipitate decisions, he calls "patience" crucial to the intuitive process. "It's easy to step in and say I have a feeling we ought to do this or that. But then you haven't let your managers weigh in with their feelings first." At the same time, he warns that the perfectionist who keeps waiting for new information never gets anything done. "Intuition is picking the right moment for making your move," adds Jensen, who spent three years as a tight end for the Baltimore Colts.

REVELING IN "CALCULATED CHAOS"

There is, in fact, considerable evidence that the wholly analytical creature pictured at the corporate pinnacle is so much folklore. That, anyway, is the view of Professor Henry Mintzberg of the McGill University Faculty of Management, who has been dissecting and writing about the executive animal for a dozen years.

According to Mintzberg, the CEO pays lip service to systematic long-range planning, elaborate tables of organization, and reliance on computers and esoteric quantitative techniques (more folklore). In reality he's a "holistic, intuitive thinker who revels in a climate of calculated chaos." Mintzberg portrays the CEO as working at an unrelenting pace, jumping from topic to topic, disposing of items in ten minutes or less, and "constantly relying on hunches to cope with problems far too complex for rational analysis."

No criticism intended. The puckish thirty-nine-year-old professor has immense admiration for the CEO's innate sense of direction, which he claims is much more reliable than that of the analytical consultant who is forever devising inflexible guidance systems for unmapped business terrain. "After all," says Mintzberg, "the intuitive Eskimo crosses the ice cap without a compass." The intuitive executive, he explains, solves problems in four interrelated stages set forth in Gestalt psychology: preparation ("creativity favors the prepared mind"), incubation ("letting the subconscious do the work"), illumination ("waking up in the middle of the night and shouting, 'Eureka, I've got it!' "), and verification ("then working it all out linearly").

In performing all of his tasks, the CEO—as students of intuitive decision-making have noted—must know how to read a lot more than words. He assimilates gestures and moods, and thrives on head-to-head encounters with both colleagues and competitors. His own language suggests this hunger for sensory information. He wants to get the "big picture," the "feel of a situation," and "hot gossip" and "cold facts."

This ability to absorb all manner of information stems from the fact that chief executives seem to be "right-brain dominated." It was long known that the right hemisphere of the brain controls the left side of the body—and vice versa. Only recently, however, was it discovered that the two sides of the brain seem to specialize in different activities. The left appears to handle the logical, linear, verbal functions. The right takes care of the emotional, intuitive, spatial functions. Therefore, as in baseball, a savvy board of directors might pick an intuitive right-brained CEO to pitch for the company.

To confirm this application of the right-brain, left-brain theory to business, Robert Doktor, a University of Hawaii business-school professor, wired up a number of CEOs to an electroencephalograph to find out which hemisphere they relied on most. The right hemispheres won hands (or should it be heads?) down.

It was only a question of time before word of the right-brained boss would leak out and somebody would develop a market for the "soft information"—gossip, clues, insights, and other intangibles—on which the intuitive mind feeds. Infer-mation, as the Williams Inference Service of New York calls itself, now sells educated hunches ("disciplined intuition" is the term it uses) to companies such as Travelers and IU International.

"Lead time is the most valuable thing a corporation can have," claims Bennett Goodspeed, marketing chief for Williams. "Yet by the time the numbers are in on any new trend, the change is obvious to everyone." Williams combs hundreds of trade and technical journals for early, isolated clues that, when connected, may convey an "unintended message." But, as Goodspeed laments, corporations resist change. He points out that of six vacuum tube manufacturers, only one had the foresight to switch to transistors.

A MASQUERADE OF MEMORIES

In today's unpredictable environment it's hard to tell whether even the "best" hunches will work. A CEO may come up with an ingenious concept that he can't sell—leaving him feeling as if he's suspended on a limb after the tree has fallen. Aware that universities were concerned about the "social content of their investments," Howard Stein, chairman of Dreyfus Corp., launched a special mutual fund in 1972 composed only of companies that strictly complied with environmental safeguards and fair-employment practices. "Ironically, this Third Century Fund has outperformed most others," reports Stein, "but the colleges call it a 'do-good attempt' and stuck to traditional investments."

In addition, William F. May, chairman of American Can Co., warns that "you have to be alert not to let bad memories masquerade as intuition." He cites his company's experience with the two-quart milk container, which failed miserably when it was first introduced in 1934. The company revived the idea in 1955 in the belief that its time had come. "Our executives turned it down," says May ruefuly. Today, American Can's competitors have two-quart containers in every dairy case.

One area where the hunch player has repeatedly scored is in figuring out the fickle American appetite. Confronted in 1960 with what his lawyer called a bad deal—$2.7 million for the McDonald name—Ray Kroc says: "I closed my office door, cussed up and down, threw things out of the window, called my lawyer back, and said: 'Take it!' I felt in my funny bone it was a sure thing." Last year, systemwide sales of Kroc's hamburger chain exceeded $4.5 billion.

PRECOGNITION AND PROFITS

This ability to decipher the telltale signs of the future puts an enormous premium on what the parapsychologists (ESP specialists) call "precognition." Almost two decades of testing executives have uncovered a close link between a CEO's precognitive and profit-making abilities. In research conducted at the New Jersey Institute of Technology, engineer John Mihalasky and parapsychologist E. Douglas Dean found that more than 80 percent of CEOs who had doubled their company's profits within a five-year period proved to have above-average precognitive powers. (The executives had to predict a 100-digit number that would be randomly selected by a computer anywhere from two hours to two years later).

Mihalasky visualizes precognition as a flow of information particles moving forward and backward in time. He uses the stock-market crash of 1929 to illustrate his point. For "precognitive" investors, there was strong evidence that it was coming and that there would be violent repercussions afterward.

"If something goes beyond the logic that we understand," cautions Mihalasky, "we say forget it." In any case, "the biggest roadblock to intuitive decision-making is not having the guts to follow a good hunch." Although Mihalasky admits that the world is full of "psi-hitters" and "psi-missers," he offers certain recommendations for inducing intuition: (1) Concentrate on what is unique. (2) Be aware of the gaps in your knowledge. (3) Make connections between diverse factors. (4) Avoid becoming over-loaded with information.

While executives may hide the importance of the hunch, nonbusiness leaders are not so reluctant to acknowledge their indebtedness to it. Helen Gurley Brown confides that she uses "secret personal knowledge" in editing *Cosmopolitan*. "When I read a manuscript, even if it's not well written, only intuition can say this is truth, readers will like it. Or intuition may tell me that a piece by a Pulitzer prizewinner is a phony."

Dr. Jonas Salk, discoverer of the polio vaccine, says: "Intuition is something we don't understand the biology of yet. But it is always with excitement that I wake up in the morning wondering what my intuition will toss up to me, like gifts from the sea. I work with it, and rely upon it. It's my partner." After tedious experiments seeking ways to immunize against polio, Salk made an intuitive leap to the correct vaccine. R. Buckminster Fuller, creator of the geodesic dome, says: "I call intuition cosmic fishing. You feel a nibble, then you've got to hook the fish." Too many people, he claims, get a hunch, then light up a cigarette and forget about it.

Artists, certainly, always assumed that creativity doesn't spring from a deductive assault on a problem. Yet there are instances where a melding of the intuitive and deductive helped them produce magnificent results. From Leonardo da Vinci's pen came detailed drawings of the first flying machine. Both Robert Fulton, inventor of the steamboat, and Samuel Morse, inventor of the telegraph, started out life as artists. But intuition led them elsewhere.

Today, it is an explorer back from outer space, Edgar Mitchell, who has turned into intuition's most fervent evangelist—and almost a mystic as well. A doctor of science from M.I.T., Navy captain, and the sixth man on the moon, he believes that "man's potential knowledge is more than the product of his five senses."

Following that journey, Mitchell founded the Institute of Noetic Sciences (Greek for *intuitive knowing*) in California, and not long ago became a director of two computer-software companies—Information Science in West Palm Beach and Forecast Systems in Provo, Utah. In all three endeavors, his aim is to help his fellow man—especially the businessman—develop intuitive decision-making powers to the point where, as he says, "they can control the scientific beast."

EXPLORING INNER SPACE

In preparing for a lunar flight, Mitchell explains, "we spent 10 percent of our time studying plans for the mission, and 90 percent of our time learning how to react intuitively to all the 'what if's.' " At Forecast Systems, Mitchell and his associates use this same approach to help clients identify potential problem areas. They interview managers, foremen, and workers to uncover their fears about all the things that might go wrong. "With a computer printout the resulting 'fault tree' in front of him, a CEO can almost smell those failures before they occur," says Mitchell, explaining "failure analysis," a space-age spinoff.

However methodical, even scientific, Mitchell and other researchers may be, the explanations of intuition and its powers remain elusive. All of the parts, added up, fall short of making a sum called the hunch. But the businessman like David Mahoney or Ray Kroc who has relied on an occasional hunch to solve an important business problem cares less about analyzing the phenomenon than seeing the results. Often, these can be spectacular.

In the future, it will probably be sparks thrown off by minds trained in still newer disciplines which produce the best hunches. Not that this amorphous, intuitive power will be any more measurable then. Of course, that is simply a hunch.

BEHAVIOR

It sometimes seems uncomfortably trite to say that management is getting things done through people. But that is nevertheless both true and crucially important. And that is why behavior in organizations is so fundamental to the civilization enterprise.

Always the point of departure here must be that people work, just as they engage in other activities, to get more of what they want. With that in mind, Edward Lawler III first addresses issues involving the "payoff" required to engage the motivation of the current generation of new workers. Stephen Kerr, does some rounding out of the basic concepts by emphasizing that organizations most dependably get from their members what these people believe they are being rewarded to do. We are next reminded by Edmund Gray, by way of a retrospective look at the Non Linear Systems "experiment," that it may be possible to become too narrowly preoccupied with the behavioral dimension of organizations as such. Richard Steers and Richard Mowday then look closely at one of the larger thrusts of thinking about motivation these days—job enrichment.

Sami Kassem takes off from the proposition that great novels can make a significant contribution to our understanding of the world we live in. In particular, he feels that Leo Tolstoy's War and Peace has instructive things to say about leadership and power in interaction with organization structure and processes. Howard Smith, taking off from a phrase in Edwin Markham's "The Man With the Hoe," emphasizes the importance of not making "stupidity assumptions" about workers bargaining with their more powerful partners in the organization. Focusing especially on what we often think of as the hardest case of all from the standpoint of the firm use of authority, military organizations, Morris Janowitz traces the development in large-scale bureaucracies of a much more flexible exercise of authority.

Of course, however, we prefer to think about the use of power and authority in organizations in terms of leadership. James Owen surveys for

233

us a great deal of what probably is, and what may not be, so in this realm. His conclusion is that we must still understand leadership as an important part of the art of management. A more explicitly contingency view of leadership is described by Chester Schriesheim, James Tolliver, and Orlando Behling. Their emphasis is the importance of keeping the leadership responsibility in perspective with other aspects of the manager's task. Bruce Harriman then discusses possibilities and processes in the realm of communication as one of the key ways managers effectively go at their responsibilities.

Just as people can develop neurotic symptoms, thereby becoming less competent for standard functioning, so can organizations. Jerry Harvey and Richard Albertson use this analogy to describe how organizations become neurotic—and how organizations that have become thus ineffective may be nursed back to better health. Patrick Connor examines more candidly than is customary the underlying premises that support this kind of organizational development work. This section is then concluded with an analysis by Martin Evans of why organizational development has been less successful than its most enthusiastic proponents once hoped.

These articles examine a wide variety of aspects of the vast realm of relationships known as organizational behavior. They should be very useful, therefore, in helping students round out a number of their understandings in this realm.

Edward E. Lawler III

University of Michigan

COMPENSATING THE NEW-LIFE-STYLE WORKER

Never before in the history of American business has there been so much discussion of problems in dealing with younger workers. The problems are, of course, part of a larger societal issue, reflected in much concern with the generation gap, Consciousness III, new life-style, and young people in general.

There is a good reason for the last few years' focus on the younger generation. All generations are different, but this one is in a sense *more* different. That is, its values, attitudes, and norms depart more radically from those of the immediately preceding generation than did those of earlier generations from their immediate predecessors'. It is precisely because of this leap that so many organizations have found it difficult to deal with the workers who are now joining them in large numbers.

These young people have failed to respond to traditional organizational practices in a number of areas, including selection, leadership, communication, and compensation. In this article the emphasis will be on compensation practices and how they will have to be changed if they are going to be compatible with the values and attitudes of many of the new-life-style workers—with the implication that many of the same kinds of changes are also needed in other areas.

Edward E. Lawler, III, "Compensating the New-Life-Style Worker," *Personnel*, May-June 1971, pp. 19–25.

235

Just who is this "new" worker, and what is he like?

Many of those who are beginning business careers accept the traditional American values, the Protestant-ethic approach to life; they present no particular problem. Others constitute groups in some ways different, yet similar—the culturally deprived, and the middle- or upper-class workers who reject traditional values and are committed to a self-actualizing approach to life. Although these two groups have disparate backgrounds, they share many attitudes and values that organizations find hard to understand and even harder to adapt to. Therefore these attitudes and values need to be examined:

Immediacy of Gratification. The currently popular term the "now generation" expresses the tendency of this generation to demand immediate action and results. Its members will have none of the view that some things must wait, that you can't change the world overnight. They are impatient and want to make tangible, basic changes this minute. It follows that when they perform in a way that they feel deserves a reward, they are not content to wait; they want the reward now.

Bases of Authority. In most business organizations authority historically has been based on position, and in society it has been based on age and position, but today's younger generation does not go along with these criteria of authority. Its criteria are personal integrity, expertise, and accomplishment. Moreover, it wants greater influence in decisions that affect people. For example, a study by D. A. Ondrack has shown that over the last 15 years college students' scores on Rokeach's dogmatism scale have gone down. Low scorers on the scale are likely to prefer participative decision making; to question the basis of authority; to be liberal, experimental, and intolerant of ambiguity; and to evaluate critically the legitimacy of authority and messages that come from authority figures.

Traditional Ways of Doing Things. The younger generation is often described as being very skeptical about traditional ways of doing things, unwilling to believe that "the right way" is automatically "the way it's always been done." This attitude ties in with the rejection of traditional authority; in both cases, this generation is saying that it has to be convinced by evidence or logic that a particular action is right. Often, the only means of getting young people's commitment to a particular action is to have them involved in the decision process.

Hypocrisy and Openness.   Personal integrity, openness, a willingness to confront issues, and letting people know where they stand are all high values of the now generation. Indeed, its members have an exaggerated fear and mistrust of decisions and actions that are taken in secret or behind closed doors and that are not open to close public scrutiny.

Mobility.   Change and personal mobility are not feared by the new-life-style worker; rather, he seems to seek them out. Many of these workers are concerned primarily with their own intellectual and emotional growth, and they recognize that to realize these aims they may have to be mobile. Thus, they are willing to change jobs, companies, and geographical locations frequently in the search for personal development.

WHERE OPINIONS DIFFER_____

Although the culturally deprived worker and the well-educated younger worker share many of the same values and attitudes, they part company when it comes to attitudes about material goods. Today's college graduate often seems to have a very cavalier attitude toward money and at times a contempt for the material goods it can purchase. Some even scorn the materialism of our society to the point of joining communes. More and more college students are turning down high-paying careers for lower-paying, to them more rewarding, ones. The disadvantaged worker, on the other hand, is demanding a greater share of the material goods that we are producing. He wants money and goods that it can buy. These groups thus differ widely in the kinds of rewards they want from work. This is not to say that money isn't important to the college-educated youth: it is important, but not to the same extent that it is to the less well-off, culturally deprived worker.

The two also differ in the kind of financial remuneration they want, because for them it serves different purposes. The culturally deprived worker needs cash to cover his day-to-day expenses, whereas the more affluent college-educated employee, if he is concerned about his pay, often wants special fringe benefits, such as time off to work on community problems. In either case, what the younger workers want in the way of compensation is quite different from the package that suits the older employee.

ADJUSTING PAY PRACTICES

It is obvious that many established compensation practices do not fit the attitudes and values of the new-life-style worker. In fact, some of the most common practices, such as secrecy and authoritarian decision making, represent the very characteristics of large organizations to which the younger generation objects most strongly. Eventually, compensation practices will have to change to accommodate the preferences of these new workers, because business needs them now and they, of course, represent the "establishment" of tomorrow. The only real question is how rapidly and how willingly companies are going to make these changes. Undoubtedly, some will change only after great pressure, but others will recognize that change is inevitable and will take the initiative.

What are these changes that will make pay practices more compatible with the values and expectations of the new kind of employee? It is impossible to predict all of them, but some can be pinpointed:

Immediacy of Reward.   The typical pay plan calls for raises to be given at regularly scheduled and often widely separated intervals. For example, many organizations have annual salary reviews, and raises are given out to all employees once a year. But a year can seem like an eternity to the kind of worker we are concerned with. Telling him that if he works hard now he will earn more money next year probably has no motivational effect on him at all, because he simply doesn't think that far in advance. He lives in the here-and-now and so responds best to short-term rewards and incentives.

Particularly in the case of the ghetto resident holding his first job, it is important that small, frequent raises be given if he is performing well. This recognition is preferable to giving a larger raise at a later time, because it provides more immediate feedback and goals to work toward. It also gives the company a means of building trust: It can promise something (a raise if performance is acceptable) and make good on that promise early in the relationship with an employee. The idea of giving immediate rewards is not new: learning and motivation theorists have for a long time pointed out the obvious advantages. However, the advent of the new-life-style worker now gives them added significance and suggests that the practice be extended beyond piece-rate and other incentive plans.

Elliott Jaques' work on time span of discretion is most relevant to the idea of giving immediate rewards. He points out that jobs differ in terms of the length of time it takes to identify how well employees are performing in them. As a rule, poor performance in lower-level jobs shows up very quickly, whereas poor performance in higher-level jobs may take years to show up. One inference from this fact is that the time between salary reviews may have to vary widely from one level to another. The yearly time interval that is commonly used for all levels may in fact be correct for many upper-level jobs (those the new breed of employee will eventually attain) but not for lower-level jobs (where they are now). *base on variability of the length to identify performance at different levels*

Participation in Pay Decisions. Pay plans have almost always been administered in a very authoritarian manner, even in companies that have moved toward Theory Y decision making. The superior decides who should receive raises, and the personnel or compensation department decides the type of pay plan that is used, the fringe benefits, and the rates that are paid for each nonunion job. The employee has no say at all, and the possibility of his having one never occurs to anyone, the assumption being that the workers' preoccupation with bettering their own pay would make it impossible for them to behave responsibly in these matters.

There is sound evidence, however, that the new-style workers who want to participate in some of the decisions concerning their pay should be allowed to. One study that I made showed that when workers were given the opportunity to participate in the design of an incentive plan they did behave responsibly, designing one that was not only effective but less expensive than the one management had in mind.

Companies that have had employees participate in job evaluation studies and salary surveys have hit on an easy and obvious way to increase employee involvement in pay decisions. In some cases, this involvement may lead to the employees' deciding the same thing that would have been decided if they had not participated. It may also turn out that they decide the traditional way of doing things is best, but this is all to the good. Young people today mistrust tradition: they have to discover things for themselves, even if this may sometimes mean that they in effect end up rediscovering the wheel.

Among compensation managers these days, there is considerable talk about employees' selecting the fringe benefits that they want, so that their benefits package will fit their individual needs. This smorgasbord approach has the double advantage of letting workers make important decisions about their pay at a relatively low cost to the organization.

In a few companies employees have been involved in deciding what their raises should be. This kind of participation as a general practice is a long way off, however, because it is so difficult to build the openness and trust that it requires, but as more of the younger generation grow into positions of authority, it, like participation in other areas, will be more common. Without waiting for that day, however, if the pay plans of organizations are to keep pace with the beliefs of this new group of employees they are going to have to make room for greater participation generally in decisions concerning pay.

Openness. Secrecy about management salaries is taken for granted in almost all business organizations, but it is a practice very likely to change as a result of the new workers' arrival on the scene. Secrecy is impossible if employees won't cooperate, and everything that is known about the younger generation suggests that it is something that they are not likely to go along with, because they strongly believe in openness and confrontation. In fact, the ones I have interviewed see salary secrecy as absurd and as a sign of how "up tight" most bureaucratic organizations are. At the lower managerial levels of many companies secrecy has already broken down, because the younger managers openly discuss their pay with each other. As these managers are promoted, it can be expected that secrecy will break down at the higher levels, too.

The disappearance of this secrecy may not be a bad thing, provided organizations prepare for it by participatively developing defensible pay systems. At the moment, many companies keep pay secret for the very good reason that they simply cannot justify their current pay systems. Since it is unlikely that they are going to be able to keep pay secret much longer, it behooves them to prepare now for the time when pay will be more open to scrutiny.

There is also evidence that secrecy has a number of dysfunctional consequences that are not generally recognized. It has been shown, for example, that where secrecy exists managers overestimate the pay of other managers at their own levels and at levels below them, so they are more dissatisfied with their pay than they would be if they knew the actual pay received by others. In addition, they tend to underestimate the pay of managers above them, with the result that promotion seems less attractive. Thus, making pay more public might actually be a step forward from the company's point of view.

Individualizing Compensation Plans. It has been suggested that organizations use smorgasbord, or cafeteria-style, benefits plans, so that individuals can pick the fringe benefits they want. In addition to the psychological advantage of allowing them to make important decisions about their pay, with the ever-increasing diversity in the working population, such plans seem to be the only way that companies can tailor benefits to the specific needs of their employees. The ghetto resident, the young college graduate, the older manager, and the older blue-collar worker—not to mention top executives—do not want or need the same fringe benefits. This situation is usually handled by giving somewhat different plans to managers and workers, but it is a solution that really doesn't individualize the plans enough. Often, there is more similarity among certain groups of managers and workers—for example, older managers with families and older workers with families—than there is among all the nonmanagerial or all the managerial employees.

In the case of the now-generation workers we are discussing, there is particular interest in portability of pensions, because these workers are so much more mobile than their older counterparts. But these younger workers are only reinforcing a broader trend, and it looks as if companies must make pensions portable or the federal government will intervene and require that it be done.

Speaking more generally, if the importance of pay fluctuates among various groups, then the importance of flexible pay plans will increase. It doesn't make sense to put a person who doesn't value pay on a pay-for-performance plan. Some other source of motivation must be found—job redesign, leadership, what have you. The point is that as individual differences multiply the organization will have to multiply its efforts to adapt to the individual in setting pay practices. This may mean placing only those people who value compensation on incentive plans: therefore, a concomitant adjustment in placement procedures seems to be in the wind.

If these prognostications about the impact of the new-life-style worker are correct, the next decade will be a difficult one for company managers, and especially for those who administer compensation. What they are doing will be questioned closely, and they will be asked to make major changes in pay practices by some employees at the same time they are told by others that pay is really not very important. Aside from this confusion, some of the changes demanded will require basic shifts in management philosophy. For example, openness about salaries and participation in salary decisions are totally incompatible with an authoritarian management style—and management style is, after all, set by top executives, In the end, of course, many of these changes will come about, because of the pressures exerted by the new generation—but not without perhaps unprecedented stress on the "older generation."

Steven Kerr

University of Southern California

ON THE FOLLY
OF REWARDING A,
WHILE HOPING FOR B

Whether dealing with monkeys, rats, or human beings, it is hardly controversial to state that most organisms seek information concerning what activities are rewarded, and then seek to do (or at least pretend to do) those things, often to the virtual exclusion of activities not rewarded. The extent to which this occurs of course will depend on the perceived attractiveness of the rewards offered, but neither operant nor expectancy theorists would quarrel with the essence of this notion.

Nevertheless, numerous examples exist of reward systems that are fouled up in that behaviors which are rewarded are those which the rewarder is trying to *discourage*, while the behavior he desires is not being rewarded at all.

In an effort to understand and explain this phenomenon, this paper presents examples from society, from organizations in general, and from profit making firms in particular. Data from a manufacturing company, and information from an insurance firm are examined to demonstrate the consequences of such reward systems for the organizations involved, and possible reasons why such reward systems continue to exist are considered.

Steven Kerr, "On the Folly of Rewarding A, While Hoping for B," *Academy of Management Journal*, December 1975, pp. 769–783.

SOCIETAL EXAMPLES_____

Politics

Official goals are "purposely vague and general and do not indicate . . . the host of decisions that must be made among alternative ways of achieving official goals and the priority of multiple goals. . ." (8, p. 66). They usually may be relied on to offend absolutely no one, and in this sense can be considered high-acceptance, low-quality goals. An example might be "build better schools." Operative goals are higher in quality but lower in acceptance, since they specify where the money will come from, what alternative goals will be ignored, etc.

The American citizenry supposedly wants its candidates for public office to set forth operative goals, making their proposed programs "perfectly clear," specifying sources and uses of funds, etc. However, since operative goals are lower in acceptance, and since aspirants to public office need acceptance (from at least 50.1 percent of the people), most politicians prefer to speak only of official goals, at least until after the election. They of course would agree to speak at the operative level if "punished" for not doing so. The electorate could do this by refusing to support candidates who do not speak at the operative level.

Instead, however, the American voter typically punishes (withholds support from) candidates who frankly discuss where the money will come from, rewards politicians who speak only of official goals, but hopes that candidates (despite the reward system) will discuss the issues operatively. It is academic whether it was moral for Nixon, for example, to refuse to discuss his 1968 "secret plan" to end the Vietnam war, his 1972 operative goals concerning the lifting of price controls, the reshuffling of his cabinet, etc. The point is that the reward system made such refusal rational.

It seems worth mentioning that no manuscript can adequately define what is "moral" and what is not. However, examination of costs and benefits, combined with knowledge of what motivates a particular individual, often will suffice to determine what for him is "rational."[1] If the reward system is so designed that it is irrational to be moral, this does not necessarily mean that immorality will result. But is this not asking for trouble?

_____

[1] In Simon's (10, pp. 76–77) terms, a decision is "subjectively rational" if it maximizes an individual's valued outcomes so far as his knowledge permits. A decision is "personally rational" if it is oriented toward the individual's goals.

War

If some oversimplification may be permitted, let it be assumed that the primary goal of the organization (Pentagon, Luftwaffe, or whatever) is to win. Let it be assumed further that the primary goal of most individuals on the front lines is to get home alive. Then there appears to be an important conflict in goals—personally rational behavior by those at the bottom will endanger goal attainment by those at the top.

But not necessarily! It depends on how the reward system is set up. The Vietnam war was indeed a study of disobedience and rebellion, with terms such as "fragging" (killing one's own commanding officer) and "search and evade" becoming part of the military vocabulary. The difference in subordinates' acceptance of authority between World War II and Vietnam is reported to be considerable, and veterans of the Second World War often have been quoted as being outraged at the mutinous actions of many American soldiers in Vietnam.

Consider, however, some critical differences in the reward system in use during the two conflicts. What did the GI in World War II want? To go home. And when did he get to go home? When the war was won! If he disobeyed the orders to clean out the trenches and take the hills, the war would not be won and he would not go home. Furthermore, what were his chances of attaining his goal (getting home alive) if he obeyed the orders compared to his chances if he did not? What is being suggested is that the rational soldier in World War II, *whether patriotic or not*, probably found it expedient to obey.

Consider the reward system in use in Vietnam. What did the man at the bottom want? To go home. And when did he get to go home? Whan his tour of duty was over! This was the case *whether or not* the war was won. Furthermore, concerning the relative chance of getting home alive by obeying orders compared to the chance if they were disobeyed, it is worth noting that a mutineer in Vietnam was far more likely to be assigned rest and rehabilitation (on the assumption that fatigue was the cause) than he was to suffer any negative consequence.

In his description of the "zone of indifference," Barnard stated that "a person can and will accept a communication as authoritative only when . . . at the time of this decision, he believes it to be compatible with his personal interests as a whole" (1, p. 165). In light of the reward system used in Vietnam, would it not have been personally irrational for some orders to have been obeyed? Was not the military implementing a system which *rewarded* disobedience, while *hoping* that soldiers (despite the reward system) would obey orders?

Medicine

Theoretically, a physician can make either of two types of error, and intuitively one seems as bad as the other. A doctor can pronounce a patient sick when he is actually well, thus causing him needless anxiety and expense, curtailment of enjoyable foods and activities, and even physical danger by subjecting him to needless medication and surgery. Alternately, a doctor can label a sick person well, and thus avoid treating what may be a serious, even fatal ailment. It might be natural to conclude that physicians seek to minimize both types of error.

Such a conclusion would be wrong.[2] It is estimated that numerous Americans are presently afflicted with iatrogenic (physician *caused*) illnesses (9). This occurs when the doctor is approached by someone complaining of a few stray symptoms. The doctor classifies and organizes these symptoms, gives them a name, and obligingly tells the patient what further symptoms may be expected. This information often acts as a self-fulfilling prophecy, with the result that from that day on the patient for all practical purposes is sick.

Why does this happen? Why are physicians so reluctant to sustain a type 2 error (pronouncing a sick person well) that they will tolerate many type 1 errors? Again, a look at the reward system is needed. The punishments for a type 2 error are real: guilt, embarrassment, and the threat of lawsuit and scandal. On the other hand, a type 1 error (labeling a well person sick) "is sometimes seen as sound clinical practice, indicating a healthy conservative approach to medicine" (9. p. 69). Type 1 errors also are likely to generate increased income and a stream of steady customers who, being well in a limited physiological sense, will not embarrass the doctor by dying abruptly.

Fellow physicians and the general public therefore are really *rewarding* type 1 errors and at the same time *hoping* fervently that doctors will try not to make them.

---

[2] In one study (4) of 14,867 films for signs of tuberculosis, 1,216 positive readings turned out to be clinically negative; only 24 negative readings proved clinically active, a ratio of 50 to 1.

GENERAL ORGANIZATIONAL EXAMPLES

Rehabilitation Centers and Orphanages

In terms of the prime beneficiary classification (2, p. 42) organizations such as these are supposed to exist for the "public-in-contact," that is, clients. The orphanage therefore theoretically is interested in placing as many children as possible in good homes. However, often orphanages surround themselves with so many rules concerning adoption that it is nearly impossible to pry a child out of the place. Orphanages may deny adoption unles the applicants are a married couple, both of the same religion as the child, without history of emotional or vocational instability, with a specified minimum income and a private room for the child, etc.

If the primary goal is to place children in good homes, then the rules ought to constitute means toward that goal. Goal displacement results when these "means become ends-in-themselves that displace the original goals" (2, p. 229).

To some extent these rules are required by law. But the influence of the reward system on the orphanage's management should not be ignored. Consider, for example, that the:

1. Number of children enrolled often is the most important determinant of the size of the allocated budget.
2. Number of children under the director's care also will affect the size of his staff.
3. Total organizational size will determine largely the director's prestige at the annual conventions, in the community, etc.

Therefore, to the extent that staff size, total budget, and personal prestige are valued by the orphanage's executive personnel, it becomes rational for them to make it difficult for children to be adopted. After all, who wants to be the director of the smallest orphanage in the state?

If the reward system errs in the opposite direction, paying off only for placements, extensive goal displacement again is likely to result. A common example of vocational rehabilitation in many states, for example, consists of placing someone in a job for which he has little interest and few qualifications, for two months or so, and then "rehabilitating" him again in another position. Such behavior is quite consistent with the prevailing reward system, which pays off for the number of individuals placed in any position for 60 days or more. Rehabilitation counselors also confess to competing with one another to place relatively skilled clients, sometimes ignoring persons with few skills who would be harder to place. Extensively disabled clients find that counselors often prefer to work with those whose disabilities are less severe.[3]

Universities

Society *hopes* that teachers will not neglect their teaching responsibilities but *rewards* them almost entirely for research and publications. This is most true at the large and prestigious universities. Cliches such as "good research and good teaching go together" notwithstanding, professors often find that they must choose between teaching and research oriented activities when allocating their time. Rewards for good teaching usually are limited to outstanding teacher awards, which are given to only a small percentage of good teachers and which usually bestow little money and fleeting prestige. Punishments for poor teaching also are rare.

Rewards for research and publication, on the other hand, and punishments for failure to accomplish these, are commonly administered by universities at which teachers are employed. Furthermore, publication oriented resumés usually will be well received at other universities, whereas teaching credentials, harder to document and quantify, are much less transferable. Consequently it is rational for university teachers to concentrate on research, even if to the detriment of teaching and at the expense of their students.

By the same token, it is rational for students to act based upon the goal displacement which has occurred within universities concerning what they are rewarded for. If it is assumed that a primary goal of a university is to transfer knowledge from teacher to student, then grades become identifiable as a means towards that goal, serving as motivational, control, and feedback devices to expedite the knowledge transfer. Instead, however, the grades themselves have become much more important for entrance to graduate school, successful employment, tuition refunds, parental respect, than the knowledge or lack of knowledge they are supposed to signify.

It therefore should come as no surprise that information has surfaced in recent years concerning fraternity files for examinations, term paper writing services, organized cheating at the service academies, and the like. Such activities constitute a personally rational response to a reward system which pays off for grades rather than knowledge.

[3] Personal interviews conducted during 1972–1973.

BUSINESS RELATED EXAMPLES

Ecology

Assume that the president of XYZ Corporation is confronted with the following alternatives:

1. Spend $11 million for antipollution equipment to keep from poisoning fish in the river adjacent to the plant; or
2. Do nothing, in violation of the law, and assume a one-in-ten chance of being caught, with a resultant $1 million fine plus the necessity of buying the equipment.

Under this not unrealistic set of choices it requires no linear program to determine that XYZ Corporation can maximize its probabilities by flouting the law. Add the fact that XYZ's president is probably being rewarded (by creditors, stockholders, and other salient parts of his task environment) according to criteria totally unrelated to the number of fish poisoned, and his probable course of action becomes clear.

Evaluation of Training

It is axiomatic that those who care about a firm's well-being should insist that the organization get fair value for its expenditures. Yet it is commonly known that firms seldom bother to evaluate a new GRID, MBO, job enrichment program, or whatever, to see if the company is getting its money's worth. Why? Certainly it is not because people have not pointed out that this situation exists; nummerous practitioner oriented articles are written each year to just this point.

The individuals (whether in personnel, manpower planning, or wherever) who normally would be responsible for conducting such evaluations are the same ones often charged with introducing the change effort in the first place. Having convinced top management to spend the money, they usually are quite animated afterwards in collecting arigorous vignettes and anecdotes about how successful the program was. The last thing many desire is a formal, systematic, and revealing evaluation. Although members of top management may actually *hope* for such systematic evaluation, their reward systems continue to *reward* ignorance in this area. And if the personnel department abdicates its responsibility, who is to step into the breach? The change agent himself? Hardly! He is likely to be too busy collecting anecdotal "evidence" of his own, for use with his next client.

Miscellaneous.   Many additional examples could be cited of systems which in fact are rewarding behaviors other than those supposedly desired by the rewarder. A few of these are described briefly below.

Most coaches disdain to discuss individual accomplishments, preferring to speak of teamwork, proper attitude, and a one-for-all spirit. Usually, however, rewards are distibuted according to individual performance. The college basketball player who feeds his teammates instead of shooting will not compile impressive scoring statistics and is less likely to be drafted by the pros. The ballplayer who hits to right field to advance the runners will win neither the batting nor home run titles, and will be offered smaller raises. It therefore is rational for players to think of themselves first, and the team second.

In business organizations where rewards are dispensed for unit performance or for individual goals achieved, without regard for overall effectiveness, similar attitudes often are observed. Under most Management by Objectives (MBO) systems, goals in areas where quantification is difficult often go unspecified. The organization, therefore, often is in a position where it *hopes* for employee effort in the areas of team building, interpersonal relations, creativity, but it formally *rewards* none of these. In cases where promotions and raises are formally tied to MBO, the system itself contains a paradox in that it "asks employees to set challenging, risky goals, only to face smaller paychecks and possibly damaged careers if these goals are not accomplished" (5, p. 40).

It is *hoped* that administrators will pay attention to long run costs and opportunities and will institute programs which will bear fruit later on. However, many organizational reward systems pay off for short run sales and earnings only. Under such circumstances it is personally rational for officials to sacrifice long term growth and profit (by selling off equipment and property, or by stifling research and development) for short term advantages. This probably is most pertinent in the public sector, with the result that many public officials are unwilling to implement programs which will not show benefits by election time.

As a final, clear-cut example of a fouled-up reward system, consider the cost-plus contract or its next of kin, the allocation of next year's budget as a direct function of this year's expenditues. It probably is conceivable that those who award such budgets and contracts really hope for economy and prudence in spending. It is obvious, however, that adopting the proverb "to him who spends shall more be given," rewards not economy, but spending itself.

TWO COMPANIES' EXPERIENCES

A Manufacturing Organization

A midwest manufacturer of industrial goods had been troubled for some time by aspects of its organizational climate it believed dysfunctional. For research purposes, interviews were conducted with many employees and a questionnaire was administered on a companywide basis, including plants and offices in several American and Canadian locations. The company strongly encouraged employee participation in the survey, and made available time and space during the workday for completion of the instrument. All employees in attendance during the day of the survey completed the questionnaire. All instruments were collected directly by the researcher, who personally administered each session. Since no one employed by the firm handled the questionnaires, and since respondent names were not asked for, it seems likely that the pledge of anonymity given was believed.

A modified version of the Expect Approval scale (7) was included as part of the questionnaire. The instrument asked respondents to indicate the degree of approval or disapproval they could expect if they performed each of the described actions. A seven point Likert scale was used, with one indicating that the action would probably bring strong disapproval and seven signifying likely strong approval.

Although normative data for this scale from studies of other organizations are unavailable, it is possible to examine fruitfully the data obtained from this survey in several ways. First, it may be worth noting that the questionnaire data corresponded closely to information gathered through interviews. Furthermore, as can be seen from the results summarized in Table 1 (see pp. 252–253), sizable differences between various work units, and between employees at different job levels within the same work unit, were obtained. This suggests that response bias effects (social desirability in particular loomed as a potential concern) are not likely to be severe.

Most importantly, comparisons between scores obtained on the Expect Approval scale and a statement of problems which were the reason for the survey revealed that the same behaviors which managers in each division thought dysfunctional were those which lower level employees claimed were rewarded. As compared to job levels 1 to 8 in Division B (see Table 1), those in Division A claimed a much higher acceptance by management of "conforming" activities. Between 31 and 37 percent of Division A employees at levels 1–8 stated that going along with the majority, agreeing with the boss, and staying on everyone's good side brought approval; only once (level 5–8 responses to one of the three items) did a majority suggest that such actions would generate disapproval.

Furthermore, responses from Division A workers at levels 1–4 indicate that behaviors geared toward risk avoidance were as likely to be rewarded as to be punished. Only at job levels 9 and above was it apparent that the reward system was positively reinforcing behaviors desired by top management. Overall, the same "tendencies toward conservatism and apple-polishing at the lower levels" which divisional management had complained about during the interviews were those claimed by subordinates to be the most rational course of action in light of the existing reward system. Management apparently was not getting the behaviors it was *hoping* for, but it certainly was getting the behaviors it was perceived by subordinates to be *rewarding*.

An Insurance Firm

The Group Health Claims Division of a large eastern insurance company provides another rich illustration of a reward system which reinforces behaviors not desired by top management.

Attempting to measure and reward accuracy in paying surgical claims, the firm systematically keeps track of the number of returned checks and letters of complaint received from policyholders. However, underpayments are likely to provoke cries of outrage from the insured, while overpayments often are accepted in courteous silence. Since it often is impossible to tell from the physician's statement which of two surgical procedures, with different allowable benefits, was performed, and since writing for clarifications will interfere with other standards used by the firm concerning "percentage of claims paid within two days of receipt," the new hire in more than one claims section is soon acquainted with the informal norm: "When in doubt, pay it out!"

The situation would be even worse were it not for the fact that other features of the firm's reward system tend to neutralize those described. For example, annual "merit" increases are given to all employees, in one of the following three amounts:

1. If the worker is "outstanding" (a select category, into which no more than two employees per section may be placed): 5 per cent
2. If the worker is "above average" (normally all workers not "outstanding" are so rated): 4 per cent
3. If the worker commmits gross acts of negligence and irresponsibility for which he might be discharged in many other companies: 3 per cent.

Now, since (a) the difference between the 5 per cent theoretically attainable through hard work and the 4 per cent attainable merely by living until the review date is small, and (b) since insurance firms seldom dispense much of a salary increase in cash (rather, the worker's insurance benefits increase, causing him to be further overinsured), many employees are rather indiffer-

TABLE 1
Summary of Two Divisions' Data Relevant to Conforming and Risk-Avoidance Behaviors (Extent to Which Subjects Expect Approval)

Dimension	Item	Division and Sample	Total Responses	Percentage of Workers Responding		
				1, 2, or 3 Disapproval	4	5, 6, or 7 Approval
Risk Avoidance	Making a risky decision based on the best information available at the time, but which turns out wrong.	A, levels 1–4 (lowest)	127	61	25	14
		A, levels 5–8	172	46	31	23
		A, levels 9 and above	17	41	30	30
		B, levels 1–4 (lowest)	31	58	26	16
		B, levels 5–8	19	42	42	16
		B, levels 9 and above	10	50	20	30
	Setting extremely high and challenging standards and goals, and then narrowly failing to make them.	A, levels 1–4	122	47	28	25
		A, levels 5–8	168	33	26	41
		A, levels 9+	17	24	6	70
		B, levels 1–4	31	48	23	29
		B, levels 5–8	18	17	33	50
		B, levels 9+	10	30	0	70
	Setting goals which are extremely easy to make and then making them.	A, levels 1–4	124	35	30	35
		A, levels 5–8	171	47	27	26
		A, levels 9+	17	70	24	6
		B, levels 1–4	31	58	26	16
		B, levels 5–8	19	63	16	21
		B, levels 9+	10	80	0	20

ent to the possibility of obtaining the extra 1 percent reward and therefore tend to ignore the norm concerning indiscriminant payments.

However, most employees are not indifferent to the rule which states that, should absences or latenesses total three or more in any six-month period, the entire 4 or 5 percent due at the next "merit" review must be forfeited. In this sense the firm may be described as *hoping* for performance, while *rewarding* attendance. What it gets, of course, is attendance. (If the absence-lateness rule appears to the reader to be stringent, it really is not. The company counts "times" rather than "days" absent, and a ten-day absence therefore counts the same as one lasting two days. A worker in danger of accumulating a third absence within six months merely has to remain ill (away from work) during his second absence until his first absence is more than six months old. The limiting factor is that at some point his salary ceases, and his sickness benefits take over. This usually is sufficient to get the younger workers to return, but for those with 20 or more years' service,

TABLE 1 (continued)

Conformity	Being a "yes man" and always agreeing with the boss.	A, levels 1–4	126	46	17	37
		A, levels 5–8	180	54	14	31
		A, levels 9+	17	88	12	0
		B, levels 1–4	32	53	28	19
		B, levels 5–8	19	68	21	11
		B, levels 9+	10	80	10	10
	Always going along with the majority.	A, levels 1–4	125	40	25	35
		A, levels 5–8	173	47	21	32
		A, levels 9+	17	70	12	18
		B, levels 1–4	31	61	23	16
		B, levels 5–8	19	68	11	21
		B, levels 9+	10	80	10	10
	Being careful to stay on the good side of everyone, so that everyone agrees that you are a great guy.	A, levels 1–4	124	45	18	37
		A, levels 5–8	173	45	22	33
		A, levels 9+	17	64	6	30
		B, levels 1–4	31	54	23	23
		B, levels 5–8	19	73	11	16
		B, levels 9+	10	80	10	10

the company provides sickness benefits of 90 per cent of normal salary, tax-free! Therefore. . . .)

CAUSES

Extremely diverse instances of systems which reward behavior A although the rewarder apparently hopes for behavior B have been given. These are useful to illustrate the breadth and magnitude of the phenomenon, but the diversity increases the difficulty of determining commonalities and establishing causes. However, four general factors may be pertinent to an explanation of why fouled up reward systems seem to be so prevelant.

Fascination with an "Objective" Criterion

It has been mentioned elsewhere that:

> Most "objective" measures of productivity are objective only in that their subjective elements are a) determined in advance, rather than coming into play at the time of the formal evaluation, and b) well concealed on the rating instrument itself. Thus industrial firms seeking to devise objective rating systems first decide, in an arbitrary manner, what dimensions are to be rated, . . . usually including some items having little to do with organizational effectiveness while excluding others that do. Only then does Personnel Division churn out official-looking documents on which all dimensions chosen to be rated are assigned point values, categories, or whatever (6, p. 92).

Nonetheless, many individuals seek to establish simple, quantifiable standards against which to measure and reward performance. Such efforts may be successful in highly predictable areas within an organization, but are likely to cause goal displacements when applied anywhere else. Overconcern with attendance and lateness in the insurance firm and with number of people placed in the vocational rehabilitation division may have been largely responsible for the problems described in those organizations.

Overemphasis on Highly Visible Behaviors

Difficulties often stem from the fact that some parts of the task are highly visible while other parts are not. For example, publications are easier to demonstrate than teaching, and scoring baskets and hitting home runs are more readily observable than feeding teammates and advancing base runners. Similarly, the adverse consequences of pronouncing a sick person well are more visible than those sustained by labeling a well person sick. Team-building and creativity are other examples of behaviors which may not be rewarded simply because they are hard to observe.

Hypocrisy

In some of the instances described the rewarder may have been getting the desired behavior, notwithstanding claims that the behavior was not desired. This may be true, for example, of management's attitude toward apple-polishing in the manufacturing firm (a behavior which subordinates felt was rewarded, despite management's avowed dislike of the practice). This also may explain politicians' unwillingness to revise the penalties for disobedi-ence of ecology laws, and the failure of top management to devise reward systems which would cause systematic evaluation of training and develop-ment programs.

Emphasis on Morality or Equity Rather than Efficiency

Sometimes consideration of other factors prevents the establishment of a system which rewards behaviors desired by the rewarder. The felt obligation of many Americans to vote for one candidate or another, for example, may impair their ability to withhold support from politicians who refuse to discuss the issues. Similarly, the concern for spreading the risks and costs of wartime military service may outweigh the advantage to be obtained by committing personnel to combat until the war is over.

It should be noted that only with respect to the first two causes are reward systems really paying off for other than desired behaviors. In the case of the third and fourth causes the system *is* rewarding behaviors desired by the rewarder, and the systems are fouled up only from the standpoint of those who believe the rewarder's public statements (cause 3), or those who seek to maximize efficiency rather than other outcomes (cause 4).

CONCLUSIONS_____

Modern organization theory requires a recognition that the members of organizations and society possess divergent goals and motives. It therefore is unlikely that managers and their subordinates will seek the same out-comes. Three possible remedies for this potential problem are suggested.

Selection

It is theoretically possible for organizations to employ only those individuals whose goals and motives are wholly consonant with those of management. In such cases the same behaviors judged by subordinates to be rational would be perceived by management as desirable. State-of-the-art reviews of selection techniques, however, provide scant grounds for hope that such an approach would be successful (for example, see 12).

suggest little success in this area

Training

Another theoretical alternative is for the organization to admit those employees whose goals are not consonant with those of management and then, through training, socialization, or whatever, alter employee goals to make them consonant. However, research on the effectiveness of such training programs, though limited, provides further grounds for pessimism (for example, see 3).

Altering the Reward System

What would have been the result if:

1. Nixon had been assured by his advisors that he could not win reelection except by discussing the issues in detail?
2. Physicians' conduct was subjected to regular examination by review boards for type 1 errors (calling healthy people ill) and to penalties (fines, censures, etc.) for errors of either type?
3. The President of XYZ Corporation had to choose between (a) spending $11 million dollars for antipollution equipment, and (b) incurring a fifty-fifty chance of going to jail for five years?

Managers who complain that their workers are not motivated might do well to consider the possibility that they have installed reward systems which are paying off for behaviors other than those they are seeking. This, in part, is what happened in Vietnam, and this is what regularly frustrates societal efforts to bring about honest politicians, civic-minded managers, etc. This certainly is what happened in both the manufacturing and the insurance companies.

A first step for such managers might be to find out what behaviors currently are being rewarded. Perhaps an instrument similar to that used in the manufacturing firm could be useful for this purpose. Chances are excellent that these managers will be surprised by what they find—that their firms are not rewarding what they assume they are. In fact, such undesirable behavior by organizational members as they have observed may be explained largely by the reward systems in use.

This is not to say that all organizational behavior is determined by formal rewards and punishments. Certainly it is true that in the absence of formal reinforcement some soldiers will be patriotic, some presidents will be ecology minded, and some orphanage directors will care about children. The point, however, is that in such cases the rewarder is not *causing* the behaviors desired but is only a fortunate bystander. For an organization to *act* upon its members, the formal reward system should positively reinforce desired behaviors, not constitute an obstacle to be overcome.

It might be wise to underscore the obvious fact that there is nothing really new in what has been said. In both theory and practice these matters have been mentioned before. Thus in many states Good Samaritan laws have been installed to protect doctors who stop to assist a stricken motorist. In states without such laws it is commonplace for doctors to refuse to stop, for fear of involvement in a subsequent lawsuit. In college basketball additional penalties have been instituted against players who foul their opponents deliberately. It has long been argued by Milton Friedman and others that penalties should be altered so as to make it irrational to disobey the ecology laws, and so on.

By altering the reward system the organization escapes the necessity of selecting only desirable people or of trying to alter undesirable ones. In Skinnerian terms (as described in 11, p. 704), "As for responsibility and goodness—as commonly defined—no one . . . would want or need them. They refer to a man's behaving well despite the absence of positive reinforcement that is obviously sufficient to explain it. Where such reinforcement exists, 'no one needs goodness.' "

REFERENCES_____

1. Barnard, Chester I. *The Functions of the Executive* Cambridge, Mass.: Harvard University Press, 164).
2. Blau, Peter M., and W. Richard Scott. *Formal Organizations* (San Francisco: Chandler, 1962).
3. Fiedler, Fred E. "Predicting the Effects of Leadership Training and Experience from the Contingency Model," *Journal of Applied Psychology*, Vol. 56 (1972), 114–119.

4. Garland, L. H. "Studies of the Accuracy of Diagnostic Procedures," *American Journal Roentgenological, Radium Therapy Nuclear Medicine*, Vol. 82 (1959), 25–38.

5. Kerr, Steven. "Some Modifications in MBO as an OD Strategy," *Academy of Management Proceedings*, 1973, pp. 39–42.

6. Kerr, Steven. "What Price Objectivity?" *American Sociologist*, Vol. 8 (1973), 92–93.

7. Litwin, G. H., and R. A. Stringer, Jr. *Motivation and Organizational Climate* (Boston: Harvard University Press, 1968).

8. Perrow, Charles. "The Analysis of Goals in Complex Organizations," in A. Etzioni (Ed.), *Readings on Modern Organizations* (Englewood Cliffs, N. J.: Prentice-Hall, 1969).

9. Scheff, Thomas J. "Decision Rules, Types of Error, and Their Consequences in Medical Diagnosis," in F. Massarik and P. Ratoosh (Eds.), *Mathematical Explorations in Behavioral Science* (Homewood, Ill.: Irwin, 1965).

10. Simon, Herbert A. *Administrative Behavior* (New York: Free Press, 1957).

11. Swanson, G. E. "Review Symposium: Beyond Freedom and Dignity," *American Journal of Sociology*, Vol. 78 (1972), 702–705.

12. Webster, E. *Decision Making in the Employment Interview* (Montreal: Industrial Relations Center, McGill University, 1964).

Edmund R. Gray

Louisiana State University

THE NON LINEAR
SYSTEMS EXPERIENCE:
A REQUIEM

The organizational changes instituted in 1960–1961 at Non Linear Systems, Inc. (NLS), a small manufacturer and marketer of digital electrical measuring instruments, represent one of the most celebrated and ambitious "field experiments" in a business firm since the famous Hawthorne Studies performed by the Western Electric Company between 1927 and 1932. NLS instituted a package of drastic changes, the most important of which were the following:[1]

Organizational Structure. A flat structure with wide spans of management consisting of three levels was established: an executive council made up of the president and seven vice-presidents; approximately thirty managers of departments, project teams, and marketing regions; and the worker level, including assistant managers in some of the larger departments. The executive council functioned primarily as a planning and policymaking

Edmund R. Gray, "The Non Linear Systems Experience: A Requiem," *Business Horizons*, February 1978, pp. 31–36.

NOTE: The author gained first-hand knowledge of Non Linear Systems, Inc. while conducting a field research project there in 1961. More recent information on the company has been gleaned from secondary sources. The recent portion of the study was funded by a grant from the LSU Foundation.

[1] For a more complete description of these organizational changes, see Cyril O'Donnell, *Cases in General Management*, rev. ed. (Homewood, Ill.: Richard D. Irwin, 1965), pp. 36–59.

body. The several department managers reported to the whole council rather than to individual members and were delegated almost complete authority for operational matters. Prior to the organizational changes, NLS had a traditional hierarchical structure with typical reporting arrangements.

Work Organization. Assembly line operations were eliminated and replaced by instrument assembly teams. A typical team consisted of three to twelve workers and an assistant manager. Under this arrangement, batches of instruments were completely built and checked out by a single team. Ideally, the teams would plan their own work and the members would assist each other in performing the overall task.

Wage Changes. Hourly wages were eliminated, and all workers were placed on straight salary with a minimum of $100 per week established (this was $24 higher than the lowest wage on the hourly scale in 1960). Time clocks were eliminated and workers were not docked for absence. Moreover, a policy of continuous employment without layoffs was announced.

Accounting Changes. The accounting department as such was expunged. The record-keeping function was reduced to a minimum and placed with the individual departments. A policy of "say it, don't write it" was established.

During the early years after the initiation of the changes, both the company and its president, Andrew F. Kay, were praised lavishly by scholars, journalists, and practitioners for their willingness to engage in such an ambitious experiment. It was frequently suggested that the results proved the validity of the underlying behavioral theory.

In 1965, with diminishing sales and increasingly unfavorable competitive conditions, NLS introduced such extensive structural modifications "as to signify the end of the experiment."[2] Again, in 1970, additional reactionary changes were initiated.

With the abandonment of the "experiment," critics were quick to blame the behavioral theories presumably being tested. Richard Farson, for example, asserted, "I think we now know that human relations don't have a lot to do with profit or production."[3] Erwin Malone in his analysis suggested that the NLS experience demonstrates that participative management does not work.

In my opinion the early advocates of the experiment were engaging in

---

[2] Erwin L. Malone, "The Non Linear Systems Experiment in Participative Management," *The Journal of Business of the University of Chicago* (January 1975), p. 57.

[3] *Business Week* (January 20, 1973), pp. 99–100.

wishful thinking rather than dispassionate judgment, while the more recent critics have been too sweeping in their denouncement of the applicability of behaviorial theory to industrial settings. In this paper I have attempted to place the NLS experience in a more objective perspective. To do this it is necessary to dispel three popular misconceptions: that it was a scientific experiment, that it tested participative management, and that it tested the theories of the leading behavioral writers of the day.

NOT AN EXPERIMENT

Although the term "experiment" is usually applied to the organizational changes at NLS in 1960–1961, those changes cannot be considered an experiment in the scientific sense of the word. James L. Gibson and associates state that for an investigation to be considered an experiment, it must contain two essential elements—the manipulation of some variable (independent variable) by the researcher, and the observation or measurement of the results (dependent variable) while maintaining all other factors unchanged.[4] Where possible it is advisable to establish separate control and experimental groups to monitor unanticipated variables. The experimental methodology permits the researcher to conclude that any changes in the dependent variable are attributable to changes in the independent variable.

A well-known example of a field experiment in industry is the Sears, Roebuck study on "flat" versus "tall" organization structures in the late 1940s. Two groups of similar stores were observed. In the experimental group of stores, thirty departmental managers reported to the store manager and assistant manager. The other group of stores (the control group) was structured in the traditional way with an additional level of management between the department heads and the store manager. The quantitative results clearly show that, at least for Sears, Roebuck, the flat structure was more effective.[5]

Unlike Sears, NLS failed to meet the requirements of scientific experimentation in two fundamental ways. First, a single independent variable was not manipulated. Instead, numerous major changes were introduced into the organization almost simultaneously, so that it would have been impossible to attribute results at a later date to specific independent variables. Second,

---

[4] James L. Gibson, John M. Ivancevich, and James H. Donnelly, *Organizations: Structure, Process Behavior* (Dallas: Business Publications, 1973), p. 14.

[5] Harold Koontz and Cyril O'Donnell, *Management: A Systems and Contingency Analysis of Managerial Functions*, 6th ed. (New York: McGraw-Hill, 1976), pp. 291–292.

dependent variables were not established prior to the introduction of the changes and then later measured. Malone has emphasized that one of the principal problems in attempting to evaluate the NLS experience is the fact that the company kept few records; hence, measurable data for analysis was not available.

If the NLS executives had been interested in scientific experimentation (and there is no indication they were), they could have introduced changes one at a time, establishing experimental and control groups where feasible, and observed changes in selected dependent variables. It is regrettable that the firm did not proceed with this approach; opportunities for experimentation in ongoing business firms have been extremely limited, principally because managers are hesitant to interrupt operations and risk poorer results. NLS management was perfectly willing to accept the risks of experimentation but was unwilling to practice the patience, discipline, and reservation of judgment required by scientific methodology. Apparently, they had made up their minds that certain theories and applications would work and wanted to demonstrate this to the world as soon as possible.

TESTING PARTICIPATIVE MANAGEMENT

In his analysis, Malone suggests that the NLS experience represents a test of participative management. Moreover, he seems to conclude that the evidence demonstates the bankruptcy of the participative approach in all but the most environmentally favorable situations. A basic problem I have with this conclusion is that participative management is not a single technique or approach but rather a generic term encompassing several different approaches. NLS encouraged and practiced some forms of participation but discouraged other forms.

Marshall Sashkin has distinguished four basic types of participation: goal- setting, decision-making, problem-solving, and the development and implementation of change. He also has asserted that participation may be implemented on an individual, dyadic, or group basis.[6] The principal form of participation designed into the structure at NLS was problem-solving, defined as nonprogrammed decision-making. Group problem-solving was encouraged and, in fact, demanded by the system at all levels. Thus, at the

---

[6] Marshall Sashkin, "Changing Toward Participative Approaches: A Model and Methods," *Academy of Management Review* (July 1976), p. 76.

executive council level, decisions affecting the company as a whole were made by the entire council. In the instrument assembly department, with specialization eliminated, group problem-solving became a way of organizational life. The several engineering project teams also relied heavily on group problem-solving. The company salesmen, on the other hand, tended to utilize individual goal-setting and problem-solving approaches.

Horizontal problem-solving among the various departments was especially critical because of the lack of direct supervision from the vice-presidential level. To facilitate this coordination, formal weekly meetings of the managers of the five production-oriented departments were held. These managers also interacted during the week as problems arose.

Surprisingly, some of the more successful forms of participation practiced in organizations today, particularly joint goal-setting, problem-solving, and decision-making between hierarchical levels, were discouraged at NLS. In other words, participation was primarily lateral at each scalar level rather than vertical between levels. Goal-setting for the instrument assembly department is illustrative of this lack of vertical participation. The executive council would establish production quotas for instrument assembly on a quarterly basis. The department manager would then distribute the work load among the various teams who, in turn, would work out the detailed plans.

In another example, the executive council unilaterally set maximum and minimum inventory levels for the materials department at $200,000 and $175,000. The department was then free to plan its purchases within these limits.[7]

Vertical interaction was probably greatest between the executive council and the engineering project teams. The typical procedure was for a team to be assigned the development of a new instrument with preliminary specifications prepared by the council. Upon receiving the specifications, the project manager would negotiate with the council until mutual agreement was reached as to exactly what the team would do. But even under these conditions, engineers were heard to complain that vertical communication was difficult because they were dealing with a faceless plural executive rather than a single superior.[8]

Perhaps the most startling omission in participation was the fact that the organizational changes were planned and executed solely by top management, primarily Andrew Kay, with the aid of outside consultants. Discussions were held with employees prior to the changes, but it would appear

[7] *Business Week*, p. 100.
[8] O'Donnell, *Cases in General Management*, p. 58.

that the primary purpose of these meetings was to "sell" and educate the employees rather than to gain their input.[9] Although it is recognized that participation is not universally necessary for successful change, it is incongruous that such dramatic changes based on behavioral management theory would be introduced without significant employee participation.

TESTING BEHAVIORAL THEORY

— various behav theory that supposedly being implemente were misapplied ie, Maslow, McGregor

NLS executives publicly stated that the organizational changes of 1961–1962 were based on the writings of Abraham Maslow, Douglas McGregor, Peter Drucker, and other leading behavioral scholars of the day. Let us now look at what these writers said and how it relates to what NLS did.

The concepts which appeared to have the greatest influence on Kay and his advisors were Maslow's "hierarchy of needs" and McGregor's "Theory Y." Maslow states that human needs are structured in a series of levels—physiological, safety, social, esteem, and self-realization—and when those on a lower level are generally fulfilled, those on the next level will demand satisfaction. "Theory Y" is a set of assumptions about human nature which asserts that people are not inherently lazy or dishonest, and that they have the capacity to learn and accept responsibility under proper conditions. McGregor contrasted it with "Theory X," which states that the average individual inherently dislikes work, avoids responsibility, and must be controlled and coerced to put forth a fair day's work.

The NLS reorganization was to a large degree aimed at creating a working environment in which employees could satisfy their full range of needs and thereby realize the assumptions of "Theory Y." Thus, the elimination of hourly wages, raising the general wage level, and the no-lay-off policy were directed at fully satisfying the employee's lower-level needs. The elements of autonomy, ambiguity, and job enrichment were designed into the system for the purpose of providing the opportunity for higher-level need satisfaction.

In designing a structure to accomplish their goals, the NLS executives had to innovate because Maslow and McGregor provided little guidance. Maslow was a psychologist who developed a general theory of human motivation. He did not concern himself with business firms and the practical problems of creating an internal environment where high-level needs could

---

[9] During my research at the firm I learned that several members of the executive council as well as others in the organization were highly skeptical of the package of changes.

be fulfilled.[10] McGregor, on the other hand, was concerned with the business firm and its management. His focus, however, was not on suggested applications but, rather, was on the assumptions of managers and a critique of their traditional practices, which were a logical consequence of what he believed to be faulty assumptions ("Theory X"). He did, however, endorse two specific techniques, the "Scanlon Plan" and "Management by Integration and Self-Control."

The Scanlon Plan has two essential features: a profit-sharing scheme based on cost reduction, and an employee-suggestion system which utilizes a series of committees to receive and evaluate ideas for improving productivity.[11] NLS, curiously, did not incorporate either of these features into its new structure. Instead of profit sharing, all workers were placed on a high straight salary, as noted earlier. Moreover, there was no formal suggestion system at NLS. Of course, the high degree of horizontal interaction encouraged the flow of ideas at the operating level, but the paucity of interaction between the departments and the executive council tended to hinder the consideration of more far-reaching suggestions.

"Management by Integration and Self-Control" was McGregor's version of Peter Drucker's "Management by Objectives." It required subordinate input into the establishment of specific goals for a limited time period and joint appraisal by the superior and subordinate of the results.[12] Conversely, major objectives and guidelines at NLS were set from above and formal appraisals were not required.

An important influence on the thinking of the organization designers at NLS was Drucker's classic, *The Practice of Management*. This book is replete with original concepts, the most significant of which was "Management by Objectives." However, as demonstrated above, NLS completely eschewed this idea.

The Drucker concept with which Kay and his advisors were most intrigued was "the eight objectives of business." Drucker argued convincingly that it is a basic fallacy for a firm to concentrate on profit as its sole objective, as economists have traditionally asserted, because it tends to misdirect managers' attention to the short run at the expense of the long run. As an alternative to profit maximization, Drucker suggested eight critical areas

---

[10] Maslow was a Visiting Fellow at NLS during the summer of 1962, well after the major organizational change had been put into effect. While there, he developed the impressions which became the basis for his book, *Eupsychian Management* (Homewood, Ill.: Richard D. Irwin, 1965).

[11] Douglas McGregor, *The Human Side of Enterprise* (New York: McGraw-Hill, 1960), pp. 110–123.

[12] McGregor, *The Human Side . . .* , *pp. 61–76.*

where objectives should be set: market standing, innovation, productivity, physical and financial resources, profitability, manager performance and development, worker performance and attitude, and public responsibility.[13] He saw these as areas where planning and control were essential to the long-run viability of the business. In essence he was recommending a comprehensive strategic planning focus for the firm. NLS, however, carried his idea a step further and incorporated it directly into its formal organization structure. Thus, the executive council was created with each position corresponding to one of Drucker's key planning areas.[14]

In my opinion, this corruption of Drucker's concept led to some of the major internal problems at NLS. The executive council became essentially an aloof, top heavy, eight-man planning group. Its members were former line executives, most of whom were uncomfortable in their new staff assignments. Moreover, their ill-defined position descriptions caused confusion, frustration, and, in one or two cases, guilt feelings resulting from a perceived lack of contribution. In any event, the structure that emerged at NLS went far beyond what Drucker had in mind.

Rensis Likert was another important behavioral scholar whose ideas were occasionally linked to the thinking at NLS. His early book, *New Patterns in Management*, presented the results of his research on the principles and practices followed by managers achieving the best results. The most famous concept to come out of this work is the "Linking Pin Function," which stresses the need for effectively functioning interlocking groups that connect the various hierarchical levels in the organization. The importance of the "Linking Pin Function," according to Likert, is that it provides for upward communication and influence in the organization.[15] However, as discussed earlier, the NLS structure mediated against vertical groups and upward communication.

According to company executives, the accounting changes instituted were inspired to a large degree by Carl F. Braun's succinct little monograph, *Objective Accounting*.[16] Braun pleads for internal accounting information that is significant, timely, and understandable. He severely criticizes standard cost accounting procedures and offers a number of practical suggestions for improving the effectiveness of internal accounting. Predictably, how-

[13] Peter F. Drucker, The Practice of Management (New York: Harper and Bros., 1954).

[14]. Actually, manager performance and development, and worker performance and attitude were handled by the same executive, and the eighth member of the council was the president, whose primary function was to coordinate the council's activities.

[15] Rensis Likert, *New Patterns in Management* (New York: McGraw-Hill, 1961).

[16] Carl F. Braun, *Objective Accounting: A Problem of Communication* (Alhambra, Calif.: C. F. Braun & Co., 1958).

ever, nowhere in the book does he recommend eliminating the accounting department or reducing accounting information to the minimum that is required for government reports. As with many of the other NLS innovations, these changes involved rather questionable extensions of an author's ideas.

What can be learned from the NLS experience? The most obvious conclusion is that a favorable environment and sagacious strategy can overcome the inadequacies of structure, but once the environment turns hostile, structural faults quickly become manifest and untenable. But what were the structural inadequacies at NLS? Malone has suggested that the executive council concept, the dearth of vertical communication, and the wage and lay-off policies were major flaws in the system. He also seems to feel that the team production concept was a moderate success. Subjectively, I tend to agree with him. Objectively, however, almost nothing about the experience can be concluded with any degree of certainty because of three fundamental errors in the design of the new structure. First, many changes were implemented simultaneously, thereby confounding any results which might have been obtained. Second, little, if any, usable data upon which to draw conclusions was generated. Contrast this with the Hawthorne studies, where various changes were introduced sequentially, and data was systematically collected for future scholarly analysis. Finally, the various behavioral theories that supposedly were being implemented were to a large degree misapplied. Hence, all that was being tested was the organization architects' unique interpretations of these concepts.

NLS is one of the few firms that has been willing to incur the risk of large-scale behavioral experimentation. It is unfortunate that the undertaking failed, but the real tragedy is that so little was learned from it. Perhaps the most important lesson to emerge from the experience is how *not* to proceed with organizational experimentation or change.

Richard M. Steers
Richard T. Mowday

University of Oregon

THE MOTIVATIONAL PROPERTIES OF TASKS

Dating from the industrial revolution, managers have shown concern for discovering more efficient methods of task accomplishment. During the scientific management movement of the early 1900s, this concern reached its zenith as managers increasingly fractionated employees' jobs in attempts to maximize productivity. The human relations movement that followed raised concern for the effects of such job fractionation on employee attitudes and performance. Contemporary approaches to management on the shop floor have attempted to satisfy the concerns of both scientific management and the human relations advocates by stressing the need to improve simultaneously "concern for people" and "concern for production." Many see job redesign or job enrichment as the answer to this dilemma.

Interest in job design has prompted research on the effects of task variations on employee performance and attitudes. These studies have generally been of two types. First, a small number of field experiments have been conducted to evaluate longitudinally the actual implementation of job enrichment in organizations. Although these studies vary widely in terms of methodological sophistication, the results generally—but not always—sug-

Richard M. Steers and Richard T. Mowday, "The Motivational Properties of Tasks," *Academy of Management Review*, October 1977, pp. 645–658.

gest that increased employee motivation and satisfaction often result from job enrichment (8, 18, 21, 28, 43). Unfortunately, studies employing field experimental procedures are rare and some of the largest and best known job redesign efforts have never been systematically evaluated. In many instances, only anecdotal evidence (generally positive) is available for evaluation of job enrichment as an organizational change strategy.

The second and more common type of study involves examining the relationships between perceived job characteristics and employee reactions at a single point in time. The general conclusion emerging from these correlational studies is that "enriched" jobs are often associated with reduced turnover and absenteeism, improved job satisfaction, improved quality of performance and—in some but certainly not all cases—improved productivity (2, 10, 11, 25, 30, 38, 42).

Although such studies abound, the type of research methodology typically employed suggests caution in interpreting the results. Correlating perceived job characteristics with employee satisfaction at one point in time provides a static comparison, revealing little about how employees react to *changes* in their jobs. Further, asking job incumbents to describe their jobs along a number of prespecified dimensions (e.g., amount of variety, autonomy and feedback) makes it difficult to assess whether such perceptual measures reflect the actual objective characteristics of the job or characteristics of the individual providing the perceptions. For instance, it is not possible to determine whether enriched jobs lead to increased satisfaction (as most authors suggest), or alternatively, whether highly satisfied employees describe their jobs more positively (i.e., as more challenging) than those who are less satisfied.

While empirical research examining the impact of task characteristics on employee reactions is extensive, comprehensive theoretical models which attempt to predict and explain the results of this research remain limited. Emphasis on repeated correlational studies of perceived task characteristics at the expense of model development has impeded understanding of this important area of organizational behavior (OB). In the absence of such models, it is difficult for researchers and practicing managers to develop a comprehensive understanding of how changes in the job affect employee motivation. Further, it is not possible to state precisely under what circumstances changes in the job would be expected to result in improved satisfaction and performance and when such positive outcomes would not be expected. Increased attention to these issues is necessary if job redesign efforts are to move beyond the simple assertion that "job enrichment works."

CONCEPTUAL MODELS OF
TASK DESIGN

In view of the limited amount of work on conceptual models of the motivational properties of tasks, this article attempts to make two contributions to understanding this important topic. First, it summarizes and evaluates the available models of task motivation. Second, based on this review, it identifies specific directions for future research and model-building.

Seven existing conceptual models explicitly examine the way in which task design influences motivation, performance, and satisfaction. These models are summarized in Table 1 and Figures 1 and 2. Each model is evaluated in terms of its utility for understanding motivational processes. Following this review, conclusions are drawn and recommendations for future research suggested.

Two-Factor Theory

Herzberg (15) was one of the first to suggest a model of the motivational properties of task design based on his two-factor theory of satisfaction. In a study of the determinants of job satisfaction, Herzberg and his associates found that individuals tended to describe satisfying experiences on the job in terms of factors that were intrinsic to the content of the job itself. Termed "motivators," the factors most commonly associated with high satisfaction were achievement, recognition, the work itself, responsibility, advancement, and growth (15). Conversely, dissatisfying experiences, termed "hygiene" factors, tended to come about as a result of extrinsic, non-job-related factors, such as company policies, salary, co-worker relations, and supervisory style (see Table 1). The implications of this research for task design and motivation are fairly obvious. If one wishes to improve motivation and satisfaction, jobs should be designed to allow greater scope for personal achievement and recognition, more challenging and responsible work, and increased opportunities for advancement and growth.

Although Herzberg's approach to job enrichment has proven intuitively appealing to many managers, his work has been criticized by researchers as being deficient in several major aspects. First, King (17) identified five alternative interpretations of the theory and noted that each implied a different criterion of "proof" to establish the empirical validity of the model. This suggests that Herzberg failed to provide an unambiguous statement of the two-factor theory. Second, Herzberg failed to take individual differences

Hauer,

TABLE 1
Conceptual Models of the Motivational Properties of Tasks

Models	Basic Components of the Model

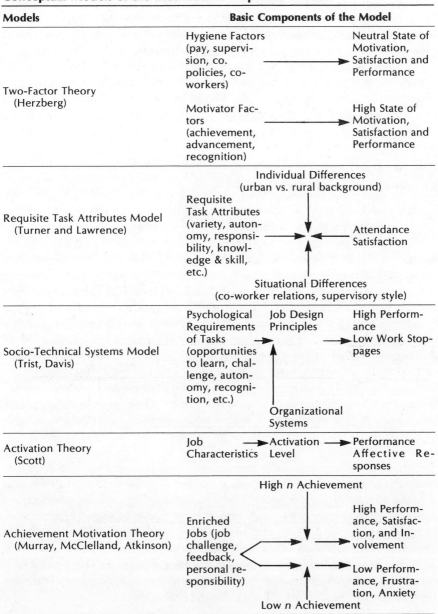

into consideration in predicting the outcomes of job enrichment (16). This failure and the somewhat limited sampling of jobs in his original study made the theory difficult to reconcile with the results of other research (45). Third, Herzberg's theory generally has not been supported by subsequent research using different research designs. Finally, the model provides little in the way of an explanation of *how* such factors as responsibility and achievement result in higher satisfaction, let alone higher motivation.

For these reasons, there is considerable doubt about the efficacy of the two-factor theory either as a model of the determinants of job satisfaction/dissatisfaction or as an empirically-verified guide for job redesign efforts. Herzberg's theoretical statement and research have stimulated interest in job design on the part of others and this may represent one of his more significant contributions to the field.

Requisite Task Attributes Model

Turner and Lawrence (42) developed a classification of job characteristics that were believed to lead to higher levels of satisfaction and attendance on the job. Six important task characteristics were identified: (a) variety; (b) autonomy; (c) responsibility; (d) knowledge and skill; (e) optional interaction; and (f) required interaction (see Table 1). Turner and Lawrence measured incumbents' perceptions of their jobs on each of these dimensions and developed a measure of "task scope" (i.e., a weighted index of the job characteristics). They found that task scope was positively related to attendance but had no simple relationship to job satisfaction. But when individual differences in the form of urban/rural background were taken into account employees from urban settings were more satisfied with low scope (i.e., "unenriched") jobs and employees with rural background reported higher satisfaction in high scope (i.e., "enriched") jobs. Their model also takes into consideration the influence of situational factors (e.g., satisfaction with supervision, work group, etc.) as moderating the task scope–employee reaction relationship.

Although Turner and Lawrence's work has proven influential among researchers in subsequent job design studies, their model fails to take into account adequately many process considerations. It does not provide clues concerning the process through which task characteristics influence employee attitudes and behavior. In addition, the task characteristics they identified were based on an a priori classification scheme and little attention was given to establishing empirically their importance to respondents. In the absence of such information, it is not possible to conclude that the six task attributes they identified are the most salient ones from a motivational standpoint. Despite these concerns, Turner and Lawrence have made a substantial contribution to subsequent job design efforts by focusing attention on the need to consider the influence of individual and situational differences on employees' reaction to jobs.

Socio-Technical Systems Model

For a number of years, Trist (41) and his colleagues have been engaged in research on the relationship between the individual, the job, and the larger organizational system. They have been highly critical of the "machine theory" of organizations inherent in scientific management for its general failure to consider social and psychological consequences of job design. Rather than stress either the technological requirements of the organization or the needs of the individual, they suggest that the important concern in job design is optimizing the match between the two. This is done largely through an analysis of group processes as they relate to individual outcomes.

Trist offered a set of general socio-technical principles of job design based on the "psychological requirements" of the job (see Table 1). These psychological requirements are described as the need for the job to provide: (a) reasonably demanding content; (b) an opportunity to learn; (c) some autonomy or discretion in decision making; (d) social support and recognition; (e) a relationship between what is produced and the employee's social life; and (f) the feeling that the job leads to a desirable future. The general psychological requirements of the job translate into job design "principles":

1. An optimum variety of tasks within the job.
2. A meaningful pattern of tasks that relate to a single overall task.
3. An optimum length of work cycles.
4. Discretion in setting standards of performance and feedback on results.
5. Extending the boundary of the job to include "boundary tasks."
6. Tasks that require some degree of skill and are worthy of respect in the community.
7. Tasks that make a perceivable contribution to the overall product.

The socio-technical approach facilitates understanding of task design by focusing attention on interactions between individuals, groups, and the nature of the tasks as they relate to other subsystems and the larger organization. But before this approach can serve as a useful guide to research and practice, further refinements in the theory appear necessary.

First, consideration must be given to identifying how individual differences affect employee reactions to task design. For example, it is not clear whether the psychological requirements of the job are the same for each individual. Second, greater specificity is necessary concerning the influence of situational factors on task design-outcome relationships. Although the socio-technical approach differentiates between several types of systems in terms of their impact on task design, the discussion remains somewhat abstract. Third, the theory does not specify *how* task characteristics influence employee reactions; thus more attention must be given to process considerations. The origin and empirical validity of psychological requirements of the job as a process explanation remain in doubt. Finally, the theory is difficult to translate into specific organizational change strategies designed to improve satisfaction and performance. For instance, it is not clear what is meant by "optimum" variety or a "meaningful" pattern of tasks. Before the socio-technical approach can serve as a useful guide to research and practice, task design principles must be defined operationally and increased specifity must be built into the theory.

Activation Theory

This model represents a physiological process explanation for the effects of task design on performance and affective responses in the work place. Scott (32) reviewed the results of research on brain stimulation, suggesting that the degree of "activation" of an individual is a major determinant of a number of behaviors. Activation—defined as "the degree of excitation of the brain stem reticular formation" (32)—has been found to have a curvilinear relationship to performance on a variety of tasks. Research has shown that performance suffers at very low or very high levels of activation. Optimal behavioral efficiency is predicted when activation is at a moderate or "characteristic" level. The "characteristic" activation level is viewed as a function of bio-chemical structure and thus can be expected to differ across individuals.

Based on this line of research, jobs which are dull and repetitive and call for habitual responses (i.e., provide low levels of activation) may lead to decreased levels of performance. As jobs are enriched to include more variety and responsibility, activation would be expected to increase to a point more closely approaching an optimal level in terms of behavioral efficiency, and thus result in improved levels of performance.

Activation theory presents an intriguing explanation for the effects of job design on individual reactions. But at this time its utility in the work place appears limited. At its present level of development, Scott concludes that activation theory does not allow precise statements concerning how or when to enrich jobs in the work place. Research is needed to provide measures of activation level and to define the "optimal" level of activation for each individual before this theory can serve as a useful guide in organizations.

Achievement Motivation Theory

Although the achievement motivation model dates from the 1930s and the work of Murray (26), its application to the issue of job design and performance is relatively recent (22, 34, 35, 37, 39). This model posits that individuals exhibit varying levels of need for achievement (n Ach), along with other needs. Need for achievement represents an experienced need to accomplish something important or compete with a standard of excellence (24). Employees who have a high n Ach tend to seek challenging tasks, prefer to assume personal responsibility for task accomplishment, and like situations where they receive clear feedback on performance. Low n Ach employees prefer situations where risk levels are low and responsibility for task accomplishment is shared with others.

When employee n Ach is considered as it relates to variations in the nature of the job, the theory would predict that enriching a job by providing more responsibility, challenge, and feedback would lead to increased performance, involvement, and satisfaction for high need achievers. Results from several studies provide support for this hypothesis (22, 35, 39).

But enriching the job of a low need achiever would at best have no impact on performance and could lead to increased frustration, anxiety, and job dissatisfaction. It could increase the chance of failure, threatening other needs that may be important to the individual (e.g., self-esteem, affiliation). For such low need achievers, other motivational strategies than job enrichment seem in order, such as the use of peer group pressure, more effective leader behavior, or stronger performance–reward contingencies. The most successful applications of behavior modification (14) have been performed on employees typically characterized by a low n Ach (e.g., hard-core unemployed, unskilled workers).

While studies consistently support the utility of considering n Ach in a model of task motivation, several limitations must be acknowledged. The model places too much emphasis on a single individual difference variable (n Ach). Murray's (26) original formulation of a need-press model of motivation employed a variety of needs. Subsequent research by Atkinson (1), McClelland (24), and others have concluded that n Ach represents the most prominent need insofar as task motivation and performance are concerned. Even so, more complex analyses are needed to take a more comprehensive approach to the problem.

A second criticism is that, with few exceptions, the *n* Ach model has been studied under laboratory conditions; its applicability to the work situation remains to be established firmly. Field study evidence supports the hypothesis that *n* Ach moderates the job scope–performance relationship (22, 35, 39). But no such moderating effect was found for the job scope–satisfaction relationship (36, 40).

Third, as with other formulations (e.g., Hackman and Oldham), the model refrains from specific managerial recommendations for employees with *low* need strengths, concentrating instead on high need strength individuals. There is an implicit assumption here that low need achievers are motivated by the inverse of that which motivates high need achievers. Such a conclusion does not follow from the theory and is contrary to existing studies. Instead, other needs (e.g., affiliation, autonomy, dominance) emerge to motivate low need achievers, and these other needs are frequently cued by factors unrelated to the job itself. Despite such criticisms, achievement motivation theory has received fairly consistent support in terms of predicting general individual reactions to task design.

Job Characteristics Model – integrates much of earlier work

Hackman, Oldham, Janson, and Purdy (13) recently presented a new strategy for job enrichment that builds upon and integrates much of the earlier work of Turner and Lawrence (42), Trist (41), and Hackman and Lawler (10). Their model includes both content and process considerations and represents one of the most detailed approaches to implementation of job enrichment in the work place.

The model begins by identifying the "critical psychological states" associated with high levels of internal motivation, satisfaction, and quality of performance (see Figure 1). These psychological states are believed to be: (a) experienced "meaningfulness" of the job; (b) experienced "responsibility" for outcomes; and (c) knowledge of actual results When these psychological states are present, they are thought to lead to low absenteeism and turnover and high levels of internal motivation, satisfaction and quality of performance.

Five characteristics of the job (core job dimensions) are viewed as leading to these psychological states. Skill variety (i.e., tasks that challenge the individual's skills and abilities), task identity (i.e., completing a "whole" and identifiable piece of work) and task significance (i.e., impact on the lives of others) lead to experienced meaningfulness of the job. Task autonomy leads to experienced responsibility for outcomes on the job. Finally, feedback concerning effectiveness of the employee's efforts provides a knowledge of results on the job. The model further specifies that these job characteristics are built into the task through five "implementing concepts" of job design: (a) combining tasks; (b) forming natural work units; (c) establishing client relationships; (d) vertical loading; and (e) opening feedback channels.

Thus the model specifies that job characteristics lead to critical psychological states which, in turn, lead to positive outcomes in the work place. But Hackman and associates point out that this may not be true for all employees or in every work situation. The extent to which job enrichment can be

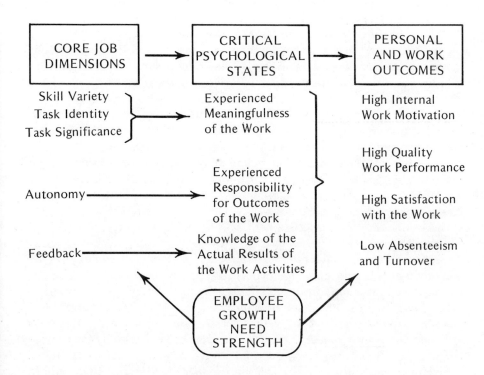

FIGURE 1 The Job Characteristics Model of Work Motivation
Source: J. Richard Hackman and Greg R. Oldham. "Development of the Job Diagnostic Survey," Journal of Applied Psychology, Vol. 60 (1975), 159–170. Copyright 1975 by the American Psychological Association. Used by permission.

expected to have positive consequences is dependent on the "growth need strengths" (GNS) of employees. The model predicts that employees with a strong need for personal accomplishment, learning, challenge, and growth will respond favorably to job enrichment. Individuals low in GNS will not respond in a similar fashion. Unfortunately, only weak support for this hypothesis emerged in their studies.

In subsequent research, Oldham, Hackman, and Pearce (27) examined the moderating influence of several situational factors on the task characteristic-employee reaction relationship. They found that employees who are satisfied with the work context (e.g., pay, job security, co-workers, and supervision) were more likely to respond favorably to enriched jobs. Such results suggest a "two-factor" theory of job design in which employee reactions to contextual factors are viewed as necessary but insufficient conditions for satisfaction with the work itself to result from enriched jobs.

Although the Hackman and Oldham (11) model is fairly recent, it has made an important contribution to the field of job design. For the practicing manager, it provides a detailed procedure for conducting a diagnosis of the work place to determine whether or not job enrichment is a useful organizational change strategy. But from a conceptual standpoint, their model appears incomplete. The explanation of how task characteristics "cause" high internal motivation and satisfaction is not well integrated with current theory and research on motivation. Moreover, the empirical status of such concepts as "experienced meaningfulness of the job" and "experienced responsibility" is somewhat ambiguous. Even if it were possible to develop operational definitions of such concepts, the present model does not go far enough in specifying how such "critical psychological states" affect motivation.

Studies generally have failed to support the model's predictive power with respect to employee performance, although support for its predictions of perceived motivation and job satisfaction are found (12). Dunham, Aldag, and Brief (6) have also noted the instability of the factor structure of the JDS, the instrument designed to measure job scope. Finally, there is a problem with the model's primary moderator variable: growth need strength. GNS purports to include such diverse (and often unrelated) needs as achievement, autonomy, self-esteem, feedback, and personal growth. In the absence of clear evidence of construct validity for the GNS notion, its theoretical status must remain in doubt. In fact, one advantage of the achievement motivation model discussed earlier is that the concept of n Ach represents a more specific need than the notion of GNS. If, as has been pointed out by Steers and Spencer (39), n Ach represents a more powerful moderator of the task characteristic-performance relationship, the utility of the broader (less specific) concept of GNS remains questionable. Despite such problems, the work of Hackman and Oldham represents a major advancement over some of the earlier and more simplistic prescriptions for job design (e.g., "job enrichment works"). But before their theory can be widely accepted as a general model of the effects of job design, more research is needed.

Expectancy Theory

A model that holds particular promise for understanding how task variations influence motivation is expectancy theory (29, 45). Expectancy theory posits that human behavior in organizations is a function of three related factors: (a) an employee's belief that effort will lead to a desired level of performance (termed "effort-performance expectancy"); (b) an employee's belief that such performance will lead to the receipt of desired rewards (termed "performance-outcome expectancies"); and (c) the value or "valence" associated with performing the task, task accomplishment, and extrinsic rewards resulting from performance. It is generally believed that when these factors are combined in a multiplicative fashion they reflect the employee's desire or motivation to perform the task.

Expectancy theory represents one of the most comprehensive motivational models developed to date. For this reason, it is a valuable model for explaining why variations in task characteristics influence an employee's motivation to perform. An expectancy theory approach to job design was first suggested by Lawler (19) and later by Hackman and Lawler (10), Staw (33), and Schwab and Cummings (31). Staw's (33) expectancy theory model is discussed here, because it is felt that it represents the most explicit explanation of the effects of task design on employee motivation and performance.

Staw (33), like others, views job enrichment as a strategy designed to increase a person's level of *intrinsic* motivation by altering the characteristics of the work performed. Such an approach can be contrasted with techniques designed to increase extrinsic motivation (as can be seen in many wage incentive, or piece-rate, pay plans). As a motivational strategy, increasing intrinsic motivation appears to have several advantages over extrinsic approaches. First, the reduced need for extrinsic rewards to motivate behavior may represent a cost savings to the organization. Second, there is a reduced need to monitor task behavior because the motivation to perform at high levels has been internalized by the individual. Finally, such intrinsic approaches avoid many problems associated with the introduction of incentive systems in organizations (20).

Within an expectancy theory framework, task characteristics are viewed as influencing motivation through three factors: (a) the intrinsic valence associated with task behavior; (b) the intrinsic valence associated with task accomplishment; and (c) the perceived probability that effort will lead to task accomplishment. As suggested in Figure 2, greater employee effort and performance are expected when task characteristics "cue" motivationally relevant responses in terms of expectancies and valences. Such a conclusion follows from existing research on expectancy theory.

A consideration of the amount of autonomy on the job provides one example of how task characteristics can influence motivation within an expectancy theory framework. Previous research has pointed to a positive relationship between autonomy and employee performance (2, 10). The explanation is relatively straightforward. An employee with more autonomy has greater control over the means of task accomplishment. Fewer outside sources of influence and interference exist. Consequently, the employee's beliefs that effort will lead to actual task performance (E → P expectancy) should be higher than for an employee with less autonomy. Increased autonomy may also increase the performance-outcome expectancy due to increased employee ownership of the task. Given greater control over the task, task accomplishment may lead to increased intrinsic rewards—a feeling of accomplishing something important and worthwhile. Finally, autonomy in some cases may increase the valence which an employee attaches to successful task accomplishment. Research by Vroom (44) and others suggests that when an employee plays a more central role in developing the

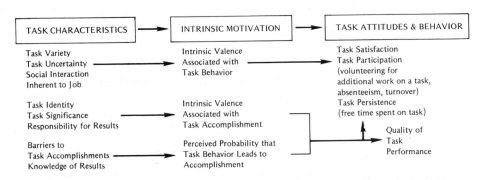

FIGURE 2 An Expectancy Theory Model of the Motivational Properties of Tasks
Source: Barry M. Staw. Intrinsic and Extrinsic Motivation (Morristown, N.J.: General Learning Press, 1976). Copyright 1976 by General Learning Press. Used by permission.

means to task accomplishment, he or she may become more ego-involved in the outcome and place a higher value on actual accomplishment.

Another example is provided by the task characteristic of feedback on performance. Some research has shown that providing employees with greater knowledge of results on task performance tends to increase effort and performance (4, 23, 38). Feedback on performance probably serves a gyroscopic function vis à vis expectancies by continually clarifying effort-performance beliefs. The more feedback is received, the greater the understanding of the relationship between effort and performance. Moreover, feedback may serve as an extrinsic reward (e.g., supervisory praise) by providing positive reinforcement for task performance.

Similar arguments can be advanced for other task characteristics (variety, task identity, social interaction opportunities, etc.). The general conclusion is that variations in an employee's task characteristics influence effort because they affect the major components which determine willingness to perform. In general, higher levels of performance can be expected when employees experience increased intrinsic motivation.

Although expectancy theory has received widespread attention recently, several aspects of the model appear troublesome. First, while the empirical evidence for the model is consistently supportive, the magnitude of the findings is somewhat weak, suggesting that other variables influence motivation and performance. Second, there is ambiguity concerning how to operationalize and measure expectancies and valences. Third, individual differences have fairly consistently been omitted in tests of the model, although their role has been suggested by the theory. Finally, little in the way of experimental evidence has emerged concerning the theory. It would be useful to see task characteristics systematically manipulated to study their effects on expectancies and valences and on subsequent effort. This remains to be done. Even so, expectancy theory appears to offer a conceptual richness that facilitates better understanding of how task design influences employee motivation.

CONCLUSIONS AND SUGGESTIONS FOR FUTURE RESEARCH

While the origins of these models of task motivation are diverse, their major purpose remains the same: to explain the manner in which task variations influence employee effort and performance. The *a priori* assumption of all the models is that task design represents an important factor in determining such behavior. While some models go further to suggest that individual or situational differences often represent important moderators, the assumption that enriched jobs motivate is ever present.

When the models are compared, several important conclusions emerge. Recommendations for future research on the topic follow directly from these conclusions.

Content vs. Process Models. First, no firm conclusion can be drawn concerning which model is "best." The answer to this question lies in the uses to which one wishes to put the models. Some models, like the two-factor theory, offer specific recommendations for managers who want to redesign jobs. These models, called "content theories" by Campbell et al., (3) simply identify those variables (achievement, recognition, etc.) which have been found to be related to performance. They say little about the underlying processes by which such variables influence behavior. Other models, like activation theory and expectancy theory, place greater emphasis on understanding motivational processes and the enduring relationships between major variables. These models are called "process theories" by Campbell et al. While useful from an analytical standpoint, process theories are often too abstract to be of much use to managers. Models are needed to simultaneously satisfy both the need to understand motivational processes and the need for action recommendations for management. The models proposed by Hackman and Oldham (11, 12) and Trist (41) have attempted such an integration, but more explicit formulations are necessary.

Derivation and Importance of Task Characteristics. Second, the derivation and importance of various task characteristics remain ambiguous. The task characteristics that are typically studied are based most often on conceptual (rather than empirical) classification schemes. Such non-empirical approaches raise questions concerning the relevance of the selected task characteristics for motivation and performance. Perhaps other more important characteristics have not been defined into the existing models. Few serious attempts have been made by investigators to examine the relative importance of each task characteristic in influencing behavior. While the determination of such weights is easily accomplished, it remains to be done.

Role of Individual Differences. Three of the seven models allow for little, if any, explicit recognition of the role of individual differences as potential moderators of the effects of task design (two-factor theory, socio-technical systems, and activation theory). Those models that explicitly recognize such differences provide little systematic examination of their magnitude or diversity. (The one possible exception is expectancy theory which lends itself easily to an examination of the role of individual differences). Most often, we are simply told that individuals with "higher-order need strengths" respond more positively to enriched jobs than individuals without such need strengths. Such a conclusion is ambiguous both in terms of identifying what is involved in such a loose "construct" and in terms of suggesting implications for management. In contract, the achievement motivation model has been more explicit in focusing on one specific individual characteristic as it relates to motivation. But this latter model has tended to ignore other important individual difference factors.

Future research should examine a wider array of individual factors which potentially influence the way employees respond to their jobs, such as the level of employees' skills and abilities. For individuals whose skill and ability levels are low relative to the demands of the job, providing greater amounts of autonomy and variety may increase frustration in task accomplishment and actually result in decreased performance.

Dubin's (5) research on the central life interests of industrial workers suggests that not all employees seek intrinsic satisfaction in the work setting. Providing increased opportunities for intrinsic satisfaction through job enrichment may not result in higher levels of motivation and satisfaction for individuals with a "non-work" central life interest. Such individuals are more likely to bring an instrumental orientation to the job and seek primary satisfaction in settings other than the final work place.

Finally, individual differences may affect the influence of task characteristics through the perceptual process (31). Different employees may see the same job in quite different ways in terms of task scope. Individual differences may act as an independent variable influencing perceived task characteristics, instead of a variable moderating the relationship between task characteristics and motivational outcomes. Employee personality characteristics and satisfaction with the job may influence how the task is perceived, independent of its actual characteristics. If, as suggested by Vroom (44) and others, employees behave in accordance with their perceptions of a job (instead of how it "really" is), then perceptual variations across employees represent an important concern for researchers and managers. For instance, if a high need achiever does not believe that the job is challenging, he or she may lower aspiration levels accordingly. Thus, not only do managers have a responsibility to redesign jobs so they are more motivating for employees; they must also see to it that employees realize the extent and nature of such changes. If job redesign does not result in a more enriched job in the eyes of employees, there is little reason to believe they will respond in the predicted fashion (21).

Role of Situational Differences. Besides individual differences, variations in the immediate work environment must also be considered as potentially important moderators of the effects of task design. Several authors (13, 41, 42) have recognized that job redesign efforts must be viewed within the context of the sub-system. For instance, increasing the amount of autonomy on a job already characterized by high role ambiguity may result in increased frustration and decreased satisfaction and performance. Increasing the amount of feedback and knowledge of results on very simple and repetitive tasks may not increase performance because it does not provide new information.

A great deal of research demonstrates that work group and supervisory relations represent important influences on how employees react to their jobs. Research on employee compensation (20) has repeatedly shown how peer group pressure, a situational factor, can negate the motivational potential of a piece-rate incentive system and result in employees intentionally restricting their income. Similar consequences may follow when job enrichment is introduced into a work environment characterized by a high degree of employee suspicion and distrust of management's intentions. Negative attitudes by employees toward one aspect of the work environment (e.g., supervision) may generalize into negative attitudes toward the job as a whole, again affecting effort and performance (27). At a minimum, employees may expect that increased demands placed upon them as a consequence of job enrichment should be met with compensation increases (9). Perhaps it is because of such concerns that many job redesign efforts (particularly the most successful ones) have been attempted only in specially chosen locations or were preceded by extensive employee-selection processes and attempts to develop a suitable "climate" into which job changes were to be introduced (7).

Lack of Empirical Support. A disturbing feature in all seven models is the dearth of empirical support. Theories are often accompanied by a scant array of correlational findings of modest magnitude. Based on such meager data, support for the model is claimed. Instead of continuing in this path, each model should be treated as a set of hypotheses and such hypotheses should be tested under experimental (as opposed to correlational) conditions. Several models should be examined simultaneously to determine their respective power in predicting effort and performance. For example, the magnitude of support for achievement motivation studies is generally stronger than that for the job characteristics model (12, 39), but no direct comparisons have yet been made.

Costs of Job Redesign. Finally, future research should examine the costs associated with job redesign, relative to benefits that are likely to accrue. There is a notable tendency to stress the positive benefits to the organization likely to result from enriching jobs (e.g., reduced turnover and absenteeism, increased quality of work). But there is evidence that such efforts may also result in increased training time and costs of production (7). From the organization's perspective, the critical question is whether the benefits to be derived from job enrichment outweight the costs involved in implementing and maintaining the program. It is doubtful whether organizational change strategies such as job enrichment can continue to be taken seriously when fundamental questions of costs and benefits are ignored.

In summary, what is needed to advance understanding of the motivational properties of tasks is a greater willingness by researchers to move beyond simplistic research designs and atheoretical analysis and spend the time necessary to develop more sophisticated and empirically validated models of the effects of task characteristics. In addition, practicing managers must exhibit a greater openness to experiment with job design changes and systematically evaluate the outcomes of such efforts. More rigorous studies are needed, not just more studies. Such efforts would benefit the field of organizational behavior and would also have useful implications for the practice of management.

REFERENCES _____

1. Atkinson, John W. *Introduction to Motivation* (Princeton, N. J.: Van Nostrand, 1964).
2. Brief, Arthur P., and Ramon J. Aldag. "Employee Reactions to Job Characteristics: A Constructive Replication," *Journal of Applied Psychology*, Vol. 60 (1975), 182–186.
3. Campbell, John P., Marvin D. Dunnette, Edward E. Lawler III, and Karl E. Weick. *Managerial Behavior, Performance, and Effectiveness* (New York: McGraw-Hill, 1970).
4. Cummings, Larry L., Donald P. Schwab, and M. Rosen. "Performance and Knowledge of Results as Determinants of Goal-Setting," *Journal of Applied Psychology*, Vol. 55 (1971), 526–530.
5. Dubin, Robert. "Industrial Workers' Worlds: A Study of the Central Life Interests of Industrial Workers," *Social Problems*, Vol. 3 (1956), 131–142.

6. Dunham, Randall B., Ramon J. Aldag, and Arthur P. Brief. "Dimensionality of Task Design as Measured by the Job Diagnostic Survey," *Proceedings, Annual Meeting of the Academy of Management, Kansas City, August 11–14, 1976,* pp. 89–93.

7. Fein, Mitchell. "Job Enrichment: A Reevaluation," *Sloan Management Review,* Vol. 15 (1974), 69–88.

8. Ford, Robert N. "Job Enrichment Lessons from AT&T," *Harvard Business Review,* Vol. 51 (1973), 96–106.

9. Foy, N., and H. Gadon. "Worker Participation: Contrasts in Three Countries," *Harvard Business Review,* Vol. 54 (1976), 71–83.

10. Hackman, J. Richard, and Edward E. Lawler III. "Employee Reactions to Job Characteristics," *Journal of Applied Psychology,* Vol. 55 (1971), 259–286.

11. Hackman, J. Richard, and Greg R. Oldham. "Development of the Job Diagnostic Survey," *Journal of Applied Psychology,* Vol. 60 (1975), 159–170.

12. Hackman, J. Richard, and Greg R. Oldham. "Motivation through the Design of Work: Test of a Theory," *Organizational Behavior and Human Performance,* Vol. 16 (1976), 250–279.

13. Hackman, J. Richard, Greg R. Oldham, R. Jason, and K. Purdy. "A New Strategy for Job Enrichment," *Technical Report No. 3* (New Haven: Yale University, 1974).

14. Hamner, W. Clay, and Ellen P. Hamner. "Behavior Modification on the Bottom Line," *Organizational Dynamics,* Vol. 4 (1976), 2–20.

15. Herzberg, F., B. Mausner, and B. Snyderman. *The Motivation to Work* (New York: Wiley, 1959).

16. Hulin, Charles L. "Individual Differences and Job Enrichment—The Case Against General Treatments," in J. R. Maher (Ed.), *New Perspectives in Job Enrichment* (Princeton, N.J.: Van Nostrand Reinhold, 1971).

17. King, Nathan. "Clarification and Evaluation of the Two-Factor Theory of Job Satisfaction," *Psychological Bulletin,* Vol. 74 (1970), 18–31.

18. Koch, James L. "Effects of Feedback on Job Attitudes and Work Behavior: A Field Experiment," *Technical Report No. 6* (Eugene, Ore.: University of Oregon, 1976).

19. Lawler, Edward E. "Job Design and Employee Motivation," *Personnel Psychology,* Vol. 22 (1969), 415–444.

20. Lawler, Edward E. *Pay and Organizational Effectiveness: A Psychological View* (New York: McGraw-Hill, 1971).

21. Lawler, Edward E., J. Richard Hackman, and S. Kaufman. "Effects of Job Design: A Field Experiment," *Journal of Applied Social Psychology,* Vol. 3 (1973), 46–62.

22. Litwin, George H., and Robert A. Stringer, Jr. *Motivation and Organizational Climate* (Boston: Harvard University Press, 1968).

23. Locke, Edwin A., Norman Cartledge, and Claramae S. Knerr. "Studies of the Relationship Between Satisfaction, Goal-Setting, and Performance," *Organizational Behavior and Human Performance,* Vol. 5 (1970), 135–158.

24. McClelland, David C. *The Achieving Society* (Princeton, N.J.: Van Nostrand, 1961).
25. Melcher, Arlyn J. *Structure and Process of Organizations* (Englewood Cliffs, N.J.: Prentice-Hall, 1976).
26. Murray, Henry A. *Explorations in Personality* (New York: Oxford University Press, 1938).
27. Oldham, Greg, J. Richard Hackman, and Jon L. Pearce. "Conditions Under Which Employees Respond Positively to Enriched Work," *Technical Report No. 10* (New Haven: Yale University Press, 1975).
28. Paul, W. J., K. B. Robertson, and F. Herzberg. "Job Enrichment Pays Off," *Harvard Business Review*, Vol. 47 (1969), 61–78.
29. Porter, Lyman W., and Edward E. Lawler III. *Managerial Attitudes and Performance* (Homewood, Ill.: Irwin, 1968).
30. Porter, Lyman W., and Richard M. Steers. "Organizational, Work, and Personal Factors in Employee Turnover and Absenteeism," *Psychological Bulletin*, Vol. 80 (1973), 151–176.
31. Schwab, Donald P., and Larry L. Cummings. "A Theoretical Analysis of the Impact of Task Scope on Employee Performance," *Academy of Management Review*, Vol. 1 (1976), 23–35.
32. Scott, William E. "Activation Theory and Task Design," *Organizational Behavior and Human Performance*, Vol. 1 (1966), 3–30.
33. Staw, Barry M. *Intrinsic and Extrinsic Motivation* (Morristown, N.J.: General Learning Press, 1976).
34. Steers, Richard M. "Effects of Need for Achievement on the Job Performance-Job Attitude Relationship," *Journal of Applied Psychology*, Vol. 60 (1975), 678–682.
35. Steers, Richard M. "Task-Goal Attributes, n Achievement, and Supervisory Performance," *Organizational Behavior and Human Performance*, Vol. 13 (1975), 392–403.
36. Steers, Richard M. "Factors Affecting Job Attitudes in a Goal-Setting Environment," *Academy of Management Journal*, Vol. 19 (1976), 6–16.
37. Steers, Richard M., and Daniel N. Braunstein. "A Behaviorally-Based Measure of Manifest Needs in Work Settings," *Journal of Vocational Behavior*, Vol. 9 (1976), 251–266.
38. Steers, Richard M., and Lyman W. Porter. "The Role of Task-Goal Attributes in Employee Performance," *Psychological Bulletin*, Vol. 81 (1974), 434–452.
39. Steers, Richard M., and Daniel G. Spencer. "The Role of Achievement Motivation in Job Design," *Journal of Applied Psychology*, in press.
40. Stone, Eugene F., Richard T. Mowday, and Lyman W. Porter. "Higher-Order Need Strength as a Moderator of the Job Scope-Job Satisfaction Relationship," *Journal of Applied Psychology*, in press.
41. Trist, Eric. "A Socio-Technical Critique of Scientific-Management." Paper presented at the Edinburgh Conference on the Impact of Science and Technology, University of Edinburgh, May 1970.

42. Turner, A. N., and P. R. Lawrence. *Industrial Jobs and the Worker* (Boston: Harvard University Press, 1965).
43. Umstot, Denis D., Cecil H. Bell, and Terrence R. Mitchell. "Effects of Job Enrichment and Task Goals on Satisfaction and Productivity: Implications for Job Design," *Journal of Applied Psychology*, Vol. 61 (1976), 379–394.
44. Vroom, Victor H. *Some Personality Determinants of the Effects of Participation* (Englewood Cliffs, N.J.: Prentice-Hall, 1960).
45. Vroom, Victor H. *Work and Motivation* (New York: Wiley, 1964).

M. Sami Kassem

University of Toledo

TOLSTOY ON ORGANIZATION

Some hundred years ago, Count Leo Tolstoy's *War and Peace* appeared in its final version. In the multitude of reviews of that monumental work, analysts have set out to prove that Tolstoy was a novelist, a philosopher, a historian, a moralist, a theologist, an artist, and/or a social critic of his time. None of the reviewers, so far as I know, have demonstrated that he was also a prophet of modern organization theory. Much of what Tolstoy had to say on organization has a peculiar relevance today, and numerous so-called modern organization theories support his views in a fascinating way. Tolstoyism was, in a sense, the forerunner of behaviorism, and this article will attempt to support that assertion. First, however, I shall refresh the reader's memory regarding the landmark novel in order to provide background for an appreciation of Tolstoy's theory of organization.

Like Boris Pasternak's *Doctor Zhivago*, Tolstoy's *War and Peace* is an epic novel. Its hero was to be a participant in the Russian Decembrist Revolt of 1825 which, incidentally, was the forerunner of the "back to the people" movement of the seventies and the revolutionary movement which eventually culminated in the downfall of the Tsardom and the 1917 Revolution. But in studying the Decembrist conspiracy, Tolstoy's thoughts went back to the period in which it had ripened—to the French invasion of Russia in 1812. The story of the Napoleonic invasion, the part played in it by the aristocracy from which the Decembrists came, and the causes of the tremen-

M. Sami Kassem, "Tolstoy on Organization," *Business Horizons*, April 1977, pp. 9–15.

dous upsurge of national feeling which swept through the whole of Russia offered Tolstoy the basic ingredients that make up this historical work.

Throughout the work, Tolstoy has infused many of his views on organizations, how they are structured and run, and who runs them. His method is to use the French and Russian military organizations as cases for discussion. In order to sift out the relevant material, certain chapters of this voluminous novel will be examined, along with the two epilogues which contain most of Tolstoy's views on organization. The logic underlying my presentation is simple. Given the nature of man, the basic task of organization theory is to find an answer to the twin questions of organization design and administrative action. My analysis follows this design quite closely. It begins with Tolstoy's concept of man, moves into an examination of his views on organizations and their leadership, and is followed by an evaluation of these views in the light of contemporary organizational literature. The article concludes with some remarks on the potential contributions of popular literature to the study of organizations.

CONCEPT OF MAN

The key thesis of *War and Peace*, expressed throughout the fictional and historical characters and fully developed in the Second Epilogue, is that man's freedom to chart his own destiny and shape his own history is limited. This is so because he is subject to both natural laws and organizational codes. Once he has become acquainted with these constraints, man is expected to respect them and subject himself to their influence. Despite learning that his will is subject to laws, however, man does not and cannot behave accordingly. Instead of submitting to these laws and codes, he is constantly trying to get around them and, thereby, increase his feelings of freedom. According to Tolstoy, man must feel free in order to live. However, this feeling can be a false one, and it is ultimately the perception of freedom and not freedom itself which is enjoyed and is the goal which motivates behavior and propels action. According to the author, "all man's efforts, all his impulses to life, are only efforts to increase his freedom of action." As an actor in a social system, man can't operate free-handedly; there is always a certain measure of freedom and a certain measure of inevitability in what he does. A belief in free will is essential to his existence—it is an acknowledgement of his consciousness. But necessity is also essential. The two concepts are used in defining each other—the interaction of form and substance. Without these concepts, Tolstoy contends "any representation of man's life is impossible." All that we know of the life of man is merely the relation of Freedom to Necessity; that is, an avowal of the laws of Reason."

Many examples in the novel document Tolstoy's conception of man. Pierre's decision to marry Helene is not a free one; fate brings him and Natasha together, chance unites Princess Marya and Nikolai, Sonya is doomed to become an old maid. The same concept is also expressed in the historically dubious contrast between Kutuzov, the old, one-eyed Russian general, and Napoleon, the Emperor of France—between the man who knows he cannot lead, and, therefore, never makes a plan or gives an order but lets himself be carried along by events, and the man who thinks he is leading and, therefore, imposes his will on the course of history.

ORGANIZATION STRUCTURE_____

In the early chapters of Part II, Tolstoy illustrates the pyramidal nature of the military organization. The hierarchy is graphically described through conversation among rank and file soldiers and the officers. Tolstoy then depicts Kutuzov (general in charge of all operations) and the general staff of the Russian-Austrian Alliance. Finally, he proceeds to show how an individual (in this case Nikolai Rostov) becomes part of the whole and takes his place as a smooth-working cog in the military machine. Tolstoy further emphasizes this hierarchical structure and the huge gap between the commanders and the rank and file soldiers later in Part II. He points out that the unselfish soldiers who accept anonymity contribute more heroism to their cause than do the self-conscious men at the top.

In Part V of *War and Peace*, Tolstoy describes the derivation of power in organizations, first in light of how it is viewed by the traditionalists, and then in its evolutionary form. Here, too, he describes the power structure through the actions and thoughts of his characters. In the traditional view, all power emanates from God and is issued down through the chain of being. In the novel, all power emanates from Alexander, the Emperor of Russia. This power is his "divine right." The emperor delegates power to the hierarchy if he desires to do so. Those below the emperor obey him because he must know what is right. Soldiers must only obey orders, die if necessary, and accept punishment if they are punished.

Tolstoy does not condemn the blind obedience which is characteristic of this form of power because he shows that it is based on a rational system of ethics and, therefore, completely logical in the eyes of those who submit to it. The example used is that this rational system of ethics demands the same acquiescence of Alexander (the emperor) to God as it does of Rostov (a soldier) to Alexander.

Tolstoy does not, however, believe that the traditional view of power is relevant to modern organizational life. The latter sections of Part V describe the waning power of a static, ethically based society and the rise of a new order where the "free" individual is ascendant. In Tolstoy's view, power must flow upwards rather than downwards, that is, be granted by the masses. He synthesizes the antithetical concepts of free will and necessity to show how power must come from below. For example, in one instance, Alexander (the divine-right sovereign), in the crisis of the Napoleonic invasion, convened even the lowliest to advise him. The national emergency demanded the response of its citizens as free men, not as servants of the king, in order to overcome the threat to their existence. Here Tolstoy shows how the old order gives way to the new through historical necessity; masses of men must act as free individuals who define themselves through a mass goal.

In the Second Epilogue, Tolstoy sums up his views on organization structure and power as follows:

> For common action people always unite in certain combinations, in which regardless of the difference of the aims set for the common action, the relation between those taking part in it is always the same.
>
> Men uniting in these combinations always assume such relations toward one another that the larger number take a more direct share, and the smaller number a less direct share, in the collective action for which they have combined.
>
> Of all the combinations in which men unite for collective action one of the most striking and definite examples is an army.
>
> Every army is composed of lower grades of the service—the rank and file—of whom there are always the greatest number; of the next higher military rank—the corporals and noncommissioned officers—of whom there are fewer, and of still higher officers of whom there are still fewer, and so on to the highest military command which is concentrated in one person.
>
> A military organization may be quite correctly compared to a cone, of which the base with the largest diameter consists of the rank and file; the next higher and smaller section of the cone consists of the next higher grades of the army, and so on to the apex, the point of which will represent the commander in chief.
>
> The soldiers, of whom there are the most, form the lower section of the cone and its base. The soldier himself does the stabbing, hacking, burning, and pillaging and always receives orders for these actions from men above him, he himself never gives an order. The noncommissioned officers (of whom there are fewer) perform the action itself less frequently than the soldiers, but they already give commands. An officer still less often acts directly himself, but commands still more frequently. A general does nothing but command the troops, indicates the objective, and hardly ever uses a weapon himself. The commander in chief never takes direct part in the action itself, but only gives general orders concerning the

movement of the mass of the troops. A similar relation of people to one another is seen in every combination of men for common activity—in agriculture, trade and every administration. *[Emphasis added.]*

> *And so without particularly analyzing all the contiguous sections of a cone and of the ranks of an army, or the ranks and positions in any administrative or public business whatever from the lowest to the highest, we see a law by which men, to take associated action, combine in such relations that the more directly they participate in performing the action the less they can command and the more numerous they are, while the less their direct participation in the action itself, the more they command and the fewer of them there are; rising in this way from the lowest ranks to the man at the top who takes the least direct share in the action and directs his activity chiefly to commanding.*
>
> *This relation of the men who command to those they command is what constitutes the essence of the conception called power. (II, pp. 818–820)*

Our presentation thus far leaves some doubt in the reader's mind that Tolstoy is more of a classicist than behavioralist in his views on organization. It would be obviously unfair, in the light of other evidence, to convey this impression and to support such a characterization. For, in addition to his democratic political theory of power he, in the later chapters of Part III, recognizes that besides the existing protocol within the hierarchy, there operates another and more actual system of subordination which, for example, allows a captain and a lieutenant to talk while a general respectfully listens. This system represents what would be termed the informal organization structure and gives an illustration of how decisions are actually made in an organization.

THEORY OF LEADERSHIP_____

Tolstoy's theory of leadership is part and parcel of his inquiry into the causes of historic events and the forces that move nations. He rejected the "Great Men" theory developed by biographical and general historians. As a believer in destiny, he argued that the men historians identified as great were merely labels on events, not prime movers. And, like all labels, they have the least possible connection to the event itself. Furthermore, he believed that leadership was overrated because leaders can do little more than reflect whatever historical processes are at work in the society. According to Tolstoy, the best leaders are the ones who, instead of making history, carry it out with a minimum of fuss. They sense which way history is going and place themselves in its forefront. These kinds of leaders perceive, more often through intuition than through cool calculation, what the constructive forces at work in their societies are, and then help them along. Their behavior may appear less adventurous and heroic than that of the great men, but it is possible that their work will be more lasting.

Throughout the Second Epilogue, Tolstoy contrasts in vivid detail the leadership behavior of Napoleon and Kutuzov—the former exemplifies what historians regard as a great man, and the latter personifies what the author considers an effective leader. These historical figures are painted "in motion" like the fictional ones. Consider the following behavioral portrait he draws of Napoleon and compare it with that of Kutuzov.

A man of will (Napoleon) wishes to impose his ideas on his followers and on the nations which he dominates. He wants everyone to submit to him. He treats his generals like children. He brutalizes them, scolds them and gives them no responsibility. He never fails to remind them that they owe him everything. This is illustrated by Napoleon's letter to Murat when the latter, on the eve of Austerlitz, took it upon himself to negotiate an armistice with the advanced guard of the Prince of Bagration. Napoleon severely reminds him that it is not for him to take such initiatives, that he should merely obey orders.

Similarly, Napoleon puts Talleyrand, who took the liberty of trying to negotiate with the enemy, firmly in his place. In the anger for which he was famed, Napoleon says to him, "You're nothing but s____ in a silk stocking." During the same session, he says to his face, "You didn't tell me that your wife is unfaithful with San Carlos."

During the battle of Borodino, described by Tolstoy, Berthier puts forward the name of a division which could be sent as a reinforcement. Napoleon accepts, then changes his mind for no apparent reason and without explanation. The eve of the battle, he visits the troops, inspects them, gives orders, but explains nothing. By adopting this aloof and scornful attitude and by ridiculing those who serve him, he believes himself to be proving his power, his authority. He does not treat them like intelligent, responsible men. His attitude is not helpful: when he criticizes, it is not to help his men prove themselves, but to assert his personal image on everyone and particularly on history. (The historical accounts of that era prove this fact. The Battle of Auerstadt, won by one of his generals, is put in the background to make way for the Battle of Iena, won by Napoleon.)

Yet Napoleon is pictured as a benevolent autocrat who manifests concern for his troops, especially the old guard. At Borodino he enquires whether they have received their biscuit and rice rations. Not trusting Rapp, his *aide-de-camp*, he checks this out himself. Nevertheless, he was a megalomaniac who, at the gates of Moscow, was dreaming about the attitude he would take when the leading citizens arrived to hand the keys of their city to him, and dreaming of the charitable work he would do in the name of his mother.

Finally, Napoleon is shown as consciously posing for history. When de Beausset shows him the portrait of his son, Napoleon assumes the pose he believes he would be expected to take, as he does when he enters Moscow. He poses for posterity. He tries to influence the times. All these postures are negated by Tolstoy. Each step of Napoleon's is shown to be of no purpose. For example, during battle he continues giving orders that no longer have any meaning and which do not correspond to reality; the situation changes too rapidly for one man to be able to influence it. This man who believes he is influencing the times is merely serving them. They are predetermined and Napoleon's influence is trifling.

For Douglas McGregor, Napoleon was a follower of Theory X. He made a certain set of motivational assumptions about his men and acted accordingly. One cannot delegate authority to followers; one must discipline them and reward them when necessary. Napoleon might cover his companions with gold, titles and decorations and be very surprised to see them betray him.

In contrast, Kutuzov incarnates the Russian soul, the Russian people. He does not take himself for a genius, he is not eternally posing for historians of future generations, he never makes a plan, he never gives an order, he lets himself be carried along by events. "He plainly had no patience with book-learning and intelligence, he had some other and more decisive form of knowledge," wrote Tolstoy. And he possessed that decisive knowledge because he was Russian, and therefore had a sense of fatality. He knew that it is useless to try to change things. He did not actively intervene during the battle. Instead, he waited.

For Tolstoy, this waiting is a great art. Kutuzov foresees the outcome and its significance. He has one goal in mind: the liberation of Russia. Having established the people's aim, he foresees that things will work out and tries, as far as possible, to restrain his assistants who wish to fight. He does not want any unnecessary loss of life and does not wish to worsen the living conditions of his men. And, unlike Napoleon, Kutuzov is not a strong personality, but an incarnation of the people, hence his modesty. He allows his assistants to speak their minds to such a degree that the German generals assigned to him have little respect for him. Tolstoy writes:

> The people, by strange ways, chose him [Kutuzov] because they recognized that the old man who had fallen out of favour possessed a superhuman sixth sense; they chose him against the will of the tsar, and made him their representative in a people's war. It is this "trait" alone that raised him to the position of supreme power, in which, as a commander in chief, he strove with all his might, not to slay and exterminate, but to save and spare.

By comparing Napoleon, who wants to be a great man in history, and Kutuzov, who incarnates the Russian people, Tolstoy outlines the parallel between free will and fatalism. He tries to belittle the role of Napoleon, who manages by details. By contrast, he elevates and exalts the role of Kutuzov, who manages by exceptions. He justifies what the historians called the negligence, incapability and indecision of Kutuzov and turns it into a strategy. Here, the writer is transformed into a hagiographer. Chauvinism makes his hand heavy; everything is rose-colored on the Russian side, black on the French.

EVALUATING TOLSTOY'S THEORY

If the preceding exposition is correct, I would be prepared to argue that Tolstoy was among the first to detect the imperfections of the conventional organizational wisdom and to lay the foundation for modern organization theory. His theory seems to meet both the general and special requirements of an overall organization theory. For one thing, it is complete, coherent, valid and consistent. For another, it provides valuable guidelines to the twin questions of organization design and administrative action. Finally, the guidelines it provides appear to be consistent with modern theory and research in organizational behavior. To be sure, let us review the elements of his theory and see how this theory might have influenced contemporary literature.

Concept of Man

Tolstoy was among the early philosophers to recognize the complex nature of man. He believed that man is not entirely free to do what he wants, and to choose what is in his best interests. This is simply because there are limits on his freedom of action, such as organizational rules, societal norms and supernatural laws. "Although man plans, God has a plan for him," writes Tolstoy.

Tolstoy's concept of bounded freedom is interesting for three reasons. First, it is a literary example of the impact of organizational constraints on the activities of the individual. Second, it emphasizes Tolstoy's wish to deflate the importance of the self and magnify the importance of other irrational, intangible and incomprehensible phenomena. Finally, the concept of limited freedom and its corollary, self-denial, though appearing foreign to the Western observer, are very much a part of the Oriental culture in general and the Russian culture in particular.

Concept of Organization

Tolstoy believes that organizations are necessary social tools that enable man to accomplish action that he cannot carry out alone. Because man cannot work well and think well simultaneously, he has built structures that allow some men to think and plan while others work. This separation of planning from doing has been identified by Frederick Taylor as a key principle of scientific management.

Like Max Weber and Fredrick Taylor, Tolstoy claims that his organizational model applies equally well to all types of human organizations. But, unlike them, his model takes into account nonrational considerations which induce employees to cooperate fully with the organization. Tolstoy was perceptive enough to recognize that human organizations are not what classical writers assumed them to be—well-oiled machines that function without static or friction. Far from it. They have imperfections of their own which he considered not only ordinary, but also desirable.

For one thing, these imperfections—which later came to be labeled as the "informal organization"—help increase workers' quest for freedom, reinforce their feelings of autonomy and eventually increase their willingness to work. For another, the informal organization helps reduce anomie, the workers' feeling of isolation. Therefore, it was Tolstoy, not Fritz Rothlisburger or Elton Mayo, who first discovered the informal organization and it is he who is the forefather of the modern human relations movement.

Concept of Power

Anticipating Chester Bernard and Rensis Likert, Tolstoy rejected the traditional view of the downward flow of power. He believed that what is obeyed is determined not by the one in command, but by the individual who is being commanded. He even claims that subordinates can render their superiors impotent without consciously opposing them. Like Bernard, Tolstoy makes no distinction between power and authority. He defines power as the collective will of the people transferred conditionally by their expressed or tacit consent to their chosen leader. It is the part of the cooperative system that men have formed out of their own free will to accomplish common goals—the relationship between the commanding few and the commanded majority.

Concept of Leadership

A corollary of Tolstoy's political theory of power is a democratic conception of leadership. Anticipating much of what Likert, McGregor and Fred Fiedler had to say about leadership, Tolstoy believes that an effective leader derives his influence from his followers. His job is entirely different from theirs: he expresses their will, shares their goals, considers their feelings, worries about their welfare, enlists their opinions, does the most thinking (plans), never takes part in direct action, sees what is important (manages by exceptions), knows how and when to use his authority, and most important of all, he acts according to the law of the situation.

Is this simply a kind of harmless nonsense, perhaps copied from a modern textbook on executive leadership? Lest this might be viewed as such, let me refer the reader back to the novel again, especially to the comparison Tolstoy makes between Napoleon and Kutuzov. Though Tolstoy appears to the Western observer as a fatalist who turns a blind eye on Kutuzov's positive generalship qualities, there is no doubt that the symbolically passive general acts in the novel. He rescues his army from danger; he makes important decisions; he refuses to defend Vienna. He chooses between different courses of action (to retreat, not to make a stand at Krems). He guides the spirit of the army as far as he is able. And in this, there is nothing incompatible with Tolstoy's central idea. The point is that he knows instinctively when events are beyond his control and submits accordingly. His impassivity on really important occasions reflects a logical and consistent policy which in those contexts shows responsibility and wisdom. Whether, in fact, the real Kutuzov was such a wise and consistent leader is beside the point. He is shown throughout *War and Peace* as a man who is guided by events which he knows are too big for him, and not as one seeking, like Napoleon, to impose his will upon them.

Although *War and Peace* is primarily an epic novel, a considerable part of it, perhaps as much as 100 pages, deals with organizations and their administration. As our analysis suggests, Tolstoy treated these themes with great skill and penetration. His treatment more or less presaged current thinking. Anyone who lives in an organizational society recognizes what he has described as a familiar scene, perhaps a daily experience. But by reading this classic novel, those who study or practice administration can gain something of a new perspective on their roles (and also learn something about administration in nineteenth century Russia).

What is true of *War and Peace* may also be true of other administrative novels. My argument is a familiar one: a great deal of value can be learned about organizations and their managements, and learned painlessly, while engaged in recreational reading of works of novelists who set action in and about organizations. Through such reading one not only learns new things but also understands old things better. Additionally, one can get from literary treatments of organizations what professional and scholarly literature omits or slights—the subjective, the emotional, the valuational, the concrete, the remote, and distant. Students and managers of organizations ought to be aware of and exploit the novel as an additional source of information in their field.

ACKNOWLEDGMENT

The author wishes to thank G. Allen Brunner, Steven Spirn, and Giorgio Inzerelli for their suggestions during the writing of this article.

Howard R. Smith

University of Georgia

"BROTHER TO THE OX"

The other day we were talking about motivation in a supervisor training program. "How," a female supervisor wanted to know, "can I motivate some of my girls to do their best—and make a lot more money, too?" "O.K.," I said, "suppose you are right that some of these girls could do much more than they are doing. Let's figure how they would come out under your pay program if they did."

Here's the way it worked out. A particular girl she had in mind was producing 60 percent of the standard for the job—and drawing $2.15 an hour. She could "easily" have done 120 percent; others around her, girls no more quick or competent than she, were doing that regularly. And if she would produce that well, she would ge $2.82 per hour.

As we got into these calculations, I think the supervisor was herself suprised at what they showed. The difference between what the employee was acutally earning and what she could have earned had she pushed herself was $26.80 for a 40-hour week—which came to $18.00 to $20.00 a week after deductions.

Frankly, I was a little taken aback by her suprise. Might there not be many situations in which giving up $18.00 to $20.00 a week in exchange for the comfort of "coasting" on the job would be seen as a very acceptable tradeoff? To what extent, I find myself wondering, are managers out of touch with the kinds of tradeoff decisions their people often find desirable?

Howard R. Smith, "Brother to the Ox," *Management Review*, November 1975, pp. 4–12.

A "STUPIDITY ASSUMPTION"?

Douglas McGregor performed a yeoman service for our thinking by focusing attention on the assumptions we were making. In particular, he highlighted some assumptions that were getting in our way—assumptions such as the one asserting that "the average human being has an inherent dislike for work and will avoid it if he can." The question for us, however, is whether we are now making a different assumption that may also be leading to trouble. It might be called "the stupidity assumption." It would read like this: "The average human being is too unsophisticated to know when he is being offered a poor deal."

How often do we, as the supervisor in my recent training program, diagnose as inadequate motivation the failure of workers to seize opportunities they might well not see as desirable. Do we frequently, in other words, fail to look at what we are doing with, for, and to workers in terms of the "bargain" they see themselves getting.

There is, by the way, little question that bosses are quite alert to the "bargain" dimensions of what they are doing. Thus I asked this particular supervisor why her organization would keep a 60 percent performer around. Her reply was candid and revealing. "Because," she said, "in ourlabor market that's what we have to hire to get the employees we need."

Surely no one really doubts that workers keep as close a watch on their "trade terms" with organizations. Witness this situation that came out of another training program: We were talking about absenteeism. One first-line supervisor asked if he might tell the group about a case he had recently run into. Pressured by his own absenteeism problem to do some investigating, he had found one man who over the preceding 12 months had managed to be away from work exactly—no more, no less—one day every week. The teller of this story had then confronted his man with this information and was told, "Of course! I work it out that way because I can't live on three days' pay a week."

THE SHADOW OF THE SPEEDUP

Often there seems to be an undercurrent of suprise when these kinds of things surface—as if a stupidity assumption really is operating. Note yet another recent exchange:

"How," one supervisor wanted to know, "do you motivate a man who doesn't want money?" Of course I asked, "What makes you think he doesn't want money?" The answer came quickly back, "Because he could make a lot more of it than he does, but he won't do it." He then elaborated by saying that this man was so good on his machine that he could make 150 percent on incentive instead of the 115 percent he was averaging.

My next question was almost as obvious. "If," I said, "he started regularly making 150 percent, how long would you let him do that?" I was not prepared for what happened next. The entire group burst out laughing.

In retrospect it is clear enough what they thought was funny. Even to these quite low-level bosses, it was immediately evident that a consistent 150 percent incentive payment would be seen by the company as a "bad bargain"—to be forthwith worked out differently. Is it not, then, worth particular note that they evidently did not see a similar "bad bargain" for the worker who vigorously increases his output only to lose much of what he thought he would gain?

AN ERA OF BROKEN PROMISES

As I reflected on this one, however, it seemed clear that I was no longer dealing with isolated instances. For this situation pointed backward in time to a broad pattern of just such thinking that shaped a major characteristic of an entire era of management. That era was called, among other things, "scientific management." Scientific management vigorously pioneered the idea of incentive compensation: Workers who did better than others in their production would fare better on payday in proportion to their higher output. By using incentive compensation programs, the sizeable problem of worker "soldiering" was at the very least supposed to become much smaller.

It is now history that things did not work out that way. In the late 1920s it was discovered that the problem F. W. Taylor had dedicated his genius to resolve was as pervasively troublesome as ever. Moreover, it can be argued persuasively that as much as anything else it was the stupidity assumption that got in the way.

Like the boy who cried wolf, managers may have been fairly successful in getting workers to respond to attractive-looking incentives—for a time. But then, almost invariably it seemed, would come the speedup, a reengineering of equipment or job making possible a downward readjustment of compensation. After bargain-conscious workers had experienced that frustration only a few times, they devised a response that has been quite standard ever since.

Just as the worker I was told about acted, superficially, as if he did not want money, so did workers much more generally defend themselve against "promises" that would probably be broken. Of course no one will play hard at a game he is almost certain to lose. Workers, accordingly, systematically kept (keep) their distance from a game in which the odds were (are) so evidently stacked in favor of the house. Which is to say that managers practicing the speedup will surely learn a lot about the slowdown.

EVERYONE TO HIS OWN TRADEOFFS

Does that not, in truth, suggest the workings of a presupposition, dating from some time ago, that workers are too unsophisticated to know the difference between a good deal and a poor one? Here's another episode that emphasizes once again that dysfunctions flowing from this assumption may still be more troublesome than would easily be guessed.

The supervisor that told this story was thoroughly upset. For more than a year two of his girls, close friends of one another, had consistently produced at 125 percent of standard on incentive. Then, quite abruptly, they decided to limit their output in order to, as they put it, "live a little." And so, each matching the other's production piece by piece, they reduced what they were turning out by a quite noticeable 10 percent. When they candidly told their boss what they were doing—and why—in response to his query, they were quite surprised that he was disturbed by the fact that they were not "doing their best."

Perhaps it is only a detail that these girls were fired; alas, they had been both careless and candid vis-à-vis a management that could not take this sort of thing in stride. But it is worth a pause to note the bargaining double standard implicit in this situation, the stupidity assumption that, though bosses will bargain toward their employees, the latter will not bargain back.

For example, note how incentive pay is typically related to output—as we offer these kinds of bargains to workers. It is not at all to criticize if we recognize that in practice we do arrange for the company to have—to dispose of—the largest proportion of added revenue from marginal output increases. The other side of that, of course, must be its consequences vis-à-vis the tradeoff choices workers make.

Put more pointedly, incentive compensation is perhaps primarily useful to managers as it helps them calculate more closely their most basic tradeoff. Almost by definition, therefore, this way of doing can also assist workers more carefully to calculate their most basic tradeoff. Not only are low-level employees sophisticated enough to know the difference between good bargains and bad ones, they are sophisticated enough to devise improvements in what they are getting. To be sure, employers and employees are working toward very different tradeoffs—money versus output in one case, money versus "living a little" in the other. But whoever supposes that workers would not make as much use of this kind of opportunity as their bosses may be caught up in assumptions that can get cripplingly in the way.

"BROTHER TO THE OX"

Of course, nothing here depends upon being more dramatic, or saying things more harshly, than is warranted by the facts. It is, for example, recognized that there were (are) many reasons for "tightening loose rates" in an incentive compensation system. More broadly, behavior that seems irrational from one perspective may be quite rational when viewed more fully. It is understood, furthermore, that the case here for a stupidity assumption is based primarily on circumstantial evidence. Unfortunately, it is the way of assumptions that they operate at a low level of visiblity.

But perhaps a few more substantive obversations can also be made. Thus it is surely no coincidence that the term "paternalism" became a way of describing a fundamental approach to employer-employee relationships. It may, too, take some of the sting out of the idea of assuming others to be stupid to think of childhood as our model of stupidity. None of this however, alters the unilateralness of parents (managers) caring/planning for children (workers), which is what paternalism has always meant. It was in this spirit of organizations as responsible for their people, and therfore not with tongue in cheek, that the president of the Reading Railroad in 1904 asserted that:

> The rights and interests of the laboring man will be protected and cared for not by labor agitators but by the Christian men to whom God in his infinite wisdom has given the control of the public interests of the country.

In other words, if it were only a caricature when Herman Wouk in one of his novels described the United States Navy as an organization designed by geniuses to be run by idiots, nevertheless something very real was being caricatured. Might not much the same thing be said about all complex organizations put together by way of narrow worker specialization—and that includes a very large proportion of such organizations? And at that point it is all too easy to recall that the "father" of scientific management himself once said:

Now one of the very first requirements for a man who is fit to handle pig iron . . . is that he shall be so stupid and phlegmatic that he more nearly resembles . . . the ox than any other type.

To be sure, students of Taylor insist tht it is unfair to suggest that this reflects his thinking. And, again, there is nothing to be gained by exaggertation. Remember, however, the childhood model of stupidity—and then put that model side by side with this vignette from Taylor's justly famous conversation with Schmidt, the pig-iron handler:

Now hold on, hold on. Your know just as well as I do that a high-priced man has to do exactly as he's told from morning till night. You have seen this man [the supervisor] here before, haven't you?

No, I never saw him.

Well, if your are a high-priced man, you will do exactly as this man tells you tomorrow, from morning till night. When he tells you to pick up a pig and walk, you pick it up and you walk, and when he tells you to sit down and rest, you sit down. You do that right straight throughout the day. And what's more, no back talk. Now a high-priced man does just what he's told to do, and no back talk. Do you understand that? When this man tells you to walk, you walk; when he tells you to sit down, you sit down and you don't talk back at him. Now you come on to work here tomorrow morning and I'll know before night whether you are really a high-priced man or not.

THE ASSUMPTIONS OF JOB ENRICHMENT_____

There is, or course, no way to guess how widely the stupidity assumption still lives among us. Very possibly it is quite vigorous—if only in its "wishful thinking" manifestation. However, rather than indulge in gross speculation to little purpose, perhaps this discussion would be a useful backdrop against which to say some things about job enrichment. And be it most emphatically noted that these things are not said in any spirit of objecting to or antagonism toward job enrichment.

The basic thesis of job enrichment is that the job itself can be an effective motivator. Put more starkly, though surely no less accurately, job enrichment builds on the expectation that workers in an enriched job situation will not have to be paid more money to produce more.

Here is a most interesting follow-on from the rise and fall of the scientific management movement. Given the history of broken promises that became much of what that philsoophy meant to workers, the principal thrust of "the gospel of efficiency" was to deenrich workers jobs in an effort to obtain more output, while giving them in return a minimum amount of additional compensation. Job enrichment—appropriately, by contrast—endeavors to obtain more output by enriching workers' jobs, while giving them in return a minimum amount of additional compensation.

Of course, half a loaf is better than no bread. That job enrichment will often be seen as more desirable than job deenrichment hardly requires argument. And that getting no more money for doing enriched work is preferable to naked speedup can also be taken for granted. But it does not follow that these truisms move us beyond the stupidity assumption. Though workers frequently do trade off working conditions against take-home pay, the world we live in is really put together very differently than the job enrichment thesis suggests.

"THEY DON'T WANT RESPONSIBILITY ANY MORE"

Overwhelmingly in that world, and very particularly at higher levels in organizations, those who have enriched jobs receive larger compensation in addition. More concretely, within a given organization there will likely be a fairly close correlation between the enrichment of work and the financial compensation that goes with it. Thus a promotion typically means a greater job challenge *and* more money; a man slected for a sizeable delegated responsibility—delegation, of course, being one of the primary forms of job enrichment—will expect to be paid more for taking on these added responsibilities. Indeed, in this realm of relationships, powerful sentiments of equity attach to the equivalents established between responsibility—which is to say, enrichment—and pay.

In short, where the prevailing compensation pattern calls for paying more expressly for the doing of higher-level work, the job enrichment formula asks people to increase their contribution for nothing—except for the "joys" of, quite literally, doing more. But preferring, under certain circumstances, enriched to deenriched work is not the same thing as preferring or enjoying work. Moreover, being willing, again under certain circumstances, to give up economic job rewards in exchange for noneconomic compensations is not the same thing as being eager to do that. And choosing a best among available alternatives is not a commitment not to count costs relative to values. When, then, assumptions are made that build on these possibilities, as if workers do not know what is happening to them, does that not once again highlight a bargaining double standard that may prove not to be as useful as many are hoping?

Indeed, is there not here something of the Aesop's Fable about the wolf and the crane? The wolf, remember, had a bone caught in his throat. He asked the crane to remove it—for a handsome reward. The crane agreed, and putting his head into the wolf's mouth, took out the bone. He then asked for his payment. To which the wolf replied: "My good fellow, you have had your head between a wolf's jaws and you are still alive. Is that not reward enough for you?"

Two cases in point—to make sure no one supposes this emphasis to be only theoretical. In a very large organization an interviewee was complaining about his span of control, wishing it were only about half as wide. In substantial part for fun, I turned to my colleague and said, "How about that! Here's a man who would rather not have more job 'enrichment." But our informant was in no mood for jesting about his choice of tradeoffs. "Of course," he retorted, "any time I can give up problems without reducing my salary—I'll take that any day." Might there not be a lot of that around— people who take on what is called job enrichment as a burden in order to get paid for it?

And that situation then makes it difficult to know how another kind is to be understood. How often we hear it said, "They don't want responsibility." The last time I heard that was in connection with a job rotation training program in a large savings and loan organization. The employees would be put, successively, into a half-dozen departments for a learning period— in the process working nowhere long enough to become either really familiar with the work or "one of the gang" doing it. At the end of about two years the successful candidate would be eligible for a sort of lead-man job.

The complaint was that employees were not putting themselves into this program much any more. At the time this came up in a group discussion, the relevant box score looked something like this. Bear in mind the discomfort that typically goes with living in a learning situation. In the history of this program, ten people had gotten all the way through it. Of these, two had in fact been promoted—while in that same period four others had been put into these lead-man jobs who had not gone through the program. The increase in pay that would go with one of these promotions would come to something like $300 a year before deductions.

Now why were people not eagerly taking on this opportunity? Was it because they did not want responsiblity—or was this situation seen as some combination of a game not really worth working hard to win, and not likely to be won in any case? How much, shall we suppose, did the designers of this program think a small amount of job enrichment and four more after-deductions dollars a week would be worth to these workers?

WALKING IN THE OTHER FELLOW'S SHOES

To repeat, there is no purpose here of assaulting any route to enhanced productivity that works. But it is very important not to expect too much from approaches that only minimally take into account the tradeoffs workers see as appropriate or desirable—that go at employees as if they are not quite bright about their own affairs.

Edwin Markham, in his famous poem *The Man With the Hoe,* may have put this in just the right perspective:

> *Bowed by the weight of centuries he leans*
> *Upon his hoe and gazes at the ground,*
> *The emptiness of ages in his face,*
> *And on his back the burdens of the world. . . .*
> *   dead to rapture and despair,*
> *A thing that grieves not and that never hopes,*
> *Stolid and stunned, a brother to the ox?*

Note that there is here no denial that many workers in Markham's time—which, incidentally, was also Taylor's—were suggesting that that group would not always be that way.

> *How will the future reckon with this man?*
> *How answer his brute question in that hour. . . .*
> *When this dumb terror shall rise to judge the world,*
> *After the silence of the centuries?*

Surely, that is much of what we are up against on the motivation front. Because our workers have done a lot of growing up as human beings they are no longer "brother to the ox" among us. And we must therefore look very carefully at whatever dealing with them we are accustomed to build around a stupidity assumption.

Which is to say, as in a very popular song of recent vintage, we may have ahead of us a lot walking in the other fellow's shoes.

Morris Janowitz

University of Chicago

CHANGING PATTERNS OF ORGANIZATIONAL AUTHORITY

Current sociological perspectives toward organization have brought into focus the informal and interactive processes which modify legal and formal authority structures.[1] Empirical research in this area emphasizes an equilibrium analysis—the striving to achieve adjustment, balance, and the like. What processes favor or hinder a large-scale bureaucracy in the maintenance of its organizational identity under pressure of internal and external demands? Equilibrium analysis focuses on limited time spans, and as a result organizational change is seen only as it takes place within definite and prescribed limits.[2]

Much less emphasized is the necessity of focusing on the long-term transformations of administrative organization. Developmental analysis which seeks to understand organizational change can take the form of a concern with the restructuring in the pattern and character of authority.

Morris Janowitz, "Changing Patterns of Organizational Authority," *Administrative Science Quarterly*, March 1959, pp. 473–93.

[1] This article is part of a study, "The Professional Soldier and Political Power," supported by a grant from the Commitee on National Security Policy Research of the Social Science Research Council.

[2] See David Easton, "Limits of the Equilibrium Model in Social Research," in Heinz Eulau, Samuel Eldersveld and M. Janowitz, eds., *Reader in Political Behavior* (Glencoe, Ill., 1955), pp. 397–404.

Developmental analysis is not descriptive history, but it is analysis with a strong concern for the historical context.[3]

As organizational forms have grown more complex, bureaucratic authority has tended to be transformed. In order to maintain their organizational effectiveness authority systems have had to become less arbitrary, less direct, and even less authoritarian. The significance of persuasion has grown with the growing complexity of society. From this point of view there has been under industrialism a relative shift in the basis of authority from status toward morale in all types of bureaucratic organizations. An authority system based on status is an expression of a simple division of labor where co-ordination involves no more than compliance or adherence to rules, the morale system implies that co-ordination is too complex to be mechanical and requires positive involvement and incentives.

In this analysis the relative shift in forms of authority is described in terms of the shift from discipline based on *domination* to that involving *manipulation*, concepts which will be elaborated later. While the analysis is applied to the military establishment, since it can be considered the bureaucratic prototype, the transformation is also found in other authority structures. One major proposition is that the military despite its rigid hierarchical structure, has nevertheless been forced to modify its authority system from domination and rigid discipline to more indirect forms of control, as have other types of bureaucracies. In its own terms, the recent transformation of military authority may be even more extensive than that found in nonmilitary organizations. Of course, a shift in authority from domination to manipulation is hardly an all-or-none change; we are only speaking of trends and countertrends.

A second basic proposition, therefore, emerges—that the shift in organizational control to an emphasis on manipulation and persuasion is highly unstable and transitional. Already one can see the outlines of emerging patterns of authority which will be required if the military establishment is to achieve its organizational goals. For lack of a better term, such a change from present forms might be called a "fraternal type" of authority system. Moreover, these transformations of authority relations in the military establishment in some respects anticipate and foreshadow developments in civilian bureaucracies. Thus the similarities and differences between the military establishment and other types of large-scale organizations require continual comparison.

The contemporary military establishment has for some time tended more

[3] See Heinz Eulau, H. D. Lasswell's Developmental Analysis, *Western Political Science Quarterly*, 40 (June, 1958), 229–242.

and more to display characteristics typical of any large-scale nonmilitary bureaucracy. This is the result of technological change, which vastly increases the size of the military establishment, elaborates its interdependence with civilian society, and alters its internal social relations. Nevertheless the typical sociological analysis of military organization does not take into account the consequences of these trends and continues instead to emphasize its authoritarian, stratified-hierarchical, and traditional dimensions as a basis for distinguishing the military from the nonmilitary bureaucracy.[4]

Thus Campbell and McCormack in their study "Military Experience and Attitudes toward Authority,"[5] supported by a United States Air Force research contract, began with the hypothesis that air cadet training would increase authoritarian predispositions among the officer candidates. Since they assumed that the dominant characteristics of military organization were its authoritarian procedures, the consequences of participation in its training program would of necessity heighten authoritarian personality tendencies among those who successfully passed through such training. (Authoritarian personality tendencies imply both the predisposition arbitrarily to dominate others of lower status and simultaneously to submit to arbitrary higher authority.)

When the results of the research, as measured by the well-known authoritarian "F" scale, showed a decrease in authoritarian traits among cadets after one year of training, the authors were tempted to conclude that perhaps their research tools were inadequate.[6] Now even a superficial examination of the organizational processes of combat flight training would have indicated an emphasis on group interdependence and on a team concept of coordination to ensure survival which should have cautioned these researchers against their initial hypothesis.[7]

The view with which these social scientists approached the military

[4] Samuel A. Stouffer, *et al.*, *The American Soldier* (Princeton, 1949), I, 55; Arthur K. Davis, Bureaucratic Patterns in the Navy Officer Corps, *Social Forces*, Dec. 1948, pp. 143–153; Arnold M. Rose, The Social Structure of Army, *American Journal of Sociology*, 51 (March 1946), 361–364; Felton D. Freeman, The Army as a Social Structure, *Social Forces*, 27 (Oct. 1948), 78–83; Harold Brotz and Everett K. Wilson, Characteristics of Military Society, *American Journal of Sociology*, 51 (March 1946), 371–375; C. D. Spindler, The Military—A Systematic Analysis, *Social Forces*, 27 (Oct. 1948), 83–88; Charles H. Page, Bureaucracy's Other Face, *Social Forces*, 28 (Oct. 1949), 88–94.

[5] Donald T. Campbell and Thelma H. McCormack, Military Experience and Attitudes toward Authority, *American Journal of Sociology*, 62 (March 1957), 482–490.

[6] T. W. Adorno *et al.*, *The Authoritarian Personality* (New York, 1950), pp. 222–280.

[7] In fact, there is some empirical evidence that selection boards in the Air Force tend to select for promotion the less authoritarian officers, presumably in part through selecting well-liked men (E. P. Hollander, Authoritarianism and Leadership Choice in a Military Setting. *Journal of Abnormal and Social Psychology*, 49 (1954), 365–370).

establishment is partly based on civilian ideology. Partly, as Hans Speier points out in his critique of the *The American Soldier* research series, such a view exaggerates the differences between military and civilian organizations by overlooking what is common to large-scale organizations in general.[8] Many of the bureaucratic features of military life are in fact to be found in civilian organizations in varying degrees.

MILITARY STRUCTURE
AND COMBAT GOALS

One can hardly deny the significant differences that exist between military and non-military bureaucracies. The goals and purposes of an organization supply a meaningful basis for understanding differences in organizational behavior, and the military establishment as a social system has its special and unique characteristics because the possibility of hostilities are an ever-present reality.

A realistic appraisal of the implications of combat and combat preparation on military organization obviously starts with the social consequences of the changing technology of warfare. Although the narrowing distinction between the military establishment and non-military bureaucracies does not eliminate fundamental differences, three trends need to be emphasized.

First, military technology both extraordinarily increases the destructiveness of warfare and widens the scope of automation in the use of new weapons. It is a commonplace that both of these developments tend to weaken the distinction between military roles and civilian roles. Nevertheless, conventional units employing the airplane, the submarine, and airborne assault troops need to be maintained for limited warfare. Despite the growth of missile systems manned auxiliary methods for the delivery of new weapons require organization similar to conventional combat units. Even more important, no military system can rely on expectation of victory based on the initial exchange of firepower, whatever the forms of the initial exchange. Subsequent exchanges will involve units and formations—again regardless of their armament—which are prepared to carry out the struggle as soldiers, that is, subject themselves to military authority according to plan and continue to fight. The automation of war civilizes wide sectors of the

---

[8] Hans Speier, "The American Soldier and the Sociology of Military Organization," in *Studies in the Scope and Method of "The American Soldier"* ed. by Robert K. Merton and Paul F. Lazarsfeld (Glencoe, Ill., 1950), pp. 106–132.

military establishment, yet the need to maintain combat readiness and to develop centers of resistance after initial hostilities ensures the continued importance of military organization and patterns of authority.

Second, it can be argued that the revolution in military technology shifts the military mission from that of preparation for the use of violence to that of deterrence of violence. There can be no doubt that this shift in mission is having important effects on military thought and authority. Military elites are more and more forced to concern themselves with broad ranges of political, social, and economic policies. Again, there are limits to the consequences of this trend. The role of deterrence is not a new one for the military. Historically the contribution of the military to the balance of power was not the result of its civilian character. On the contrary, the balance-of-power formula operates, when it does, because the military establishment was prepared to fight effectively and immediately.

With the increase in the importance of deterrence, military elites have become more and more involved in diplomatic and political warfare, regardless of their preparation for such tasks. Yet the specific and unique contribution of the military to deterrence is the threat of violence which has currency—that is, the threat can be taken seriously because the possibility of actual violence is real. The types of weapons available do not alter this basic formula. In short, deterrence still requires an organization prepared for combat.

Third, the assumption that military institutions, as compared with civilian institutions, are resistant to change has been eliminated as the process of innovation in the military establishment itself has become routinized. Analysis of the relative impact on technological development of the requirements of war versus the requirements of civilian economic entrepreneurship has produced volumes of historical writing. Schumpeter in his brilliant analysis of modern imperialism argues that capitalist economic organization succeeded only as it opposed the military establishment.[9] For him the technological development of the capitalist economic system stood in opposition to the interests of the feudal aristocratic elements, which, unable to find their place in the changing social order, supplied the ideology and personnel for the military and imperialistic expansions from Western Europe up through the nineteenth century. In this view capitalism produced social change through technological innovation in order to accumulate capital and to make profits. By contrast, the military, concerned with honor and a way of life, stood in opposition to social change and technological innovation and accepted new developments in military organization with great reluctance.

[9] Joseph Schumpeter, *The Sociology of Imperialism* (New York, 1955).

In all probability military organizations of the middle of the nineteenth century were strongly resistant to technological innovation and derived their goals and tasks from other sectors of society—from the religious, from the political, or merely from a negative effort to escape the powerful dogmas of capitalist profit and business pacifism.

However, it is impossible to find support for Schumpeter's view of the antagonisms between business enterprise and the military order as a basis for understanding social change during the twentieth century. Military institutions, because of the nationalism on which they rest and the vast resources they command, can no longer be thought of as merely reacting to external pressures. The articulation of the military establishment with the business enterprise system is indeed too complex to be considered as simple antagonism. Moreover, the military creates requirements of its own for technological innovation which modify industrial organization. The classical view of the military standing in opposition to technological innovation is inapplicable as the present cycle of the arms race converts the armed forces into centers of support and concern for the development of new weapons systems.

Leadership based on military customs must share power with experts not only in technical matters but also in matters of organization and human relations. Specific organizational adaptations of the military even foreshadow developments in civilian society, since the military must press hard for innovation and respond rapidly to the strains created. For example, the continual need for retraining personnel from operational to managerial positions and from older to newer techniques has led to a more rational spreading of higher education throughout the career of the military officer rather than the concentrated dosage typical of the civilian in graduate or professional school.

There are of course powerful pressures against innovation. As long as imponderables weigh heavily in estimating military outcomes, and as long as the "fighter" spirit is required for combat, the military establishment cannot become completely technological in its orientation. The heroes of former engagements can with some validity press their personal experiences as a basis for decision making. The need to protect privilege as well as all the classic devices of bureaucratic behavior—military or civilian—imply that outmoded militarism persists even though technological necessity becomes dominant. Nor does acceptance of technological change necessarily imply acceptance of changes in approach toward political and diplomatic conflict. The residues of conservative military authority become manifest at times in an overemphasis on the use of force to regulate competing national interests.

Thus neither the increased automation of military technology, nor the military shift in mission from war making to deterrence, nor the decline in traditional military opposition to innovation can give a completely civilian form to military institutions. The function of military authority—the key to military organization—is undergoing systemic change; yet the character of military authority remains an expression of organizational requirements for combat and combat preparation—goals unique to military and military-type organizations.

CHANGING MILITARY AUTHORITY: FROM DOMINATION TO MANIPULATION

Although a preponderance of military personnel is engaged in administrative and logistical operations, military authority, if it is to be effective, must strive to make combat units its organizational prototype.[10] For combat the maintenance of initiative has become a crucial requirement of greater importance than the rigid enforcement of discipline. In the concise formulation of S.L.A. Marshall:

> The philosophy of discipline has adjusted to changing conditions. As more and more impact has gone into the hitting power of weapons, necessitating ever widening deployments in the forces of battle, the quality of the initiative in the individual has become the most praised of the military virtues.[11]

Close-order formations based on relatively low firepower could be dominated and controlled by direct and rigid discipline. But continuously since the development of the rifle bullet more than a century ago, the social organization of combat units has been altering so as to throw the solitary soldier on his own and his primary group's social and psychological resources. In World War II and again in the Korean conflict, the United States organizational crisis centered on developing the ability of the infantry soldier to make the fullest use of his weapons. The decision to fire or not to fire rested mainly with dispersed infantrymen, individually and in small primary groups. Thus the military with its hierarchical structure, with its

[10] The distinction betwen logistics and combat is a functional distinction and not a formal organizational distinction. It too is more and more difficult to make as the military establishment becomes more complex.

[11] S. L. A. Marshall, *Men against Fire* (New York, 1947), p. 22.

exacting requirements for co-ordination, and with its apparently high centralization of organizational power must strive contrariwise to develop the broadest decentralization of initiative at the point of contact with the enemy. Any new nuclear weapons systems short of total destruction creates the same organizational requirements.

The combat soldier—regardless of military arm—when committed to battle is hardly the model of Max Weber's ideal bureaucrat following rigid rules and regulations. In certain respects he is the antithesis of this. He is not detached, routinized, and self-contained; rather his role is one of constant improvisation. Improvisation is the keynote of the individual fighter or combat group, from seeking alternative routes to a specific outpost to the retraining of whole divisions immediately before battle. The impact of battle destroys men, equipment, and organization, which need constantly and continually to be brought back into some form of unity through on-the-spot improvisation. In battle the planned division of labor breaks down.

The military organization of today is forced to alter its techniques of training and indoctrination. Rather than attempting to develop automatic reaction to combat dangers, it requires a training program designed to teach men not only to count on instruction from superiors but also to exercise their own judgment about the best response to make when confronted by given types of danger. The designation "combat team" exemplifies the goals of such indoctrination since it emphasizes the positive contributions of each person regardless of rank.

Obviously technology conditions these changing internal social relations in the military. Modern weapons involve a complex division of labor and high levels of technical skill. The morale and co-ordination of the individual members of a group cannot be guaranteed by authoritarian discipline. The complexity of the machinery and the resultant social interdependence produce an important residue of organizational power for each participating member. All the members of a military group recognize their mutual dependence on the technical proficiency and level of performance of others as well as on the formal authority structure. Moreover, the increased firepower of modern weapons causes military forces to be more and more dispersed so that each unit becomes more and more dependent on its own organizational impetus.

Thus the impact of technology has forced a shift in the functions of military authority. Military authority must shift from reliance on practices based on *domination* to a widening utilization of *manipulation*. By domination we mean influencing an individual's behavior by giving explicit instruction as to desired behavior without reference to the goals sought. Domination involves threats and negative sanctions rather than positive incentives.

It tends to produce mechanical compliance. By manipulation we mean influencing an individual's behavior by indirect techniques of group persuasion and by an emphasis on group goals. Manipulation involves positive incentives rather than physical threats; though it does retain the threat of exclusion from the group as a form of control. The indirect techniques of manipulation tend to take into account the individual soldier's predispositions.

Despite its hierarchical structure and despite its legal code the military establishment presents a striking case of this shift from domination to increased reliance on manipulation. The transformation can be seen in every phase of organization behavior—for example, the narrowing of the differences in privileges, status, and even uniforms of the enlisted man and the officer, the development of conference techniques of command from the smallest unit to the Joint Chiefs of Staff themselves, or the rewriting of military law into the new Uniform Code. The report of the Doolittle inquiry following World War II on officer-enlisted man relations represented a high point in this development. Emphasis on manipulative control varies as between the various services, depending mainly on the rate and nature of technological change. The Air Force in some respects has gone the farthest in modification of its organizational behavior.

THE INSTABILITIES OF MANIPULATIVE AUTHORITY

The long-term outcome of the current transformation of the military from an organization having an underlying emphasis on domination to one showing increased reliance on manipulation is problematic. It is abundantly clear that present forms are highly transitional. Since the shift in military authority is a function of organizational requirements, it is not surprising that armies in totalitarian political systems display these same features. The organizational effectiveness of the Wehrmacht was based on highly developed practices of manipulation and group cohesion, within the context of radical repression of political and ideological deviation.[12]

Likewise the contradictory interplay of practices designed to stimulate group initiative and those required for organizational coordination are again general contemporary bureaucratic processes which are certain to create

---

[12] Edward A. Shils and Morris Janowitz, Cohesion and Disintegration in the Wehrmacht in World War II, *Public Opinion Quarterly*, 12 (1948), 280–315.

built-in strain and dilemmas in any large-scale bureaucracy. It can be argued that they are more extreme in military than in civilian organizations. In the military the requirements for initiative in the face of combat are very great, and simultaneously the professed need for more rigid organizational coordination is powerfully sanctioned. Organizations can and do function effectively despite internal strains and dilemmas, but the military has special characteristics which complicate and disrupt the successful incorporation of authority based on indirect control, group decision, and other manipulative techniques.

Devices for maintaining organization balance are slow to develop under these conflicting requirements. Thus, for example, it requires extensive training and great expertise to develop an officer cadre that is skilled in applying indirect techniques of control and whose use of indirect techniques of leadership will be accepted by subordinates as valid rather than mere sham. Likewise, the gap between formal regulations and the informal realities of command is especially great. This gap becomes a source of tension and confusion.

Equally disruptive to indirect discipline is the ideological orientation of portions of the military elite. In the United States and elsewhere the military elite holds a conservative ideological and political orientation which often is alarmed by and misinterprets the new requirements of military authority.[13] Segments of the military elite see the new requirements as potentially undermining the fundamental basis of authority and as threatening decision making on the strategic level. Their interest in technological change is not necessarily accompanied by an interest in organizational change. They fail to see how manipulative techniques supply the basis for developing the necessary strong subleadership required to operate effectively within a closely supervised larger military unit. In fact, they fail to see that indirect and manipulative control of rank-and-file leadership based on positive group cohesion is essential to maintain both decentralized initiative and operational control over widely dispersed military formations.

Furthermore, it does not necessarily follow that indirect organizational control interferes with strategic or tactical decisions. On the contrary, staff work in support of the strategical commander has traditionally been extensive before the commander arrives at a decision. The requirements of command have pushed this form of decision making down to the lowest operational units, and it is understandable that such a trend is resisted by

[13] C. S. Brown, "The Social Attitudes of American Generals, 1898–1940." Unpublished doctoral dissertation, University of Wisconsin.

military traditionalists. Typically, military elites are concerned that indirect control should not undermine the authority structure, and therefore they repeatedly attempt to limit the scope of manipulative and group consensus procedures on the part of lower commanders. As a result, as the older techniques of military domination break down under technological requirements, newer forms based on manipulation emerge highly unstable and laden with dilemmas.

The outlines of dysfunctional responses by military authority to the strains of organizational change are all too obvious. A number, illustrative of United States experiences but more generally applicable, are worthy of note—organizational ridigity, ceremonialism, and exaggerated professionalism.

Organizational Rigidity

Organizational rigidity means the handling of new problems through the mechanical application of traditional practices rather than by innovation. Some degree of organizational rigidity develops in any military establishment as soon as combat ends and the organization tends to return to simple forms of routine. But disruption follows the efforts to re-establish traditional discipline. The lessons of the necessity of initiative remain alive in those units whose routine training most closely approximates actual combat or is most hazardous, whereas concern with traditional discipline is a particular expression of ritualism among members of the military elite, who see their particular weapons systems becoming obsolete with no opportunity of regaining their organizational dominance.

Some quarters in the United States military have pointed to the events in Korea as justification for traditional discipline. There is no doubt that during the first phases of the Korean conflict ground troops lacked sufficient exposure to realistic training. However, improvised and realistic adaptations having little or nothing to do with formal discipline produced in Korea one of the most effective military forces in recent American military history. The performance of military units in Korea is a striking example of the conditions under which civilian apathy was prevented from influencing battle behavior by the performance of a professional officer corps, especially its junior elements, who were convinced that their organizational integrity was at stake.

The Womble committee of the Department of Defense, which sought to investigate the professional status of officers as an aftermath of the Korean conflict, issued a report in 1953 that contained strong overtones of concern for traditional forms of discipline and officer prerogatives.[14] The report, written as a reaction to the results of the Doolittle Board, dealt not only with basic matters of pay and promotion in the military establishment but gave emphasis to a formalism which seemed to be more oriented toward past ideology than the realities of military life.

A return to an organizational structure based on domination can only be achieved at a high cost. The repressive mechanisms of a totalitarian state are needed to enforce consistently such a high level of conformity; indeed we are now witnessing the partial renunciation of such levels of repression by totalitarian elites themselves. Given American cultural traits, the officer corps runs the risk of losing its most creative intellects, while the noncommissioned ranks, as discipline becomes harsher, attract those who are unsuccessful in civilian life. Besides, any widespread and conscious effort to reimpose stricter discipline is tempered by the political pressures that draftees can exert.

Ceremonialism

Since any serious return to the discipline of domination is blocked by the realities of military life and by civilian political pressures nostalgia for the past expresses itself in increased ceremonialism. Ceremonialism refers to those organizational processes that are conventional gestures and formal observances. The opportunities and evidence for increased ceremonialism are ample, from the reintroduction of the dress sword for naval officers to more close-order military parades.[15]

Ceremonialism is functional when it contributes to a sense of self-esteem and to the maintenance of organizational efficiency. Psychologically it is a device for dealing with the fear of death. But at what point does it interfere with the realistic requirements of the military establishment? Military ceremony seems at times to be a device for avoiding concern with unsolved problems of military management. Much of the increased ceremony appears to focus on patterns of social intercourse outside the military role. Ceremony thereby becomes a substitute for career satisfactions and a device for regulating the off-duty life of the military officer. As such it is a profound

[14] Department of Defense, Press Release, Dec. 3, 1953, "Final Report—Ad Hoc Committee on the Future of Military Service as a Career that Will Attract and Retain Capable Career Personnel."

[15] The close-order drill parade which was introduced with the advent of musketry was not only ceremonial but also a training exercise for the field of battle. Today a fire demonstration would be the appropriate equivalent of a combined combat training exercise and public spectacle.

source of tension between the professional soldier and the citizen soldier. Both the latter and the public at large often fail to see its purpose or significance.

Exaggerated Professionalism

Because of the drive for efficiency in the military establishment ritualist tendencies toward ceremonialism are diverted and are more easily expressed in the form of exaggerated professionalism. Professionalization can be defined as the process by which the members of an occupation develop a training procedure, a body of expert knowledge, and a set of operating standards. To speak of overprofessionalization implies that concern with the forms of professional status outweigh concern with functional performance.

Overprofessionalization is an expression of professions with low social status—and officership, despite public acclaim of individual military heroes—is a low-status profession. The results of a national sampling of opinion placed the prestige of the officer in the armed services below not only that of physician, lawyer, scientist, college professor, and minister but also that of public school teacher.[16] In this respect there is much similarity between the army officer and the social worker, especially since they are both professional groups dedicated to doing other peoples' "dirty work."

Overprofessionalization leads to an exaggerated concern with the specification of missions and roles and to organizational morale based on parochialism rather than on a sense of competence. The result is an emphasis on mechanical principles of military science at the expense of creative problem solving. Exaggerated professionalism increases interest in status differentials and, given the low ceiling on income and prestige in the military, results in an intensification of the struggle for minor advantages.

The professional status of the troop leader versus the technical and logistical expert becomes particularly acute and contributes to the dilemmas of developing consistency in authority patterns. In order to enhance the authority of those responsible for operational formations strenuous efforts must continually be made to differentiate the "fighter" from logistical personnel on the basis of pay, dress, and status. Yet the maintenance men press heavily for rewards and for control over the conditions of their employment, and technical specialists demand both special consideration

---

[16] Public Opinions Survey, Inc., Princeton, "Attitudes of Adult Civilians toward the Military Service as a Career," prepared for the Office of Armed Forces Information and Education, Department of Defense, Washington, 1955.

for their professional qualifications and at the same time the status and authority of combat personnel.

Moreover, the authority systems of technical and logistical formations are at variance with those of combat units. Here professional perspectives increase organizational strains. The leaders of technical units operate without recourse to authoritarian domination and often decry the disciplinary character of operating and line units. Yet they fail to recognize that combat units must develop much higher levels of positive group identification than technical units in order to be able to seek and to face danger. On the other hand, troop and operational commanders see in the standard operating procedures of technical and logistical units bureaucratic resistance to military effectiveness. Exaggerated professionalism deepens these differences.

THE PROSPECTS FOR ORGANIZATIONAL BALANCE: FRATERNAL-TYPE AUTHORITY

Each of these illustrative responses—organizational rigidity, ceremonialism, and exaggerated professionalism—has an adaptive counterpart simultaneously at work. The functional adaptations if successful would seem to be transforming the authority system of the military into a "fraternal type" order—the recognized equality of unequals—which theoretically would permit initiative and creativity within a hierarchical organization. The organizational behavior of the emerging fraternal type authority system would have two elements. On the one hand, the formal structure of authority is recognized and accepted by those in both superordinate and subordinate roles. There is less attempt to hide the facts of power and authority, as can be the case when manipulative practices become extreme. On the other hand, from the highest levels of the organization down to the very bottom, technical and interpersonal skill plus group loyalty qualify subordinate personnel for effective but circumscribed participation in the decision-making process. Since strategic decisions are centralized, the authority system accepts the decentralization of implementation as a desirable goal rather than as a threat to its existence. The gap between formal organization and the actualities of infomal procedures is thereby reduced. Fraternal-type authority is only one possible outcome of present tensions.

At the risk of a dangerous analogy the outcme of the shift in authority from *domination* to *manipulation* can be highlighted. Organizational behavior based on domination is the authority system analogous to the classical authority of the father over his son, comprehensive and absolute. Under fraternal-type authority the system reflects the authority of the older brother over the younger, circumscribed and functional. Although the older brother's superior authority cannot be denied because of the biological facts of age and the forms of family structure, the younger brother has his forms of equality because of the very same considerations.

More revealing than this analogy undoubtedly are the procedures and processes for modifying authority in the military which have the potential to render the fraternal type of discipline effective and functional.

1) *Organizational rigidity* does not develop if fraternal-type authority becomes established. Not only is traditional discipline seen as ineffective, but those in authority consider undue reliance on powerful negative sanctions as personally degrading. Instead there is a growing concern with those managerial techniques involved in the successful exercise of authority. The military career becomes defined as a career of managerial skill; true it is a career that is unique since it involves leading men into battle, but it is still an honorable managerial career, which ultimately requires public respect.

Thus the adaptive segments of the military elite seem to be interested in overcoming the types of criticism that the citizen soldier is prone to level at the military mind. In order to negate the criticism that many of those exercising authority are unqualified for their jobs, the commander must demonstrate his ability to exercise authority. If he performs the same task as his men, it is not simply a manipulative device—"Look we are all in it together"—but rather to show that he has passed the initiation rite and is fully qualified. In order to avoid the charge of senseless and arbitrary exercise of authority, he is careful to explain his "reasons why" whenever possible.

But most crucial under an ideal type system of fraternal authority is the fact that the officer must avoid exercising his authority as if he assumed a low level of intelligence among his subordinates. The fraternal-type organization is based on the assumption of open equality: any individual who can demonstrate his competence can rise. Since in the United States military establishment some enlisted personnel can and do become officers, this assumption is grounded in reality. Most social deficiencies in a man's background that might hinder his exercise of authority can be erased by military education. Thus officers exercising fraternal-type authority must assume that each soldier is a potential officer. This is like civilian society's dogma about the possibilities of social mobility.

Concern with technical competence, explanations of the purposes of commands, and assuming high performance potentials among subordinates are all incompatible with a continued demonstration by military leaders that the sanctions they hold in reserve are severe and ultimate. There is something of the older aristocratic outlook to be found in the successful and competent leader who is aware that to threaten is to demonstrate actual or potential weakness. He rather attempts to base his authority on his very presence and on his expertise. The older military dictum that authority inheres in the office rather than in the occupant is being modified to a considerable extent. "You salute the bars, not the man," is no longer tenable. The attempt is made to justify authority on the basis of personal qualities as well as role criteria.

2) A military elite concerned with adaptation avoids *ceremonialism* and concentrates instead on developing organizational cohesion and group solidarity. Cohesion and solidarity on the job are a function of technical competence and of the quality of interpersonal relations among the members and leaders of a military unit. Social research has emphasized the importance of practices which promote cohesive primary group relations if complex organizations are to operate effectively. The standardized procedures for replacing the human components of military organization operate to weaken social solidarity. A wide variety of techniques are available and are being employed to assist in the maintenance of primary group solidarity. These range, for example, from the modification of the replacement system from one based on individuals to one based on groups and units to special training academies for noncommissioned officers who figure so prominently in maintaining group cohesion. Fundamentally under a fraternal-type authority system, especially in a democratic society, organizational *esprit de corps* rather than ideological indoctrination supplies the basis for positive morale. This is strikingly the case for the Israeli Army which can be considered a military formation closely approximating the fraternal type of authority.

In addition, the military must have institutional devices for linking military life to family life and for controlling the tensions between these two spheres. In the past garrison life resulted in an intermingling of place of residence and place of work, especially during peacetime. Although these practices may have served to isolate military from civilian society, the military community was a source of social cohesion for its members both to the soldiers and to their families. The changing technology of warfare and changing patterns of military life are eliminating the geographically isolated military community. Now the military must assume on an organized basis many of the services rendered informally to military families on the basis of self-help. It is indeed striking to realize the extent to which the military has built into it many of the features of the welfare state. Private commercial interests are continually criticizing the military for its organizational socialism, but these features are important sources of its organizational solidarity.

3) The military establishment incorporating adaptive change would be constantly altering the content and scope of professional roles in order to avoid the dangers of a rigid division of labor and *exaggerated professionalism*. One measure of adaptation is the extent to which the classic struggle between the troop commander, the manager of men and machines, and the staff officer, the manager of plans and organizational co-ordination, can be overcome.

Professional training must be concerned with exposing the individual to a wide variety of experiences so that he can broaden his perspective and be prepared to deal with new and emerging tasks. If it is true that combat requires authority oriented toward maintaining initiative among a group and possessing the skills of indirect control, then the skills of the combat commander and the staff officer are in effect converging. Skill in interpersonal relations even more than technical competence is necessary. (One is struck by the number of United States higher staff officers who have combined achievement in both spheres as a result of their World War II experiences.) Thus the job requirements of the successful professional soldier in an adaptive army are not those of a disciplinarian, although he must be prepared to use the powerful sanctions at his disposal. This is not to deny that an important element of tension still exists between the emotional and technical requirements of many of the initial assignments of a combat officer, such as the fighter pilot or paratrooper, and the emotional and technical requirements of a commander. Yet for all those who survive the rigors of indoctrination, training, and initial assignment, the professional career of the officer holds the prospect of permitting the development of general managerial skills applicable in a wide range of assignments.

The changing content of professionalism in the military establishment alters the relationship between the civilian and military elites. It is not only the greater size of the military establishment and the increased importance of policies of national security which pose the problem of the interjection of the military elites into roles traditionally reserved for civilian leaders. More fundamentally it is the fact that the type of training and experience of military leadership are more relevant for and have greater transferability to civilian bureaucracies—both economic and governmental.

CONCLUSIONS

Throughout this analysis it has been assumed that the military establishment as a social system is no longer a major point of resistance to technological change—at least no more resistant than might be expected by an elite involved in a highly dangerous task. Organizational adaptations to these technological changes have been analyzed mainly in terms of the requirements of the military system of authority. The result has been a transformation of military authority from one based on domination to one employing more and more techniques of manipulation. Organizational processes of manipulative discipline are unstable and transitional. Adaptive and maladaptive responses in organizational behavior can be observed whose final outcome remains problematic. One possible functional outcome would be a "fraternal type" of authority which would maintain organization co-ordination and yet ensure the high levels of initiative required for combat. Whether such an organizational transformation develops depends not only on factors within the military organization but also on political and ideological considerations in civilian society which are not discussed here. The conditions under which selective service and conscription are modified or abandoned as air formations and nuclear weapons become more dominant will be extremely important. But even with professional armies, so to speak, there can be no possibility of a successful return to earlier forms of military authority, although one common response to the strains of change is an effort to reconstitute past arrangements.

Finally, these processes by which organizational authority is being transformed in the military are present in all types of large-scale bureaucracies. The movement from domination to manipulation seems to be a general pattern of social change. The fact that it is present even in the military is of particular theoretical importance.

James Owens

The American University

THE USES OF LEADERSHIP THEORY

Carl L. was facing a crisis. A technician by background and now in his late thirties, he had recently become manager of a group of technicians and found himself in the midst of almost open rebellion. He knew the job well and was outstanding in his abilities to organize, handle detail, plan, and control. His technicians were competent. But the group's morale had fallen to a point where all spirit and will seemed suctioned out of the group; the talent was there in abundance but simply not operating. What had gone wrong? And what should he do about it? His career depended on the answers.

Carl's managerial failure and variations of it are, unfortunately, commonplace incidents within organizations, despite the personal tragedy and organizational nightmares involved.

What had gone wrong in Carl's group? Probably leadership, that still mysterious and only vaguely understood ingredient which must be created and sustained daily by a manager; with it, other managerial skills and resources come to life and work; without it, managerial skills and group talents become paralyzed—and work results grind to a halt.

This article aims (1) to present a practical framework, consisting of essential leadership theory, which can serve to facilitate a manager's understanding, analysis and evaluation of his personal leadership skills; and (2) to report on a composite managerial opinion about leadership practices, drawn

James Owens, "The Uses of Leadership Theory," *Michigan Business Review*, January 1973, pp. 13–19.

327

from the author's work with many practicing managers over the past seven years, summarizing the insights of these managers themselves based on their years of practical experience.

Thus, my intent is to present a blend of research theory and practical *managerial experience* as, hopefully, a rich information-base for any manager seriously intent on improving his own managerial performance and career growth.

TRAIT THEORY VERSUS BEHAVIOR THEORY

The earliest studies of leadership hypothesized that what makes a leader (manager) effective is his personality, what he is as a person. Proponents of this "trait theory" searched for some set of built-in traits which successful leaders possess and ineffective leaders lack, such as "aggressiveness," "self-control," "independence," "friendliness," "religious orientation," "optimism," and many others. Decades of social science research, when finally tallied, added up disappointingly to very ambiguous results: effective leaders were found to be sometimes aggressive, self-disciplined, independent, friendly, religious, and optimistic—but often none or few of these things.

The mystery of leadership was not so easily or simplistically to be revealed and entered, definitively, into neat columns. Such research proved what most managers know intuitively, sometimes from bitter experience—such as Carl's—that effective leadership is one of the most complex phenomena in human relations and an ever-elusive riddle to those who must master it. (The obvious irony here is that the successful manager must master this phenomenon in practice, if not in theory and understanding, because—unlike social scientists—his very survival, as a career manager, depends on it!

A "behavior theory" of leadership then came upon the scene: what makes a leader effective is (quite independently of his personality) simply what he does. Much less ambitious than trait theory, behavior theory tried to search out the right things that effective leaders do: such as how they communicate, give directions, motivate, delegate, plan, handle meetings, and so on. The value of the theory, to the extent it was valid, was its implication that "leaders need not be born to it but could be trained to do the right things," independently of their inner personality traits. Unfortunately, this approach, too, missed the essence of leadership and proved to be not only unambitious but too often degenerated into mechanical "techniques" and other superficial "gimmicks," which, on the job, emerged as robot-like counterfeits of genuine leadership—and thus failed.

The decades of work by both camps, however, were not wasted. It seems clear, today, that, on balance, there is truth—and valuable knowledge—to be gained from each theory.

THE USES OF TRAIT THEORY

Although trait theory advocates failed to build a comprehensive model of leadership, their work articulated and forced into sharp focus a practical truth: one's personality, what he fundamentally is as a person, is an ever-present and massive influence on how, and with what success, he functions as a manager.

The personality of a man is his inner life, including such inner elements as background, life history, beliefs, life experiences, attitudes, prejudices, self-image, fears, loves, hates, hopes, and philosophy of life. In this sense, a man is like an iceberg: only a small fraction of what he is appears above the surface (his observable behavior, what he does); the rest is his inner life, the seven eighths of the iceberg that lie, unobservable, below the surface.

However, the manager's inner personality causes—or "spills over" into—his behavior which, in turn, affects others with whom he works, eliciting from them either cooperative or resistance reactions. And, therein lies the manager's fate: cooperative reactions from his people spell success; resistance reactions, however irrational from the manager's viewpoint, usually assure his failure (as, probably, in the case of Carl).

Any attempt to "formulize" this cause-effect process in the form of simple one-to-one correlations, such as trait Z_1 causing invariably behavior Z_2 causing invariably effect Z_3, is doomed to failure—as the efforts of the trait-theorists proved. However, it is clear that there is an influential relationship between a manager's total personality and his success, as a manager, on the job. I have submitted this precise concept to several thousand practicing managers over the years and, based on their experience, virtually all acknowledge its validity. For example, most of these managers concluded that a manager who is naturally low in his ability to trust others, has little chance to succeed; despite his best efforts, he will be unable to delegate properly and thus becomes a "bottle-neck," as work piles up on his desk, and a source of frustration to people who want a chance to get involved and grow. Or, a manager whose personality requires a high degree of security in his life, is unable to take any risks, and thus fails because he decides and does nothing! Or, a manager who struggles within himself with a poor self-image and an inherent low level of self-confidence, avoids decisions and radiates, as a kind of "self-fulfilling prophesy," certain failure. Other examples include the effect on managerial success of personality characteristics like racial prejudice, intolerance for unfamiliar ideas, dislike or distrust of the young, respect for (or general cynicism about) other people because of their background, sex, intelligence, experience, or appearance, and so on.

The virtually unanimous opinion of these thousands of practical managers has been that any manager, who genuinely has ambitons for managerial growth and advancement, can achieve it only if he adds to his efforts a periodic evaluation of his total personality, especially his attitudes, and their effect on his people as well as the success (or failure) they produce for him. Such a manager, who is capable even of managing his own career, will find that most of his personality characteristics are assets; but, if he pursues the search objectively, he will find, too, that some are liabilities. These he must begin to change, if he can or wishes; and, if he can not, then he must, as a mature person with mature judgment, assess himself carefully and find the kind of job that fits his personality.

In short, these managers believe—and I do too—that a manager can grow in his managerial career only if he grows as a total personality, which he is long before he begins to function as a manager. What a man is and brings to the office in the form of a total personality largely determines what and how he does and with what degree of success. What this means is that personal growth as a human being underlies and becomes, to a great extent, the real foundation upon which managerial and career growth can develop. Managerial success is not a peripheral set of "techniques"; it is a working-out of one's essential being in the form of action.

THE USES OF BEHAVIOR THEORY

What "behavior theory" has taught us, over the years, is that, within certain limits imposed by the inner personality of the individual, each person has the capability of cultivating habits of behavior (by act of will) which optimize his effects upon people. Many of us feel moody, but, by act of will, virtually never act moody. Constructive habits of courtesy, self-control, two-way communication, delegation and interest in the problems of others can be learned and practiced, by act of will.

The most important contribution of "behavior theory," however, is the development of a classification of leadership behaviors (styles) which provides a manager an analytical tool with which he can consciously and intelligently build a personally successful leadership style.

A MATRIX OF
LEADERSHIP STYLES_____

Probably the most practical contribution of research to the day-to-day life of the manager is the analytic model of leadership styles—their description and properties. Virtually all of the managers to whom I have presented this classic model agree that it clarifies their options and serves well as a means for productive analysis and evaluation of their personal leadership styles as well as their relative success.

The exact form of the leadership matrix varies as do its details but the following version is standard. The brief descriptions of each style are, of course, stereotyped and oversimplified for purposes of clear identification and analysis. Also, they are defined in neutral language, avoiding, as much as possible, either favoring or disparaging overtones at this point. The five leadership styles, which comprise the matrix, are as follows:

1. The Autocratic Leader: The autocrat has authority, from some source such as his position, knowledge, strength, or power to reward and punish, and he uses this authority as his principal, or only, method of getting things done. He is frankly authoritarian, knows what he wants done, and how, "tells" people what their work-assignments are, and demands unquestioning obedience. The autocrat ranges from "tough" to "paternalistic" depending on how much he stresses, as motivation, threat and punishment in the former case or rewards in the latter. The "tough" autocrat demands and gets compliance, "or else." The "paternalistic" autocrat demands and expects compliance but mainly on a "father-knows-best"—and often very personal—relationship, implying personal dependence, rewards, and security. The autocrat permits people little or no freedom.

2. The Bureaucratic Leader: Like the autocrat, the bureaucrat "tells" people what to do, and how, but the basis for his orders is almost exclusively the organization's policies, procedures, and rules. For the bureaucrat, these rules are absolute. He manages entirely "by the book," and no exceptions are permitted. He treats rules and administers their force upon people as a judge might treat—and permit no departure or exception from—laws, including their every technicality. Like the autocrat, the bureacrat permits people little or no freedom.

3. The Diplomatic Leader: The diplomat is an artist who, like the salesman, lives by the arts of personal persuasion. Although he has the same clear authority as the autocrat, the diplomat prefers to "sell" people and operate, as much as possible, by persuasion and broadscale individual motivation of people. He will "revert," if necessary, to the autocratic style, but prefers to avoid this. Some term him a "sell-type" leader who uses a large variety and degree of persuasion-tactics, ranging from simple explanation of the reasons for an order to fullscale bargaining with people. He will usually relate his organizational goals to the personal individual needs and aspirations of his people. Such a leader retains his authority in that he knows and will insist on a particular course of action; but, he provides some—limited—freedom to his people in that he permits them to react, question, raise objections, discuss, and even argue their side of the issue.

4. The Participative Leader: The participative leader openly invites his people to participate or share, to a greater or lesser extent, in decisions, policy-making and operation methods. He is either a "democratic" or a "consultative" leader.

The "democrative" leader "joins" his group and makes it clear, in advance, that he will abide by the group's decision whether arrived at by consensus or majority vote. (This style is sometimes seen in the operations of research and development groups.).

The "consultative" leader consults his people and invites frank involvement, discussion, pro and con argument, and recommendations from the group, but makes it clear that he alone is accountable and reserves the final decision to himself.

In both forms of the participative style of leadership, people are given a high degree of freedom—as they are, too, in the Free-Rein style.

5. The Free-Rein Leader: The "free-rein" leader (the analogy, of course, is to a horseman who has left the reins free) does not literally abandon all control. He sets a goal for his subordiate as well as clear parameters such as policies, deadlines, and budget and then drops the "reins" and sets his subordinate free to operate without further direction or control, unless the subordinate himself requests it.

THE "BEST" LEADERSHIP STYLE

Despite certain implications in the literature that there is a "best" and ideal leadership style, the managers I surveyed categorically reject this simple solution suggested by some social scientists. Their virtually unanimous view was that the "best" leadership style depends on:

(a) the individual personality of the manager himself ("Trait theory" revisited);
(b) the individual followers, the kind of people they are and the kind of work they do;
(c) and, the particular situation and circumstances on any given day or hour.

In short, no "cookbook" or formulized recipe for effective leadership "rang true" as realistic with these managers. The complexity and mystery of leadership does not permit simplistic approaches.

Only a manager, himself, examining, and exploring the varieties of leadership styles, their advantages and weaknesses, as well as the people and the situation with which he is dealing, can decide what is the "best" leadership style for him, and with them, and in this particular situation. It must be an act of individual judgment. A theoretical framework can assist, as can the opinions of thousands of managers, but the choice and practice of leadership style must always remain the act of judgment of the individual manager.

Some authors have coined the expression "tool box approach" for this necessity that faces managers of choosing the "right style" at the "right time" in the "right situation" (as opposed to the easy and utopian formula of a single, predominant leadership style for all people and all situations).

A SUMMARY OF MANAGERS' VIEWS_____

Working closely over the years with many practicing managers, I have had the opportunity to learn much of what they learned about leadership—based, not on textbook abstractions, but realistically on years of hard experience. The essential results of this seven-year informal survey of these managers are organized below as telegraphic propositions expressed as either advantages or weaknesses of each classic leadership style. Each proposition is a kind of composite view representing a virtual consensus of the opinions of these managers. Naturally, they are general statements and, as such, allow for exceptions in individual cases. Even so, these propositions are experience-based insights of managers themselves and should be helpful to any manager seriously intent on evaluating and improving his own leadership.

1.The Autocratic Leadership Style:

(a) Advantages:

—When appropriate, can increase efficiency, save time and get quick results, especially in a crisis or emergency situation.
—The paternalistic form of this style of leadership works well with employees who have a low tolerance for ambiguity, feel insecure with freedom and even minor decision-making requirements, and thrive under clear, detailed, and achievable directives.
—Chain of command and division of work (who is supposed to do what) are clear and fully understood by all.

(b) Weaknesses:

—The apparent efficiency of one-way communication often becomes a false efficiency since one-way communication, without "feedback," typically leads to misunderstandings, communication breakdowns and costly errors.
—The autocratic manager must really be an expert, not just think he is, because he receives little, if any, information and ideas from his people as inputs into his decision-making. He is really alone in his decision-making and this is generally dangerous in today's environment of technological and organizational complexity.
—The critical weakness, however, of the autocratic style is its effect on people. Many managers pine for the good old days when the boss gave orders and people obeyed meekly and without question. These managers, however, agree that—like it or not—those days are gone forever. Today, most people resent authoritarian rule which excludes them from involvement and reduces them to machinelike cogs without human dignity or importance. They express their resentment in the form of massive resistance, low morale and low productivity (if not downright work stoppage or sabotage). This is especially true, today, with technical or educated people, youths entering the job market, and members of most minority groups.

2.The Bureaucratic Leadership Style:

(a) Advantages:

—Insures consistency of policy and operations which can be critical in industries where legal paramenters are common (banking, sales, etc.). Every manager must be a bureaucrat to some reasonable extent.

—Consistent application of personnel-related rules, for one and for all, contributes a sense of fairness and impartiality in the manager's many and complex dealings with people.
—People know where they stand. Most decisions concerning them are by known—and accepted—rule, predictable, objective (rather than by the whim or mood of a manager)—and there is security and a sense of fairness.

(b) Weaknesses:

—Inflexibility in situations where exceptions to rules should be made or requested.
—Paralysis in situations not covered by rules or where rules are ambiguous (as is often the case: policies and rules represent legislation for the majority of situations but can never substitute for individual human judgment in a particular specific situation.)
—The reaction of people working under a strongly bureaucratic manager is essentially the same as described above in the case of the autocratic manager: again, resentment, resistance, and low morale.

3.The Diplomatic Leadership Style:

(a) Advantages:

—People cooperate and work more enthusiastically if managers take even a few minutes—and respect people enough—to give them the simple reasons and explanations of the reasons that make a particular task important—rather than just a blind chore.
—A manager's personal effort to explain to or persuade a subordinate is usually received as an important compliment and show of respect—and usually appreciated and responded to with a high degree of cooperation and effort.
—This style of leadership is indispensable for the legions of so-called "staff" people (and even "line" people who realize the inadequacy of their real authority). They must achieve the results, for which they are accountable, "unfairly" deprived of the clear-cut authority required and, therefore, are utterly dependent on the skills of persuasion to get the help and cooperation needed.

(b) Weaknesses:

—Some people interpret efforts to persuade them, rather than order them, as a sign of weakness and, thus, lose respect for a manager.

—the basic weakness, however, of the diplomatic style is the same as the pitfall always facing those who use consistently the "tool-box" approach to leadership; namely, hypocrisy. Unless handled with judgment, skill and sincerity, the diplomatic style—as well as any "tool-box" approach with people—quickly degenerates and "comes through" to people as insincerity, frank manipulation and exploitation—and is, thus, deeply resented and resisted. And, naturally, a complete failure.

—Anyone employing the diplomatic style must be a skilled and competent salesman, who usually "wins" the "sale." A salesman routinely expects and invites objections—a manager who operates this way must be able to convince and "sell" people, or he will be forced to "revert" (hypocritically) to a frank autocratic order. The effect of this on people is both obvious and disastrous.

4.The Participative Leadership Style:

(a) Advantages:

—When people participate in and help formulate a decision, they support it (instead of fighting or ignoring it) and work hard to make it work, because it's their idea and, now, part of their life and their "ego."

—The manager consistently receives the benefit of the best information, ideas, suggestions, and talent—and operating experience—of his people. The rich information-source which they represent becomes his and a key input into his decision-making.

—Group discussion, even though time-consuming, before a decision is made, can force critical information to the surface which, when considered, improves decision-making—or, in some cases, actually averts a disaster which would have occurred if key operating-level information were not made available.

—This style of leadership permits and encourages people to develop, grow and rise in the organization (both in terms of responsibility they can assume and service they can contribute).

—Most people work better, more enthusiastically and at a high level of motivation when they are given a reasonable degree of freedom to act and contribute. Because, thus, they enjoy a sense of personal importance, value and achievement. (Unlike human cogs in machine-like organizational systems.)

—Most importantly, as already implied above, the participative manager establishes a work climate which easily unleashes the enormous power of people who are motivated by—and will strive hard for—goals which they help create and in the accomplishment of which they gain deep personal satisfaction in the form of recognition, sense of accomplishment, sense of importance and personal value. In short, the participative manager has the critical factor of built-in personal motivation working for him.

(b) Weaknesses:

—The participative style can take enormous amounts of time and, when used inappropriately, be simply inefficient.
—Some managers "use" the democratic style as a way of avoiding (or abdicating) responsibility.
—People resent the invitation to offer recommendations when such recommendations are consistently ignored and rejected. It follows that any manager, who must reject a recommendation, should quickly explain why such recommendations had to be rejected.
—Use of participative styles can easily, if not handled well, degenerate into a complete loss of managerial control.

5.The Free-Rein Leadership Style:

(a) Advantages:

—This style comprises the essence of full managerial delegation with its benefits of optimum utilization of time and resources.
—Many people are motivated to full effort only if given this kind of free-rein.

(b) Weaknesses:

—Very little managerial control and a high degree of risk.
—This style can be a disaster if the manager does not know well the competence and integrity of his people and their ability to handle this kind of freedom.

CONCLUSION

Leadership is still an art despite the efforts of social science researchers to make it a science. The summaries, here, of essential leadership theory and managerial opinion (based on experience) are presented only as a help to (not a substitute for) the final individual judgment of the manager as he lives with his particular people in his particuular situation.

Every such manager, however, must operate by some leadership style or styles and it is hoped that the ideas presented above will aid the manager in his analysis, evaluation and development of his own personal leadership style.

Chester A. Schriesheim

University of Southern California

James A. Tolliver

Michigan State University

Orlando C. Behling

The Ohio State University

LEADERSHIP THEORY: SOME IMPLICATIONS FOR MANAGERS

In the past seventy years more than 3,000 leadership studies have been conducted and dozens of leadership models and theories have been proposed.[1] Yet, a practicing manager who reads this literature seeking an effective solution to supervisory problems will rapidly become disenchanted. Although we have access to an overwhelming volume of leadership theory and research, few guidelines exist which are of use to a practitioner. Nevertheless, interest in leadership—and in those qualities which separate a successful leader from an unsuccessful one—remains unabated. In almost any book dealing with management one will find some discussion of leadership. In any company library there are numerous volumes entitled "Increasing Leadership Effectiveness," "Successful Leadership," or "How to Lead." Typical management development programs conducted within

Chester A. Schriesheim, James M. Tolliver and Orlando C. Behling, "Leadership Theory: Some Implications for Managers," *MSU Business Topics*, Summer 1978, pp. 38–40.

339

work organizations and universities usually deal with some aspect of leadership. This intensity and duration of writing on the subject and the sums spent annually on leadership training indicate that practicing managers and academicians consider good leadership essential to organizational success.

What is meant by leadership, let alone *good* leadership? Many definitions have been proposed, and it seems that most are careful to separate management from leadership. This distinction sometimes becomes blurred in everyday conversations. The first term, *management*, includes those processes, both mental and physical, which result in other people executing prescribed formal duties for organizational goal attainment. It deals mainly with planning, organizing, and controlling the work of other people to achieve organizational goals.[2] This definition usually includes those aspects of managers' jobs, such as monitoring and controlling resources, which are sometimes ignored in current conceptualizations of leadership. *Leadership*, on the other hand, is a more restricted type of managerial activity, focusing on the interpersonal interactions between a leader and one or more subordinates, with the purpose of increasing organizational effectiveness.[3] In this view, leadership is a social influence process in which the leader seeks the voluntary participation of subordinates in an effort to reach organizational objectives. The key idea highlighted by a number of authors is that the subordinate's participation is voluntary.[4] This implies that the leader has brought about some change in the way subordinates want to behave. Leadership, consequently, is not only a specific process (more so than management), but also is undoubtedly political in nature. The political aspect of leadership has been discussed elsewhere, so at this point it suffices to note that a major implication of leadership's political nature is that such attempts at wielding influence will not necessarily succeed.[5] In fact, other types of managerial tasks may have a stronger influence on organizational effectiveness than those interpersonal tasks usually labeled leadership.[6]

Despite this shortcoming, the examination of leadership as it relates to interpersonal interactions is still worthwhile simply because managers may, in many cases, have more control over how they and their subordinates behave than over nonhuman aspects of their jobs (such as the amount and types of resources they are given). In addition, some information does exist concerning which leadership tactics are of use under various conditions. For this information to be of greatest use, however, practicing managers should have some concept of the direction leadership research has taken. Thus, before attempting to provide guidelines for practitioners, we shall briefly review major approaches to the subject of leadership and point out their weaknesses and limitations.

BASIC APPROACHES TO LEADERSHIP_____

Thinking concerning leadership has moved through three distinct periods or phases.

The Trait Phase

Early approaches to leadership, from the pre-Christian era to the late 1940s, emphasized the examination of leader characterisitcs (such as age and degree of gregariousness) in an attempt to identify a set of universal characteristics which would allow a leader to be effective in all situations. At first a few traits seemed to be universally important for successful leaders, but subsequent research yielded inconsistent results concerning these traits; in addition, research investigating a large number of other traits (about one hundred) was generally discouraging. As a result of this accumulation of negative findings and of reviews of this evidence, such as that conducted by R. M. Stogdill, the tide of opinion about the importance of traits for leadership effectiveness began to change.[7] In the late 1940s, leadership researchers began to move away from trait research. Contemporary opinion holds the trait approach in considerable disrepute and views the likelihood of uncovering a set of universal leadership effectiveness traits as essentially impossible.

The Behavioral Phase

With the fall of the trait approach, researchers considered alternative concepts, eventually settling on the examination of relationships between leader behaviors and subordinate satisfaction and performance.[8] During the height of the behavioral phase, dating roughly from the late 1940s to the early 1960s, several large research programs were conducted, including the Ohio State University leadership studies, a program of research which has received considerable publicity over the years.

The Ohio State studies started shortly after World War II and initially concentrated on leadership in military organizations. In one of these studies, a lengthy questionnaire was administered to B-52 bomber crews, and their answers were statistically analyzed to identify the common dimensions underlying the answers.[9] This analysis discovered two dimensions which seemed most important in summarizing the nature of the crews' perceptions about their airplance commanders' behavior toward them.

Consideration was the stronger of the two factors, and it involved leader behaviors indicative of friendship, mutual trust, respect, and warmth.

The second factor was Initiation of Structure, a concept involving leader behaviors indicating that the leader organizes and defines the relationship between self and subordinates.[10]

In subsequent studies using modified versions of the original questionnaire, Consideration and Structure were found to be prime dimensions of leader behavior in situations ranging from combat flights over Korea to assembly line work.[11] In addition, studies were undertaken at Ohio State and elsewhere to compare the effects of these leader behaviors on subordinate performance and satisfaction. A high Consideration–high Structure leadership style was, in many cases, found to lead to high performance and satisfaction. However, in a number of studies dysfunctional consequences, such as high turnover and absenteeism, accompanied these positive outcomes. In yet other situations, different combinations of Consideration and Structure (for example, low Consideration-high Structure) were found to be more effective.[12]

Similar behaviors were identified and similar results obtained in a large number of studies, such as those conducted at the University of Michigan.[13] Although the display of highly Considerate–highly Structuring behavior was sometimes found to result in positive organizational outcomes, this was not true in all of the cases or even in most of them.[14] The research, therefore, clearly indicated that no single leadership style was universally effective, as the relationship of supervisory behavior to organizational performance and employee satisfaction changed from situation to situation. By the early 1960s this had become apparent to even the most ardent supporters of the behavioral approach, and the orientation of leadership researchers began to change toward a situational treatment.

The Situational Phase

Current leadership research is almost entirely situational. This approach examines the interrelationships among leader and subordinate behaviors or characteristics and the situations in which the parties find themselves. This can clearly be seen in the work of researchers such as F. E. Fiedler, who outlined one of the first situational models.[15]

Fiedler claims that leaders are motivated primarily by satisfactions derived from interpersonal relations and task-goal accomplishment. Relationship-motivated leaders display task-oriented behaviors (such as Consideration) in situations which are either moderately favorable or unfavorable. Task-motivated leaders display relationship-oriented behaviors in favorable situations and task-oriented behaviors in both moderately favorable and unfavorable situations. Fiedler's model specifies that relationship-motivated leaders will be more effective in situations which are moderately favorable for the leader to exert influence, and that they will be less effective in favorable or unfavorable situations; the exact opposite is the case for task-motivated leaders. (They are most effective in favorable or unfavorable situations and least effective in moderately favorable ones.) According to Fiedler, the favorableness of the situation for the leader to exert influence over the work group is determined by (1) the quality of leader-group member relations (the warmer and friendlier, the more favorable the situation); (2) the structure of the tasks performed by the leader's subordinates (the more structured, the more favorable); and (3) the power of the leader (the more power, the more favorable the situation).[16]

A number of other authors propose similar types of interactions among the leader, the led, and the situation. We will not review all these other models, but the situational model of Victor Vroom and Phillip Yetton deserves mention.[17] Their model suggests the conditions under which the leader should share decision-making power. Five basic leadership styles are recommended. These range from unilateral decisions by the leader to situations in which the leader gives a great deal of decision power to subordinates and serves as a discussion coordinator who does not attempt to influence the group. Which style is recommended depends upon the leader's "yes" or "no" response to seven quality and acceptability questions which are asked sequentially. In those cases where more than a single style is suggested, the leader is expected to choose between recommendations on the basis of the amount of time to be invested. While this model, as is the case with most of the situational models, has not been fully tested, the literature supports the basic notion that a situational view is necessary to portray accurately the complexities of leadership processes.

ORGANIZATIONAL IMPLICATIONS

What does this discussion of leadership theory and research have to do with the practice of management?

Selection does not seem to be the primary answer to the organization's need to increase the pool of effective leaders. The results of the numerous trait studies summarized by Stogdill and others indicate that the search for universal personality characteristics of effective leaders is doomed.[18] This statement requires qualification, however. It should be recognized that the assertion concerns leadership effectiveness, which is only one aspect of managerial effectiveness. A manager may contribute to organizational effectiveness in many ways other than by being an effective leader. The role of selection in picking effective managers, as distinguished from effective leaders, consequently may be much greater. Furthermore, present disappointment with attempts at leader selection is derived from research which has sought to identify universal characteristics of effective leaders, consequently may be much greater. Furthermore, present disappointment with attempts at leader selection is derived from research which has sought to identify universal characteristics of effective leaders in all situations. Summaries such as Stogdill's demonstrate that leadership effectiveness is highly dependent upon the relationship between leader characteristics and the demands of particular situations, and thus universal approaches will not work. Exploration of leader traits as they relate to performance in particular situations may reveal that careful selection has some potential. Unfortunately, given the many situational factors which appear to influence leadership effectiveness, it seems unlikely that selection procedures will be able to follow typical actuarial (statistical) selection procedures.[19] (It appears almost impossible to gather enough individuals in identical jobs to do this.) However, this does not preclude the use of clinical (judgmental) techniques for selection of leaders.

A further limitation on selection procedures as ways of increasing the pool of effective managers and/or leaders within organizations is the dynamic nature of managerial jobs and managers' careers. If, as research seems to indicate, leadership success is situation-specific, then the continual and inevitable shifts in the nature of a manager's assignment and his or her movement from one assignment to another may make the initial selection invalid.

Another implication is that existing forms of leadership training appear to be inappropriate, based on the evidence outlined here. There are two reasons for this. First, the majority of such training programs are based upon the assumption that there exists one best way to manage. Great emphasis usually is placed on an employee-centered (Considerate) approach or one which combines a concern for employees with a concern for high output (Initiating Structure). For example, the Managerial Grid and its associated Grid Organizational Development Program are popular approaches to management and organizational development.[20] Both are based on the premise that a managerial style which shows high concern for people and high concern for production is the soundest way to achieve excellence, and both attempt to develop this style of behavior on the part of all managers.[21] Rensis Likert's "System-Four" approach to managerial and organizational development, although different from the Grid approach, also assumes that one best way to manage exists (employee-centered leadership).[22] Clearly, these ideas are in conflict with the evidence and with contemporary opinion.

The other limitation of leadership training is that it seems ineffective in changing the behavior of participants. Leadership training aimed not directly at leadership behavior itself, but at providing diagnostic skills for the identification of the nature of the situation and the behaviors appropriate to it, appears to offer considerable potential for the improvement of leadership effectiveness. Obviously, however, additional research is needed to identify the dimensions of situations crucial to leadership performance and the styles effective under various circumstances.

Fiedler's suggestion that organizations engineer the job to fit the manager also has potential.[23] However, the idea is impractical, if not utopian. Application of this approach is limited because we have not identified the crucial dimensions of situations which affect leadership performance. Also, while the overall approach may offer theoretical advantages when leadership is treated in isolation, it ignores dysfunctional effects on other aspects of the organization's operations. Leadership effectiveness cannot be the only concern of administrators as they make decisions about job assignments. They must consider other aspects of the organization's operations which may conflict with their attempts to make good use of leadership talent. Some characterisitics of the job, task, or organization simply may not be subject to change, at least in the short run. Thus, engineering the job to fit the manager may increase leadership effectiveness, but this approach seems risky, at least for the forseeable future.

It should also be noted that it is not unusual for work organizations to use traits and trait descriptions in their evaluations of both leadership and managerial performance. A quick glance at a typical performance rating form usually reveals the presence of terms such as *personality* and *attitude* as factors for individual evaluation. Clearly, these terms represent a modern-day version of the traits investigated thirty years ago, and they may or may not be related to actual job performance, depending upon the specifics of the situation involved. Thus, some explicit rationale and, it is hoped, evidence that such traits do affect managerial performance should be provided before they are included in performance evaluations. Just feeling that they are important is not sufficient justification.

INDIVIDUAL IMPLICATIONS

The implications of our discussion of leadership theory and research for individual managers are intertwined with those for the total organization. The fact that leadership effectiveness does not depend on a single set of personal characteristics with which an individual is born or which the individual acquires at an early age should provide a sense of relief to many managers and potential managers. Success in leadership is not limited to an elite, but can be attained by almost any individual, assuming that the situation is proper and that the manager can adjust his or her behavior to fit the situation. The process leading to effective leadership, in other words, is not so much one of changing the characteristics of the individual as it is one of assuring that he or she is placed in an appropriate situation or of teaching the individual how to act to fit the situation.

Thus, a manager's effectiveness can be improved through the development of skills in analyzing the nature of organizational situations—both task and political demands. Although it is difficult to provide guidelines, some recent research points to tentative prescriptions.[24]

Generally speaking, a high Consideration–high Structure style often works best. However, this approach cannot be used in all instances because dysfunctional consequences can result from such behaviors. For example, upper management sometimes gives highly considerate managers poor performance ratings, while in other instances high Structure has been related to employee dissatisfaction, grievances, and turnover. It sometimes will be necessary for a manager to choose between high Consideration and high Structure, and in these cases an individual'a diagnostic ability becomes important.

If the diagnostician (manager) has little information, it is probably safe to exhibit high Consideration. Although it does not guarantee subordinate performance, its positive effects on frustration-instigated behavior—such as aggression—are probably enough to warrant its recommendation as a general style. However, in some situations Structure probably should be emphasized, although it may mean a decrease in subordinate perceptions of Consideration. Although the following is not an exhaustive list of these exceptions, it does include those which are known and appear important. The individual manager, from a careful analysis of the situation, must add any additional factors that can be identified.

Emergencies or High-Pressure Situations. When the work involves physical danger, when time is limited, or when little tolerance for error exists, emphasis on Initiating Structure seems desirable. Research has demonstrated that subordinates often expect and prefer high Structure in such instances.

Situations in Which the Manager Is the Only Source of Information. When the leader is the only person knowledgeable about the task, subordinates often expect him or her to make specific job assignments, set deadlines, and generally engage in structuring their behavior. This does not mean that the leader cannot be considerate if this is appropriate.

Subordinate Preferences.   There is limited evidence that some subordinates prefer high Structure and expect it, while others expect low Consideration and are suspicious of leaders who display high Consideration. Other preference patterns undoubtedly exist, and managers should attempt to tailor their behavior to each individual employee, as the situation dictates.

Preferences of Higher Management.   In some instances, higher management has definite preferences for certain leadership styles. Higher management sometimes prefers and expects high Structure and low Consideration, and rewards managers for displaying this behavioral style. The manager should be sensitive to the desires of superiors, in addition to those of subordinates. While it is not possible to specify how these expectations may be reconciled if they diverge, compromise or direct persuasion might be useful.[25] Once again, the success of these methods probably will depend both upon the situation and the manager's skill. This leads to the last point—adaptability.

Leader Ability to Adjust.   Some managers will be able to adjust their behavior to fit the situation. For others, attempts to modify behavior may look false and manipulative to subordinates. In these instances, the manager probably would be better off keeping the style with which he or she is most comfortable.

LIMITATIONS AND CONCLUSION

The situational approach avoids the major shortcomings of both the trait and behavioral approaches to leadership. However, the implicit assumption that hierarchical leadership is always important has recently come into question. Steven Kerr, for example, points out that many factors may limit the ability of a hierarchical superior to act as a leader for subordinates.[26] Factors such as technology (for example, the assembly line), training, clear job descriptions, and the like, may provide subordinates with enough guidance so that supervisor Structure may be unnecessary to ensure task performance. Also, jobs which are intrinsically satisfying may negate the need for supervisor Consideration, since Consideration is not needed to offset job dullness.

Another problem with the situational approach, and with leadership as a major emphasis in general, is that effective leadership may account for only 10 to 15 percent of the variability in unit performance.[27] While this percentage is certainly not trivial, it is clear that much of what affects performance in organizations is not accounted for by leadership. While studying and emphasizing leadership certainly has its merits, it could be argued that there is much to be gained by treating leadership effectiveness as but one component of managerial effectiveness. As an earlier publication emphasized:

> It is necessary to note that leadership is only one way in which the manager contributes to organization effectiveness. The manager also performs duties which are externally oriented so far as his unit is concerned. For example, he may spend part of his time coordinating the work of his unit with other units. Similarly, not all of the manager's internally oriented activities can be labeled leadership acts. Some of them concern the physical and organizational conditions under which the work unit operates. For example, the manager spends part of his time obtaining resources (materials, equipment, manpower, and so on) necessary for unit operations. This is an essential internally oriented activity but hardly constitutes leadership. Clearly, the manager must perform a mix of internal and external activities if his unit is to perform well. Leadership is only one of the internal activities performed by managers.[28]

Thus, the manager should not overemphasize the importance of leadership activities, especially if this causes other functions to be neglected.

For managers to be effective as leaders, they must attempt to be politically astute and to tailor their behaviors, taking into account differences in subordinates, superiors, and situations. Leadership should be kept in perspective. Clearly, it is important, but it cannot be treated in isolation: the importance of leadership depends upon the situation, and the practicing manager must take this into account.

REFERENCES

1. R. M. Stogdill, *Handbook of Leadership* (New York: The Free Press, 1974).
2. A. C. Filley, R. J. House, and Steven Kerr, *Managerial Process and Organizational Behavior*, 2nd ed. (Glenview, Ill.: Scott, Foresman, 1976). See also R. C. Davis, *Industrial Organization and Management* (New York: Harper, 1957).
3. C. A. Gibb, "Leadership," in Gardner Lindzey and Elliot Aronson, eds., *The Handbook of Social Psychology* (Reading, Mass.: Addison-Wesley, 1969), vol. 4.

4. See, for example, R. H. Hall, *Organizations: Structure and Process* (Englewood Cliffs, N.J.: Prentice-Hall, 1972).

5. C. A. Schriesheim, J. M. Tolliver, and L. D. Dodge, "The Political Nature of the Leadership Process," unpublished paper, 1978.

6. For examples of other types of managerial tasks which may have more of an impact on organizations, see J. P. Campbell, M. D. Dunnette, E. E. Lawler, and K. E. Weick, *Managerial Behavior, Performance, and Effectiveness* (New York: McGraw-Hill, 1970).

7. R. M. Stogdill, "Personal Factors Associated with Leadership: A Survey of the Literature," *Journal of Psychology* 25 (January 1948): 35–71.

8. T. O. Jacobs, *Leadership and Exchange in Formal Organizations* (Alexandria, Va.: Human Resources Research Organization, 1970).

9. A. W. Halpin and B. J. Winer, "A Factorial Study of the Leader Behavior Descriptions," in R. M. Stogdill and A. E. Coons, eds., *Leader Behavior: Its Description and Measurement* (Columbus: Bureau of Business Research, The Ohio State University, 1957).

10. Ibid., p. 42.

11. Stogdill and Coons, *Leader Behavior.*

12. Steven Kerr, C. A. Schriesheim, C. J. Murphy, and R. M. Stogdill, "Toward a Contingency Theory of Leadership Based upon the Consideration and Initiating Structure Literature," *Organizational Behavior and Human Performance* 12 (August 1974): 62–82.

13. See, for example, Daniel Katz, Nathan Maccoby, and Nancy Morse, *Productivity, Supervision, and Morale in an Office Situation* (Ann Arbor: Survey Research Center, University of Michigan, 1951).

14. Kerr et al., "Contingency Theory."

15. See F. E. Fiedler, "Engineer the Job to Fit the Manager," *Harvard Business Review* 43 (September-October 1965): 115–22.

16. F. E. Fiedler, *A Theory of Leadership Effectiveness* (New York: McGraw-Hill, 1967).

17. V. H. Vroom and P. W. Yetton, *Leadership and Decision-Making* (Pittsburgh, Pa.: University of Pittsburgh Press, 1973).

18. R. M. Stogdill, "Personal Factors."

19. Kerr et al., "Contingency Theory."

20. R. R. Blake and J. S. Mouton, *The Managerial Grid* (Houston, Texas: Gulf, 1964), and *Building a Dynamic Corporation Through Grid Organizational Development* (Reading, Mass.: Addison-Wesley, 1969).

21. Ibid., p. 63.

22. Rensis Likert, *New Patterns of Management* (New York: McGraw-Hill, 1961), and *The Human Organization: Its Management and Value* (New York: McGraw-Hill, 1967).

23. Fiedler, "Engineer the Job."

24. Kerr et al., "Contingency Theory."

25. See Filley, House, and Kerr, *Managerial Process*, especially pp. 162–80; and George Strauss, "Tactics of Lateral Relations," in H. J. Leavitt and L. R. Pondy,

eds., *Readings in Managerial Psychology*, 1st ed. (Chicago: University of Chicago Press, 1964), pp. 226–48.

26. Steven Kerr, "Substitutes for Leadership: Their Definition and Measurement," unpublished paper, 1978.

27. O. C. Behling and C. A. Schriesheim, *Organizational Behavior: Theory, Research and Application* (Boston: Allyn and Bacon, 1976).

28. Ibid., p. 294.

Bruce Harriman

Chairman, Aristorius Corporation, Woburn, Massachusetts

UP AND DOWN THE COMMUNICATIONS LADDER

Effective interpersonal communication has long been recognized as basic to any ·successful human enterprise. In fact, the problem of communicating has become the number-one cliché of our time. Satirist Tom Lehrer became so weary of hearing about the problem of communicating between young and old, rich and poor, black and white, that he said, "It seems to me that if someone is having all that trouble communicating, the very least he can do is shut up!"

Ignoring that good advice, my company has developed a theory of communications that, once recognized and applied, has helped solve problems in attitude and operational effectiveness.

Serious communications problems in the company were documented in a study made in 1969 by a New England Telephone task force and Daniel Yankelovich, Inc. This study team uncovered a strong desire on the part of employees to play a larger role in decisions affecting their jobs and the company. The findings also indicated that most employees wanted to improve the company's overall effectiveness as well as their own jobs.

Bruce Harriman, "Up and Down the Communications Ladder," *Harvard Business Review*, September-October 1974, pp. 143–151. Copyright © 1974 by the President and Fellows of Harvard College; all rights reserved.

Editor's note: Readers interested in this piece may wish to refer to Dan H. Fenn, Jr., and Daniel Yankelovich, "Responding to the Employee Voice," HBR May-June 1972, p. 83.

At the same time, higher management saw the need for an accurate, timely, and unfiltered flow of communications from within the company that would help it perceive and react to change in an effective manner.

Accordingly, the company developed a program to respond to those needs and desires. Since it is based on the theory of up-and-down communications, we call it the "upward communications program." In this article, I first examine the theory itself and explain how it works to the advantage of individual managers as well as the organization. Then I describe the design, implementation, and results to date of my company's program. In the final section I offer suggestions for improved up-and-down communications channels that may be useful to other organizations.

THEORY OF UP-AND-DOWN COMMUNICATIONS

The theory that guided our 1969 study and resulting program is that communications in a hierarchical society or organization work according to the principle that governs gravity.

Downward communications are usually better than anyone realizes and frequently more accurate than those at higher levels want them to be. Conversely, upward communications have to be pumped and piped, with a minimum of filters, in order to be effective.

The reason for this difference is a phenomenon of human perception whereby persons in a subordinate position must, for survival or success, develop a keen understanding of the true motives, character, and personality of those in positions of power over them. For example, to survive in a white society, most blacks have developed their perception of a white person's basic intentions and attitude in the same manner that a blind man develops an acute sense of hearing.

In one study, researchers found that role taking—empathizing with and acting to please superiors—will increase in accuracy in inverse proportion to the perceiver's power in the structure. They also suggest that role-taking ability may result from the person's position rather than from a static personality trait.[1] To me this says, "Where you stand depends on where you sit."

Applying the theory of up-and-down communications to a business

---

[1] D.L. Thomas, D.D. Franks, and J.M. Calonico, "Role Taking and Power in Social Psychology," *American Sociological Review*, October 1972, p. 605.

organization, we determine that subordinates "read" their bosses better than is usually realized and bosses "read" their subordinates less well than they think.

Yet most management methods run counter to this theory; for example, formal job appraisals are always the boss's appraisal of the subordinate. Further, we have all noted that when bosses complain about communications in their organizations, they invariably mean that their subordinates have not heard them clearly and effectively. Most formal company communications programs and media are aimed from the top down. Few formal programs are designed so that subordinates can talk and bosses listen.

Downward Communications

The key aspect of downward communications is that subordinates react most effectively to those matters that they judge to be of greatest *personal* interest to the boss. Among the various commands, policies, practices, and suggestions that come from above, subordinates select those most in keeping with their perception of their bosses' character, personal motivation, and style and give them priority.

This tendency helps explain why some directives of a given manager "go off in the fog," while other directives get effective response. And it indicates why it is that what is communicated well through one boss fails to come through from another. The effectiveness of communications changes to the degree that each boss's personal interest is aroused in dealing with a particular situation. In short, "whatever turns you on" is the common reaction of subordinates to superiors. (This explanation ignores the needs, attitudes, and conditioning of the subordinates, which will be discussed shortly in my review of the upward communications phenomenon.)

Downward communications, however good, must ensure that employees act in the best interests of the company and not just in the interest of the boss; the two conflict occasionally. To improve downward communications, four principles must be followed:

1. Know yourself.
2. Be yourself.
3. Send selective signals.
4. Listen for signals.

Know Yourself. First, if subordinates react to their keen perception of what the boss really is and what he is most personally "turned on" by, then the boss had better examine himself very thoroughly. One of the best ways to gauge subordinates' perception is by their responses. Which of the many downward communications get fast reaction in your group? Which ones have to be pushed? Listen more sensitively to what people are trying to tell you about yourself. Seek upward appraisal from those subordinates closest to you and whose judgment you trust.

Jerry Rose has pointed out, "One of the privileges of power, perhaps an overlooked one, is the privilege of insensitivity to the negative attitudes of others."[2] If managers are aware of their insensitivity, they can improve their job performance in direct proportion to the degree that they receive and respond to upward communications.

Since I became more conscious of subordinates' reactions based on upward perception, I have discovered some things I didn't know about my own job interests and preferences. The key was to examine what was succeeding or failing in my organization. For example, in the first months of my present assignment our budgetary methods and controls were not satisfactory. I discovered that our department heads and staff members were reacting to my personal aversion to prolonged analysis of numbers. I now force myself to give priority to this necessary work and, therefore, so do my reporting people.

The whole area of upward perception and performance appraisal remains to be studied definitively, but an informal trial in our company suggested that appraisals by the subordinate of the boss are most accurate, appraisals by the boss of the subordinate are less accurate, and self-appraisal is the least accurate—as measured against quantifiable results. Careful studies could establish or refute this premise. If true, however, the real trick will be to utilize these appraisals without seriously threatening levels of supervisory authority.

Be Yourself. The second point is to be yourself—whatever that is. Once subordinates have "read" a boss's personal characteristics and methods of communicating, a change of style or signals is destructive to the organization's goals. This warning does not mean that managers should not adjust their methods of supervision as required. In fact, such change is the object of improved boss-subordinate communications.

Simply stated, supervisors should always act in a manner that is most natural to them. Whether the supervisor is a Casper Milquetoast or King Kong, he is most effective when using his natural personality and methods of expression. Too many times higher-level managers have worked hard to

<hr>

[2] J.D. Rose, "The Role of the Other in Self-Evaluation," *The Sociological Quarterly*, Fall 1969, p. 470.

change a tough guy into a human relations star or a reserved person into a tiger only to wonder later what went wrong with results after the subordinate caved in and changed his style. Sometimes managers try to change themselves on their own initiative to match the kind of managerial type they think their boss prefers. Once a manager's true personality and style are perceived by his subordinates, they know how to react. If he changes all his signals, the result will be confusion and a less effective organization.[3]

A classic example of the dangers of trying to change a tiger's stripes occurred in our company some years ago. As part of a human relations training program, we gave two days of instruction to all managers in Roger's nondirective interview technique. We called it "understanding listening." This technique involves person-to-person discussions in which the supervisor refrains from making any definite comment of his own during the discussion. Theoretically, this procedure leads to clearer expression by the subordinate and helps the manager understand better what is on the subordinate's mind.

The result of the program was that bosses refrained from making their own opinions and directives clear to their subordinates. Confusion and frustration multiplied in those organizations headed by dedicated graduates of understanding-listening training. We stopped the training, assessed what was happening, and then told our managers to return to their natural manner of running their jobs. We now use understanding-listening as a specific technique primarily in interviewing candidates for employment.

(ie, so that communication effective)

3) **Send Selective Signals.** Assuming you really know yourself and behave naturally, you must then learn to control the signals you send so that all your communications are effective.

Signals in interpersonal communications are many and varied. The words you use, tone of voice, facial expressions, gestures, body attitude are all signals. What you choose to write rather than communicate orally may signal the relative importance of a message. So too may be covering a subject in private rather than at a group meeting. All these signals and many more are read by people to determine not only what is being communicated but also how important the subject is to the communicator.

If you are communicating on a subject that really interests you, relax and don't worry about signals. Just get all the facts clear and the reaction will be in proportion to your personal interest in the subject. But when you must communicate policy, practice, or whatever on subjects that interest you less

[3] For further discussion of these ideas, see Theodore Levitt, "The Managerial Merry-Go-Round," HBR July-August 1974, p. 120

or to which you are personally opposed to some degree, then candor is the key.

Make it clear that something must be done because it is the law, or larger corporate considerations require it, or because budget controls demand it. Never suggest a "them" (external or higher authority) versus "me" or "us" feeling on your part.

This will fail for several reasons. First, if the immediate boss does not feel personally responsible for a given matter, the subordinates will not either. Second, it confuses people to see conflict between different levels of authority. If employees respond to one, will they fail to satisfy another? Finally, it's an obvious "cop-out" that lessens the boss in the eyes of subordinates, thus lessening the total effectiveness of the group. Just make it as clear as possible *why* something must be done even though it is not a prime personal interest of yours.

Thus subordinates can, without confusion, give high priority to a program or directive that is not the boss's "thing." However, if the boss is not conscious of the signals he uses, the areas of personal interest to him will get most of their attention.

This signaling technique worked in the budget control problem mentioned earlier. I acknowledged to my subordinates that budgetary analysis and control were not my favorite pastimes but that I saw them as top priorities for the subordinates and me. I then insisted on budget reviews and commitments in detail whenever we got together. They got the message.

Listen for Signals. The fourth principle, listening, is a shorthand introduction to the need for good upward communications. There are situations in which downward communications are either (a) effective in terms of useful action or (b) ineffective because of subordinates' perception of their bosses. The problem is to relieve (b). The best solution is to establish a good balance of two-way communications by deliberately improving upward communications. Bosses will then get a feedback on the effectiveness of their downward communications. Thus a continuing cycle of up-and-down signals will restore balance to what is usually a downward and less effective information flow.

Upward Communications

Before discussing how to establish good upward communications, I shall restate the theory. The better the interpersonal perception, the better the communications. Upward communications are poor in most hierarchical organizations because perception downward is poorer than perception upward. Add to that the "filters" of management levels that dilute upward communications. As you go higher, the word gets more garbled, edited, or, even worse, eliminated entirely.

New England Telephone found that the upward communications program developed as a result of our study is a very effective tool in overcoming this problem. I shall briefly summarize our study techniques and findings, then go on to what we are at present doing and experiencing in our own program.

First, we surveyed hundreds of companies in the United States and Canada for communications programs and also sought enlightenment from many colleges and business schools. Seventy-five companies were studied in depth. Seven U.S. and Canadian companies were finally selected for intensive study.

We encountered no experts, studies, or programs on upward communications. Most corporate communications programs dealt with downward communications, and the few that were aimed upward were individual techniques, such as employee suggestion plans, methods for answering questions, or ways of letting off steam. Although we found no comprehensive communications programs, we did discover individual techniques of merit that could be combined under one umbrella. Then we studied and interviewed, in groups and individually, our own employees, from the president to those with less than one year's service.

UPWARD COMMUNICATIONS PROGRAM

The upward communications program that resulted from this study started in New England Telephone in 1970 and is still evolving. It is now fully implemented in all five divisions in Massachusetts, including corporate headquarters in Boston, after an 18-month trial period in one area.

Private Lines

Our upward communications program started with "private lines," which permit all employees to question or discuss anonymously any matter of concern, from corporate policies to personal job-related problems, with any responsible official in the company. The "lines" can be either mailed in on a freely available form or called in to the full-time coordinating staff that administers the program, which then transmits them to those in the company who have the responsibility and/or expertise required in each case.

We select key private-line questions and answers of general interest for publication in the company newspaper. It is the most widely read column in the paper.

The practice of telephoning questions via the coordinators is growing because it permits personal discussion between one of the coordinators and the questioner that hones the points and aims the question to the right person. It further allows the coordinator to determine how to handle sensitive personal situations. Problems are sometimes resolved or questions answered by the coordinator during the discussion. On some occasions, our employees are willing, when reequested by the program coordinator, to forgo their anonymity to get a problem solved.

To date, we have processed more than 2,500 questions or comments. The most prevalent categories employees ask questions about are working conditions; benefits; promotions, transfers, and assignments; and wages and compensation. Under the category of working conditions, the number-one problem revealed has been inadequacies in the physical environment of the job. We have been quite successful in improving these conditions and thus job performance.

An ongoing survey of employee reaction to the private-line program shows that 79 per cent of the participating employees are satisfied with the response to their questions, and 93 per cent said they would use the program again. The source of employee-coordinator communications is about 75 per cent nonmanagement and 25 per cent management.

The numbers, however, are unimportant compared with the number of major policy reviews and changes undertaken, personnel problems solved, and levels of awareness increased. Even more revealing is that practically all communications have been serious, thoughtful, and concerned with the welfare of the total company. The true value of the program is apparent in the growing respect and importance accorded it since its inception.

Private lines have contributed to changes in policies and practices such as physical working conditions, employee benefits, career planning programs, training programs, specific work practices, and internal communications media. Personal job-related questions have ranged from female toilet facilities in previous all-male locations to "How can you get ahead in this outfit?" A comment to our president was, "You visited our office but didn't meet all of us individually." That one led to a review of how visits from the brass would be conducted.

One articulate white male manager anonymously expressed dismay that the corporate affirmative action program's goals and timetables for the progress of women and minorities cut into the promotion opportunities on which he and his colleagues had been planning. This statement was published along with our reply acknowledging that the competition for promotion had increased. His strong, candid letter, plus our equally candid reply, turned out to be one of the most effective airings to date on this sensitive issue.

Task Teams Work on Local Problems

Another part of the program is the task teams, which consist of nonmanagement employees who live or work in a given community or area. The teams are created following a survey of company problems in a specific location. Employees volunteer to serve on a seven-member panel that addresses itself for a total of 16 hours of company time per project to some or all of the identified local problems. Team members have participated during off-hours on their own initiative, and several have done so while on vacation. Their recommendations are sent to a middle management interdepartmental committee from the area in question. The committee has 30 days to respond.

To date, over 90 per cent of all team recommendations have been accepted and implemented. Operating teams have improved in a majority of the cases. Teams have handled sticky local problems such as parking for employees, cafeteria food, local public relations, working conditions, and interdepartmental orientation. The team in my home town ran a telephone open house to improve local public relations. I doubted that it would succeed, but it was standing room only for two straight nights and I still hear favorable comments from townspeople.

A good example of the range and effectiveness of task teams is the activities of the Northampton, Massachusetts team. This team studied and made workable recommendations on the following: comptometer training for clerks, static on the piped-in music system, air circulation in the office, employee-management relations in the engineering group, cleanliness of the operator positions, interdepartmental tours for employees, processing of incoming calls in the construction planning group, scheduling of routine maintenance work, administration of Centrex customer accounts, and follow-up training for business office representatives.

False Starts and Surprising Side Effects

One of the first programs started during the trial period was called the management council, which consisted of interdepartmental middle management people selected from among volunteers to attack specific operating problems identified by higher management They were compensated above regular salary for this assignment. However, this part of the program proved redundant to normal management channels and was abandoned.

The council did, however, conceive the idea of an interdepartmental team of first-line management people in each locality. These "coordinating action teams" meet regularly to act on local interdepartmental operations problems. Now on trial in several areas, these teams appear more viable than the council that spawned them.

Coordinating action teams, if successful, can fill a major gap in our operations. Currently our interdepartmental management teams start at the second level of management. The task teams are proving successful with nonmanagement people. We are certain that coordinating action teams are a vehicle for getting more meaningful and effective participation from our first-line management people.

One happy result we did not foresee was that the coordinating staff which administered the entire upward communications program has become a major factor in itself. The program staff has personally talked to over 500 employees who have participated in the program. Many personal and business problems have been resolved in this manner because of the person-to-person nature of the contacts. Whenever employees are contacted by a coordinator, they are surprised and pleased to find that corporate management is concerned enough with their well-being to call them.

The staff has been very careful never to assume roles or responsibilities not assigned to it, but the members have helped solve problems that needed a sensitive, objective ombudsman as a catalyst.

Cost of Program . . .

The full-time coordinating staff consists of a director and two assistants. Their salaries plus the lease on their off-company premises and associated expenses make up most of the allocated cost of our program. Add to this the expense of private-line forms and report forms, and the total allocated annual cost of the program is about $100,000 to serve over 38,000 employees in Massachusetts.

. . . **Versus Results.** The problems uncovered are often very personal. There are cases involving management people who are uncomfortable with their responsibilities and want to be transferred or demoted but don't know how to discuss it with their supervisors. Wives of some of these people initiate or participate in the contacts.

In one case, a clerk with nine months' service was complaining about the atmosphere at her job location. She respected her supervisor but thought she was overburdened and thus unresponsive to the needs of individuals in her group. The clerk agreed to a face-to-face meeting with her supervisor and the district manager in the coordinators' office. The upshot was that more supervision was added to the group, and current feedback tells us that the situation is vastly improved.

My favorite story is of the time our upward communications director made an off-hours phone call to an employee who had sent in a private-line question. He reached an intercept operator who referred him to another number. The employee answered at the new number and, as they discussed the problem, the director kept hearing sounds of merriment in the background. When asked about the change of telephone number, the employee told him she had recently married and moved to a new apartment. He asked, "When did you get married?" She answered, "Today. I'm at my wedding reception now." She stopped his apologies by saying, "I would talk to you anytime about the problems we're having at the office." Not typical, but indicative.

The coordinating staff not only runs the total program, provides the personal touch, and protects anonymity where required, but it also produces useful feedback for management on the program. This feedback is produced in several ways:

- —The staff provides copies of completed, but anonymous, private-line questions and answers to managers who may be interested or involved. This is not done in cases where the employee might be identified.
- —It maintains private-line reference binders for management on questions of general interest. These binders are used frequently on matters of policy and practice.
- —It publishes questions and answers of interest to all in the "nitty-gritty" column of the company newspaper.

MAKING UPWARD
COMMUNICATIONS WORK

The upward communications program has not solved all our management problems, but we are rapidly improving our overall operating effectiveness, and we believe the program has enhanced our efforts.

Our upward communications director summed it up in a recent interview when he said, "We are responsive to employee concerns. The program lends itself to that. They're able to tell us what's wrong, and then we follow through by identifying their problems and getting management people involved in these concerns so that action can be taken. In 99 percent of the cases, we can do something and when we do, it has to reflect in the ways we do business—ranging from productivity to public relations."

With very little modification the key points underlying our upward communications program can be applied to any business anxious to improve internal communications. In summary, the points are:

1. The majority of nonmanagement and management people want to help the company perform its functions more responsively. Achieving this goal requires a program to help employees cope with their work problems and enhance their involvement in their jobs and the company. Therefore, the program should be considered a management tool and not a cathartic outlet or morale booster.

2. The program must be very carefully structured and introduced into a trial area with thorough person-to-person discussion. A one-year trial period is necessary to establish a credible record of positive results. Gradual expansion of the program to other areas must have the same careful introduction as the initial trial. This will ensure commitment at the top and credibility down the line. Rapid or miraculous results should not be expected even where acceptance is good.

3. Different individuals and groups have differing communications needs, and these needs shift as circumstances change. Thus only a multipurpose communications system developed step by step can provide channels covering the entire company as well as programs tailored for local or special requirements.

4. Such a program cannot be a part-time responsibility run by just anyone. Absolutely essential to the success of the program is the full-time coordinating staff, made up of a few management people selected on the basis of proven human relations skills and strong personal commitment to the program. This staff should be in a location that permits private, face-to-face discussions. In addition, special toll-free phone lines might be provided to facilitate and encourage direct calls from employees to the coordinators.

5. Anonymity is required in that portion of the program which involves questions to management. In general, managers can be questioned or given opinions on any matter concerning the company except items subject to union bargaining or grievances. Anonymity not only protects the questioner but protects all intervening levels, thus assuring nonfiltered yet nonthreatening communications.

6. Managerial commitment is assured by allowing area or divisional managers to choose whether to join the program or to create their own mechanisms. In keeping with the basic theory, if the boss doesn't buy it, the program will die; therefore it is much better not started at all. Generally speaking, the delegation for implementing a total system is not effective below the fourth or fifth level of management. But lower-level participation in implementing local aspects of the system is possible.

7. The program must produce *visible results.* This is the cruncher. Fast, candid, visible, and sensitive response by top managers is the key. They must be ready to have policies and practices questioned—and what is worse, questioned accurately and articulately. They must be prepared to reexamine and change policies, to tell employees facts that hitherto were not generally disseminated, and to admit they are wrong on occasion.

We at New England Telephone are only in the early stages of understanding and utilizing the potential of upward perception. We have not yet fully achieved a total system of upward communication designed to tap the various primary categories of communications needs. Also there is much to do to improve our understanding and handling of downward communications. Still we think we have learned a few things about interpersonal communications in a structured situation and about making this knowledge work to our organization's benefit.

Jerry B. Harvey

George Washington University

D. Richard Albertson

University of Puget Sound

NEUROTIC ORGANIZATIONS: SYMPTOMS, CAUSES AND TREATMENT

PART I

Organizations, like individuals develop neuroses. The toll on an organization's behavior, measured in terms of production, efficiency, absenteeism, turnover, overhead and morale, is tremendous. And since each of these organization variables has personal antecedents, the price paid by individual organization members, measured in terms of misery and loss of self-esteem and confidence, is inestimable. But organizations, like people, can be cured of neurotic behavior and returned to a state of healthy functioning. The purpose of this article is to describe the symptoms of organization neurosis, to identify some of its causes, and to define a course of treatment for restoring neurotic organizations to health. Implicit throughout are descriptions of the role and function of an organization consultant in the process of diagnosis and treatment.

Jerry B. Harvey and D. Richard Albertson, "Neurotic Organizations: Symptoms, Causes and Treatment," Part 1, *Personnel Journal*, September 1971, pp. 694–699; Part 2, *Personnel Journal*, October 1971, pp. 770–783.

364

SYMPTOMS OF ORGANIZATION NEUROSIS___

Perhaps the most effective way to get a feel for the symptoms of organization neurosis is to read summaries of interviews with several employees including the head of one neurotic organization.

INTERVIEW I___

Consultant: How are things going on the job?

Employee A: Terrible. I hate to come to work. And once I'm here, I don't get anything done. We just sit around and gripe. The only thing I look forward to is vacation.

Consultant: What's the problem? What's causing the trouble?

Employee A: We have a couple of problems. First, we have a lousy boss. He never holds up our end with the higher ups. And second, at least two of the five units making up this division should not be reporting to him. Putting Sales and Research under the same man is absurd. In a lot of ways they are competitive. There is no reason for them to work together. They never have and never will.

Consultant: Have you ever confronted your boss with his failure to "carry the flag?"

Employee A: Hell, no. Do you think I'm crazy or something?

Consultant: What about the problem with Sales and Research? What are you doing to solve that?

Employee A: Just last week we met and agreed to operate under a combined budget.

INTERVIEW II___

Consultant: How are things going on the job?

Employee B: Pretty bad. This is a frustrating place to work. Right now I'm looking for another job. I take as much vacation and sick leave as I can. And I don't get anything done when I'm here. Really, I'm just marking time, hoping things will get better.

Consultant: What's causing all the frustration?

Employee B: Well, for one thing our organization set-up doesn't make sense. Whoever designed it must have been crazy. Having Sales and Research report to the same man is unworkable. We spend half our time fighting one another. In addition, our boss doesn't represent our viewpoint to the top.

Consultant: Are you taking any steps to deal with the problems you just described?

Employee B: Yes, just last week the president instructed my boss to get us together to solve the morale problem. It's beginning to cut into everyone's production. The last quarter was very poor from a profit standpoint. And two of our best researchers took jobs with another company.

Consultant: What did you do?

Employee B: We had an all day meeting and agreed to operate under a combined budget. That should force us to work together more effectively.

Consultant: One other question. What about your boss? Has he ever asked whether he is doing an adequate job of carrying the division's viewpoint to the top?

Employee B: Yes, just the other day, he said he had heard by the grapevine that we thought he wasn't giving us good representation with the president and his staff.

Consultant: What did you say?

Employee B: I said I thought he was doing a good job.

INTERVIEW III

Consultant: What problems and issues are facing your division at the present time?

Boss: Well, morale is at an all time low. We have had a couple of good people quit and go to other companies. And production is down. The heat is on me and everyone else. I've about given up.

Consultant: What's the cause of it?

Boss: One big problem is the way we are organized. My boss gave me several units that don't have any reason to work together. In fact, two of the units are actually competitive in a functional sense. With that kind of arrangement, it's impossible to build teamwork among the staff.

Consultant: What have you done about it?

Boss: Well, last week I gave a pep talk to the staff at our weekly meeting and said we had to work together more effectively. And to insure that we do, we developed a unit budget that ties each subgroup's performance into the over-all performance of the division.

Consultant: Have you ever thought about telling your boss that the way you are organized does not make sense?

Boss: I've tried, but I can't seem to make him understand.

Consultant: Have you really pushed him hard?

Boss: I'm not about to do that. He might think I am not an effective manager.

As can be seen by the interviews, the neurotic organization exhibits a number of specific symptoms which are collectively expressed by its members.

Its members complain of frustration, worry, backbiting, loss of self-esteem and a general sense of impotence. They do not feel their skills are being adequately used. As a result, they become less efficient and look for ways to avoid the job, such as taking vacation, taking sick leave, and "giving up" or "opting out" of trying to solve the problems they see as causing the pain.

BLAMING OTHERS FOR THE PROBLEMS

Its members attempt to place much of the blame for the dilemma on others, particularly the boss. In "backroom" conversations among subordinates, he is termed as incompetent, ineffective, "out of touch" or as a candidate for transfer or early retirement. To his face nothing is said, or at best, oblique or misleading information is given concerning his impact on the organization.

SUBGROUP FORMATION

As pain and frustration become more intense, the personnel form into identifiable subgroups. These subgroups may develop on the basis of friendship with trusted acquaintances meeting during coffee or over lunch to share rumors, complaints, fantasies, or strategies for dealing with the problems at hand. The most important effect of such meetings is to heighten the over-all anxiety level in the organization rather than to help to realistically cope with its problems.

AGREEMENT AS TO PROBLEMS

Its members generally agree as to the character of problems causing the pain. For example, in the interviews related above, organization members agree that the organization has two basic problems: 1) The composition of the units reporting to the same superior is inappropriate, and 2) There is a failure to communicate the urgency of the composition issue to upper levels of management. The first problem reflects an important *task* issue (Benne and Muntyan, *Human Relations in Curriculum Change*, 1951), i.e., how to organize effectively. The second reflects an equally important *maintenance* concern (Benne and Muntyan, *ibid.* 1951), i.e., how to work together in such a way that the organization functions effectively. That agreement as to task and maintenance issues bridges both hierarchical and functional lines. Stated differently, the boss and his subordinates see the problems in the same way as do employees from Sales and Research. Although organization members may be unaware of the degree to which they agree with one another, the reality is they do agree.

MEMBERS ACT CONTRARY TO DATA AND INFORMATION THEY POSSESS

Perhaps the most unique characteristic of neurotic organizations is that its members act in ways contrary to the data and information they possess. In analogous terms, it would be as if an outside observer viewed the following vignette involving twenty people from a neurotic organization:

Observer: (Approaching a group sitting around a camp fire) How are things going?

Organization Members: (Who are holding their hands over an open fire) Awful. It's too hot. We are burning up. The pain is excruciating. Our hands are too close to the coals.

Observer: What do you intend to do about it?

Organization Members: Move our hands closer to the fire, what else?

Although the analogy may sound absurd on the surface, it is certainly no more absurd than the following conversation which occurred in an actual organization.

Consultant: You say there is no possible functional relationship among the groups reporting to your boss and it is impossible to build one.

Organization Members: Yes, that's right.

Consultant: What do you propose to do about it?

Organization Members: Meet more often so we will have more opportunities to learn to work together.

It is this characteristic which really defines neurotic organization behavior the same way it defines neurotic individual behavior. The individual who consistently acts contrary to his best "internal signals" becomes neurotic, and if he acts in concert with a variety of others, the organization as an entity develops neurotic symptoms. Stated conversely, any human system must act congruently with reality if it is to function effectively.

MEMBERS BEHAVE DIFFERENTLY OUTSIDE THE ORGANIZATION

Finally, the key to the diagnosis of organization neurosis is the fact that outside the organization context, members do not either suffer the pain nor demonstrate the irrational behavior (such as behaving contrary to their own views of reality) that they demonstrate in their day-to-day work. Outside the organization, individual members get along better, are happier, and perform more effectively than they do within it, a fact that heightens their discomfort when living and working within the organization.

CAUSES OF NEUROTIC ORGANIZATION BEHAVIOR

Given a description of organization neurosis, the question is then, "Why do organization members engage in behavior which is both individually and organizationally destructive?" Basically, there are two reasons.

LACK OF AWARENESS

First, organization members are unaware of their behavior and the consequences it has for them as individuals and for the organization as an entity. Such lack of awareness may involve any of three levels. At the most superficial level, an organization member may be unaware of the degree to which the information and feelings he possesses are shared by others in the organization. Thus, he may feel as if he is alone in his diagnosis of the organization's problems. Or, he may feel that, at most, the subgroup to which he belongs agrees as to the character of the organization's problems. He seldom realizes that his understandings and beliefs are widely shared across functional and hierarchical lines and that he is not an isolate.

Consultant: Do you think people other than yourself believe that the unit needs to be reorganized?

Employee: Well, several guys that work with me agree on that issue, but I doubt if any others do.

Consultant: What would you say if I told you that virtually everyone in the division feels the same as you do about that issue.

Employee: I'd say you must be kidding.

Since that lack of agreement reflects a simple information gap, it is the simplest form of unawareness to correct.

At a second level, organization members may be unaware of the dysfunctional group norms and standards which inhibit or prevent their coping with the problems at hand. It is at the normative level that the difference between individual and organization neurosis is most clearly articulated. Individual neurosis stems from *personal* dynamics unique to the individual. Organization neurosis stems from *collective* dynamics unique to the organization. Thus, organizations develop social norms and standards, neurotic in character, the breaking of which by individual members results in the application of social pressure to conform. For example, some organizations develop dysfunctional norms mitigating against open discussion of important organization issues.

Organization Member A: I think we ought to confront the issue of whether we are appropriately organized. I personally don't think these units belong together.

Organization Member B: Oh, knock it off! Let's not get involved in something like that.

Organization Member D: What are you trying to do? We don't need things stirred up any more than they already are.

Organization Member C: Yes, the problems aren't as bad as you crack them up to be. We really work together rather well. I move we change the subject.

As one consultant put it, "fish are the last to know that they are in water." So it is with organization members. They are frequently the last to know of the dysfunctional norms which govern and occasionally consume them. However, as Lewin (*Field Theory in Social Science*, 1947) has demonstrated, behavior rooted in group standards and norms is easier to change than behavior rooted in individual character structure. Because of this principle, organization neurosis is potentially more amenable to change than the individual variety.

Finally, a third level relates to the degree to which organization members are unaware of the manner in which they contribute to maintaining the problems. For example, some members may see the part others, particularly the boss, play in maintaining destructive organization norms and standards, but few sense their own roles in the process.

Consultant: You say your boss is at fault; that he should demand to his superior that the situation be changed.

Employee A: Absolutely. He is doing a lousy job.

Employee B: You can say that again.

Consultant: Have you or any other members of your division ever demanded of your boss that he do a better job of representing your group to the President?

Employee A: No. That's not what I'm around here for.

Employee B: Me neither.

Employee C: I think it would be foolish and disrespectful to do something like that.

Consultant: It seems to me as if you may be doing exactly the same thing you don't want your boss to do.

Employee C: (Lamely) We are?

It is as if the identification with superiors, other peers, or the organization itself is so great that employees lose their capacities to understand either their individual or collective contributions to the dysfunctional organization process. Since the dynamics supporting such lack of awareness tend to be so deep within the individual and group psyche (Freud, *Group Psychology and the Analogy of the Ego*, 1951) they are the hardest to identify, make explicit, and change.

FANTASIES ABOUT CONSEQUENCES OF ALTERNATIVE ACTIONS

Even when organization members are aware of the degree to which they agree as to the substance of the problems, are knowledgeable about the group norms and standards which prevent their coping effectively with those problems and are cognizant of their own unique ways of maintaining those dysfunctional norms and standards, they still may be unable to take effective problem-solving action. Again, the question is "Why?"

In most cases, the inaction relates to rich and varied fantasies organization members have about possible negative consequences which may befall them if they do act. The fantasies have a mythlike quality (Bradford and Harvey, *Training and Development Journal*, Vol. 6, No. 3, 1970) which are frequently unrelated to reality.

Consultant: Each of you seems to agree this division needs to be reorganized and that the present format is unworkable. Why don't you suggest to your boss that you reorganize?

Employee A: He might fire us for treading on his territory. He's supposed to think of that, not us.

Employee B: The new organization might be worse than the present one. It's not worth taking the chance.

Employee C: I'm sure things will get better if we just wait it out. Life isn't as bad as we make it out to be.

Employee D: I've got a mortgage payment on the house. I can't afford to do anything that rocks the boat.

Consultant: Is there any possibility that things might get better if you do something other than wait?

Various Employees: We doubt it.

The fantasy-like quality comes from the fact that the projected outcomes are seldom if ever tested for reality. In general, such fantasies reflect a tremendous amount of underlying anxiety and concern that has to be taken into account in any process designed to treat the "neurosis."

The symptoms of a neurotic organization described above serve, in effect, as a diagnostic checklist for identifying organization neurosis.

Jerry B. Harvey

George Washington University

D. Richard Albertson

University of Puget Sound

NEUROTIC ORGANIZATIONS: SYMPTOMS, CAUSES AND TREATMENT

PART II

In Part I of this article, a neurotic organization was defined as one in which organization members feel pain, frustration and loss of self esteem. They agree among themselves as to the problems causing the pain, but usually take collective action essentially contrary to the data, information and feelings they possess for solving the problems. This, in turn, increases the frustration and loss of self esteem and leads to the emergence of other symptoms. It was pointed out that these same people do not suffer similar pain or demonstrate irrational behavior outside the organization.

Some of the causes for such behavior were identified as lack of awareness of self-destructive organization patterns and fantasized consequences of pursuing problem solutions whose outcome is uncertain or unknown.

In this part of the article, procedures for treating organization neurosis

Jerry B. Harvey and D. Richard Albertson, "Neurotic Organizations: Symptoms, Causes and Treatment," Part 1, *Personnel Journal*, September 1971, pp. 694–699; Part 2, *Personnel Journal*, October 1971, pp. 770–783.

will be discussed. Like individual neurosis, it can be treated, and like the individual variety, the treatment is complex.

The first step is to collect data from a representative sample of organization members. It is particularly important that more than one level of the organization be represented in the data collection, since issues of hierarchy and authority are generally central to the kinds of problems identified. On the basis of their experiences with a variety of organizations, the authors have found that open-ended interviews conducted around three basic questions produces the data required. These questions are:

1. What issues and problems are facing the organization at the present time?
2. What is causing these problems?
3. What strengths are available in the organization to solve the problems?

Interviews last 45 minutes to an hour. Basic to their success is that they be conducted by someone who can view the organization from an essentially objective standpoint. Although it is possible that an inside consultant with enough functional autonomy can achieve and maintain the kind of objective detachment required, an outside consultant is generally preferred. An outsider is less likely to be caught up in the dysfunctional processes underlying the neurosis and, therefore, is less likely to have distorted perspectives of the organization and its problems.

Essentially, verbatim notes are taken by the consultant. When all interviews are completed, the data from interviewees are sorted into themes[1] which are identified with nonevaluative titles. Actual statements of organization members are grouped under each theme. A typical set of themes and supporting statements are shown in Exhibit I.

Exhibit I

Examples of Themes, Supporting Data and Summary Statements

Theme 1: Division Composition

1. The composition of this division does not make sense.
2. This division is a group of independent units operating under an umbrella.

---

[1] A theme is arbitrarily defined as an issue or concern which is spontaneously mentioned by at least 50 per cent of the organization members interviewed.

3. It is not a group. It is a collection of units just thrown together.
4. Research does not belong in the division.
5. The way the division is constituted is inappropriate.
6. The division needs to be subdivided.
7. It is a mixture of apples and oranges.
8. The division is made up of remnants of an earlier era. There is not much logic to it.
9. What we have is a variety of sub-groups.
10. Units do not have much in common.
11. It is not a group in any sense.

Summary Statement

The present composition and/or structure of the division is inappropriate, out of step with the opportunity to accomplish our purposes, and should be changed.

Theme 2: Collaboration within the Division

1. Some staff members do not communicate with anyone.
2. No communication within division.
3. Staff share few common goals—the exception is survival.
4. There's no relationship between some units, like Sales and Research.
5. There's too much time talking as a group. The subjects talked about are not perceived as making much difference.
6. There is no support. I occasionally feel close to harassment. We frequently talk to other staff members rather than confronting the person we should talk to.
7. Within the division some are more willing to jump unit lines than others.
8. Other units in the division fight each other for stature.
9. Some units in the division are pro-active while others sit around waiting to be told what to do.
10. Each unit is a kingdom unto itself.

Summary Statement

In general, units within the division do not work together.

Theme 3: Top Leadership

1. The boss is too nice and that causes people to take advantage of him.
2. His style keeps us from confronting problems even when conflict is there.
3. The boss is unable to carry the "flag." I don't know why.
4. He has not been able to change or get the attention of top management.
5. He spends a lot of time telling the group that everything is okay—all is right with the world—but that is not true.
6. His style is not congruent with the confrontation style that works in the organization today.
7. He sometimes has to support positions that he does not believe in and that makes him ineffective in dealing with top management.
8. His inability to be defensive and hostile gets him in trouble.

Summary Statement

The boss's style is not of a confronting nature.

Theme 4: Pain

1. We are suffering from . . .
2. I feel no support and occasionally feel close to harassment.
3. People who are committed are frustrated as well.
4. Nothing feeds failure like failure.
5. Creativity is squelched.
6. Joe Smith is being stifled.
7. We want to contribute in a positive way, but can't.
8. There is a lot of insecurity and morale is very low.
9. The division is not conducive to good mental health and working conditions.

Summary Statement

Most division personnel are frustrated, worried, and feel insecure; morale is low.

It should be stressed that the data must be verbatim accounts of what the organization members said relative to each theme. The data must not be a summary of what the consultant would like organization members to say or believe. Throughout the process of consultation, the actual data contributed by organization members, not the consultant's biases and prejudices, must be the topic of exploration.

DATA FEEDBACK TO
ORGANIZATION MEMBERS

After data are collected and sorted into themes, the consultant presents both the themes and supporting statements to the interviewees in a modified version of a confrontation session (Beckhard, 1967). During this session, which usually requires several hours, organization members are encouraged to discuss, clarify, and modify both the themes and supporting statements. Whenever organization members are satisfied that the themes and the supporting data are accurate reflections of their own feelings and knowledge, they are asked to develop a single summary statement which adequately summarizes the data contributed under each theme. Examples of summary statements are also contained in Exhibit I.

After each theme has been discussed and a summary statement developed, organization members are asked to vote publicly as to whether they agree or disagree with the content of the summary statement.

Votes are counted and if a clear majority do not agree with a summary statement, the consultant works with the group to clarify the reasons for the disagreement. Discussion continues until the statement is modified so that most organization members can agree with it, or until the statement is eliminated because it does not actually reflect their feelings and attitudes.

Taking a public vote is important because it transfers ownership of the themes and the supporting data from the consultant to the organization members themselves. Stated differently, the vote forces the organization members to accept responsibility for the validity or lack of validity of the data they contributed.

Once the data are identified as belonging to organization members rather than the consultants, the next step is to ask each member to "own up" (Argyris, 1962) to his individual contribution to each issue represented by the various themes.

Thus, each organization member is asked to produce a series of written statements according to the following directions:

For each of the summary statements, write a few sentences describing the way in which you contribute to the issue which is summarized. Your descriptions will belong to you. Although you may want to share your thoughts with others later on, there will be no requirement to do so.

Here, the purpose is to help each organization member focus on his possible contribution to maintaining the process causing the problems. It also helps to set a norm of examining one's own contribution to the organization's problems rather than blaming others.

SHARING THE THEORY

One of the most important steps in the treatment process involves the sharing of the consultant's theory with organization members. Again, organization members' own views of reality, which they have affirmed through a public vote, is central to the presentation process. The rationale for presenting the model is that theory itself is a powerful intervention. In brief, it helps organization members to diagnose and understand organization problems and to plan action steps which do not foster the continuation of those problems.

Basically, the theory is presented by the consultant as follows:
When organization members:

1. Experience pain and frustration.
2. Agree with one another as to the problems and causes.
3. Act in ways contrary to their own thoughts, feelings, and information.

the following assumptions should be tested:

1. Organization members are implicitly or explicitly collaborating with one another to maintain the status quo,
2. Organization members have fantasies about the disastrous consequences of confronting those issues and concerns they know and agree cause the pain and frustration.

At this point, the consultant helps organization members apply the model to their own lives by "walking them through" an actual case involving their own organization.

Consultant: In this organization you agree that you are unhappy and frustrated (Theme 4), that the organization is inappropriately constituted (Theme 1), and that units do not work well together (Theme 2). Yet, when asked by top management to make a proposal for solving the problems of this organization, what happened?

Organization Member: We made a proposal.

Consultant: What did you say in the proposal?

Organization Member: That we develop a matrix organization and operate under a combined budget.

Consultant: What will that decision require?

Organization Member: Well, for one thing, a lot more teamwork.

Consultant: Is that decision congruent with the reality that everyone feels the organization is inappropriately constituted and that the various sub parts do not work well together?

Organization Member: Oh, hell! We've done it again, haven't we?

Using members' own data forces them to become aware of the discrepancy between their own views of reality (We don't work well together) and the actions they take which, in effect, deny that reality (making decisions which require working more closely together). This new awareness confronts them with the necessity of making a conscious choice to explore alternatives based on their views of reality (for example, dissolving the division and reorganizing, a solution which may require working more closely together). This new awareness confronts them with the necessity of making a conscious choice to explore alternatives based on their views of reality (for example, dissolving the division and reorganizing, a solution which may require painful shifts in job, status, and location) or continuing to act on the basis of irrational fantasies which are individually and organizationally destructive (organizing in a way that denies their beliefs that the composition of the division is inappropriate.)

If the consultant is to be effective in helping the organization alter its destructive patterns, he must continue to help members confront the basic discrepancy which exists between their views of reality and the decisions they make.

CONSULTANT FUNCTIONS IN CHANGE PROCESS

Throughout the data feedback session, and in other encounters within the organization, events occur which mirror the problems organization members have in working during their day-to-day activities. In these encounters, the consultant has a variety of functions all of which require his being sensitive to underlying emotional and process issues. Examples of these include:

1. Building Awareness of Dysfunctional Group Standards and Norms

The process of presenting data to the persons who contribute it helps organization members become aware of the degree to which they agree with one another about the character of the organization's problems. In effect, the sharing of data assists in solving problems stemming from an "information gap." However, the consultant must also help organization members become aware of dysfunctional norms and group standards which inhibit their capacity to cope with problems identified in the data sharing stage.

Organization Member: (to consultant) I did not like being forced by you to fill out the questionnaire regarding my contribution to maintaining the problems. When you asked me to do that, I felt very manipulated. I didn't think the process would lead to anything and still don't. I just filled it out to suit you. It sure didn't suit any need of mine.

Consultant: I wonder how many others felt that way.

Various Members: I did.

Consultant: In some ways, that is similar to the tendency of members of this organization to act contrary to their own best views of reality.

Organization Member: I don't understand that either. We just did as we were told. What's wrong with that?

Consultant: Well, it looks as if most of you did not want to respond to the questionnaire because you didn't think it was relevant. Yet everyone responded and nothing was said at the time. That's very similar to not confronting the problem of reorganization even though there is uniform agreement that reorganization is needed.

Organization Member: You got us again.

Consultant: I didn't get you.

Organization Member: Yeah. We got ourselves. We contributed to the problem again.

Previous Member: Yes, but he still makes me mad, catching us.

2. Coping with Feelings

As the previous vignette indicates, the members of a neurotic organization, like neurotic individuals, demonstrate extreme difficulty in the area of learning new behavior. They find it difficult to appraise the past in the light of the present. As a consequence, they find it hard to assimilate and utilize new knowledge, although it may be all around them and clearly apparent to an outsider. They seem to be restricted to coping responses rooted in history. Although these responses may be inadequate and dysfunctional, organization members persist in using them and even exert a tremendous amount of collective energy in trying to maintain them.

Much of that energy in a change process may be directed against the consultant in the form of anger and resentment or lavish praise.

Organization Member: He makes me mad, catching us that way.

Organization Member: He doesn't make me mad. He sees things none of the rest of us see. He's doing a great job.

The feelings of ambivalence are understandable for the consultant, in ways similar to the individual therapist, represents both a threat and a promise to organization members.

It is important for the change process that the consultant understand this and be prepared to cope with such feelings when they arise, because in any organization change process, as in an individual therapeutic process, there is an initial period of disorganization and anxiety before new, more functional norms and standards are developed.

The coping can take two forms. One is to help members learn from their feelings.

Consultant: Both comments may reflect some reality and some fantasy. For example, I don't think I "caught" anyone. And I also doubt that I'm the only one who sees what I reported. I would like to check that out with others here.

The other form of coping is more pragmatic. The authors suspect that it is around this issue that many organization change processes are terminated. Thus, organization members must be informed in advance of the possible turmoil they may feel and of the potential positive consequences. Otherwise, a change process may be stopped at the very time constructive change takes place. In short, just as it is with a neurotic individual, the neurotic organization is its worst enemy.

3. Encouraging Fantasy and Reality Testing

One of the basic reasons for acting contrary to one's view of reality are fantasies about the consequences for alternative actions. Again, underlying these fantasies is a great deal of emotionality and concern that must be dealt with if organization members are to clearly differentiate between fantasy and reality. One way to facilitate the process of clarification is to encourage the process of fantasizing.

Consultant: One of the reasons people sometimes act contrary to what they really know is that they have notions about what will happen if they actually do what needs to be done.

Organization Member: What do you mean?

Consultant: Well, one of the reasons people may not want to question whether Jim (the boss) is confronting enough in upholding the viewpoint of this organization to top management is that they don't know what he might do to those who question his actions.

Organization Member: Damn right. He might fire me. (nervous laughter)

Another Member: Or send me back to the production line.

Another Member: Or get back at me when annual reviews come along.

Interviewer: Has anyone in this group ever questioned Jim's actions before?

Organization Member: I have.

Consultant: What did he say?

Organization Member: He said "thanks" and that he was unaware of what he was doing.

Another Member: Same thing happened to me.

Consultant: I wonder if all of the worries you have voiced are justified? Do they have any reality?

Organization Member: It doesn't sound like they do.

COACHING

Although organization members may (a) have full access to information, (b) be aware of dysfunctional norms and standards, (c) understand the way they contribute to maintaining those norms, and (d) be able to distinguish between fantasized consequences and reality, they still may not be able to develop new ways of coping. Therefore, a third function of a consultant in a change process is to "coach" organization members in new behaviors. Such coaching can take place in group meetings, in private conversations, and in various sub group configurations.

Organization Member: Okay, I want to tell Jim (the boss) that I don't think he is holding up our end with the President. What do I say? Do I say "Jim, you are a lousy manager." That doesn't seem to make much sense.

Consultant: One alternative would be to admit your own feelings about Jim and what he is doing.

Organization Member: What do you mean?

Consultant: Well, you might say, "When I don't feel you represent us at the top it makes it a lot harder for me to do my job in addition to making me downright angry." That way you're not saying Jim is personally incompetent. You're saying what his actions do to you.

Organization Member: Hmm. I've never thought of that approach before.

4. Other Functions

Obviously, organizations cannot be "cured" of neurotic behavior in a single session. About all that can be expected in a brief meeting is that organization members may develop some awareness of the degree to which they agree with one another on important issues and of the manner in which they contribute to maintaining dysfunctional organization procedures. They may also become aware of the degree of discomfort they feel with the situation and of their motivation and readiness to change it. In addition, in one meeting organization members may decide whether the consultant and his approach might be helpful to them in coping with their problems.

Assuming that the decision is affirmative, there are several additional roles that the consultant may play, all of which involve building awareness, coping with feelings, encouraging fantasy, and coaching in new behavior. These roles include:

1. Attending regular work meetings of various organization units to serve as an observer, confronter, reality tester.
2. Individual coaching sessions with key organization members concerning their roles in the process. Since the role of the superior of the unit is always central to the underlying problems of an organization (Crockett, 1970), coaching sessions with him can have an unequal impact on the organization's operations.
3. Working with the organization to develop acceptable measures of progress and improvement. Sometimes individually tailored measures are developed and sometimes "packaged" research materials such as Likert scales (1967) are employed. Whatever measures are used, they must be acceptable and agreed upon collaboratively by both the organization members and the consultant. If such agreement is reached, it is far more likely that organization members will accept measures of progress or regression as valid and as reflecting reality. Collaborating in the development of such measures also helps members to learn to act on the basis of their own view of reality. Thus, such measures do not contribute to maintaining the very norms and standards which are the targets of change.
4. Helping develop reasonable expectations about speed of change. As can be understood from the preceding discussions, the processes

supporting organization neurosis are complex, and the skills needed to change those processes cannot be learned quickly. As a consequence, the "do-it-tomorrow" perspective, frequently characteristic of organization members, is unrealistic. However, to the extent that there are ways of measuring progress which are agreeable to organization members and the consultant, periodic assessment of results can be made. Time, thus, becomes less important as an absolute variable in the evaluation process, since it may be viewed in the light of whatever positive or negative results are achieved.

In summary, the treatment of organization neurosis involves the use of consultants who help members (a) collect reality centered information about the organization, (b) gain understanding of the dysfunctional norms and standards which keep them from using whatever information is available, (c) help them in differentiating reality from fantasy when assessing alternative solutions to the problems which are identified, and (d) assist them in developing the skills necessary to implement realistic alternatives. Although organization neurosis involves complex long-term treatment, change is possible and well worth the effort in terms of both economic and humanistic savings.

REFERENCES

1. Beckhard, R., "The Confrontation Meeting," *Harvard Business Review*, Harvard University, March-April 1967, Vol. 45, No. 2, pp. 149–154.
2. Argyris, C. *Organizations and Innovation*, Richard Irwin, Homewood, Illinois, 1965.
3. Crockett, W. J., "Team Building—One Approach to Organization Development," *Journal of Applied Behavioral Science*, Vol. 6, No. 3, 1970, pp. 291–306.
4. Likert, R., *The Human Organization*, McGraw Hill. New York, 1967.

Patrick E. Connor

Oregon State University

A CRITICAL INQUIRY INTO SOME ASSUMPTIONS AND VALUES CHARACTERIZING OD

Not since Taylorism has a set of ideas about management and organization engendered so much controversy and commentary as organization development (OD). The intent of this article is to add to the clamor. The scope of the addition is relatively narrow: this is a normatively based inquiry, containing first a descriptive discussion of dominant assumptions and values contained in OD, some of which have not been treated previously, and second, a pessimistic examination of some OD implications.

It is not the purpose to give a lengthy examination to all the nuances of OD philosophy and practice. Detailed discussions of its fundamental properties can be found elsewhere (2, 3, 4, 8, 16, 17, 19, 21, 25, 26, 32). The term "organizational development" subsumes a large variety of activities (7, 18, 48), and a precise definition equally applicable to all its forms is probably impossible. In fact, one has a difficult time even deciding what to call OD—movement, process, philosophy, and approach all seem to be both appropriate and inappropriate terms. But review of the principal OD literature does reveal a fairly high level of consensus about its essential nature. Beckhard captures this essence:

P. E. Connor, "A Critical Inquiry into some Assumptions and Values Characterizing OD," *Academy of Management Review*, October 1977, pp. 635–644.

385

Organizational development is an effort (1) planned, *(2)* organizationwide, *and (3)* managed *from the* top, *to (4) increase* organization effectiveness *and* health *through (5) planned* interventions *in the organization's "processes", using behavioral-science knowledge (2, p. 9) (emphasis in original).*

This effort is rooted in relatively explicit values (1, 5, 16, 17, 19, 21, 25, 26, 32, 34, 43), and directed specifically at the organization, not the individual or small group. (17, 21, 34)

ASSUMPTIONS AND VALUES IN OD

Examination of the descriptive, prescriptive, and empirical OD literature quickly reveals foundational premises. This discussion focuses at two levels: assumptions underlying and values reflected in OD philosophy and practice. Arbitrariness in distinguishing between assumptions and values is inevitable, owing to the amorphous character of the two concepts. In fact, assumptions probably reflect values. But it is useful analytically to separate working suppositions from abstract ideals. (38)

Assumptions

Assumptions characterizing OD have frequently been examined, catalogued, and discussed. (2, 4, 7, 16, 17, 19, 21, 25, 26, 32, 34) The lists of assumptions produced usually resembles that elaborated by French and Bell (17, pp. 65–72):

1. Most individuals have drives toward personal growth and development.
2. Most people desire to make, and are capable of making, a higher level of contribution to the attainment of organizational goals than most organizational environments will permit.
3. One of the most psychologically relevant reference groups for most people is the work group, including peers and superordinates.
4. Most people wish to be accepted and to interact cooperatively with at least one small reference group, and usually with more than one group.
5. Group members, not just the leader, are critical to group effectiveness.
6. Suppressed feelings adversely affect problem solving, personal growth, and job satisfaction.

7. The level of interpersonal trust, support, and cooperation is lower in most groups and organizations than necessary or desirable.
8. Policies and practices of the larger organization affect the small work group—and *vice versa.*
9. Win-lose conflict strategies are ultimately deleterious to overall organizational effectiveness.
10. OD interventions, if they are to succeed, must be reinforced by the organization's total human resources system.

Beyond these, several other assumptions underlie OD philosophy and practice. First, organizations are most realistically described using an open-systems model. (3) Interdependencies among management, work group, task, individual, process, technology, and so on, are critical to effective organizational functioning. These interdependencies are the basis for the organization's requiring a high level of inter-personal effectiveness on the part of members (17, 21, 32, 34). This requirement is discussed below.

Second, contemporary human and organizational values are both in transition and approaching convergence:

> *Growing evidence strongly suggests that humanistic values not only resonate with an increasing number of people in today's world, but also are highly consistent with the effective functioning of organizations built on the newer organic model (32, p. 11).*

OD proponents assume that this convergence of values of people and organizations is in the direction of a humanistic position (4, 7, 32). In general, this evolution is producing:

> *a new concept of man, based on increased knowledge of his complex and shifting needs . . . ; a new concept of power, based on collaboration and reason . . .; and a new concept of organization values, based on humanistic existential orientation (8, p. 188).*

Third, there is increasing requirement for developing social technologies to effect task performance. Lundberg laments: "competencies for initiating and facilitating change in complex, modern social organizations have lagged behind technological, informational and other competencies" (31, p. 1). People active in OD assume that the Tayloristic quest for the one best way (or set of ways) remains a viable paradigm on which to base organizational improvement. Huse (25) identifies techniques used in various situations: job design, psychodrama, team building, organization grid, job expectation technique, third-party intervention, and process consultation. This long but instructive list includes techniques in the OD proponent's tool kit for improving performance—more variegated than the classicists', but a tool kit nonetheless.

Fourth, western society (and therefore the western organization) is characterized by continual and significant growth. This assumption is the most difficult to capture. Intuitively (and this is the basis of observation), it appears that OD's chief thematic emphasis is the need for planned change. Discussion of organic organizational systems pervades OD literature; environmental turbulence is at least implicitly attributed to forces accompanying growth, rather than to a realignment of existing forces. The reader is invited to join in pondering this one.

Values

Many OD writers explicitly identify values underlying organization development (5, 17, 21, 25, 26, 31, 32, 34, 43). But there are a few values beyond those usually discussed.

First, dominant in all OD theory and practice is the value of rationality (18). This value appears in two forms, scientific and organizational. *Scientific* rationality is the basis of OD's emphasis on "an orderly process of inquiry, data gathering, and testing of hypotheses" (17, p. xv). Conscious and systematic utilization of the Lewinian change model (unfreezing, change through experimentation, refreezing) in particular, and continual experimentation with intervention methods in general, indicate a strong value commitment to a rationality which is usually labeled scientific (1, 2, 16, 17, 19, 26). Owing to the emphasis on technique rather than theory building and testing, this rationality probably ought to be labeled engineering.

Few writers reflect very explicitly on their commitment to *organizational* rationality, although this latter commitment seems much the stronger. In Beckhard's definition, increasing organizational effectiveness is the driving element. More than anything else, OD seems rooted in the imperatives of organizational effectiveness. Common to the numerous descriptions of OD is an emphasis on improving organizational performance (17, 31, 32, 34).

Second, OD reflects trimodal humanism. Commitment to traditional humanistic concerns of individual growth, development, dignity, worth, and meaning is the primary mode (5, 17, 21, 25, 32, 34). The literature reflects a strong proclivity for collective behavior as the most efficacious means to both improved organizational performance and the goals of the humanism (2, 17, 21, 25, 26, 32, 33, 34, 43). This collectivism is the secondary mode. Finally, OD proponents reveal a clear anti-bureaucratic (in the Weberian sense of the term) stance. Such classic bureaucratic prescriptions as rigid hierarchy, centralization of authority, and highly formalistic rules and regulations are considered inconsistent with the humanistic goals of OD (2, 5, 17, 34, 43). Wilcox commented that to OD advocates:

> (1) The hierarchical form of organization . . . is inimical to, and destructive of, the human personality. (2) Contemporary organizations fall into two major categories, the first of which is identified with the traditional and prevailing form of hierarchical organization, and the second which is supportive of the needs and requirements of the human personality (49, p. 54).

Third, and seemingly inconsistent with the foregoing, OD literature reveals an elitist value posture. Strauss observed that "in resolving the alleged conflict between the individual and the organization, stress is placed on changing people. The [humanistic revolution] is to be imposed benignly from the top" (42, p. 15). This observation squares with Beckhard's (2) description of OD, cited earlier. But interventions seem not "managed from" the top so much as restricted to the higher echelons of the organizational hierarchy. Rettig and Amano (37), for example, found various OD programs aimed primarily at the managerial ranks; involvement by nonmanagers was considerably less. OD's lack of success in addressing the total organization (7) may reflect this elitist perspective. Developing top management is not the same as developing the organization.

Fourth, and perhaps most significant, OD is strongly characterized by a clinical emphasis (17, 21, 25). Therapy is not just incidental; for many OD practitioners it is the focal thrust of the activity:

> Believing that people have vast amounts of untapped potential and the capability and desire to grow, to engage in meaningful collaborative relationships, to be creative in organizational contexts, and to be more authentic, we feel that the most effective change interventions are therapeutic in nature. Such interventions focus directly on the hang-ups, both personal and organizational, that block a person from realizing his potential. We are referring to barriers in himself, in others around him, and in the ongoing culture (43, p. 26).

SOME CRITICAL OBSERVATIONS

Several areas of concern are suggested by the kinds of assumptions and values identified here. The first two have to do with the essential character of OD, while the remainder relate to the organization and its inhabitants.

A Belief, Not a Science

Despite the protestations of OD advocates, "it is a bit premature to conclude that OD is truly a scientific method [and] it is downright misleading to suggest that OD's utility has been proven scientifically valid" (42, p. 14). This state of affairs reflects the confused status of the term "organization development." Kahn (26) suggests it is not a scientific concept, having no precise definitions, no specifiable elements, no systematic theory; Weisbord (47) admits to being unable to decide whether it is art, science, notion, or fantasy.

Conceptual ambiguity leads to research problems. Seldom are there any hypothesized relationships between independent and dependent variables (48). Research procedures tend to be equally problematic. OD researchers seem inordinately casual about testing the validity of their techniques:

> In summary, most OD research uses poor research designs. The measures are subject to halo errors and poor reliability. The designs are frequently inadequate for making causal inferences. Statistical comparisons are weak and infrequently used. Finally, Hawthorne and experimenter bias effects provide highly plausible alternative hypotheses (48, p. 70).

Confidence in reported OD results depends on one's confidence in the methods employed to produce those results. Considering the brief laundry list of OD techniques mentioned under the heading of assumption three: what is the empirical evidence, collected within the framework of commonly accepted social-scientific protocols, that those techniques are as effective as they are touted to be?

OD proponents also must face the larger issue of scholarly/scientific orientation. There is a noticeable lack of emphasis in OD literature on scholarship and science as important frameworks within which OD theory and practice should advance. Bowers (7), for example, counts only 18 studies within the last 15 years that provide useful evidence about OD effectiveness. The literature is replete with articles, notes, comments, and other communications, each describing some innovative intervention, frequently inspired by an intuitive clinical insight. While it is nice to read about successes, one feels a strong need for conceptual order. Instead, OD literature gives a litany of idiosyncratic techniques.

Thus, while OD ideology and techniques are attractive, the question posed by Wilcox will not go away:

> Can such an ideology provide answers for the problems which loom before us? Or should we resist the temptations of word intoxication and strengthen our orien-

tation toward the study of empirical relationships in organizational systems. . . ?
(49, p. 61).

If OD is to deliver—and it is essentially an ideology of performance, not pneuma—then it must ultimately be rooted in scientific rationality, not metaphysical transcendence. Its values would be better served if more energy were expended gathering evidence and less in winning converts.

Is It Really Humanistic?

The second area of concern generated by an admittedly critical reading of OD literature involves the essential honesty of the movement. This is not to criticize because of discrepancies between OD philosophy and practice; that criticism has already been leveled with sufficient clarity. Rather, the concern derives from the essentially dual nature of OD. On the one hand OD advocates call for a higher quality of life for the worker, while on the other they attempt to persuade managers that their bag of tools contains just what the organization needs to be more effective (efficient?). Bowers (7) describes this "commercialism" as one of the three major problems of OD practice. Organizations frequently subscribe to OD-prescribed solutions because managers believe in the OD consultant. One must ask: where is the "ownership" in that process?

The opposite side of the credibility coin is also evident. Managers frequently use OD (or any program), not in an honest attempt to improve life, or even to solve problems, but as a rite. Its purpose, as with all rites, is to allow participants to attend to various process needs, leaving substance alone—and unaffected. OD proponents thus find themselves in the middle, trapped by the dual nature of their philosophy. Attending to that kind of process is probably better than nothing, but it certainly is not what OD is supposed to be about. One can sympathize, but the inevitable difficulty does seem to lie in the duality of OD's nature.

OD consultants resolve the conflict inherent in such a dual nature by emphasizing technique. As managers become increasingly convinced of OD's capacity for solving specific problems, their demands for specific techniques grow. OD may be on its way to becoming the acupuncture of the behavioral sciences. The organizational acupuncturist inserts a few carefully chosen needles into the proper nerve endings and twirls them, effecting changes in neural relationships. While possibly effective, organization acupuncture does not seem to embody what OD values are supposed to be. What Friedlander (18) calls the existential nature of OD does not seem well served by this sort of development.

In short, the OD movement is not immune to the seductive imperatives of *la technique* (13), in which technique drives purpose. OD consultants, like the rest of us, are frequently subject to Kaplan's law of the instrument: "give a small boy a hammer, and he will find that everything he encounters needs pounding" (27, pp. 28–29). Such central values as freedom, self-esteem, and privacy already may be suffering erosion as a result of increased OD activity (46). Is this not an overly expensive treatment for OD's dual nature?

Bowers (7) suggests that practitioners contribute to much of the movement's difficulties by failing to challenge their clients' assumption that the consultant is supposed to operate primarily as a catalyst. Consultants should deemphasize their tool-kit procedures, and emphasize their service as a "link between a body of knowledge and a client system in potential need of its selective application" (7, p. 56). A focus on improving the client-system's problem solving abilities will facilitate performance of this linking role.

The Organization

A second set of concerns involves not so much the essence of OD, but rather the object of its actions—the organization. The concerns do stem from OD's emphasis on interpersonal competence as a key element in both organizational and personal effectiveness. This set has three related components: task competence, performance evaluation, and organizational socialization.

Task Competence

Traditionally, the skills thought necessary to perform a task were principally technical: machine-design skills for a mechanical engineer, substantive knowledge and pedagogical technique for a teacher, financial–analytical skills for an accountant. Organizations and tasks have grown in size and complexity; there is no doubt that interpersonal skills are necessary. Thus, most engineers have to be able to work effectively in project teams (20, 24); teachers increasingly need to "relate" to their students, and be effective in team-teaching situations (45); and the accountant must be able to work with management, other employees, and government representatives (9). Managers' functions increasingly are described in social-skill terms. They must allocate human as well as nonhuman resources, motivate people, and coordinate the work of subordinates within their own organizational unit as well as with other administrative units (35, 41).

But acknowledging that interpersonal skills are necessary for organizational effectiveness is not to suggest that they are sufficient. Structural, technological, and other "macro" variables are important to effective organizational functioning; indeed, OD purports to include such variables in its purview. Nonetheless, despite some disclaimers (17, 32) OD remains a movement basically "aimed at changing the 'people' aspects of organizational life rather than [the] 'task' aspects" (7). This emphasis on people, their relationships, and therefore their interpersonal competencies, suggests that task skills tend to be conceptualized in interpersonal terms. Accordingly "task effectiveness" tends to mean interpersonal effectiveness, and this limited focus falls short of OD's promise to address the total organization.

Performance Evaluation

Coincidental with limiting the meaning of task effectiveness, many OD assumptions and values seem to require changes in performance evaluation criteria. If interpersonal effectiveness is critical to organizational performance, it should be an important criterion in management's evaluation of employee performance. As a corporate vice-president put it:

> the striving for quantification [in performance evaluation] must be viewed in perspective and with some caution. Some of the most important characteristics of performance do not appear to be precisely measureable, such as quality of leadership, spirit of teamwork, entrepreneurial activity, or ethical matters (15, p. 296).

Or, as Labovitz restated it somewhat more prescriptively:

> To argue that performance must be reduced to some measurable objective standard fails to take into account that organizations are not merely systems of related functions but also interpersonal social systems in which individuals are placed in close interaction with one another. If the organization is viewed in terms of a system of interpersonal relationships then [rewardable] behavior must inevitably be affected by an element of the individual's success in interpersonal relations as well as objective standards of work measurement (29, p. 294).

One major difficulty faced by industrial psychologists, administrative theorists, and practicing managers concerns development of valid methods of evaluating employee performance. This difficulty is amplified when the employee's task is not amenable to "objective" measurement, as with most white-collar, professional, and administrative personnel. It is not simple to evaluate responsibly the performance of an engineering planner in an R&D firm, a nursing supervisor in a general hospital, the director of an engineering design group, or an assistant dean in a university. One suggestion is to enlarge the scope of such performance evaluation "to include not only the individual's on-the-job behavior, but also his functioning as an integral part of the organizational system" (40, p. 15).

Such counsel does little to resolve the initial difficulty. Indeed, the difficulty becomes compounded. At the minimum, interpersonal effectiveness means ability to influence behavior (1, 21), but other things are implied. "Influence" is concerned also with attitudes, opinions, beliefs, and values (28, 38). Managers are being advised, at least implicitly, that the performance evaluation process should include evaluation of attitudes, beliefs, and even values. Subjectivity in performance evaluation may do injustice to the individual being appraised as well as to the organization (10). Bringing in values, attitudes, and beliefs as evaluative factors can only exacerbate the difficulties.

Assuredly the evaluation problem is complex. But lofty statements about employee contributions to organizational efforts, or effectiveness in the team, may do more injury than benefit. At worst, the employee is at the mercy of management's caprice: a supervisor's definition of "contribution" and "team effectiveness" may be entirely idiosyncratic, largely unmonitored and unmeasured by higher management. Tannenbaum et al. (44) report a fascinating study: a "clinically skilled interviewer" was able to predict almost perfectly supervisors' evaluations of the engineering competence of subordinate R&D engineers, by clinical evaluation of each supervisor's personal needs and interpersonal orientations. Senger (39) found managers to rank highest in overall competence those subordinates having Spranger-type values most similar to their own. Labovitz (30) reported that managerial subordinates who were identified by top management as having "high promotion potential" displayed a "people-centered orientation," while those with "low promotion potential" were "very noticeably results oriented." At best, the employee's "personality," attitudes, beliefs, and values may be judged undifferentiatingly from her or his task performance.

Thus a major effect of emphasizing some OD values may be that managers fail to focus on job performance—that is, on the outcome or result—and instead evaluate employee characteristics which may or may not be related to performance. The emphasis is on evaluating *instrumentalities* of performance effectiveness, rather than effectiveness itself.

Developing effective organizational processes is unarguably important. But it is at least equally important that managers try to find ways of evaluating subordinates' performance results, not just the means to those results. OD philosophy portends performance-evaluation systems that emphasize "right thinking."

Organization Socialization

"Right thinking" commonly expresses the notion that a person's ideas are congruent with the consensual ideas of his or her compatriots—peers, superordinates, or both. This is one aspect of the larger process of organizational socialization.

Socialization is a process by which an individual's values, attitudes, and behavior are brought into congruence with those of some significant set of others (12). Not limited to the child, "adult" socialization is a real proces (8, 11), and the organizational experience may be the basis for the dominant form of adult socialization in modern culture. (14, 36) Organizational socialization is the process by which core values, attitudes, and behavior are brought toward congruence with the demands exerted on organization members or perceived by them.

A central arena for organizational socialization lies within the interpersonal milieu. If members of organizations are required by their superordinates to exhibit behavior judged conducive to effective attainment of organizational objectives, then we would anticipate that the members will experience a drive to bring basic attitudes and even values into congruence with that behavior.

OD proponents would argue that the purpose of developing interpersonal effectiveness as a vital force in the organization is to improve the members' quality of life by increasing their behavioral options, not to reduce their options to those delimited by organizational imperatives of efficiency and rationality. This purpose may not be as real as it is apparent, since OD seems primarily occupied with increasing behavioral options that are instrumental to increased production. Not that increased production is an unworthy goal, but it is a limited one, especially in light of the stated scope of OD values and purpose.

Other socializing forces act on the individual besides those of management—for example, those of the informal group. But even groups within the organization may contribute to the individual's developing values and attitudes reflecting organizational imperatives. Empirical work shows that the small group provides an important socializing experience, and often adheres to norms not consistent with—sometimes actually dysfunctional for—attainment of formal organizational goals.

As Gross (23) points out, "formal organizational goals" usually means formal "output" goals (goals pertaining to the eventual product or service produced by the organization). Instead of focusing solely on output goals, a proper analysis should consider also what Gross calls "support" goals. His empirically based argument is that support goals are distinct from output goals, yet are just as important to effective organizational functioning. By implicitly equating "formal organizational goals" with output goals, we are likely to miss recognizing that although a set of group norms may appear to be dysfunctional (for output objectives), they may be highly functional for various organizational-maintenance goals.

The point becomes evident: the informal group often is seen as providing a mediating influence on the individual–management relationship; but this may be true only with respect to output goals, not other organizational objectives. The group, owing its existence to the organization, may provide a socialization influence largely congruent with organizational imperatives (36, pp. 156–163). Gross concludes:

> *primary controls on behavior are far from being inconsistent with institutional controls. There is an unfortunate tendency . . . to regard cliques as innocuous play groups, or else as being antithetical to the purposes of the organization, as exemplified in restriction of output. . . . It is suggested here that cliques may have quite another purpose—they may actually be essential to the very functioning of instituted organizations (22, p. 373).*

With respect to informal groups outside the organization, their potentially countervailing force may be blunted by the pervasiveness of organizational socialization. The process is not limited to the work organization and hence to the individual's role as an employee. It includes the church, fraternal lodge, junior-college evening class, summer slow-pitch softball league, weekly military reserve activities, and all the roles that the individual assumes for each. Indeed, the process may begin with the child being concerned with interpersonal effectiveness based on the imperatives of the large school organization. Is it possible for the philosophical and operational conflict inherent in the dual nature of OD to be resolved in favor of humanistic values?

A FINAL NOTE

This has been a critical reading of some OD assumptions, values, and their implications. An emphasis by management on OD values contains obvious implications for valid and reliable performance appraisal, and also may affect the formation of organizational members' beliefs, attitudes, and values. The kind of "right thinking" portended by this emphasis goes to the heart of the individual personality. Unlike the classical principles of administration, it is not simply an orthodoxy for the workplace; it is as large as life.

Such emphasis transcends organizational goal-attainment effectiveness; it presumes to interfere with the psychological and social health of the individual.

White and Mitchell (48) recently suggested that continued OD survival and prosperity will require increased theoretical and empirical rigor—in short, better science. Since OD is basically an action program, it also needs to examine critically the values that underlie it, and the actions those values suggest.

REFERENCES

1. Argyris, Chris. *Interpersonal Competence and Organizational Effectiveness* (Homewood, Ill.: The Dorsey Press, 1962).
2. Beckhard, Richard. *Organizational Development: Strategies and Models* (Reading, Mass.: Addison-Wesley, 1969).
3. Beer, Michael, and Edgar F. Huse. "A Systems Approach to Organization Development," *Journal of Applied Behavioral Science*, Vol. 8 (1972), 79–101.
4. Bennis, Warren G. *Changing Organizations* (New York: McGraw-Hill, 1966).
5. Bennis, Warren G. *Organization Development: Its Nature, Origins, and Prospects* (Reading, Mass.: Addison-Wesley, 1969).
6. Bowers, David G. "OD Techniques and Their Results in 23 Organizations: The Michigan ICL Study," *Journal of Applied Behavioral Science*, Vol. 9 (1973), 21–43.
7. Bowers, David G. "Organizational Development: Promises, Performances, Possibilities," *Organizational Dynamics*, Vol. 4 (1976), 50–64.
8. Brim, Orville, Jr., and Stanton Wheeler. *Socialization After Childhood: Two Essays* (New York: John Wiley & Sons, 1966).
9. Bruns, William J., and Don DeCoster. *Accounting and Its Behavioral Implications* (New York: McGraw-Hill, 1969).
10. Chung, Kae H. "Can We Defend Subjective Performance Appraisal?" *Academy of Management Journal*, Vol. 12 (1969), 507–510.
11. Clausen, John A. (Ed.). *Socialization and Society* (Boston: Little, Brown, 1968).
12. Dager, Edward Z. (Ed.). *Socialization* (Chicago: Markham, 1971), pp. ix–x.
13. Ellul, Jacques. *The Technological Society* (New York: Random House—Vintage Books, 1964).
14. Etzioni, Amitai. *Modern Organizations* (Englewood Cliffs, N.J.: Prentice-Hall, 1964).
15. Evans, Robert L. Personal correspondence to George H. Labovitz. Cited in George H. Labovitz, "In Defense of Subjective Executive Appraisal," *Academy of Management Journal*, Vol. 12 (1969), 293–307.
16. French, Wendell. "Organization Development: Objectives, Assumptions, and Strategies," *California Management Review*, Vol. 12 (1969), 23–34.

17. French, Wendell L., and Cecil H. Bell, Jr. *Organization Development* (Englewood Cliffs, N.J.: Prentice-Hall, 1973).
18. Friedlander, Frank. "OD Reaches Adolescence: An Exploration of its Underlying Values," *Journal of Applied Behavioral Science*, Vol. 12 (1976), 7–21.
19. Friedlander, Frank, and L. Dave Brown. "Organization Development," *Annual Review of Psychology*, Vol. 25 (1974), 313–341.
20. Glaser, Barney G. *Organizational Scientists: Their Professional Careers* (New York: The Bobbs-Merrill Co., Inc., 1964).
21. Golembiewski, Robert T. *Renewing Organizations* (Itasca, Ill.: F.E. Peacock, Inc., 1972).
22. Gross, Edward. "Some Functional Consequences of Primary Controls in Formal Work Organizations," *American Sociological Review*, Vol. 18 (1953), 368–373.
23. Gross, Edward. "Definition of Organizational Goals," *British Journal of Sociology*, Vol. 20 (1969), 277–294.
24. Hagstrom, Warren O. *The Scientific Community* (New York: Basic Books, 1965).
25. Huse, Edgar F. *Organization Development and Change* (St. Paul: West Publishing Co., 1975).
26. Kahn, Robert L. "Organization Development: Social Problems and Proposals," *Journal of Applied Behavioral Science*, Vol. 10 (1974), 485–502.
27. Kaplan, Abraham. *The Conduct of Inquiry* (San Francisco: Chandler, 1964).
28. Katz, Daniel, and Ezra Stotland. "A Preliminary Statement to a Theory of Attitude Structure and Change," in S. Koch (Ed.), *Psychology: A Study of a Science* (New York: McGraw-Hill, 1959).
29. Labovitz, George H. "In Defense of Subjective Executive Appraisal," *Academy of Management Journal*, Vol. 12 (1969), 293–307.
30. Labovitz, George H. "More on Subjective Executive Appraisal: An Empirical Study," *Academy of Management Journal*, Vol. 15 (1972), 289–302.
31. Lundberg, Craig C. "Organization Development: Current Perspectives and Future Issues." In Laurence J. Moore and Sang M. Lee (Eds.), *Scientific and Behavioral Foundation Division Analysis* (Atlanta, Ga.: AIDS, 1974).
32. Margulies, Newton, and Anthony P. Raia. *Organization Development: Values, Process, and Technology* (New York: McGraw-Hill, 1972).
33. Margulies, Newton, and John Wallace. *Organizational Change* (Glenview, Ill.: Scott, Foresman, 1973).
34. Miles, Raymond E. *Theories of Management: Implications for Organizational Behavior and Development* (New York: McGraw-Hill, 1975).
35. Parsons, Talcott. "Suggestions for a Sociological Approach to the Theory of Organizations—I," *Administrative Science Quarterly*, Vol. 1 (1956), 63–85.
36. Presthus, Robert. *The Organizational Society* (New York: Random House—Vintage Books, 1962).
37. Rettig, Jack L., and Matt M. Amano. "A Survey of ASPA Experience with Management by Objectives, Sensitivity Training and Transactional Analysis," *Personnel Journal*, Vol. 21 (1976), 26–29.

38. Rokeach, Milton. *Beliefs, Attitudes, and Values* (San Francisco: Jossey-Bass, 1968).
39. Senger, John. "Managers, Perceptions of Subordinates' Competence as a Function of Personal Value Orientations," *Academy of Management Journal*, Vol. 14 (1971), 415–423.
40. Sloan, Stanley, and Alton C. Johnson. "New Context of Performance Appraisal," *Harvard Business Review* (November-December 1968), 14–30.
41. Steiner, Ivan D. "Models for Inferring Relationships Between Group Size and Potential Group Productivity," *Behavioral Science*, Vol. 11 (1966), 273–283.
42. Strauss, George. "Organizational Development: Credits and Debits," *Organizational Dynamics*, Vol. 1 (1973), 2–19.
43. Tannenbaum, Robert, and Sheldon A. Davis. "Values, Man, and Organizations," *Industrial Management Review*, Vol. 10 (1969), 67–86, reprinted in Newton Margulies and Anthony P. Raia, *Organization Development Values, Process and Technology* (New York: McGraw-Hill, 1972).
44. Tannenbaum, Robert, Irving R. Wescheler, and Fred Massarik. "Problems of Evaluation: The Impact of Interpersonal Relations on Ratings of Performance," in their *Leadership and Organization: A Behavioral Approach* (New York: McGraw-Hill, 1961), pp. 324–332.
45. Unruh, Glenys G., and William M. Alexander, *Innovation in Education* (New York: Holt, Rinehart, and Winston, 1970).
46. Walter, Gordon A. "Organizational Development and Individual Rights," *Proceedings of the Academy of Management*, 35th Annual Meeting (1975), pp. 351–353.
47. Weisbord, Marvin R. "The Gap Between OD Practice and Theory—And Publication," *Journal of Applied Behavioral Science*, Vol. 10 (1974), 476–484.
48. White, Sam E., and Terence R. Mitchell. "Organization Development: A Review of Research Content and Research Design," *Academy of Management Review*, Vol. 1 (April 1976), 57–73.
49. Wilcox, Herbert G. "Hierarchy, Human Nature and the Participative Panacea," *Public Administration Review*, Vol. 29 (1969), 53–63.

Martin G. Evans

University of Toronto

FAILURES IN OD PROGRAMS— WHAT WENT WRONG?

Why do many packaged organizational development (OD) programs fail to produce sustained organizational change? Do they in fact fail? The evidence on this is sparse. At a conservative estimate, evaluation results are available for fewer than 10 percent of all OD programs. Some may be evaluated privately for the organizations concerned, but most are not evaluated at all. The literature on evaluation that is available tends to lack the safeguards of a research design which protects against certain alternative explanations of the observed change, such as regression toward the mean, historical change, and maturation of the individuals involved.

In any event, the research that has evaluated the impact of packaged OD programs has resulted in mixed findings. Occasionally, the programs have increased managerial effectiveness, but, more often, little effect on performance coupled with improved job satisfaction is noted among subordinates. What, then, goes wrong? At least three factors inhibit the organization from learning from such programs:

Failure to tailor the program to the needs of the organization. The introduction of such a package is rarely preceded by a diagnosis of the problems of the organiza-

Martin G. Evans, "Failures in OD Programs—What Went Wrong?" *Business Horizons*, April 1974, pp. 18–22.

tion followed by either the search for appropriate programs or by the development of a program specially designed to suit the organization.

Failure to model the appropriate behaviors in the program itself. Most OD packages are explicitly based upon a human resources model of organizational participants. Although an OD package is much more than a new motivational approach, most packages are designed to enhance individual motivation through increased participation and the engagement of the individual's higher order needs of growth and self-esteem. For example, the managerial grid of R. R. Blake and J. S. Mouton is designed to help managers integrate a concern for people and a concern for the task. In operation, however, the program models a concern for the task—that of getting people through the program. Managers are assigned to go participate with little concern for their individual needs.

The failure of the organization to reorder its personnel and reward subsystems. The former should model the appropriate new behaviors and the latter should reinforce the managers who begin to change their behavior.

For the remainder of this article, I will focus on the third set of inhibiting factors. The failure of the organization to consider a change in its personnel and reward policies stems from a misunderstanding of the nature of motivation. In the past, the focus on motivation theory has been on the nature of human needs and a growing awareness of the changing salience of such needs through the economic-social-self-actualizing-complex man sequence. The way in which the individual's behavior may be linked to the satisfaction of such needs has been ignored until recently.

A MODEL OF MOTIVATION_____

A number of writers have developed a model suggesting that motivation to perform is a function of the attractiveness, desirability, or importance of the individual's needs (this has been focused on) and the individual's beliefs as to whether or not high performance will enable him to gain satisfaction from those needs.
Thus:

$$\text{Motivation to perform} = \frac{\text{Need}}{\text{desirability}} \times \frac{\text{Belief that effort}}{\text{leads to reward}}$$

Of course, individuals have more than one need or desired reward, so that a complete understanding of motivation to perform requires a summation of these needs (for example, money, esteem, power, or promotion). It is clear that motivation will be high only when the individual believes that high performance will enable him to satisfy his needs and the needs satisfied by high performance are important to the individual. Conversely, if either beliefs or the importance of needs is low, the motivation will be low. If the individual values money, then money will not motivate him to perform if he works in an organization where salary increments are automatic and based upon seniority rather than being based specifically upon performance.

The elaboration of the model of motivation to include the individual's beliefs about the probability that performance will lead to a reward is an important step. First, there is growing evidence to suggest that this model is appropriate for individual motivation in organizations because it is a good predictor of job performance and satisfaction. Second, it introduces a set of variables—beliefs about performance-reward links—that are under the influence of the organization. The organization, through its policies and practices, determines the nature of actual performance-reward links. These, in turn, form the basis for individual beliefs about the links. The organization, whether it likes it or not and whether it recognizes it or not, influences these beliefs.

Every time the organization makes a promotion or salary raise decision based upon seniority ("Buggins' turn next" or "lateral arabesque" considerations), the individual's beliefs that performance leads to promotion or a pay raise are weakened and, consequently, the individual's motivation to perform is lessened. An individual's motivation to perform is likely to be lowered if he sees someone whom he regards as incompetent promoted. His motivation to perform is likely to be raised if he sees someone whom he regards as competent promoted, regardless of whether the individual himself is promoted.

IMPLICATIONS AND LIMITATIONS _____

Theoretically, most behavioral science OD programs such as job enrichment and the managerial grid should create conditions for strong links between high performance and the individual's own goals. I have reviewed elsewhere the research evidence that suggests the motivation for high performance is enhanced by at least four conditions:

1. The job which provides a challenge and freedom to set one's own standards creates importance for the higher order needs of self-esteem and self-actualization and provides conditions under which the individual who performs well can obtain these rewards.

2. If the individual's manager is both task and person oriented, then person-oriented supervision implies that the manager can reward the individual in a variety of ways corresponding to the individual's needs and that the supervisor perceives the particular set of needs deemed to be important by each individual; task centeredness implies that such rewards are contingent on performance.

3. If a pay raise is clearly based upon performance, the value of the raise is enhanced when it is linked with performance and is seen as an esteem type reward; when high variations in pay increases occur both between persons and over time for the same person (such variation, of course, being related to performance); and when the individual can choose the form of his pay increase (for example, substitution of the fringe benefits such as a longer holiday, shorter work week, insurance program, or pension).

4. If promotion policies are clearly based upon performance, a promotion is valued as an esteem reward when linked with performance.[1]

Such conditions are strongly emphasized by the OD packages previously mentioned. If each of these programs is properly implemented, certain expectations are aroused in the mind of the participants. These expectations may include involvement in decisions about the criteria for performance that will be applied to him and whether or not he (and his peers) have met these criteria; and the building of an organizational climate which shows concern for the individual and which facilitates a free exchange of information.

The problem is that beliefs about path-goal links are based upon history. In the past, it is likely that weak links between high performance and goal attainment have been established, while strong links between goal attainment and such conditions as seniority, keeping one's "nose clean," or not rocking the boat have been established. Consequently, when an OD program is implemented, specific attempts must be made to build strong links between high performance and goal attainment.

Despite their designers' intentions, such programs often have little impact on the infrastructure of the organization. Careful attempts are made to implement the program into the work flow and budgeting processses of the organization, but the programs are not implemented into the personnel policies of the organization—into making pay, promotion, or job transfer decisions. The necessary path-goal links between high performance and the

[1] M. G. Evans, "Managing the New Managers," *Personnel Administration* (May-June 1971), pp. 31–38.

individual's goals have not been developed; the old links of survival leading to reward remain; and motivation to perform well stays weak.

APPLICATION TO POLICY

For all managers, but especially for personnel managers, a change in emphasis in their activities is necessary. A. Bowey has pointed out that the compensation policies for lower level employees, for example, can be designed with one or more of several goals in mind: administrative ease, reduction of uncontrolled overtime, individual or group motivation, satisfied unions, optimization of work flow, and facilitation of technological change.

The following is a list of factors which should be considered in the formulation of four managerial policies.

> *Compensation policy.* What should be the nature of remuneration? The possibilities include salary, fringe benefits, and deferred payments such as pensions and stock options. How frequently should changes in remuneration be made? What should be the basis for those changes?
>
> *Promotion policy.* What should be the performance basis for promotion? What organization members will form the locus of decision making concerning promotions?
>
> *Manpower planning policy.* What will be the future vacancies in the organization, and what skills will be needed to fill those vacancies? Who are the potential candidates to fill these job openings? Are they available? Who will choose the new employees? Will the new employee need training? Will he be trained on or off the job? Again, at what levels are such decisions made?
>
> *Geographic mobility policy.* Is mobility necessary for job performance? How much mobility is needed? Who decides what the mobility requirements should be?

Compensation

As far as compensation and its form are concerned, one of the major constraints is the legal position with regard to tax of various forms of compensation. Nevertheless, most organizations, probably for administrative ease, take a system-wide approach; everyone gets the same mix of pay and fringe benefits with some minor differentiation by job level. However, any differentiation is determined by the organization, and there is little effort to tailor the compensation to match the desires of the individual, despite the fact that employees seek individual differences in the mix. If the organization were to introduce the so-called "cafeteria plan" for compensation, the individuals would be able to choose among forms of remuneration—straight salary, pension, longer holidays, or medical insurance. The probable result would be that, dollar for dollar, the organization would be distributing desirable, and thus more valuable, rewards to its members, thereby enhancing their motivation.

From an administrative point of view, the complications inherent in individual choice look nightmarish. But the problems can be handled through computerized accounting, payroll and personnel systems, or the contracting of compensation services outside the organization (for example, to banks).

The second problem is the linkage between performance and reward. A prerequisite is an assessment system that is trusted by the individuals concerned. The assessment must be tied to observable behavior and performances rather than to diffuse personality characteristics, and the system must be accepted by—and probably developed by—those who do the assessing and those who are assessed. The use of the criterion development scheme involving the retranslation of expectations method provides a vehicle for the participative development of performance criteria.[2]

In other words, assessment is an important arena for management-group participation. The management by objectives program attempts to do this, but it should probably be widened from a one-to-one basis to a one-to-all procedure. This is essential in the phase of developing desirable criteria upon which performance is to be judged.

Through this process, the organization will help resolve the individual-group performance conflict. Such a process will build systems-wide criteria into the performance criteria for groups and individuals. One criterion will involve the contribution made by the individual to the group, or by the group to the organization. For example, P. R. Lawrence and J. W. Lorsch have shown that successful integrators were rewarded for the job of facilitating the integration and contribution of two groups.

Promotion

The major implication is concerned with the criteria for promotion. If promotion is to be a motivator, it needs to be closely tied to performance and

---

[2] M. D. Dunnette, "Managerial Effectiveness: Its Definition and Measurement," *Studies in Personnel Psychology* (October 1970).

based on criteria that are shared and agreed upon by the people involved. The procedure for criteria development suggested by M. D. Dunnette and described above is appropriate here.

The second factor of importance concerns the wishes of the people involved. Are these taken into account? Can an individual refuse a particular promotion without jeopardizing his chances in the future? Is the organization living up to the values implied by its adoption of the OD program and allowing individuals to have some real choice?

Manpower Planning and Mobility

The concern in manpower planning activities and their implementation is organization centered. When decisions are made concerning the human resources available and about the kinds of on- or off-the-job training required to fit people for their managerial positions of the future, little or no account is taken of the individual's own preferences. The fact that he should be an active participant in planning his own career is often neglected. His job assignments and training are based only upon organizational considerations, rather than on an individual basis.

To be consistent with the values implied in OD, the manpower planning function must be expanded so that when the characteristics of the available human resources are gathered, the plans, aspirations, and needs of the individuals concerned must be mapped, as well as their skills, experiences, and potential.

In one OD program monitored by the author, it became clear that the OD activity did not extend to this personnel process.[3] People did not have a grasp of their potential careers in the organization. New job assignments and their implications were not explained to, or discussed with, the people concerned. Information about job changes and even work location changes were presented as *faits accomplis*. Individuals were well aware of the contrast between the way the organization was treating them, and the values implied by the OD training.

What I have suggested is that a major barrier to the effective implementation of an OD program results from its partial application to the task subsystem of the organization and from the failure of the personnel subsystem to implement its activation in a way consistent with the values implied in the OD program. As a result, the necessary beliefs about performance and reward are not established in the minds of the organization's members,

[3] S. R. Maxwell and M. G. Evans, "An Evaluation of Organizational Development: Three Phases of the Managerial Grid," *Journal of Business Administration* (Fall 1973).

who fail to see the value (or payoff) in behaving in the ways described by the program.

Some general suggestions have been made about personnel areas in which alternative policies might be appropriate and congruent with the OD values. With the use of computerized personnel and manpower records, the practical difficulties of implementing a more personalized personnel system can be overcome.

DECISION
TECHNOLOGY

Developments in decision technology are having a significant impact on contemporary management practice. We use this term to refer to the application of management science methods and the computer to support managerial decision making. Management science methods such as simulation, linear programming, PERT/CPM, and queuing theory allow management to explore the characteristics of systems that heretofore were not rigorously subjected to quantitative analysis. In many instances this exploration is made possible through the availability of the digital computer, as many of these methods have high computational requirements. The computer also plays an important role in computer-based information systems, and these systems are also having an impact on the way in which decisions are made.

The articles in this, section are designed to add depth, breadth, and perspective to your understanding of decision technology.

The first article, "Management Science and Business Practice," gives the views of C. Jackson Grayson on the relationship of management science methods to actual business practice. Mr. Grayson's perspective is especially valuable since he was trained as a management scientist, has taught management science courses, has been a university administrator, and has served as Chairman of the Price Commission in Phase II of President Richard M. Nixon's Economic Stabilization Program. In the article Mr. Grayson focuses on some of the problems associated with management scientists and their methods and what needs to be done to solve these problems.

In the next article, "A Perspective on the Implementation of Management Science," John Anderson and Thomas Hoffman suggest the need for an

409

expanded and enlightened perspective on what constitutes successful management science implementation. They present a framework for better understanding and evaluating management science implementation.

In "Corporate Planning Models," Thomas Naylor and Daniel Gattis explore the growing use of computerized corporate planning models. Based upon a survey of over 300 corporations, the authors describe who are using corporate models, why corporate models are being used, how they are used, concepts of model construction, the politics of corporate model building, and the limitations of corporate models.

Concern for the environment has led to legislation, such as the National Environmental Policy Act, which calls for the preparation of an Environmental Impact Statement (EIS) for projects that potentially affect the environment. The preparation of an EIS is in itself a complex project, and in "The Environmental Impact Statement: A PERT Network Approach," A. G. Kefalas and W. A. Pittenger describe and illustrate how PERT can be used to help manage the development of an EIS.

In "Computer Technology and Information System Performance," Hugh Watson, Ralph Sprague, and Donald Kroeber describe the computer hardware and software and performance levels that can be realized in a computer-based information system. The authors emphasize that managers must understand the relationship that exists between these two dimensions and manage their evolution in order to support organizational needs and objectives.

These articles should provide you with an increased awareness and understanding of the ways that decision technology is affecting the practice of management. It is expected that the importance of decision technology to managers and organizations will continue to grow over time.

Jackson Grayson, Jr.

Chairman of the American Productivity Center

MANAGEMENT SCIENCE AND BUSINESS PRACTICE

Management science has grown so remote from and unmindful of the conditions of "live" management that it has abdicated its usability. Managers, for their part, have become disillusioned by management science, and are now frequently unwilling to consider it seriously as a working tool for important problems. The author believes that management science can make a contribution to management; and in this article he suggests how a bridge between the two groups can be constructed. He also makes it clear that the scientists must be the ones to start construction.

What we need to do is humanize the scientist and simonize the humanist." This dictum is a popularization of C. P. Snow's view of science and the humanities as two distinct cultures, and it is all too true when applied to management. Managers and management scientists are operating as two separate cultures, each with its own goals, languages, and methods. Effective cooperation—and even communication—between the two is just about minimal. And this is a shame.

Each has much to learn from the other, and much to teach the other. Yet, despite all kinds of efforts over the years, it seems to me that the cultural and operating gap which exists between the two is not being closed. Why?

I can offer some explanations, based on my years as an academician, consultant, businessman, and, most recently, head of an organization with control over a large part of our economy—the Price Commission. I can also

Reprinted by permission of the *Harvard Business Review*. "Management Science and Business Practice," by C. Jackson Grayson, Jr., July-August 1973, pp. 41–48. Copyright © 1975 by the President and Fellows of Harvard College; all rights reserved.

411

suggest a way to build the bridge so badly needed between the two cultures and the people who make them up. This bridge must span the gap between two quite different types:

> *The management scientists.* As people, they want to help managers make decision making more explicit, more systematic, and *better* by using scientific methodology, principally mathematics and statistics. They can be found largely in universities and in staff operations of enterprises. They may belong to any of a number of professional associations, such as The Institute of Management Sciences (TIMS), Operations Research Society of America (ORSA), and the American Institute for Decision Sciences (AIDS).
>
> *The managers.* They make and implement decisions, largely by rough rules of thumb and intuition. They are the operating executives, found principally in the line.

The lines of distinction are never so pure, but most people, I believe, understand what I mean.

What I have to offer to the management scientists is a few bouquets and then a load of bricks. First, the bouquets:

> Management scientists have had *some* impact on real-world operations and managers.
>
> Some management science tools have been successfully applied in accounting, finance, production, distribution, and weapons systems.
>
> Managers do tend to give a little more conscious thought to their decision making than in previous years—but still precious little.
>
> By indicating how abysmal our knowledge is about decision making, management scientists have highlighted areas for further research.
>
> Both the faculty and the students at business schools have gained some added prestige in the business and academic communities for being more "scientific."

And now the bricks. The total impact of management science has been extremely small. Its contribution looks even smaller than it is if one compares it to the revolution promised for management offices in the early years. And the "wait-until-next-generation" theme is wearing thinner and thinner.

Let me quickly acknowledge that there are *some* management scientists who operate effectively in both cultures. But they are rare birds. Most management scientists are still thinking, writing, and operating in a world that is far removed from the real world in which most managers operate (and in which I personally have been operating). They often describe and structure nonexistent management problems, tackle relatively minor problems with overkill tools, omit real variables from messy problems, and build elegant models comprehensible to only their colleagues. And when managers seem confused or dissatisfied with the results of their activities and reject them, these scientists seem almost to take satisfaction in this confirmation of the crudity and inelegance of the managerial world.

Have I overdrawn the picture? Only very slightly.

WHY THE GULF?_____

I do not mean to say that management scientists have purposefully created this cultural gap. Most of them feel that much of what they are doing today is really helpful to managers. But I'm afraid it simply isn't so. Others argue that much of what they are doing is "pure research," which will be useful one day. I do not discount the value of pure research; some of it is needed. But the fact remains that only a small fraction of management science "results" are being used.

Those management scientists who do acknowledge a gap often excuse it by one of two reasons:

"The manager doesn't understand the power of the tools."
"He isn't sympathetic to systematic decision making and would rather fly by the seat of his pants because this is safer for his ego."

I myself am a counterexample to both these excuses. I have had some fairly good training in management science. I have done research in the area and written a book urging the use of more explicit decision tools in a specific industry—oil well drilling.[1] I have taught various courses in the area, for example, in statistics, management control systems, and quantitative analysis.

And yet, in the most challenging assignment of my life—putting together the Price Commission—I used absolutely *none* of the management science tools explicitly. One might think that in the task of developing an organization of 600 people (mostly professionals), creating a program to control

[1] *Decisions Under Uncertainty* (Boston, Division of Research, Harvard Business School, 1960).

prices in a trillion-dollar economy, and making decisions that involve costs, volume, prices, productivity, resource allocations, elasticities, multiple goals, trade-offs, predictions, politics, and risk values, an expert would have found ways to use his familiarity with management science to advantage. I did not.

A defender of the faith will quickly say that, although I did not use them explicitly, I probably used them *implicitly*, and that they helped to discipline my approach to decision making. I agree that this is probably true. But I nevertheless think it is a damning indictment that I can identify *no* incident of a conscious, explicit use of a single management science tool in my activities as head of the Price Commission.

Further, my conscience is clear. To my mind there are five very valid reasons for my rejecting the idea of using management science.

Shortage of Time

Although I thought about using management science tools on many occasions, I consistently decided against it because of the shortage of time. Management scientists simply do not sufficiently understand the constraint of time on decision making, and particularly on decisions that count; and the techniques they develop reflect that fact. They may write about time as a limitation. They may admonish managers for letting time push them into a "crisis" mode. They may recognize the constraint of time with a few words and comment on its influence. They may say that they, too, experience time constraints. But their techniques are so time consuming to use that managers pass them by.

Does this mean that all management science work ought to be thrown into shredders? No, it simply means that management scientists (a) need to get out of their relatively unpressured worlds and *experience* the impact of time on the decision-making process, and (b) need to build the time factor into models instead of leaving it as an exogenous variable.

Inaccessibility of Data

The second reason for ignoring management science in practice is related to the time problem. A manager will ordinarily use data or a management science tool only if both are conveniently, speedily accessible. If he is told that the needed data are buried in another part of the organization, or that they must be compiled, or that the model must be created, nine times out of ten he will say, "Skip it." I did, ten times out of ten.

True, many management scientists would say that I must have developed "trade-offs" in my mind, weighing the cost of obtaining data or building a model against the probable opportunity payoff, and that my mental calculator ground out negative responses on each occasion. This is perfectly plausible. Unconsciously I probably did build a number of such informal investment-payoff models.

But where does this leave us? It leaves us with management scientists continuing to construct models that call for substantial investments in design and data collection and managers discarding them. The statement is made ad nauseum that most data are not in the forms that most models call for, or that they are not complete; yet the management scientists go right on calling for inaccessible, nonexistent, or uncompiled data to suit "theoretically correct" models. And hence managers continue to say, "Skip it."

Instead of asking a manager to lie in the Procrustean bed of the theoretically correct model, why shouldn't the management scientist design a realistic model, or a realistic part of a model, or come up with a realistic data prescription? The result might be extremely crude; it might embarrass a theoretician; it might be shot down by the purist and the theoretician. But it just might be *used*.

Resistance to Change

The third reason that I did not use management science tools explicitly is that educating others in the organization who are not familiar with the tools, and who would resist using them if they were, is just too difficult a task. Management scientists typically regard this problem as outside the scope of their jobs—at most, they remark on the need to educate more people and to change organizations so they become more scientific. Or, if they *do* recognize the problem, they grossly underestimate the time and organizational effort needed to "educate and change." I suggest that management scientists do two things:

1. They should build into their models some explicit recognition of the financial and emotional cost of change of this kind and make explicit allowance for the drag of change resistance. I am quite aware that some change techniques are being used: sensitivity training, Esalen-type devices, management by objectives, quantitative analysis courses for managers, and so on. I have used them myself, and I know that they help. But the magnitude of time and energy required to install them is not generally appreciated—certainly not by management scientists— and their impact is highly overrated.

2. They should get themselves some education and direct experience in the power, politics, and change-resistance factors in the real world of management so they can better incorporate the imperfect human variables in their work.

Long Response Time

Fourth, few management science people are geared up to respond to significant management problems in "real time." Management science people in universities live largely by the school calendar, and if they receive a request for help, they are likely to respond in terms of next semester, next September, or after exams. And once again the manager is likely to say, "Skip it." Even most management science personnel in staff positions of live organizations operate in a time frame that is slower than that of the line managers. It is their nature to approach a problem in a methodical, thorough way, even when the required response time dictates that they come up with a "quick and dirty" solution.

Invalidating Simplifications

Fifth, and finally, it is standard operating procedure for most management science people to strip away so much of a real problem with "simplifying assumptions" that the remaining carcass of the problem and its attendant solution bear little resemblance to the reality with which the manager must deal. The time constraints, the data-availability questions, the people problems, the power structures, and the political pressures—all the important, nasty areas that lie close to the essence of management—are simplified out of existence so that a technically beautiful, and useless, resolution may be achieved.

This is somewhat paradoxical since management science originated in wartime Britain, when many interdisciplinary talents were forced into combination to grapple with the problems of total mobilization. That situation tolerated no fooling around. But in subsequent years management science has retreated from the immediate demands for workable results. It has increased its use of the hard sciences of mathematics and statistics, hardening itself with methodological complexity, weakening its own reliance on the softer sciences of psychology, sociology, and political science, and losing the plain, hardheaded pragmatism with which it started out.

Realizing this, many managers think it pointless to turn the really important problems over to management science. Their experience has shown them the impotence of emasculated solutions.

At the risk of repeating a tired joke, let me recall the story of the man who said he had a way to destroy all the enemy submarines in the Atlantic during World War II: "Boil the ocean." Asked next how he would do this, he replied, "That's your problem." Similarly, when managers ask management scientists how to solve a problem, they too often say, in effect, "Boil the company." They leave it to the manager to worry about shortages of time, inaccessibility of data, resistance to change, slow response times, and oversimplified solutions.

FIRING THE FURNACE

At the Price Commission we operated, I think fairly successfully, without getting the data we "should" have had, without using any explicit decision tools, without once formally consulting a management scientist, and without building models of our decision-making processes. I am not especially proud of these facts; I am a member, and an intellectually loyal member, of ORSA, TIMS, and AIDS. I believe in the general direction in which these organizations want to go. But I also have a personal dedication to action, a sense of the urgency and immediacy of real problems, and a disbelief in the genuine responsiveness of management science models to my managerial needs.

I have asked myself the question whether we might have done better by using some management science models, and my honest answer is *no*. Using models would have slowed decision making. It would have frustrated most of our personnel. Given the fact that most models omit the factors of time, data accessibility, people, power, and politics, they simply would not have provided sufficient predictive or prescriptive payoff for the required investment of energy.

Consider the severity of the demands that were made. Establishment of the Price Commission required fulfillment of seemingly impossible tasks and directives:

Create and staff a fully competent organization.
Work out regulations worthy to bear the force of law.
Keep the program consistent with policies established in Phase I and the current state of the economy.
Work in conjunction with the Pay Board, the Internal Revenue Service, and the Cost of Living Council.
Control the prices of hundreds of millions of articles and commodities in the world's largest economy.
Do not inhibit the recovery of the economy.

Do not build a postcontrol bubble.

Do all of this with a regulatory staff of 600.

Have the entire operation functioning in 16 days.

A natural first reaction to such demands might well have been General McAuliffe's famous one-word response: "Nuts!" It would have been very easy to point out, for example, that:

> Nobody could begin to do the job of price control with 600 people, even with the services of 3,000 Internal Revenue Service agents to help with enforcement. It had taken 60,000 people to handle the assignment in World War II and 17,000 in the Korean War.

> To do the job right would require a thoroughgoing study of what was involved—the resources and kinds of personnel required, the most efficient way of actually controlling prices, the optimum method of working in concert with other federal agencies—as well as the accumulation of data about the economy and the testing of various models.

> The 16-day period was too short. There was not enough time to get the Price Commission appointed, let alone to build, organize, and house the right kind of staff, promulgate regulations, and get it all functioning.

I might have pointed out these things and many others. I did not. I simply started bringing in staff, renting quarters, creating an organization, framing regulations, and developing a modus operandi. In 16 days the organization was accepting requests for price increases from U.S. business; the staff was at work—in some cases eight to an office, four to a telephone, and a good many spending up to 20 hours a day on the job.

I cite this record not to boast. Our achievement did not grow out of extraordinary capability. It was simply a matter of orientation and intuition—orientation and intuition toward action. But just as managers incline toward intuition and action, management scientists incline toward reflective thinking. They tend to be scholarly, less action-oriented, and averse to taking risks—even risk of criticism from their peers. They dissect and analyze, they are individualistic, and they are prone to trace ideas much as one can trace power flows in a mechanical system, from gear to belt to gear. They have not cared much about firing the furnace that makes the steam that drives the gear in the first place.

The manager offers an almost complete contrast. He integrates and synthesizes; he sees situations as mosaics; his thoughts and decision processes are like electrical circuits so complex you can never be sure how much current is flowing where. At the core of his value system are depth and breadth of experience, which he may even permit to outweigh facts where the whole picture seems to justify it.

For his part, the management scientist tends to optimize the precision of a tool at the expense of the health and performance of the whole. He has faith in some day building ultimate tools and devising ultimate measurements, and this lies at the foundation of his values and beliefs.

The problem, then, boils down to two cultures—the managers' and the management scientists'—and not enough bridges between them. Somebody has to build the bridges.

WHO SHALL BUILD THE BRIDGES?_____

Closing any gap requres that one or both cultures change. It is my strong belief that the management scientist must move first, and most. *The end product is supposed to be management, after all, not management science.* Further, as a philosophical point, I think science has greater relevance in our world if it moves constantly toward art (in this case the management art) than the other way around. Then, instead of moving toward increased and separated specialization, both evolve toward a mature symbiosis, a working and dynamic unity of the kind found in successful marriages, detentes, and mergers.

The management scientist is not going to find it easy or comfortable to change, and yet it is he who must change most in attitude, action, and life style. He is going to have to think in terms of the *manager's* perceptions, the *manager's* needs, the *manager's* expectations, and the *manager's* pressures— that is, if he wants to have impact in the real world of the manager. If not, he will go on missing the mark.

What, concretely, can be done? Let me offer a few suggestions to the management science people and the managers they are supposed to be helping.

Inside Operating Organizations

First, top management should not isolate the management science people but sprinkle them throughout the organization in situations where they can really go to work. It should give them *line* responsibility for results. Their natural tendencies will cause them to flock together at night or on weekends to compare and refine tools, and that, again, is as it should be; but their prime responsibility should be to the line unit, not to a management science group. To put the matter another way: management should not think of having an operating person on a management science team—it should think of having a management scientist on an operating team.

Second, managers should demand implementation by management scientists; they should not tolerate "package" solutions that leave out the complicating factors. In that way, managers can avoid simplistic, unworkable solutions that ignore the factors of time, data accessibility, unwillingness of people to change, power, and so on.

Third, even when professional management scientists are brought into companies as consultants, they are often given the easy, old problems, for the reasons that I have named. This expectational cycle has to be broken.

At the University

The same general approach is valid within universities.

First, both management science faculty and students have to get out of the isolated, insulated world of academe. They must go beyond structured cases and lectures and become directly involved in real-world, real-time, live projects, not as a way of applying what they know, but as a way of learning.

It is a mistake to teach the student linear programming or decision theory and then search for a problem to which the tool can be applied. That creates the classic academic situation from which managers are revolting—the tool in search of a problem. Instead, tackle the *real* problem. This will be frustrating, but the frustration of trying to reach a *workable* solution can be used to the teach the management scientist or student in a way that is both useful to him and to the business or government unit. The solutions thus derived may not be so elegant as they might be, but they may be used. The student who wants to reach for higher, more sophisticated theories should be treated as a special case, not the general case.

Second, management science people should stop tackling the neat, simple problems, or refining approaches to problems already solved. These projects may be easier, but working and reworking them will not help bridge the cultural gap I am talking about. Instead, tackle the *tough* problem. The management of time pressure and the use of the persuasion and negotiation required by a real, tough problem will give both the faculty member and the student some salutary discipline in convincing others to follow a strange idea, to cooperate, and to listen.

The best example of what I am describing occurred at Case Institute in the early days of Russell L. Ackoff, E. L. Arnoff, and C. West Churchman. There, faculty and student teams worked on real problems in real time in real business settings. That example does not seem to have caught on at other universities, partly because of the difficulty of doing it, and partly because it flies against the nature of the management science personality that I have described. The process is messy, people-populated, schedule-disrupting, time-demanding, and complicated by power and politics. That is exactly as it should be.

Third, faculty members should plan to get out of the university, physically and completely, for meaningful periods of time. They should plan their careers so that they schedule at least a year, periodically, in which they get direct, real-world experience in business, nonprofit organizations, or the government.

One helpful device with which I am familiar is the Presidential Personnel Interchange Program of the federal government, now in its third year. So far this year it has brought 60 business executives into government work and 18 federal government managers into business. These numbers should be expanded tremendously, and the organizations involved should include universities. The universities could well join in a three-way interchange, or start their own program with business.

Finally, universities should bring in real managers and involve them directly in problem-solving and joint-learning sessions. Doctors expect to return to medical school as part of their normal development; so should managers. The universities can offer managers an update in science; corporate managers can offer universities an update in management.

These are some of the ways to build bridges. There are other ways to tear them down, or to maintain the gap. Jargon, for example, will drive away managers. So will intellectual snobbery toward "intuitive" decision making. Management scientists should dispense with both. Managers can maintain the gap by continuing to refer to past disillusionments and never allowing management science people to tackle executive-suite programs. Managers should recognize that. In fact, defensive behavior on the part of either group can block reconciliation and progress.

People *do* exist who effectively bridge the two cultures. Such people do not always bear an identifying brand; one cannot distinguish them by their degrees, university course credits, titles, experience, or even home base. But they do have one strong, overriding, characteristic—they are *problem- and action-oriented*. They are essentially unicultural; they employ a healthy mix of science and intuition in their decision making.

WORDS TO THE WISE

I am not suggesting that the two specializations—management science and management—be destroyed. Primary bases and modes of operation can be preserved, provided that both groups are receptive to and understanding of the other's basic orientation, and that they work together in harmony, not in dissonance. And all should remember that the problem is the thing, not the methodology; the function, not the form.

My slings and arrows have been directed mostly toward management science—rightly so, I think. But managers must assist in the bridge-building process.

They should stop recounting tales of how "they never laid a glove on me" in encounters with management scientists. They should make it a point of future pride to use management science.

They should make available the real nasty, complicated decisions to management scientists.

They should not expect a lot.

They should not deride small gains.

They should hold any management science approach or individual accountable for producing *results*, not recommendations.

The management science people must play their part, too:

Get out of the monasteries, whether these are universities or staff departments.

Submerge the paraphernalia (journal articles, computer programs, cookbooks) and rituals ("sounds like a linear programming program to me" or "we need to get the facts first").

Put people, time, power, data accessibility, and response times into models and create crude, workable solutions.

Learn to live with and in the real world of managers.

Again, I submit it is the management science people who will have to change most. They should take the first step toward closing the gap between the two cultures. The consequences can only be better for managers, for management science, and for the problem itself.

John C. Anderson
Thomas R. Hoffmann

Both of University of Minnesota

A PERSPECTIVE ON THE IMPLEMENTATION OF MANAGEMENT SCIENCE

Implementation (or lack thereof) of Operations Research and Management Science (OR/MS) is becoming of increasing concern to educators, researchers, and management. An apparent problem of unsuccessful implementation exists, as evidenced by researchers' and managers' observations. But, before we prejudge this lack of success and, particularly, before we hastily press forward researching and/or developing strategies toward successful implementation, we must analyze and gain an understanding of the goals which are implied when an OR/MS effort is deemed successful.

All too often, the real meaning of implementation has been mistaught by educators, misconstrued by management in industry, and mismeasured by researchers. This article sheds some light and structure on the implementation issue. Drawing upon experiences gained as Management Scientists in industry, as researchers of OR/MS implementation, and as educators of OR/MS, the authors examine the implementation problem—and the variety of views surrounding it—and present a framework for better understanding and evaluating OR/MS implementation. This framework is then compared with practice and results as observed in research, industry and education, concluding with a proposed new emphasis for OR/MS efforts.

John C. Anderson and Thomas R. Hoffman, "A Perspective on the Implementation of Management Science," *Academy of Management Review*, July 1978, pp. 563–571.

423

THE NATURE OF THE IMPLEMENTATION PROBLEM

The sparse research evidence currently available on the implementation problem is insufficient to identify the extent of, or to completely characterize, the implementation problem. The available evidence has consistently shown results which indicate that the OR/MS implementation problem is widespread. In a study by Radnor and Niel (12), over 50 percent of the 108 large firms examined had completed and implemented only 50 percent-80 percent of OR/MS projects; several other case studies (9, 15) provided evidence of the implementation problem.

Perhaps one of the most thought-provoking comments on the subject of implementation problems came from Grayson, who said:

> I have taught various courses in the area, for example in statistics, management control systems and quantitative analysis, and yet in the most challenging assignment of my life, putting together the Price Commission, I used absolutely none of the Management Science tools explicitly. One might think . . . that an expert would have found ways to use his familiarity with management science to advantage. I did not (5).

Grayson is not alone in his sentiments. The authors have invited industrial leaders in the field of Management Science to speak to classes about real-life application of Management Science. Ensuing discussions often reveal a disappointing lack of use of Management Science and Operations Research models in management decision processes.

With this disillusioning evidence—low industrial implementation, lack of explicit use of Management Science tools, and little use of OR/MS models—evaluation is in order. But before disciplining our discipline, we must better understand the problem at hand. A systematic look at the whole of implementation of OR/MS programs is required.

IMPLEMENTATION— A VARIETY OF VIEWS

Implementation is a word which is spoken with a variety of intended meanings. At a recent conference on implementation attended by researchers and industrial managers who were studying and emphasizing the implementation of OR/MS programs, an entire evening was spent attempting to clarify and define the concept of OR/MS implementation. Even amongst "experts," the definition of implementation and the strategies necessary to obtain successful implementation were actively discussed with little or no resolution.

OR/MS implementation is, at best, a difficult concept to pin down. It is a phenomenon with many definitions in a field which defies definition, as evidenced by the discussions and disputes over many years. Many definitions of OR/MS exist, but perhaps the most widely accepted OR/MS definition is that stated by the Operations Research Society of America (ORSA): "Operations Research is the science that is devoted to describing, understanding and predicting the behavior of [complicated systems of men and machines] operating in natural environments" (11).

Given this definition, a basic goal of OR/MS (as stated by ORSA) "is assistance to executives in improving the operations under their control." Beyond this, it is necessary to state criteria for successful assistance of OR/MS. As an example, Arnoff states: "Unless our models result in decision rules and/or procedures (a) which are implemented within the managerial decision making process, (b) which really work, and (c) which lead to cost effective benefits, our efforts are not successful" (1). While perhaps not originally intended by Arnoff, this definition of succssful OR is tied directly to models in decision processes, then indirectly through these models to positive impacts on decision processes. This statement limits what is termed successful practice of OR/MS, and correspondingly successful implementation, by focusing on installation of a model. Unfortunately this view has been a predominant perspective and has lead to an undue emphasis on models rather than modeling and on the ends (decisions) rather than on the means of management decision making.

While many researchers and industrial practitioners have held the above stated narrow view of implementation, successful implementation in practice means different things to different people.

At a conference dealing specifically with implementation in the production setting, one of the OR consultants told of having developed a linear programming (LP) model for scheduling. If it had been used to schedule a prior month's activity it would have resulted in a 9 percent performance improvement. After management saw the results, they revised their rules-of-thumb: then the LP model was only 0.1 percent better. Management did not install the LP model—they simply stayed with their improved rules-of-thumb. Was the OR effort a failure?

In another instance, a scheduling model was developed and programmed using representative test data. The quality of the model was not questioned, and management learned much about the decision during the model building process. But, management then realized that the cost in people and money to create the data base necessary to use the model was too great so they did not install the model for generation of regular schedules. A failure?

Each of these involvements would be considered by some to be successful implementation of OR/MS; by others, to be a failure. This judgment depends upon one's perspective regarding implementation and primarily on the criteria involved. What is important is to critically examine the nature of possible outcomes of an OR/MS effort, so that OR/MS implementation and associated criteria can be placed into perspective and the true organizational value of OR/MS be determined.

IMPLEMENTATION— A CONCEPTUAL FRAMEWORK

What then is implementation? According to Webster's *New World Dictionary*: "Implementation is the act of carrying into effect or providing the means for carrying into effect". Note that from a management perspective, the first part of the definition focuses on the completion of a decision; in contrast, the second part highlights implementation as a *process* or means toward affecting the decision process. It follows then, the implementation may occur when a decision has been directly affected by application of the MS *concept* or *methodology* towards "describing, understanding and predicting behavior" (11). Although the describing process may be termed modeling, implementation of (use of) OR/MS should not necessarily be limited to whether a mathematical model itself was installed in a particular decision situation. What seems necessary is to define a structure which keeps successful application of OR/MS and installation of a model in proper perspective. This framework will allow us to properly analyze the implementation problem.

In an effort to gain this perspective, consider a conceptual framework which includes three factors: *installation, implementation,* and *integration* as critical dimensions of an OR/MS effort. To understand this framework the following definitions are given:

1. *OR/MS Model Installation:* Model installation implies the condition where a mathematical model was developed and installed, operating with real world data, producing its intended solution and/or results,

perhaps in an operating system intended to support the decision process.

2. *Implementation of OR/MS:* Implementation of OR/MS occurs when the *concept* or *methodology* has assisted in *describing, understanding,* and *predicting* the *behavior* of the *system* involved in the *management decision process.* The impact may be a programmed decision; or, as is more often the case, the impact may be decision support, e.g., a more consistent decision, increased or decreased confidence in a decision, increased decision timeliness, or a better understanding of the decision situation.

3. *Integration of OR/MS:* Integration of OR/MS occurs when line or staff management involved internalize concepts and perhaps methodology in their own decision processes and become capable of recognizing the need for or applying these approaches in other decisions.

It is important to recognize that an individual OR/MS effort may be considered in light of the three somewhat separate dimensions and a judgment made as to attainment of success along each dimension. One dimension focuses on model installation; a second on affecting a current decision process, and a third on management internalization of OR/MS concepts. Viewing OR/MS results with this perspective reveals eight different combinations of successes and failures as shown in Figure 1.

Implementation and Installation:
Two Dimensions of an OR/MS Effort

Consider first the two-dimensional problem on Figure 1—Implementation and Installation. Four possible conditions may exist. The first condition (No. 1) is where successful implementation and successful model installation have occurred. Certainly, almost everyone would agree that this marks successful application of both concept and methodology in the decision making problem, for a model was built and installed in a decision process successfully impacting decisions, following Arnoff's definition (1).

A second condition (No. 4) is where no model was installed and no decision impact occurred—thus, no success. This is simply a situation where a modeling approach was attempted, and the manager realized no real assistance in the decision process. If a model was built, it did not fit the decision situation and so was not installed in an operating manual or automated system supporting the decision process. While these first two conditions are widely understood and expected occurrences, the remaining two conditions (No. 2 and No. 3) require attention.

Condition No. 2 exists when a model has been unsuccessfully installed in a decision situation but the modeling process has assisted in *describing, understanding,* and *predicting* the *behavior* of the *system* involved in the *management decision process:* therefore, successful implementation has occurred. In this instance, a modeling approach was attempted which resulted in a model which was not installed in an operating manual or automated system and therefore not producing intended model output. But, along the way in developing the model, management learned—from parameterization, from design, from inputting into the model building process—something which influenced the decision.

Condition No. 3 identifies a situation where a model has been installed in a decision making situation, but is unsuccessfully assisting the management decision process, i.e., it is being circumvented or ignored by the manager. This is clearly an undesirable situation, because a model was successfully sold and installed in a decision process, but it is having no effect, or possibly

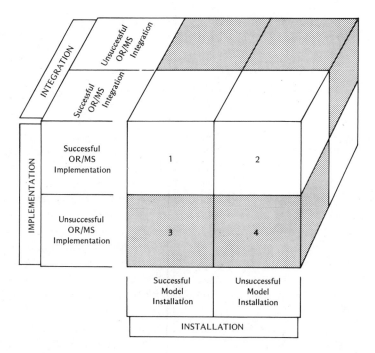

FIGURE 1   *The Result Dimensions of an OR/MS Effort*

an adverse effect, on that particular decision process. Certainly we would all agree that this is not a successful application of OR/MS.

Installation, Implementation, and Integration: Three Dimensions of an OR/MS Effort

Eight combinations of the three dimensions exist, some more prevalent than others. Consider the situation where all three goals are successfully attained (Condition 1 with successful integration). A modeling approach was employed, resulting in a model which produced its intended outputs to the decision process. The effort assisted management's decision process, management integrated concepts and/or methodology into its way of thinking as an aid for the decisions to follow. Consider the situation where successful implementation and integration occurred, yet no model was installed (Condition 2 with successful integration). The modeling approach employed did not result in a model which was producing intended outputs to the decision process, but the effort influenced management's current decision process, and management internalized concepts for ongoing decision processes. In both instances, the process of interaction between the management scientist and management, the process of model formulation, and/or the process of parameterization caused successful implementation and created internalization of concepts, whereby ongoing decision processes became more systematic, structured, and logical.

Another prevalent dimensional combination involves the situation where implementation and integration have been unsuccessful, yet model installation was "successful" (Condition 3 with unsuccessful integration). The effort produced outputs which affected neither managements' current nor ongoing decision process. Consider a final situation where attainment of all three goals is unsuccessful (Condition 4 with unsuccessful integration)—a failure, to say the least.

The four remaining dimensional combinations are found in the shaded area of Figure 1. These combinations are included to complete the conceptual framework of the results of OR/MS efforts and warrant less discussion because they are not outcomes of OR/MS efforts. While these outcomes in the shaded region may exist in limited instances, internalization of concept in ongoing decision processes (integration) is much more highly dependent upon successful implementation than model installation, as the shading in Figure 1 illustrates.

In summary, the conceptual framework illustrates alternative dimensions in viewing the success of an OR/MS effort. It begins to clarify why certain OR/MS efforts are considered a success by some and a failure by others.

One cannot simply state that successful OR/MS is concommittant with success along any one dimension. Management, faced with the realities of making decisions and seeking assistance in the process, may primarily value application along the implementation dimension. An MS analyst, on the other hand, may all too often value an involvement along the installation dimension. The individual concerned with management development may place primary value along the integration dimension—where ongoing decision processes have been enhanced.

The conceptual framework illustrates to management, OR/MS practitioners, academicians, and researchers that there may be separable goals for an OR/MS effort. One might argue that in order to gain the most out of OR/MS concept methodology and discipline, goals in all three dimensions—implementation, installation, and integration—must be kept as conscious objectives. Expediency, personal bias, and/or time pressures may force emphasis on one dimension over another in particular efforts. But for an OR/MS effort to be a viable component of organizational value, the primary objective must be implementation (assisting the management decision process) which may or may not imply model installation. Further, sustained implementation may require that we pursue the integration goal, perhaps even at the expense of installation of models. If management's decision process itself becomes more structured, systematic, and logical, better ongoing decisions will result. In addition, opportunities for acceptance of more structured and systematic MS approaches will be greater.

CURRENT PERSPECTIVES ON OR/MS IMPLEMENTATION

Recently, other authors have presented ideas pertinent to this structure. McKenney and Keen (8) pointed out that the management scientist's role can be one of either producing a product or rendering a service. Product orientation emphasizes model installation, while service orientation emphasizes the process of implementation.

In emphasizing the role of OR/MS in relatively unstructured, one-shot decisions, Hammond (6) similarly points to the distinction between a process and product orientation. He states that the goal of OR/MS in this context "should be to augment, stimulate and otherwise assist the reasoning of the manager". MS should serve as a "a decision prosthetic rather than a decision maker."

Huysman (7) discussed the difference between management action (acceptance), management change (implementation), and recurring use of the OR approach (integration), indicating various levels of management response to an OR/MS effort. Miser (10) cited ORSA's definition (11) and pointed to six categories of activity: observation, models, verification, practice, invention, and design. He lamented the over-emphasis on "modeling" so that "at times it has almost seemed as though operations research and modeling were synonymous." Unfortunately, many would even go so far as to say they were identities.

Academia has been guilty of Miser's lament—it predominantly emphasizes model construction rather than the other categories of OR/MS activity. Textbooks are notorious for their emphasis on tools and techniques; basic books concentrate on mathematical developments, devoting only a few pages to problem identification, implementation, or data requirements and support systems. Advanced courses and texts, seeking to be more theoretical, devote a still larger percentage of their coverage to models (products). As any teacher of OR/MS knows, it is far easier to teach (and test) tools and techniques (facts!) than philosophy, conceptual foundations, or implementation and integration strategies. In the extreme case, this emphasis leads to such professorial statements as: "If the management scientist develops a good model and management doesn't use it, it's management's fault." Thus, some pedagogues define successful OR/MS as simply model construction where model installation, much less implementation, is relegated to management.

OR/MS research has also emphasized models and model installation. Research aimed toward development of concept and methodology has been heavily weighted toward development of tools and techniques. Survey after survey has revealed that we have explict tools (i.e., models) that are very sophisticated and far beyond the reach of current industrial practices. Yet when it comes to basic decision processes, little progress beyond the eighteenth century has been made (4).

A second thrust of research is the area that specifically studies the implementation of OR/MS. Practically all research which measures some kind of a causal relationship between situational factors and implementation success has employed model installation as its definition of successful implementation. With this definition, several studies reported problems in data collection because management felt certain applications were successful, yet models were not installed. Bean *et al.* (2) observes that when implementation is defined as model installation, then there is no judgment concerning the quality of OR/MS work. Furthermore, this definition does not consider unused work which has been "shelved" for extenuating reasons nor the effect on organizational decision makers' thinking of unused projects and general educational activity. Bean *et al.* contend that such changes in thinking may be potentially more valuable than the project itself.

The emphasis on installation and models is not confined merely to academia and research. Woolsey (17) illustrates several examples of the application of mathematical models where the emphasis on the models caused the analysts involved to lose perspective of the problem they wished to solve. Industry practice of organizing "project teams" following project management protocols often aimed at developing a specific product (scheduling system, forecasting model, etc.) frequently overlooks the overall goal of providing decision support. In other cases, management, with an objective of improving its decision processes, frequently solicits OR/MS support; the OR/MS practitioner responds with an approach which has as an objective of building a model which then can be used in the decision process. The two groups' objectives are subtly different; often the objective of building a model, which should be a means to an end, becomes an end in itself.

OR/MS EMPHASIZING THE PROCESS OF IMPLEMENTATION

To achieve more successful application of OR/MS, changes are required in education, research, and industry. In education there is a need for more real world experience. Woolsey had chastised the OR/MS community for some time (16, 17). His points are well-taken: an education in checkers does not prepare one to play chess. One school (3) has capitalized on its proximity to industry and requires all MBA's, not just OR/MS majors, to work in interdisciplinary teams on real industry problems. Working with industry representatives, a team must identify a real problem, develop a systematic approach to solve the problem—which may or may not involve development of a model—and, finally, recommend an implementation procedure. The students find it hard but enjoyable work, a real "capstone" to their education. At the undergraduate level, more emphasis must be placed on philosophy, applications, and interpretation of results. This is achieved by using only portions of standard textbooks supplemented by readings and case studies and supported by computer programs tailored to educational rather than research use. At the departmental level, educators must work closely with colleagues in other disciplines to get them to use the OR/MS approach.

Loan of MS staff to the other areas to work with and co-teach such courses as "Management Policy" and "Business and Society," Marketing, Finance, Accounting, etc. may not go unrewarded in this regard. A similar loan of academic staff from these disciplines to co-teach management science courses emphasizing particular application areas is also helpful.

Research efforts must be directed not only at development of new tools based upon mathematical reasoning, but must also be directed at developing the role of and particular approaches for the other five areas Miser (10) cited: observation, verification, practice, invention, and design in decision processes. Continued emphasis on sophisticated models can only produce further disparity between theory and practice. Emphasis should be on refining concept and methodology to support rather than supplant basic decision processes. This research in and of itself must draw heavily from empirical study and from involved observation of implementation within real environments rather than overly simplified research frameworks within hypothetical settings. The strategy must be "real" rather than "toy" research (14). Further, the OR/MS implementation research must widen its scope to include studies which include implementation rather than just model installation. An interesting study would be to analyze conditions in which implementation occurs without model installation—a situation which has not gone entirely unnoticed by industrial management.

Industry should recognize the distinction between various goals of OR/MS involvements in order to gain maximum benefit and avoid misapplication. It should recognize the role of OR/MS as a conceptual and philosophical approach in the ongoing process of decision making, not just a set of tools for developing programmed decisions. The importance of implementation in providing decision support, or integration in providing better ongoing decision processes, as opposed simply to model installation cannot be overemphasized. OR/MS efforts should be valued not only for the solutions they may provide, but also for the logical structures their discipline may bring to bear on the decision process. Project teams should be less product-oriented and more cognizant of the interactive nature of their activities in providing decision support.

Another emphasis should be for industry to incorporate OR/MS activity within functional areas. Shycon (13) points out that most major U.S. corporations do not have simply one management science group, but a variety of such groups scattered throughout the firms. Indeed, much of the OR/MS impact takes place without the OR/MS banner as is evidenced by the commonness of marketing, inventory, and logistics planning models. This infiltration, which brings OR/MS closer to managerial decision process, should be encouraged.

As described in the conceptual framework, dimensions of OR/MS results exist and require the considered attention of the academician, reseacher, and practitioner in the planning and conduct of OR/MS efforts. Experience has shown emphasis on one dimension—installation—at the expense of the other two—implementation and integration. Focus on the latter two dimensions is vital for OR/MS to contribute to managerial decision making.

In summary, implementation occurs when the application of OR/MS *concept* or *methodology* has assisted in *describing, understanding,* and *predicting,* the *behavior* of the *system* involved in the *management decision process.* As such it may or may not involve installation of a model or integration of OR/MS. It is hoped that isolating and identifying the basic meaning and distinction between implementation, installation, and integration affords a structure that helps to understand better these phenomena and enhances the likelihood of successful OR/MS efforts.

REFERENCES

1. Arnoff, E. Leonard, "Successful Models I Have Known," *Decision Sciences*, Vol. 2, No. 2 (April, 1971), 141–148.
2. Bean, A., R. Neal, M. Radnor, and D. Tansik, "Structural Correlates of Implementation Success and Failure in U.S. Business Organizations." A presentation at the Conference on the Implementation of OR/MS Models, University of Pittsburgh, November, 1973.
3. Chervany, N. L., and J. S. Heinen, "The Structure of a Student Project Course," *Decision Sciences*, Vol. 6, No. 1 (January, 1975), 174–183.
4. Etter, W., "Benjamin Franklin and Prudential Algebra," *Decision Sciences*, Vol. 5, No. 1 (January; 1974), 145–147.
5. Grayson, C. L., Jr., "Management Science and Business Practice, *Harvard Business Review* (July-August, 1973), 41–48.
6. Hammond, John S., "The Roles of the Manager and Management Scientist in Successful Implementation," *Sloan Management Review* (Winter, 1974), 1–24.
7. Huysman, J. H., "Operations Research Implementation and the Practice of Management," A paper presented at the Conference on the Implementation of OR/MS Models, University of Pittsburgh, November, 1973.
8. McKenney, James L., and Peter G. W. Keen, "How Managers' Minds Work," *Harvard Business Review* (May-June, 1974), 79–90.
9. McKinsey and Co., Inc. "A Limited Survey of Industrial Progress in OR," in Learner, R. N. *The Management of Improvement* (New York: Reinhold Publishing Co., 1965).
10. Miser, Hugh J., "What is Operations Research?," *Operations Research*. Vol. 22, No. 4 (July-August, 1974), 903–909.

11. Operations Research Society of America: Purposes, History, Organization, Activities, Membership," (Baltimore, Maryland: Operations Research Society of America).

12. Radnor, M., and R. Neal, "The Progress of Management Science Activities in Large U.S. Industrial Corporations." *Research Monograph, #4–71* (Evanston, Ill: Graduate School of Management, Northwestern University, December, 1971).

13. Shycon, Harvey N., "All Around the Model: Perspectives on MS Applications," *Interfaces*, Vol. 4, No. 2 (February, 1974), 21–23.

14. Sprague, L. G., and C. R. Sprague, "Management Science," *Interfaces*, Vol. 7, No. 1 (November, 1976), 57–62.

15. Stimson, David H., and Ruth H. Stimson, *Operations Research in Operations Diagnosis and Prognosis* (Chicago Hospital Research and Educational Trust, 1972).

16. Woolsey, R. E. D., "A Novena to St. Jude or Four Edifying Case Studies in Mathematical Programming," *Interfaces*. Vol. 4, No. 1 (November, 1973), 32–39.

17. Woolsey, R. E. D., "Operations Research and Management Science Today , – or – Does Education in Checkers Really Prepare One for a Life of Chess," *Operations Research*, Vol. 20, No. 3 (May-June, 1972), 465–473.

Thomas H. Naylor

Duke University

Daniel R. Gattis

Affiliated with Minton Amick & Associates

CORPORATE PLANNING MODELS

Through direct personal contact we have identified nearly two thousand firms in the United States, Canada, and Europe that are either using, developing, or experimenting with some form of corporate planning models. These models represent an attempt to describe the complex interrelationships among a corporation's financial, marketing, and production activities in terms of a set of mathematical and logical relationships which have been programmed into a computer.

As recently as 1969, Gershefski was able to identify only 63 firms from a sample of 1,900 that were actually using corporate planning models.[1] In September 1974, Social Systems, Incorporated, of Durham, North Carolina, conducted a survey of 1,881 corporations which were thought to be either using, developing, or planning to develop a corporate planning model.[2] Of the 346 corporations that responded to the survey, 73 percent were either using or developing such a model. Another 15 percent were planning to develop a corporate planning model, and only 12 percent had no plans to develop a planning model.

The reasons corporate management is turning to corporate planning models include: economic uncertainty; shortages of energy and basic raw

Thomas H. Naylor and Daniel R. Gattis, "Corporate Planning Models," *California Management Review*, Summer 1976, pp. 69–78. Copyright © 1976 by the Regents of the University of California.

materials; a leveling off of productivity; international competition; tight money and inflation; political upheavals; environmental problems; and new business opportunities. That is, top management has become increasingly aware that the old ways of "muddling through" are not adequate to meet the complex problems facing corporations in the future. The need for a more systematic approach for evaluating the consequences of alternative managerial policies and socioeconomic and political events on the future of the corporation has become self-evident. A change in pricing or advertising policies affects production operations, cash flow, and the profit-and-loss statement. Difficulty in borrowing additional funds to finance inventories leads to reverberations not only in the balance sheet but also in marketing strategies and production plans.

The problem is that everything is related to everything else. Ad hoc plans that focus on only one functional area of the business are likely to be myopic and ineffective, which can lead the firm into troubled waters. In order to survive during these turbulent days, corporate plans must be both comprehensive and systematic.

Corporate planning models are an attractive, viable alternative to informal, ad hoc planning procedures. The uses of corporate planning models vary from company to company, depending on managerial objectives. The Memorex Corporation used a financial planning model to negotiate a more favorable line of credit with a bank. A Swedish shipyard employs a corporate financial model to determine which currencies to use to buy raw materials when building ships and which currencies to use when the ships are sold. Merger and acquisition decisions are evaluated with the Dresser Industries model. The treasurer of United Air Lines generates alternative financial scenarios with across-the-board fare increases, additions and deletions of different types of flight equipment, and increases in the price of jet fuel. On the other hand, American Airlines uses a corporate marketing model to forecast the profitability of different cities in its route structure. Firms like Monsanto, Tenneco, and Royster use corporate planning models to forecast cash requirements.

WHO IS USING CORPORATE MODELS?_____

In our survey we asked those firms using corporate simulation models to indicate the actual users of the model. The results are shown in Table 1. The table shows the percentage of firms in our sample for which a particular person is receiving and using information produced by the corporate model.

TABLE 1
People Receiving and Using Output from the Model

User	Percentage
Vice-president of Finance	55
President	46
Controller	46
Executive vice-president	32
Treasurer	30

TABLE 2
Sales of Firms Using Corporate Models

Sales	Percentage
Under $50 million	7
$50 million to $100 million	3
$100 million to $250 million	8
$250 million to $500 million	16
$500 million to $1 billion	21
Over $1 billion	38
No response	7
Total	100

These results are indeed encouraging, for they indicate that in approximately half of the corporations using corporate simulation models, the right people are receiving and actually using the output generated by the models. There is abundant evidence available to support the hypothesis that it is crucial to the success of any corporate modeling project to have the active participation of top management in both the problem-definition phase of the project and the implementation stage. The fact that the president and senior financial executive of half of the firms using corporate models employ these models bodes well for the future of corporate modeling.

Next we examine the relative size of the firms in our sample which are using corporate simulation models. Total sales are used as a measure of the size of these corporations. Although over half of the firms in our sample have sales in excess of $500 million, it is interesting to note that 10 percent of the users of corporate models have sales of less than $100 million. With the advent of timesharing computer languages, which facilitate the development of corporate planning models, corporate modeling is now economically feasible for firms with sales less than $10 million.

WHY ARE CORPORATE MODELS USED?

Financial applications dominate the list of reasons why corporations are using corporate planning models. Cash-flow analysis, financial forecasting, balance-sheet projections, financial analysis, pro forma financial reports, and profit planning are among the leading applications of corporate simulation models. Table 3 contains a summary of existing applications of corporate models based on our survey results. The listing shows the percentage of firms in our sample of users that make use of a particular application.

HOW ARE THEY USED?

Next we shall analyze the results of a series of questions in our survey aimed at determining how corporate models are used. Table 4 indicates that corporate simulation models are used most often to evaluate alternative policies; to provide financial projections; to facilitate long-term planning; to make decisions; and to facilitate short-term planning.

RESOURCE REQUIREMENTS

Most of the existing corporate models (67 percent) were developed in-house without any outside assistance from consultants; 24 percent were developed

TABLE 3
Applications of Corporate Models

Applications	Percentage
Cash-flow analysis	65
Financial forecasting	65
Balance sheet projections	64
Financial analysis	60
Pro forma financial reports	55
Profit planning	53
Long-term forecasts	50
Budgeting	47
Sales forecasts	41
Investment analysis	35

TABLE 4
How Corporate Models Are Used

Use	Percentage
Evaluation of policy	79
Financial projections	75
Long-term planning	73
Decision making	58
Short-term planning	56
Preparation of reports	47
Corporate goal setting	46
Analysis	39
Confirmation of another analysis	35

in-house with outside consulting; and 8 percent were purchased from an outside vendor. Eighteen man-months was the average amount of effort required to develop models in-house without outside assistance. The average cost of those models was $82,752. For these models developed in-house with the help of outside consultants, the average elapsed time required to complete the model was ten months. The average cost for those models was $29,225. In terms of computer hardware, 42 percent of the models are run on in-house computing equipment; 37 percent are run on an outside timesharing bureau; and 19 percent are run both in-house and on a timesharing bureau. Of the firms using corporate models in our sample, 62 percent run their models in conversational mode, while 56 percent utilize the batch mode of computation. In our sample of firms using corporate models, 43 percent run these models on IBM computers, 5 percent on UNIVAC, 4 percent on Honeywell, 3 percent on Xerox, 2 percent on Burroughs, 1 percent on Digital Equipment Corporation and 1 percent on NCR. FORTRAN is by far the most widely used computer language for programming corporate simulation models. Fifty percent of the existing models were programmed in FORTRAN, 8 percent in COBOL, 5 percent in PL/1, 4 percent in APL, 2 percent in Assembler, and 1 percent in DYNAMO. Another 26 percent of the models were programmed in one of over forty planning and budgeting languages that are available to facilitate the development and programming of corporate planning models. These include such languages as PSG, SIMPLAN, and BUDPLAN. These languages tend to be much more user-(management-) oriented than scientific languages such as FORTRAN, APL, and PL/1. Although firms with sales less than $100 million typically would not employ scientific programmers, it is possible to teach financial analysts a language like SIMPLAN in a matter of a few hours. With the availability of planning languages on time-sharing bureaus, much smaller firms now find it economically feasible to develop and use corporate models.

Although econometric modeling techniques are not used very extensively even by the largest corporations in the United States, Canada, and Europe, we found that 57 percent of the firms using corporate models subscribed to some national econometric forecasting service.

CORPORATE MODELING TERMINOLOGY_____

A Taxonomy for Corporate Models. In describing corporate planning models, we find it useful to employ the conceptual framework outlined in Figure 1. We shall assume that a typical corporation consists of multiple divisions. In some companies, such as General Electric, divisions are called strategic business units. In other companies they are called groups or businesses.

We further assume that the corporation is completely decentralized; that is, each division has its own separate financial, marketing, and productive activities. Although there is a centralized corporate financial function for the corporation as a whole, there are no centralized marketing or production activities for the firm.

Each division can be represented by a division model, which consists of a front-end division financial model that is driven by a division marketing model and a division production model. For example, a corporation like

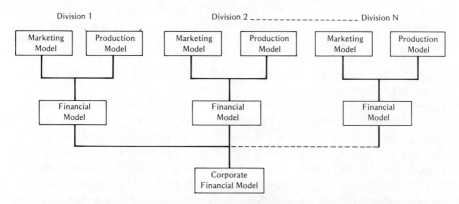

FIGURE 1   A Conceptual Framework for Corporate Models

Babcock and Wilcox has fourteen divisions. There will then be fourteen separate division models, each consisting of a separate financial, marketing, and production model. When the entire set of division models is consolidated, the result is a total corporate financial model.

In the following paragraphs we shall define exactly what we mean by division financial, marketing, and production models, as well as an overall corporate financial model. The conceptual framework described in Figure 1 is widely used among corporations that have developed some form of corporate planning model. Among the firms using this type of conceptual framework are Santa Fe, Monsanto, Dresser Industries, Honeywell, and United Air Lines.

Financial Models. The front end of every corporate planning model is an overall corporate financial model. The outputs of a corporate financial model consist of an income statement, balance sheet, cash-flow statement, and sources and uses of funds statement. In other words, the outputs take the form of the usual financial reports used by the financial management of the firm.

For a multidivisional corporation, a corporate financial model represents the consolidation of all of the separate division financial models. For example, the Dresser Industries corporate financial model is a consolidation of seven division financial models. Frequently these consolidations involve complex transfers of funds between divisions and are, therefore, not merely straightforward additions.

The individual division financial models are usually considerably less complex than the overall corporate model. A typical division model consists primarily of a profit-and-loss statement. In most corporations the concept of the balance sheet is meaningless at the division level. Revenue and sales forecasts are generated by the division marketing model. Operational and production costs associated with alternative levels of output are generated by the division production model.

The corporate financial model can be used to check the economic feasibility of alternative financial plans for the different divisions of the firm. These models can also be used to evaluate the financial impact of alternative cash management, depreciation, capital investment, and merger-acquisition.

Both division financial models and corporate financial models are relatively straightforward to develop. They are essentially definitional in concept and are based entirely on the firm's given accounting relationships.

Marketing Models. Each of the division models in Figure 1 has its own marketing model. Marketing models are used to explain or predict sales and market share by product or major project group. We shall consider two different types of marketing models—short-term forecasting models and econometric policy analysis models. Short-term forecasting models are naive, mechanistic models, devoid of any explanatory power. They cannot be used to do "what if" analysis. On the other hand, econometric models are rich in explanatory power and may be used to link sales to the national economy and to conduct marketing policy simulation experiments. With econometric marketing models, it is possible to simulate the effects on sales and market share of alternative advertising, pricing, and promotional policies.

Marketing models provide the sales forecasts that are required to drive both financial and production models. That is, sales forecasts generated by marketing models are external to both financial and production models. Table 5 indictes the extent to which forecasting models have been utilized in the corporate models in our sample.

Production Models.   Each division model in Figure 1 also contains a production model. For given levels of output, production models generate operating costs and cost of goods sold. Our approach to production models is essentially an activity-analysis approach in which the cost of operating at different levels of output is built up in terms of the resource requirements for each production process. Some firms, such as Exxon, CIBA-GEIGY, Schlitz, and Anheuser-Busch, have used mathematical programming to determine the minimum-cost production schedule for each level of output. This is one area of corporate modeling in which there is a definite need for more theoretical development as well as empirical experience.

Sales forecasts generated by marketing models provide input into production models. On the other hand, production models yield cost of goods sold and other production information required by financial models.

TABLE 5
Forecasting Techniques Used in Corporate Models

Forecasting Technique	Percentage
Growth rate	50
Linear time trend	40
Moving average	22
Exponential smoothing	20
Nonlinear time trends	15
Adaptive forecasting	9
Box-Jenkins	4

Corporate Models. Of those firms that indicated they are using a corporate simulation model, 39 percent claimed to have modeled the "total company." We suspect that this figure overstates the case and may reflect differences in interpretation of what constitutes the total company. In actual practice, relatively few firms have managed to integrate the financial, marketing, and production activities of the firm into truly integrated corporate simulation models. Three notable exceptions to this rule are CIBA-GEIGY, IU International, and Anheuser-Busch.

Each of these firms has successfully achieved development and implementation of a total corporate simulation model. The CIBA-GEIGY model is probably the most sophisticated in existence today. It is used extensively by corporate and division management to evaluate long-range plans.

Most of the corporate planning models (76 percent) in use today are "what if" models—models which simulate the effects of alternative managerial policies and assumptions about the firm's external environment. Only 4 percent of the models in our sample were optimization models in which the goal was to maximize or minimize a single objective function, such as profit or cost, respectively. However, 14 percent of the models use both approaches. The remainder of the firms in our sample either did not respond to the question or use some other approach.

DEFINITION OF VARIABLES

Fundamental to the specification of a corporate model or some component thereof is the definition of the variables to be included in the model. Figure 2 provides a framework for classifying these different types of variables.

The box in Figure 2 may represent either the corporation or the financial, marketing, or production component of the firm. Our objective is to

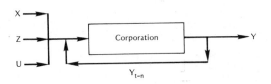

FIGURE 2   Flow Chart of Variables in a Corporate Model

formulate a set of mathematical and logical relationships between a set of output variables given by Y and a set of *input variables—X, Z, U*, and Y_{t-n}.

Output Variables.   We use the symbol Y to denote the output variables describing the behavior of a firm or one of its components. Depending on whether one is a mathematician, a statistician, or an econometrician, the Y's may be called either *dependent* variables, *response* variables, or *endogenous* variables.

The output variables of a corporate financial model are the line items of the income statement, balance sheet, cash-flow statement, or sources and uses of funds statement. Marketing output variables include market share and sales by product. Units of output and cost of goods sold represent output variables in a production model. The output variables of a corporate model are set in place when the goals and objectives of the model are defined. They basically represent the indicators by which management judges the performance of the firm or some subsystem of the firm.

External Variables.   Certain variables affect the behavior of a company but are not affected by the behavior of that corporation. These are called *external* or *exogenous* variables. We use the symbol X to represent these variables, which are too important to ignore. Causality is assumed to be unidirectional in the case of external variables. That is, X is assumed to influence Y, but Y has only a negligible effect on X. Furthermore, X is read into the model and is neither explained nor forecasted by the model.

The most obvious example of an external variable is the national economy of a country to which a corporation sells. Other external variables might include social and political events, strikes, and national disasters. "Watergate" is a good example of such an event. Wars, economic boycotts, and labor disputes are also examples of crucial external variables. Although variables of this type are difficult, if not impossible, to model and predict, it is indeed possible to model and predict the impact of such events on the future performance of the firm. This is an extremely important point.

We have often heard managers say, "We cannot use models because there are too many unpredictable, uncontrollable factors influencing the performance of our business." These managers have entirely missed the point. Consider the case of Standard Oil of Ohio (SOHIO), which owns over 50 percent of the Alaskan oil field. The financial future of SOHIO depends very much on whether the Alaskan pipeline is completed. SOHIO had no model to predict whether or not the Congress would approve the pipeline. They had no model to predict when the pipeline might be completed. But they did have a model to simulate the effects on SOHIO's financial structure of alternative (hypothesized) completion dates for the pipeline. They can project their cash requirements for alternative completion dates for the pipeline long before it is actually completed.

The interface between external events and corporate models is crucial. There must be someone on the corporate modeling team who is familiar with the global environment of the firm and can anticipate the different types of external events that may affect the firm.

Policy Variables. The policy variables are the variables over which management can exercise some degree of control. Financial policy variables might include such variables as cash-management policy, debt-management policy, taxation policies, depreciation policies, and merger-acquisition decisions. Marketing policy variables include pricing decisions, advertising policies, promotional policies, and geographic location of salesmen. Capital investment decisions, new product decisions, and plant locaton decisions are examples of production policy variables. The symbol Z is used to represent policy variables.

Random Variables. Frequently when we construct corporate planning models there may be considerable risk and uncertainty associated with particular forecasts. For example, suppose we feel it is quite likely that sales revenues will increase by 10 percent by next year. However, there is some chance that they may increase by as much as 15 percent. On the other hand, sales could decrease by 10 or 15 percent.

When we are uncertain about the exact value of a particular variable or parameter in our model, we may want to make use of a concept known as *risk analysis*. For example, we may want to treat sales as a *random variable* with a given or estimated probability distribution. We use the symbol U to represent random or probabilistic variables with a given probability distribution. By including random variables in the model we can test the sensitivity of the model to random shocks, perturbations, and extreme values.

Unfortunately, by introducing random variables into our model we increase the complexity of the analysis rather considerably. For this reason, we do not recommend the use of random variables and risk analysis with the initial formulation of corporate models. Indeed, we recommend that the model builder should spend at least a year getting acquainted with the deterministic version of his model before introducing risk analysis. Our survey of users of corporate planning models found that only 6 percent of the models in current use involve risk analysis—the remaining 94 percent are deterministic models.

Lagged Output Variables. To make the model dynamic and more realistic we also introduce lagged output variables Y_{t-n}. The rationale for including lagged output variables is that corporations are ongoing, dynamic enterprises. For example, sales today depend in part on sales last month, the month before, and the month before that. We represent lagged output variables by sequences of the following type: $Y_{t-1}, Y_{t-2}, \ldots Y_{t-n}$.

MODEL SPECIFICATION

Once we have defined the input and output variables for our model, we must then specify a set of mathematical and logical relationships linking the input variables to the output variables. The average number of equations in the models in our sample was 545. The range varied from 20 equations to several thousand equations. Most of the equations are definitional equations, which take the form of accounting identities. The average number of definitional equations was 445. The average number of behavioral (empirical) equations was only 86. Behavioral equations take the form of theories or hypotheses about the behavior of certain economic phenomena. They must be tested empirically and validated before they are incorporated into the model.

Definitional Equations. Definitional relationships are exactly what the term implies—mathematical or accounting definitions. Definitional relationships are encountered most often in the formulation of corporate financial models. They are typically defined by the firm's accountants and financial analysts. The following is an example of a definitional equation.

$$CASH = CASH(-1) + CAR + NDEBT$$

$$- NASSET - PAP - LPAY \tag{1}$$

Equation (1) is a typical cash equation in a corporate financial model. It states that beginning cash (CASH) is equal to previous period cash [CASH (-1)] plus collection of receivables (CAR) plus borrowing (NDEBT) minus the purchase of assets (NASSET) minus the payment of accounts payable (PAP) minus loan repayments (LPAY).

Equation (2) provides a second example of a definitional equation.

$$INV = INV(-1) + MAT + DL - CGS \tag{2}$$

It may be interpreted as follows. Beginning inventory (INV) is equal to previous period inventory [INV(−1)] plus new material purchases (MAT) plus direct labor costs (DL) minus the cost of goods sold (CGS).

Some definitional equations are determined by government regulations such as tax laws, investment credit allowances, and depreciation rates.

Behavioral Equations.   Behavioral relationships are hypotheses that are subject to empirical testing and validation. They are theories that reflect management's understanding of certain internal and external relationships affecting the firm.

Perhaps the best known behavioral model is what economists call the "law of demand."

$$Q = a - bP \tag{3}$$

The thrust of the specification of equation (3) is that higher prices (P) will be associated with reduced consumption of the commodity or product (Q) in question. Graphically, this hypothesis can be expressed as shown in Figure 3.

The law of demand can be tested empirically. We can collect some data on P and Q, estimate the parameters a and b, and determine whether or not there is a significant negative relationship between P and Q. (This is an oversimplification, for there are certain well-known econometric problems in dealing with such a simplistic model.)

Equation (4) represents a more realistic example of a behavioral equation.

$$SALES = a + bP + cADV + dGNP + eRD + fP_c + u \tag{4}$$

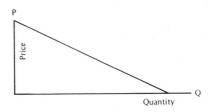

FIGURE 3   The Law of Demand

This equaton hypothesizes a linear relationship between the quantity sold of a given product and price (P), advertising expenditures (ADV), Gross National Product (GNP), research and development expenditures (RD), the price of the firm's leading competitor (P_c), and a random error term (u). If we have time series or cross-sectional data on SALES, P, ADV, GNP, RD, and P_c, we can test the statistical significance of the parameter estimates and evaluate the overall explanatory power of the model. Finally, we can simulate the effects on sales of alternative pricing, advertising, and research and development strategies. We can also experiment with alternative assumptions about the national economy as measured by GNP.

The Politics of Corporate Model Building

The political support of top management is crucial to the successful implementation of any corporate simulation model. Although suitable models and computer software are necessary for the success of corporate modeling, they are by no means sufficient. If the president of the company or at least the vice-president of finance is not fully committed to the use of a corporate model, then the results are not likely to be taken seriously and the model will see only limited use.

To get some feeling for the political environment in the firms where corporate modeling is being used, we asked a series of attitudinal questions concerning the interest of management in the corporate modeling activities of their firm. The findings displayed in Table 6 seem to imply that the corporate models included in our survey enjoy a relatively high degree of political support from management. In 60 percent of the firms using corporate models, top management is "somewhat interested" in corporate

TABLE 6
Attitudes of Management Toward Corporate Modeling

Attitude	Top Management	Planning	Finance	Marketing
Very Interested	30%	67%	54%	23%
Somewhat Interested	60	22	37	39
Indifferent	8	4	5	24
Not at all Interested	1	1	3	8
No Response	1	1	1	6

modeling, while in another 30 percent they are "very interested." On the other hand, the degree of interest in corporate modeling expressed by planning departments and finance is even higher.

BENEFITS OF CORPORATE SIMULATION MODELS

The primary benefits to be derived from the use of corporate simulation models stems from the ability to use these models to conduct "what if" experiments. That is, alternative scenarios can be generated reflecting a wide variety of different managerial policies and assumptions about the external environment in which the firm will operate. Scenarios can be produced almost as fast as the human mind can conceive of alternative policies or assumptions about economic, political, and social conditions confronting the firm.

Once one has developed an adequate data base, formulated a set of mathematical and logical relationships describing the firm's functional activities, and expressed the relationships in the form of a computer program, then one automatically has the ability to answer two other equally important questions. We call these the "what is" and "what has been" questions. That is, if one has gone to the trouble to construct a corporate simulation model, then a natural by-product of such an undertaking is the capability to access the firm's data base and ask questions about the current status of sales, cost of goods sold, cash, profitability, and so on. In other words, a corporate simulation model can be used as the front-end of a management information system.

But not only can we answer the "what is" types of questions, we can also answer the "what has been" questions. Again, using the corporate model as the front-end of a total management information system, we can interrogate the data base and produce instantaneous historical reports. We can also conduct experiments with the historical data to ascertain what might have been. In other words, we may want to evaluate the previous consequences of alternative strategies that have been used in the past as a means of providing guidance in developing long-range plans for the future.

According to our survey, the major benefits that present users of corporate models have derived include: ability to explore more alternatives; better quality decision making; more effective planning; better understanding of the business; and faster decision making.

TABLE 7
Benefits of Corporate Models

Benefit	Percentage
Able to explore more alternatives	78
Better quality decision making	72
More effective planning	65
Better understanding of the business	50
Faster decision making	48
More timely information	44
More accurate forecasts	38
Cost savings	28
No benefits	4

TABLE 8
Limitations of Corporate Models

Shortcoming	Percentage
Is not flexible enough	25
Poorly documented	23
Requires too much input data	23
Output format is inflexible	11
Took too long to develop	11
Running cost is too high	9
Development cost was too high	8
Model users cannot understand model	8
No shortcomings	9

LIMITATIONS OF CORPORATE MODELS

Opinions about the limitations of corporate models do not appear to be as intense or as well defined as opinions about the benefits of these models. The three shortcomings mentioned most often were lack of flexibility; poor documentaton; and excessive input data requirements.

THE FUTURE OF CORPORATE MODELING

As indicated previously, the number of firms using or developing corporate simulation models has increased from less than 100 in 1969 to nearly 2,000 in 1975. In a field characterized by such dramatic growth in a short period of time, one can anticipate rapid changes in both the technology and application of corporate models over the next ten years. If corporate simulation models are going to help management meet the challenges and the opportunities of the future, some changes must necessarily take place in the theory and application of these models.

First, there seems to be a definite need to make corporate simulation models more user-oriented. If top management is going to be motivated to participate in the development of a corporate model and to make use of the model once it has been completed, then both the model and the modeling language must be relatively easy to understand. Corporate models that have been written in scientific programming languages such as FORTRAN and APL do not tend to be very user-oriented. A number of the new planning and budgeting languages like SIMPLAN are highly user-oriented and greatly facilitate both the conceptualization and the coding of corporate simulation models.

Second, we anticipate that the use of production planning models linked into an overall corporate simulation model will become increasingly important. The energy crisis, shortages, and problems of declining productivity necessarily imply that greater attention will be given to production modeling than has been the case in the past.

Third, some firms may soon begin experimenting with the use of optimization techniques linked to corporate planning models. This linkage is likely to occur in two important areas. The most obvious area is in production planning, where mathematical programming routines can be used to generate the minimum-cost production plans associated with given demand forecasts. In addition, some firms are beginning to experiment with the use of goal programming and portfolio optimization models to assist in the allocation of resources among alternative divisions or strategic business units in the firm.

Fourth, although relatively few firms have successfully integrated finance, marketing, and production into a single overall corporate simulation model, there is every indication that we will see an increasing number of firms moving in this direction. In the past, these types of linkages were very cumbersome to do in conventional scientific programming languages. It was difficult to build in adaptability and flexibility. Some of the new corporate simulation languages greatly simplify the integration of finance, marketing, and production into a single corporate simulation model.

Fifth, a number of firms such as Xerox and General Electric are now beginning to experiment with models of the external environment as well as internal corporate planning models. We see this type of modeling becoming much more important during the next decade. A series of global economic, political, social, and environmental problems has given rise to a new breed of corporate futurists.

Sixth, we believe that both model builders and users of corporate simulation models are becoming increasingly aware of the importance of corporate politics in the successful implementation of a corporate planning model. Model builders are finally learning to speak the language of top management. Top management has learned to ask the right questions.

Seventh, and perhaps most important of all, we need to spend more time integrating corporate planning models into the planning process. This is the real challenge facing top management, corporate planners, and model builders alike.

REFERENCES

1. George W. Gershefski, "Corporate Models—The State of the Art," *Managerial Planning* (November-December 1969).
2. Thomas H. Naylor and Horst Schauland, "A Survey of Users of Corporate Simulation Models" (Durham, N.C.: Social Systems, Inc., 1975).

A. G. Kefalas

The University of Georgia

W. A. Pittenger

Officer in the United States Army

THE ENVIRONMENTAL IMPACT STATEMENT: A PERT NETWORK APPROACH

Since its inception, environmental legislation and its accompanying environmental controls have been the subject of considerable controversy. While some people have felt that environmental controls were long overdue, others have felt that the environmental concern became institutionalized too easily and too quickly. In any case, this institutionalization presented managers with one of the greatest challenges ever. Partly because of the novelty of the subject, and partly because of the "fuzziness" of the law, business management has thus far been rather slow to harness its analytical resources in an effort to comply with these new constraints and to control the added administrative burden involved. This paper proposes the application of an analytical tool for compiling and submitting an Environmental Impact Statement (EIS), an analytical tool long familiar to management, namely a computer-based PERT network analysis. The paper explains the logic of the

A. G. Kefalas and W. A. Pittenger, "The Environmental Impact Statement: A PERT Network Approach," *Journal of Environmental Management,* No. 3, 1975, pp. 309–327.

454

requirements of an EIS, a method for gathering and organizing the necessary data, and the types of output information generated for management control.

DEFINING THE ENVIRONMENTAL ISSUE

Few, if any, societal issues became institutionalized with such speed and ease as the environmental concern. Within a few years from the first demonstrations of ecology-minded groups, the U.S. Congress debated and finally passed into law on 1 January, 1970, the National Environmental Policy Act (NEPA). NEPA's organ for implementing and realizing society's goals for a cleaner environment is the federal Environmental Protection Agency (EPA). The EPA's 1970 mandate is summarized as follows:

> *The United States Environmental Protection Agency was established December 2, 1970, bringing together for the first time in a single agency the major environmental control programs of the Federal government. EPA is charged with mounting an integrated, coordinated attack on the environmental problems of air and water pollution, solid wastes management, pesticides, radiation, and noise.*

The true impact of environmental legislation was not felt until January, 1972—the target date set by the government for massive and rigorous industrial and municipal clean-up. While for some organizations the target date meant the end of their struggle for environmental clean-up (or at least the beginning of a serious, sound, and well-organized effort), for the majority it meant the beginning of long, tedious, and costly fights in which companies and cities battled to prove that they had exhibited "good faith" in complying with federal and state laws on air, water, and land pollution.

The NEPA authorized the EPA to identify and develop methods and procedures which would insure that presently unquantified environmental amenities and values be given appropriate consideration in decision-making along with economic and technical considerations.

In attempting to interpret and comply with environmental regulations, the manager is confronted with a gigantic puzzle whose dimensions and patterns have been constantly changed by the EPA, and whose pieces are occasionally stolen by the organized public acting as pressure groups, by city and state officials, and by the federal government.

The NEPA authorized the EPA to monitor environmental quality for virtually every industrial and municipal economic development project, from the construction and operation of dams and steel mills to shopping centers. Of particular interest is Section 102 of NEPA which requires a statement, now known as the Environmental Impact Statement (EIS), presenting "the probable impact of the proposed action on the environment."

The experience of industry and municipalities with the development and filing of environmental impact statements (EIS) has been mixed, ranging from cancellations of proposed projects to some pleasing and unexpected cost savings (*Wall Street Journal*, 1973). The cost associated with an EIS can vary from some $550 for a shopping center to the record $12 million for the 6000-page EIS for the controversial Alaskan pipeline. Time required for an EIS can range from several months to several years, as is usually the case with large projects (such as the construction of nuclear power plants).

In 1970, the Council on Environmental Quality published in the *Federal Register* the following guidelines about what should be included in an EIS:

(1) a description of the proposed action including information and technical data adequate to permit careful assessment of impact;
(2) the probable impact of the proposed action on the environment;
(3) any probable adverse environmental effects which cannot be avoided;
(4) alternatives to the proposed action;
(5) the relationship between local short-term uses of man's environment and the maintenance and enhancement of long-term productivity;
(6) any irreversible and irretrievable commitments of resources which would be involved in the proposed action should it be implemented;
(7) where appropriate, a discussion of problems and objections raised by other Federal, State, and local agencies and by private organizations and individuals in the review process and the disposition of the issues involved. This section may be added at the end of the review process in the final text of the environmental statement.
(Leopold, Clarke, Hanshaw and Balsley, 1970; p. 6).

THE DEPARTMENT OF THE INTERIOR APPROACH

The philosophy of the Department of the Interior was summarized in 1970 by the then Secretary Rogers Morton, as follows: "To be effective we must provide a system for relating large numbers of actions and environmental factors and for placing value judgments on impacts which are difficult to quantify" (Leopold *et al.*, 1970; p. 3).

At Mr. Morton's request the Geological Survey developed an Information Matrix System which provides:

> *a reference checklist or a reminder of the text of the environmental assessment to enable the many reviewers of impact reports to determine quickly what are considered to be the significant impacts and their relative importance as evaluated by the originators of the impact report (Leopold et al., 1970; p. 1).*

The evaluation of the environmental impact of a proposed action is based upon the estimation of (a) the *magnitude* of the impact upon a specific sector of the environment and (b) the degree of *importance* of the particular action on the environmental factor. A scale from 1 (minimum) to 10 (maximum) is used to estimate both the magnitude and the importance of the impact.

For all practical purposes the *magnitude* can be understood as the probability of occurrence of certain events which cause certain effects on a specific sector of the environment. *Importance*, on the other hand, refers to the actual degree of impact after the occurrence of that event has taken place. For example, oil spills and gas leakages are relatively rare phenomena and therefore will receive a low score on the magnitude scale. However, should a spillage or leakage occur, their effects on the environment will be great and therefore they should receive a high mark on the importance scale.

Nuclear power is a very good case in point. Although the probability of occurrence of a leakage of radiation from a power plant is very small and therefore the magnitude of the impact is also small, the nature of the impact of radiation on the human and physical environment is such that, despite all scientific assurances and television commercials by the Chief of the AEC, a rather high score should be and is placed on the importance scale.

The Geological Survey's Information Matrix for Environmental Impact Assessment represents a total of 8800 possible interactions between a set of (a) 100 actions which might cause environmental impacts and (b) 88 existing environmental conditions which might be affected. Each cell of the matrix must be filled with two numbers which reflect the quantification of the two criteria of environmental impact, namely magnitude and importance. Figure 1 represents a summary version of the matrix where only the main categories of actions and conditions are included along with the number of their respective subcategories.

It is fairly obvious that not all 8800 possible interactions would have to be evaluated or estimated in terms of both magnitude and importance. Some projects will require more extensive "filling" than others. The matrix does provide, however, a convenient and comprehensive look at the total situation so that the manager can plan for contingencies which will enable the firm to accomplish its objectives.

Submission of an EIS

Considerably more important than the actual compiling of an EIS is the submission of it to the appropriate agencies and the granting of the necessary permits. In completing an EIS the firm has virtual control over the resources it decides to invest in compiling it. If, for example, the firm desires to complete an EIS in, let us say, two months, it can either hire a consulting firm to help, or it can employ its own scientists to get it done. The degree of control both in terms of time and cost diminishes considerably, however, when the firm submits the EIS to an EPA office.

For the purpose of the evaluation, copies of the EIS and the comments and views of the Federal, State, and local agencies authorized to develop and enforce the environmental standards must be made to the President, to the Council on Environmental Quality, and to the public. Once the EIS is filed with the Council on Environmental Quality, any individual or organization has the right to file suit against the proposed action on the basis of insufficiency of the impact evaluation, or on the grounds that sufficient damage would be done to the environment which would warrant halting the implementation of the proposal. The conflict must then be resolved by the courts.

Preparing the EIS is in itself a complex, difficult task. Submitting it in correct order, to the proper agencies, and through prescribed channels presents almost as bewildering a problem. This process of obtaining approval for a proposal (the permitting process) can, however, be simplified through flow charting and PERT network analysis.

The Submission Process

The first step in simplifying the administrative maze is to grasp, in one macro-level view, the full range of activities and deadlines involved in the submission process. This can be done through a variety of methods, but in the case at hand the construction of a basic flow-chart model of the process probably helps to eliminate confusion. This process requires some initial research in the form of interviews and background studying, but is fruitful in that all posssible decision points, time frames, and parallel paths in the procedure become explicit for analysis. Figure 2 presents a portion of what such a flow-chart would look like for the analysis of an EIS submission. Of

I. PROPOSED ACTIONS WHICH MAY CAUSE ENVIRONMENTAL IMPACT

Proposed actions / Existing environm. conditions	A Modification of regime	B Land Transformation and construction	C Resource extraction	D Processing	E Land alteration	F Resource renewal	G Changes in traffic	H Waste emplacement and treatment	I Chemical treatment	J Accidents	K Others	Total 11 categories
	13 Sub-categories	19 Sub-categories	7 Sub-categories	15 Sub-categories	6 Sub-categories	5 Sub-categories	11 Sub-categories	14 Sub-categories	5 Sub-categories	3 Sub-categories	2 Sub-categories	100 Sub-categories
A Physical and chemical characteristics — 35 Sub-categories												
B Biological conditions — 18 Sub-categories												
C Cultural Factors — 36 Sub-categories												
D Ecological relationsh. — 7 Sub-categories												
E Others — 2 Sub-categories												
Total 5 categories — 88 Sub-categories												

II. EXISTING CHARACTERISTICS AND CONDITIONS OF THE ENVIRONMENT

The matrix combines 100 proposed actions which may cause environmental impacts and 88 existing conditions of the environment to produce an 8-800 cells matrix depicting environmental impacts in terms of:

MAGNITUDE: Degree, extensiveness, or scale of the impact on a specific sector of the environment

IMPORTANCE: Significance of the particular action on the environmental factor in the specific instance under analysis

FIGURE 1   Information Matrix for Environmental Impact Statement

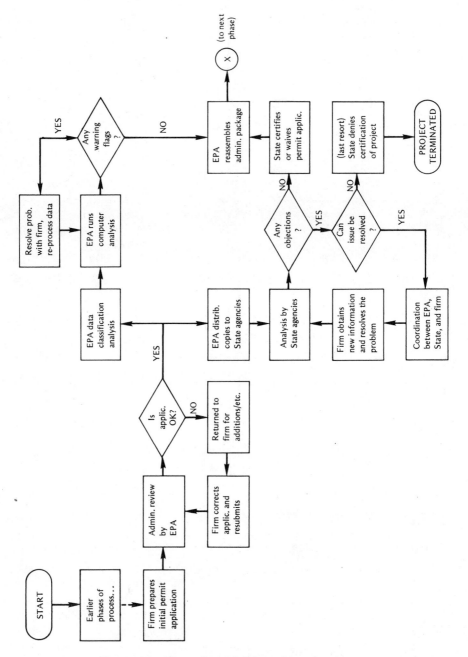

FIGURE 2   Flow Diagram of Decision Process

particular interest are the diamonds (indicating decision points in the process), and the nodes where processing continues in multiple branches. At this point the model indicates by whom the EIS is processed (outside the firm), and the possible consequences of certain decisions. It does not show what resources will be required from within the firm to accommodate this processing, nor how the firm can exert some control over its application.

Converting the Process Model to PERT

Figure 2 presents a logical view of the processing involved after the firm submits its EIS, but it does not provide the kinds of management information needed to enable the firm to guide its application through the maze with full insight into what could happen to it. This additional information which would answer questions such as: "What is this process going to cost? How long will we be in the red-tape cycle before we can begin construction?" can be generated by converting the analysis to PERT. This will re-orientate the analysis from the decisions involved to the resources (time and money) needed to push it to a successful end.

The first step in the conversion is to recognize the differences in the symbology of flow-charting and PERT networks. In the flow-chart of Figure 2, what happens inside the boxes (processing or decision-making) is the important aspect, and the lines merely connect these processing steps in an orderly manner. In a PERT network, each circle (denoting an event) merely indicates a particular "state of existence" which is different in some way from all other events. The arrows (denoting activities) indicate the actual processing involved, and can be constructed to show (by scale) the time or money consumed. At times, an important decision might not be explicit in a PERT network, since the concept of "feedback" or looping cannot be portrayed in the network. For example, the following PERT activity (linking events A and B) in Example 1 portrays the same process as the sequence of logic flow-diagram blocks in Example 2 (see next page)

Thus, while activity A–B in Example 1 could have been broken down into several smaller, successive activities linking A to B, it could not have shown the possible stumbling block inherent in the administrative decision to accept or reject the application as portrayed in Example 2. This is why it is imperative that a thorough understanding of the process be completed prior to going ahead with what are apparently the "proper" things to do.

In the illustrative case of a large utility firm contemplating the construction of a new power generating facility, the processing involved would result in the PERT network shown as Figure 3. It is important to note that, even where computer-assisted models are available to assist in the analysis

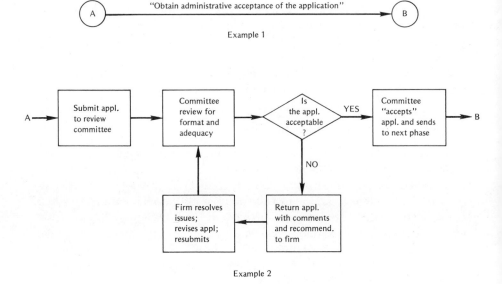

Example 1

Example 2

of the network, the construction of the network itself is an unavoidable task which must be done by human analysts.

Modifying Department of the Interior Information Matrix

After a PERT network has been constructed for the process, the next task is to obtain the information (i.e., time and cost estimates) needed to fill in the network. One way this could be approached in a systematic manner is to modify Department of the Interior's EIS Information Matrix (Figure 1), so as to identify the types and sources of required information. Figure 4 shows how the matrix could be modified to serve as a basis for the illustrative PERT network under consideration. The top (horizontal) axis would portray the activities involved in the submission process, as previously developed. The left (vertical) axis would portray, in some suitable fashion, the organizational elements of the firm involved. Intersections within the grid would be either null (indicating that this particular element is not involved in this activity), or an indication of the resources (in time and money) required for this element to do its share of the activity.

While the information within the matrix would not provide final estimates of the desired precision, the matrix would clearly indicate which elements would be involved in performing the activity, and to some extent the

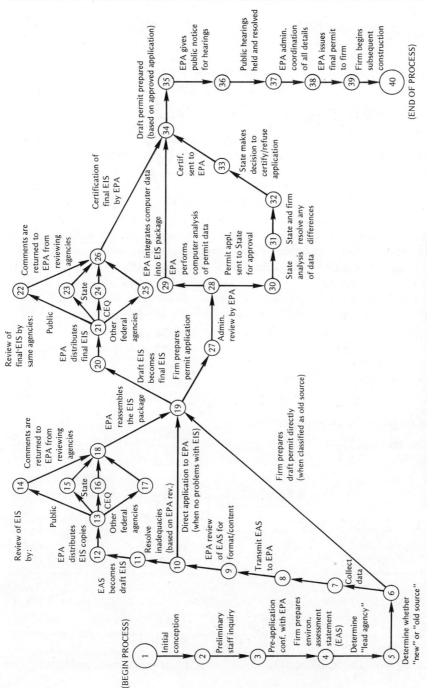

FIGURE 3 Detailed PERT Network Showing EPA Processing of EIS

resources required for their effort. At this point it would be relatively easy to construct a summary table to determine the numerical estimates required by PERT. Figure 5 shows an example of such a table used to calculate the estimates.

Implementing the Computer-Assisted PERT Analysis

At this stage of the analysis, management has a detailed PERT network showing the activities and events involved in the submission process, and has completed the estimates needed to compute the critical path and total time and cost involved. This process could be done manually, but for large networks the effort involved (and the probability of human error) leads most analysts to look for better methods. Such a tool exists in the form of computer programs which accept information about the network, compute the relevant results, and then display them in a variety of formats for user inspection. The authors used the PERT package which comes as an option to the software system for the Control Data Corporation Model 6400 computer, but other available packages would be equally acceptable. Since all of the programs commercially available will perform the same functions in computing critical path and least time/cost data, the only real measure for making one's choice of a package is the flexibility and variety of possible forms of output listings. The CDC formats provide sufficient flexibility to satisfy most typical requirements.

Description of the Computer Package

As an illustration of how the computer-generated PERT package would work, the network shown in Figure 3 was actually run, using the CDC-provided program. For each activity of the network, a card was prepared (according to the instructions which accompany the package) with the following data:

| Predecessor event no. | / | Successor event no. | / | Time estimates a / m / b | / | Activity name |

All information was extracted directly from the summary table shown in Figure 5, with the exception of "Milestone code" which will be explained shortly. The package also allows the network to be defined in terms which are suitable to the user to accommodate different time units, for example. Specific calendar deadlines, associated with the completion of certain events,

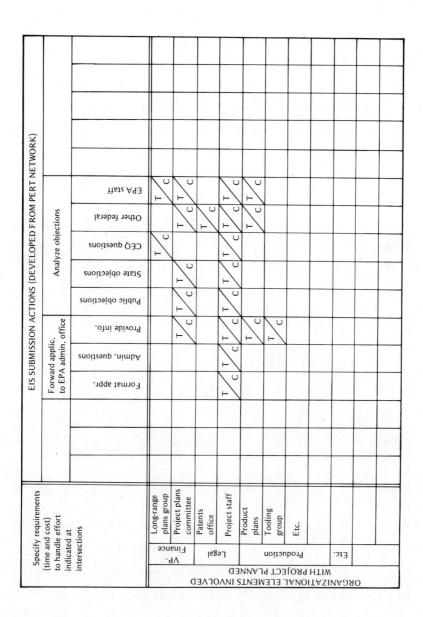

FIGURE 4   Grid Chart for Estimating Internal Resource Requirements
T = time; C = cost

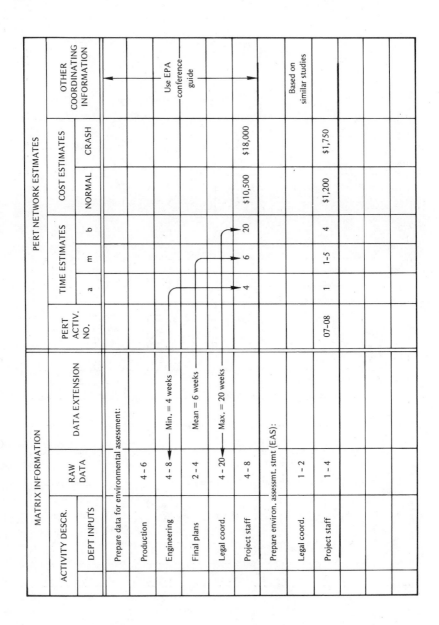

FIGURE 5 Converting Internal Estimates into PERT Estimates

can be specified, along with the operational data which explain the nature of the firm's work-week and planning calendar. The activity cards, along with a small set of package control cards, comprise the card input to the program. Most users would be able to implement the package with no prior training on either the specific package or the computer system in use, as long as they were prepared to actually use the package (i.e., they must have completed the previous phases of the analysis so as to have the proper input estimates).

Explanation of Results of Computer Run

After submitting the data for execution on the computer, the user would receive one or more output reports of the form shown in Figure 6. The output listings provide the following information:

(a) A list of all activities in the network, arranged according to the sequence specified in designated "sort-keys." The example shown lists the activities by (first) predecessor event no., then (where two or more activities have the same predecessor) by successor event no., then (similarly) by expected date (the T_E calculated from the specified time estimates, then by Latest Allowed Date (T_L in PERT jargon).

(b) Descriptive columns show the activity name, its T_L and associated completion calendar dates, the probability that the activity will be completed on time, and the amount of "slack" available at this stage for this activity.

(c) The "critical path" can be deduced from those activities shown to have zero amount of slack.

(d) The total time (and the related calendar date from the date of the project's beginning) are available under the columns corresponding to the final activity of the network.

The listing thus constructed shows all of the information generated by the computer analysis, but it can achieve significantly increased utility to the user by means of multiple reports. For example, the report shown in Figure 6 would be useful for a left-to-right overview of the entire network, but some of the available information is relatively "buried" within the report. This can be rectified by specifying (at data input time) another report arranged according to different "keys." For example, sorting the activities by the keys of (in order) "slack/predecessor/successor" would provide a list which begins by listing all the activities on the critical path of activities and events without further effort by management. The same thing could be done

PERT/Time activity report								
1st Sort key	Predecessor event no.	Name of project					Report date	
2nd Sort key	Successor event no.							
3rd Sort key	Expected date	EIS planning/scheduling simulation					03/15/75	
4th Sort key	Latest allowed date							
Event			Activ.	Dates			Remaining	
Pred.	Succ.	Activity description	time	Expected	Allowed	Prob.	Slack	Time
01	02	Initial dummy event planning	0-0	03/01/75	03/01/75		0-0	0-0
02	03	Preliminary inquiry	5-5	04/11/75	04/11/75	0-50	0-0	3-5
06	07	Determine/collect data, EAS	26-5	09/03/75		0-36	0-0	24-5
19	20	Draft EIS becomes final EIS	1-0	·11/20/75	05/20/76	0-89	25-2	37-2

FIGURE 6   Typical PERT Program Output Report

for listings which concentrate on the latest allowed calendar dates, or for time remaining for the completion of the activity.

A second type of output report which the program can generate (using the same input information) is called a "milestone report." At the time the PERT network is being constructed, it frequently becomes apparent to the analyst that some activities and events are inherently "more important" than others. Frequently, top management may wish to monitor the project, but do not wish to become mired down in all the detail of specific tasks. Milestone reports satisfy this need. If, at the time the data are recorded on cards for input to the program, a "milestone code" is attached to each activity and/or event, the program will generate a series of reports which focus on a specified level or levels of interest. Consider the three networks shown as Figure 3, 7, and 8. Figure 7 shows only those activities and events which are of interest to top management, thus allowing them to focus their attention on the critical phases of the project without excessive effort. For various departmental/project managers, the next network (Figure 8) shows the same process to a greater degree of detail, and specifies which events are included in the reports provided to top management. Lastly, (assuming that there is no utility in creating additional hierarchical layers) the final network (Figure 3) shows the network in full detail. The milestone reports generated by the computer would be in the form of a listing of events (similar to the

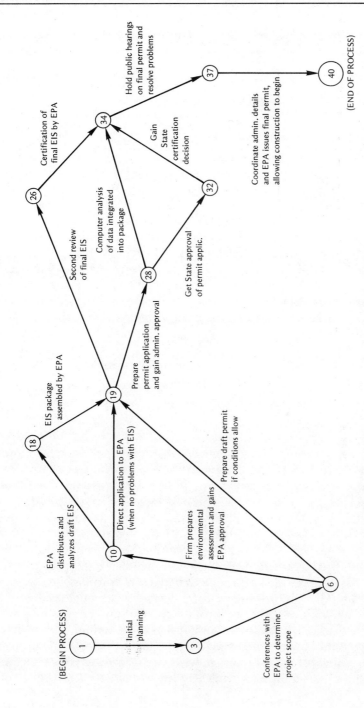

FIGURE 7 PERT Network from "Macro" Viewpoint (for Top Management)

other formats discussed above), but could immediately be transferred to graphical displays if desired.

Creating Worthwhile Information

It should be evident from the above discussion that before the computer program is called upon to provide information about the network under consideration, some forethought should be devoted to the kinds and amounts of output reports desired. As noted before, the program provides the same information in each of the activity report formats specified, but different formats emerge as being more useful than others. The computer does nothing that cannot be done by a reasonably careful human; what is gained from its use is more insight in less time, provided the package is properly utilized. Many of the reports which can be generated by the computer are suitable for distribution to various levels within the firm without the need for translation or explanation—but to gain the credibility in actual practice that is critical for their acceptance, the reports must answer the questions that management wants answered, while expending less time and money. These objectives can be achieved through the use of the package much more efficiently (after only a very short familiarization period) than they can through the efforts of numerous analysts doing the redrawing and recalculating the same data manually.

Using the Package for Sensitivity Analysis

During long-term projects such as the power utility expansion mentioned in this article, top management frequently is led to inquire (based on the information it already has received): "If we reallocate some of our internal resources from task X to task Y, what effect would that have on the project as a whole? How much would it cost to reduce the total project completion time by six months? If the project staff is limited to manual methods of analysis, the answers to these and similar questions may not be worth the cost of the effort required to get them. On the other hand, once the PERT network has been processed through its initial run, any number of variations can be examined with little extra effort, merely by varying the data pertaining to the network which is used from program input. For example, if each activity were originally described in terms of a "minimum," "most likely," and "maximum" time estimate, the original output report would provide a total time estimate for the project and the probability that the project would in fact be completed on time. This estimate would be a direct result of the

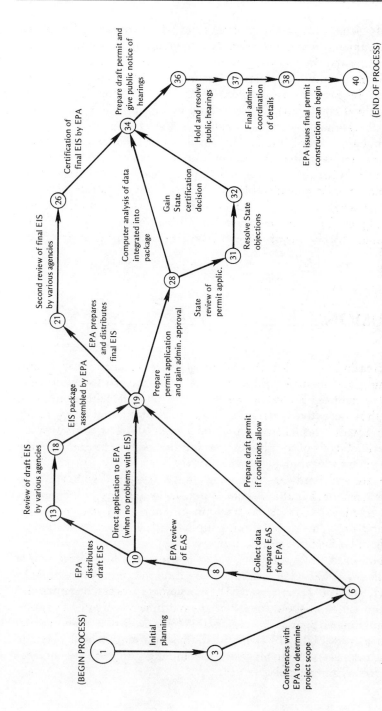

FIGURE 8 PERT Network Expanded to "Significant" Viewpoint (for Second-level Management)

variability of each of the activity times—the wider the spread between activity minimum and maximum estimates, the more variation there could be in the total time required. Now, if another computer run were to be made, using *only* the minimum time estimate for each activity, then the resultant total time for the network would constitute a "lower-time-limit" under absolutely optimal conditions. (There would be no probability associated with this time estimate, since each activity time was given as a point estimate). Similarly, a third run could be made using the maximum (pessimistic) activity time estimates, thereby providing a "worst-case" time limit. These two limits, with the original total time estimate located somewhere between could provide considerably more insight for corporate planners wondering just what the project's chances for successful completion are. Similar techniques could be employed for a break-even analysis of how much additional effort on the project would still provide a positive return on investment.

CONCLUSION

The ever-increasing external intrusion, both governmenal and public, into the functioning and management of private and semi-private enterprises has accelerated the need for extending the use of management techniques, which have thus far proved effective in dealing with internal tasks, to the task of dealing with external environmental complexity. The computerized PERT network analysis of an EIS described in this paper demonstrates the feasibility of such endeavours.

Both software and hardware technology have developed sufficiently to allow such extensions. What is needed is a meta-technology, which incorporates the creative use of managerial imagination for better problem-perception and problem-formulation, coupled with a better utilization of the powerful tool of information technology.

The computerized PERT network analysis presented here represents a small module of what may be called an External Environment MIS (ENVMIS) (Kefalas, 1975). Such an MIS will gather, process, organize and disseminate information about the external environment either as a supplement to an internal MIS, or as a separate unit. This evolution of an internal MIS toward a true total MIS (where external information will play the protagonist's role) is an inevitable process stemming from the ever-increasing demand for organizational openness.

REFERENCES_____

1. Environmental Protection Agency (1970), *Toward a New Environmental Ethic.* Washington, D.C.: U.S. Government Printing Office, p. 5.
2. Kefalas, A. G. (1975), Environmental management information systems (ENVMIS): a reconceptualization. *J. Business Res.*, July (in press).
3. Leopold, L. D., Clarke, F. E., Hanshaw, B. B. and Balsley, J. R. (1970), A procedure for evaluating environmental impact. *Geological Survey, Circular No.* 645.
4. *Wall Street Journal* (1973). September 27, p. 1.

Hugh J. Watson
University of Georgia

Ralph H. Sprague, Jr.
University of Hawaii

Donald W. Kroeber
James Madison University

COMPUTER TECHNOLOGY AND INFORMATION SYSTEM PERFORMANCE

Most managers feel uncomfortable making decisions that commit organizational resources to computers and information systems. This is understandable when one considers the potential consequences of computer-related decisions upon organizational efficiency and effectiveness, the data processing field's high and ever changing level of technology, and jargon that is almost incomprehensible to the nonspecialist. It is not surprising that many managers pass a majority of their decision-making responsibilities on to their data processing staff, a data processing steering committee, computer manufacturers' sales representatives, outside consultants, or anyone they think might be able to help. To be sure, outside advice and consultation are important; however, the manager needs a broad-based understanding of computers and information systems.

This article highlights recent advances in computer hardware and software *technology*, the *performance* capabilities of information systems, and

Hugh J. Watson, Ralph H. Sprague, Jr. and Donald W. Kroeber, "Computer Technology and Information System Performance," *MSU Business Topics*, Summer 1977, pp. 17–24.

474

the interface between these two areas. An understanding of these factors provides a basis for effective managerial action.[1]

Computer hardware and software technology and information system performance are separate dimensions of information system sophistication. However, various combinations of technology and performance can be assessed by considering rows that represent possible technological positions and columns that represent possible performance levels. A representation of this type commonly is referred to as a *matrix*. The one described above is useful both as an aid to *understanding* technology performance relationships and to *evaluating* information system efficiency. Let us begin by discussing the two matrix dimensions—technology and performance.

The familiar "computer generations" provide a convenient basis for considering information systems technology.[2] Each generation can be defined by a characteristic component technology, access or cycle time, storage capacity, programming techniques, and so on. These attributes are shown in Exhibit 1. There is general agreement on the nature and duration of the first three generations; a fourth generation is acknowledged, but it is less clearly defined in the literature.

First generation computers were based on vacuum tube technology. Memory type evolved from ultrasonic (mercury tanks), to electrostatic (vacuum tubes), to magnetic (drum and early core). The primary means of input was punched cards, while cards and printers were used for output. Programming of first generation computers was accomplished initially in machine language, later in assembly language, and still later in prototype procedure language (SPEEDCODE, AUTOCODER, FORTRAN). Commercial computers of the first generation included the UNIVAC I and IBM 650, 701, 702, 704, 705, and 709 models.

Second generation computers were distinguished by the use of transistors in place of the short-lived, heat producing vacuum tubes. Cards continued to be the most widely used medium for input, but tape, previously used only for secondary storage, proved effective for both input and output. Core became the dominant primary storage medium, while tape, disk, and magnetic cards were used as secondary storage devices. Access time in second generation computers was ten times faster than in their predecessors, and storage capacity was two to eight times greater. Although there were numerous programming developments in the second generation, FORTRAN II and COBOL were the most significant. Popular second generation computers included the UNIVAC II, IBM 1401 (card input), and IBM 1410 (tape input).

The *third generation* is characterized by widespread use of integrated circuits. Although main memory continues to be primarily core, access times

EXHIBIT 1
Attributes of the Computer Generations

Attribute	First Generation	Second Generation	Third Generation	Fourth Generation
Component technology	Vacuum tube	Transistor	Integrated circuit (IC)	Medium- or large-scale integration (MSI, LSI)
Memory type	Drum, early core	Core	Core, IC	IC
Access time	200–8 microseconds	20–1 microseconds	0.2–0.08 microseconds	0.1–0.01 microseconds
Main memory capacity	1–4K characters	2–32K characters	16–128K characters	10^5–10^{13} characters
Programming techniques	Assembly languages, early macroprogramming, FORTRAN	Procedure-oriented languages, COBOL, FORTRAN II	Procedure-oriented languages, multiprogramming, FORTRAN IV	Procedure-oriented languages, micro-programming
Other technologies	Punched card I/O and files	Card, tape I/O; tape files; early utility software (sort, tape-print, and so forth)	Tape, disk I/O; disk and drum files; advanced utility software; early data base management systems; multiprocessing	Virtual storage; data base management systems; teleprocessing; mini and micro computers
Examples	IBM 650, 701; UNIVAC 1	IBM 1401, 1410; UNIVAC II	IBM 360 series; UNIVAC 9200; Burroughs B-2500	IBM 370 series

have again been reduced by a factor of ten and storage capacity has been increased four to eight times. Third generation computers are often *systems* of hardware with a variety of input/output devices (cards, tape, disk, consoles, cathode ray tubes), a hierarchy of storage media (main core, extended core, disk, data cell, tape), and other peripheral devices (terminals, data entry stations, display stations). Third generation software improvements are most apparent in operating systems that largely control the internal functioning of the computer. Multiprogramming, a software advancement, permits the running of a second program while the central processor is not dealing with the first program. This capability increases computer efficiency. Multiprocessing, a hardware feature that allows the central processor to run two programs simultaneously, also was introduced in third generation equipment. The IBM System 360, with its many models, is most representative of this generation, but the UNIVAC 9200 and 9300, Burroughs B-2500, and RCA SPECTRA 70, also should be mentioned.

The *fourth generation*, which is just emerging, is more difficult to define. The characteristic technology probably will be medium- or large-scale integration, but holographic, laser, and grand-scale integration technologies are predicted.[3] In addition to third generation techniques, remote job entry terminals, point-of-sale terminals, and minicomputers are used for input and output. Integrated circuits are being used for main memory storage, with semiconductors and other advanced technologies predicted as major storage media. Access times have been improved by a factor of five over the third generation, and techniques that provide virtually unlimited storage have increased effective memory capacity by a factor of approximately sixteen. Only the larger models of the IBM System 370, with appropriate peripherals and features, can be considered fourth generation.[4]

SYSTEMS PERFORMANCE DIMENSION_____

The systems performance dimension reflects the various performance levels possible in an information system.[5] The levels vary from basic data processing to decision support systems. The attributes that define each level include the types of tasks performed, the nature of the data base, the use of decision models, the type of information provided, and the organizational levels served by the information system. These performance attributes are illustrated in Exhibit 2.

In the first stage, information systems perform only *basic data processing* tasks, and each task is a self-contained job (for example, payroll). No common data base exists since a separate file is maintained for each job. The

EXHIBIT 2
Attributes of Information System Performance According to Performance Level

Attribute	Basic Data Processing Systems	Integrated Data Processing Systems	Management Information Systems	Decision-support Systems
Applications	Payroll, inventory and personnel record keeping	Production scheduling, sales analysis	Production control, sales forecasting, capital budgeting	Long-range strategic planning
Data base	Unique to each application, batch update	Common to tasks within a system, batch update	Interactive access by programmers	Data base management systems, interactive access by managers
Decision capabilities	No decision models	Simple decision models	Management science models	Integrated management science and operations research models
Type of information	Summary reports	Summary reports, operational information	Scheduled and demand reports, management oriented information, structured information flows	Information to support specific decision-making responsibilities
Highest organizational level served	Submanagerial levels, lower management	Lower management	Middle management	Top management

Note: Only the most sophisticated attributes of each level are listed. Many lesser attributes are also found at each level.

output consists of processed transaction data and a limited set of summary reports. These latter are available to all managerial levels but are of limited value to middle and top management in carrying out their decision-making responsibilities (management control and strategic planning). Typically, no decision models are used.

The *integrated data processing* stage combines data processing jobs into integrated systems. Many of the tasks use more than one data file, and the same data often are used in more than one application. Still, almost all of the data processing activities involve the processing of transaction data and the generation of reports that primarily support lower management decision making. Simple decision models, such as for inventory control, begin to be included in the data processing system at this stage.

There are differences of opinion as to what constitutes a *management information system* (MIS). At one extreme are those who view it as a further integration of the processing of transaction data and the preparation of an expanded set of scheduled reports. At the other extreme are those who believe an MIS should provide all organizational elements with the information needed to function effectively. Somewhere in between are those who view the information system in terms of the beginning of an integrated data base. Demand as well as scheduled reports are generated, and these reports serve some of the information needs of middle and top management. Attempts are made to structure appropriate information flows to upper management. Decision support models commonly are used, but they are not well integrated into the information system.

Since 1970 information systems with unique characteristics and capabilities have steadily emerged.[6] These systems have been referred to by various names (management decision systems, strategic planning systems), but are now most commonly called *decision support systems*. Rather than stressing structured information flows, these systems focus on the use of decision models to support decision making. The decision-making tasks may occur at the operational level, but more commonly they are of a management control or strategic planning nature. In general, decision support systems feature an integrated system of decision models and data base to support one or more decision-making tasks.

MATRIX OVERVIEW

The dimensions of technology and performance can be combined to form an Information Systems Evolution Matrix as shown in Exhibit 3. Some general statements may be made about areas within the matrix. These will provide an introduction to the more detailed examination of the matrix cells which follows. The areas marked by X, Y, and Z indicate where information system performance is equal to, greater than, or less than the available technology.

The cells marked by Z can be categorized as *technology intensive*. That is, organizations in a Z position have considerable technology relative to their information system's performance level. For example, an organization using third generation technology with an integrated data processing system has more technology than performance.

The Y positions can be characterized as *performance intensive*. Organizations operating in this area are receiving more information system performance than might be expected given their available computer hardware and software. Relatively few organizations are in Y positions.

The X positions in the matrix represent a balance between systems technology and performance. For most organizations, X positions are preferred.

CELLS OF THE MATRIX_____

The Information Systems Evolution Matrix is composed of 16 cells representing the interaction of the four computer generations and the four performance levels. The cells can be specified through matrix notation by referring to their (row, column) position. For example, the (3,2) cell represents third generation computer technology with integrated data processing system performance. Matrix notation will be used, but not heavily relied upon, in the following discussion.

Although all matrix positions are theoretically possible, some combinations of technology and performance are rare, while others are common. The following descriptions focus on the individual matrix cells, their characteristics, cost effectiveness, frequency of occurrence, and historical place in the evolution of information systems.

In the early 1950s, when computers were first introduced for commercial purposes, almost all organizations were in cell (1,1). Early UNIVAC and IBM computers were used for basic, nonintegrated tasks such as payroll preparation and customer billing. Near the end of the first generation of computer systems, magnetic tape came into use for secondary storage. This made it possible for a few innovative organizations to begin the integration of their data files and, consequently, begin the movement to integrated data processing systems. Management information systems as they are now

EXHIBIT 3
Information Systems Evolution Matrix

	Systems performance dimension			
Systems technology dimension	Basic data processing systems (N,1)	Integrated data processing systems (N,2)	Management information systems (N,3)	Decision support systems (N,4)
First generation (1,M)	X	Y	Y	Y
Second generation (2,M)	Z	X	Y	Y
Third generation (3,M)	Z	Z	X	Y
Fourth generation (4,M)	Z	Z	Z	X

defined did not exist with first generation equipment. However, the ability to interrogate a data file, which is commonly considered to be a capability of MIS, was at the heart of several first generation computer-based library retrieval systems. Decision support systems were little more than a dream of visionaries.

Second generation systems with their faster tape drives, input/output software, greater tape storage densities, and sort/merge utility programs made integrated tape files increasingly feasible and led to a movement from basic data processing to integrated data processing systems. Some organizations, notably large manufacturing firms, aerospace firms, and Department of Defense agencies, attempted to use second generation technology to develop information systems with characteristics now attributed to an MIS. These organizations had mixed success, but in general experienced high development costs in trying to expand the capabilities of their second generation technology. Once again, as was the case with first generation technology, decision support systems did not exist.

Some organizations still are in (2,1) and (2,2) positions, but in a way different from the past. Organizations with limited data processing needs are using simple minicomputer systems for basic and integrated data processing. While the minis possess advanced component technology, their limited storage capacity, associated peripheral equipment, and operating systems properly place many of them in the second computer generation.

Some organizations, particularly smaller ones, are in (3,1) positions. Some of them did not automate until third generation equipment became available and logically entered the matrix at (3,1). Others arrived at this position as a result of one or two technological upgrades with no corresponding increase in performance. Of all the possible locations in the matrix, the most common for larger organizations are (3,2) and (3,3).[7] These organizations are realizing performance levels in keeping with their technological capabilities. The third generation is the lowest technological level at which decision support systems are feasible. Without third generation technology the software is either insufficient or inefficient for managing the data and model bases, and the hardware is deficient in data communications.

Organizations that use fourth generation equipment with basic data processing systems receive only a small portion of the potential benefits of their available technology. They are simply using their system for its number crunching ability rather than for its more diverse capabilities. Many organizations (banks and insurance companies) use and justify a (4,2) system on the basis of the huge volume of transaction data that must be processed. Many of these found that their third generation technology could be emulated on fourth generation hardware at less cost. Although these organizations may have cost-effective systems, they may be at a disadvantage with respect to competitors who use their technology more fully. Although there are few fourth generation systems (fourth generation main frame *plus* other fourth generation attributes) in use, many of them are used in (4,3) systems. Since any fourth generation hardware is quite likely a recent acquisition, many of these systems may be in the process of evolving to (4,4) cells. The relative rarity of both fourth generation technology and decision support performance combines to make a sparsely populated cell. However, decision support systems increasingly are being developed for use on fourth generation equipment.

IMPLICATIONS FOR MANAGEMENT_____

The important question for managers is: Where is my organization positioned in the Information Systems Evolution Matrix, and is it in the correct position? This question should be answered by all information specialists and by all managers who provide directional guidance to their organization's information system.

Based on our discussion of the matrix, managers should be able to identify approximately their organization's position. The second part of the question asks where the organization should be positioned. While this cannot be answered precisely, helpful directional guidance can be provided by considering once again the X, Y, and Z areas of Exhibit 3.

The Z cells have been identified as technology intensive; that is, they have relatively advanced technology in comparison to performance. Such positions are not always undesirable. For smaller organizations that obtain relatively sophisticated hardware and software capabilities to satisfy a heavy load of transaction processing, the costs of redesigning an information system to upgrade performance might not be justified by potential returns. However, managers of Z organizations usually should look to performance enhancement before authorizing additional technological upgrading. Of course, there can be exceptions. Insurance companies typically have advanced technology but elementary performance levels. While these companies often can justify their computer hardware and software on the basis of reduced clerical expenses, more can and probably should be expected of their information systems given their data processing staffs and the organizations' information needs. It is common for an organization to be temporarily in a Z position when there has been a recent technological upgrading of the system. This reflects the commonly accepted belief that it usually takes time for an information systems staff to utilize fully the new technology: consequently, a lag exists between the introduction of technology and its full utilization.

The performance intensive Y cells reflect, for the limited number of organizations positioned there, a situation in which more performance is being realized than might be expected given the available technology. Several years ago a number of banks and aerospace firms attempted to operate in Y positions and incurred heavy start-up, or pioneering, costs. Not all attempts have been unsatisfactory, however, and there is potential in some situations for substantial rewards. For example, the system might provide a unique competitive advantage for the organization, or elements of the system might be marketable as packaged software. In general, it can be said that Y positions can return big rewards but also carry risk and usually place heavy demands upon the organization's resources. Any organization contemplating moving to a Y position should ask if breaking technological ground is a valid objective.

For most organizations, X cells are the most desirable locations since they reflect a balance between technology and performance. Unless there exist strong and legitimate reasons to the contrary, managers should guide their organizations to balanced X positions. There is a tendency in some organizations to let performance consistently lag behind technology without justification. This is a natural tendency, since performance improvements require organizational, procedural, and attitudinal changes greater than those necessary for technology enhancements. Balancing information system technology and performance is the joint responsibility of management and the organization's information specialists.

SUMMARY

Information systems need to be analyzed in terms of their technology and performance. The Information Systems Evolution Matrix provides a useful framework for conceptualizing the relationship between an organization's technology and its performance capabilities. For most organizations a balance of the two is advised, even though performance-intensive and technology-intensive systems can sometimes be justified. But it is only after identifying where an organization is and where it ultimately should be in terms of technology and performance that management can provide effective directional guidance.

BIBLIOGRAPHY_____

1. A number of writers have recognized the relationship between technology and performance. See, for example, Robert J. Thierauf, *Systems Analysis and Design of Real-Time Management Information Systems* (Englewood Cliffs, N.J.: Prentice-Hall, 1975).

2. See, for example, Hugh J. Watson and Archie B. Carroll, *Computers for Business: A Managerial Emphasis* (Dallas: Business Publications, Inc., 1976).

3. Rein Turn, *Computers in the 1980's* (New York: Columbia University Press, 1974).

4. Interestingly, IBM does not refer to the System 370 series as fourth generation.

5. References to performance levels or stages are common in the literature. See, for example, Frederic G. Withington, "Five Generations of Computers," *Harvard Business Review* 52 (July-August 1974): 99–108.

6. See, for example, Michael S. Morton, *Management Decision Systems: Computer Based Support for Decision Making* (Cambridge, Mass.: Graduate School of Business Administration, Harvard University, 1971); and William R. King and David I. Cleland, "Decision and Information Systems for Strategic Planning," *Business Horizons* 16 (April 1973): 29–36.

7.-Donald W. Kroeber, "An Empirical Study of the Current State of Information Systems Evolution," Ph.D. diss., The University of Georgia, 1976.

EPILOGUE: THE FUTURE

"The trouble with our times," said Paul Valéry, "is that the future is not what it used to be." What is the future? Why suddenly is it not what it used to be? Why should a manager bother with it? This is indeed the purpose of this last section of the book: to sensitize the reader to the necessity of looking upon an organization and its place in a society as a long-range relationship rather than as an immediate and transitory phenomenon. Of the numerous approaches to futures research, we prefer and recommend the one that espouses the philosophy that the best way managers can make statements about the future of their organizations is by continuously scanning the external business environment and by organizing the search into alternative futures of their organizations. In this sense, this section of the book picks up where the Systems and Environment section ends.

The section on the future begins with Barrie James's "A Look into the Future of the Pharmaceutical Industry." James, who is a director of Strategic Planning for Merck, Sharp and Dohme International, studied the pharmaceutical industry and its external environment and published the results in a book. This article provides a summary of that work. James' recommendation of the scanning approach for the development of a future perspective of pharmaceutical managers is evident throughout the paper. In his words, "unless the pharmaceutical industry comprehends the value of the technique of influence and learns to understand and cope with social change by matching values and attitudes with those demanded by society, the industry will continue to suffer excesses of public control."

In the second selection, Theordore J. Gordon, a well-known futurist and president of the Futures Group, identifies five overriding crises that will

487

drastically affect human life in the next 20 years. These crises (1) nuclear war, (2) food scarcity, (3) deterioration of the biosphere, (4) imbalance in the distribution of wealth, and (5) material and energy shortages, will have tremendous effects upon society and its organizations such as business enterprises. Anticipating the crises, resetting organizational policies and objectives, and redesigning the organizational structure to accommodate them and even profit from an early proaction must be the job of the future manager.

The last article has a special meaning to one of the co-authors of this book—Professor Kefalas—because of the sudden death of the author with whom he was collaborating on the Project Forethought described in the paper. It is in his memory that this article closes this section of Readings in Management: Making Organizations Perform. *In "Alternative Futures for the Corporation," George T. Coker, Jr., who, until his recent death was with Shell Development Co. in Houston, Texas, speculates about the future of the corporation. His speculations are based upon his 25-year corporate experience and the experience of numerous corporate planners whose opinions and ideas he had solicited and organized as part of Project Forethought, which he created and coordinated until his death. Although Mr. Coker's dream for a fast "move toward the ultimate socializing mode in which the corporation is run entirely for the benefit of society," will never materialize for him, the probability for its materialization for us has been brought closer to realization because of concerned people like George.*

Barrie G. James

Merck, Sharp, & Dohme International

A LOOK INTO THE FUTURE OF THE PHARMACEUTICAL INDUSTRY

If we are to believe our daily diet of gloom from the media the world today is a hazardous place filled with economic, social, and political turbulence and we are slowly drifting into a new dark age. This fixation with doom has produced widespread malaise and a fear of what the future will hold.

Despite the predictions of the doomsayers the predominant issues of our time: the energy problem, economic stagnation, the population explosion, food shortages, and declining raw material reserves are all solvable. Unfortunately the pharmaceutical industry, along with the business community, has been influenced by this climate of pessimism and forecasts of the future tend to be colored by this pervasive despondency.

There is little doubt that the pharmaceutical industry will change shape, structure, size, and direction radically over the next ten to 15 years. There are, and will continue to be, exciting opportunities and challenges for the industry. However, these conditions should be placed in perspective. To look constructively at the future of the industry and to avoid the pitfall of an excessive focus on impending disaster it is necessary to look, albeit briefly, at the industry's recent past and at current trends. These two factors

Barrie G. James, "A Look into the Future of the Pharmaceutical Industry," *Medical Marketing & Media*, July 1978, pp. 13–21. © Navillus Publishing Corporation, all rights reserved.

will have a powerful influence on both the shape of the future and on the way in which the industry will develop and meet a changing and challenging environment.

The Belle Epoque

The 25 years between 1945 and 1970 were characterized by an exceptionally good operating environment for the pharmaceutical industry worldwide due to the interlinkage of a number of favorable economic, social, political, commercial, and technological conditions.

• Relative economic, social, and political stability combined with large and continuous growth in real income worldwide and particularly in the industrialized countries of North America. Western Europe, and Japan who account for the bulk of world drug innovation, production, consumption, and trade.

• Constant technological advancement culminating in the rapid development of more efficacious drugs with lower side effects and the ability to produce large quantities of drugs at low cost to the consumer.

• The formation of public and private healthcare systems in most industrialized countries together with increasing government subsidization to meet growing consumer demand for higher quality and greater quantity of healthcare services.

• Growing center and left political strength and the widespread adoption of the sociopolitical philosophy of the individual's fundamental right to health care on a "need" basis rather than the means to pay and equality of access to all services.

• The continued operation of a free market system within the growing public sector of the market with relatively low levels of government control over technology or competitive forces.

These conditions, which were instrumental in creating the modern pharmaceutical industry, have now either changed their form or have disappeared as a result of shifts in the environment.

An Era of Discontinuity

The 1970s released a flood of pent-up social and economic conditions which both radically and rapidly transformed the operating environment of the pharmaceutical industry. Many of these changes were so fundamental that they questioned the very institutions and circumstances which had created the spectacular post-1945 world growth and produced within a few years a series of new social, political, and economic orders.

These fundamental changes had an immediate and profound impact on the operating environment of the pharmaceutical industry.

Economic Environment

The early 1970s were characterized by the worldwide recession—a result of both the series of agricultural problems 1972–1974 and the 1973 oil crisis. For the first time nations became interdependent as a result of the gradual synchronization of national economies to world economic change which aided the transmission of recession factors. In reality an economic "domino" effect. The impact on the pharaceutical industry was two-fold.

• The philosophy of unlimited health care on a need basis is open to high levels of abuse and unnecessary overutilization of scarce resources and almost infinite interpretation. Services which were originally designed to cope with primary care, physicians, and hospitalization, as a result of public demand rapidly spread to secondary and even tertiary services. This expansion of services pushed healthcare costs to a point where health care now absorbs up to 10 percent of the GNP of industrialized countries. Cost control became inevitable and since the pharmaceutical industry rapidly became the sole private sector in healthcare delivery, attention was focused on the profits, pricing, and promotional activities of the industry. These moves were made despite the fact that ethical drugs rarely exceed 15 percent of total healthcare costs, have not risen in cost at anywhere near the indexed cost increases of medical personnel or hospitals, and are highly cost effective and thus of greater economic benefit than higher cost, labor intensive surgery, and capital intensive hospitalization where such substitutes exist.

• The pharmaceutical industry is highly reliant on the petrochemical industry for raw materials and packaging components and the 1973 oil crisis rapidly increased these costs. Similarly the round of inflation following the events of 1973, and which are still with us, produced very much higher energy, labor, and costs, most of which were unrecoverable due to the cost controls imposed by public healthcare services. Together with the liquidity-squeeze and currency fluctuations these factors played havoc with industry profitability and overturned the myth of the "recession-proof" nature of the pharmaceutical industry.

Political Environment

Political activity affected the pharmaceutical industry on two planes:
• The political commitment to public health care and the present pattern of state operation or virtual funding of most healthcare services has isolated

the pharmaceutical industry as almost the only private sector in the health-care market in many countries. The economic pressures and the heavy demand have outpaced the ability to fund many of these systems. Conse-quently there has been a vociferous movement for the elimination of the private sector and the accompanying profit motive from the healthcare market. Other arguments for state ownership of the pharmaceutical indus-try range from high levels of over promotion, to lack of competition and the wrongful direction of research toward commercial opportunity. State own-ership of pharmaceutical companies became a reality in Australia, Canada, France, India, Italy, and Sweden.

• The change in social attitudes produced a wave of legislation in the area of control over business activities in general and in specific pharmaceutical legislation. In the latter case the effects of legislation designed primarily to ensure greater safety and efficacy of ethical drugs have raised a number of issues. The cost of complying with the rapidly increasing and changing set of scientific criteria has become enormous and the bureaucracy necessary to evaluate product submissions has created a real time lag between develop-ment and marketing and consequently a gap in the physicians' therapeutic armamentarium between countries. Inevitably the increase in controls on safety and efficacy have served to constrain innovation by both reducing the number of new products as well as rapidly increasing R&D costs. The high publicity value of personal well-being has heightened political opportunism in the area of pharmaceutical legislation.

Social Environment

The effects of the transition towards a post-industrialized society with pragmatic social democracy in a participative society became widespread in the early 1970s and radically changed many traditional norms of society in industrialized countries.

Changes in contemporary cultural preferences, values and perceptions of need and of abuse have greatly influenced social behavior. Constant quan-titative increases in wealth have given increasing access to education, communication, mobility, and travel, and have contributed to the rise of social phenomena such as environmentalism, consumerism, feminism, and liberalism. These changes in social attitudes have also led to intense social scrutiny and public dissatisfaction with the way in which business operates, the tripartite interface between business, technology, and government, and the effects of industrialization on the social and economic systems. The greater participation in, and the growth of, wealth in the industrialized countries reoriented societal goals away from the basic economic necessities and the material pursuit of quantitative increases in the standard of living towards increases in the quality of life. This reorder of social priorities and public morality has strengthened the trend of the transfer of power away from the institutions toward the state and organized pressure groups. Changes in the social environment had both a rapid and many faceted effect on the pharmaceutical industry. In the short term the industry boomed as a result of social pressures on the political system for a greater quantity of healthcare services. This boom gave way to stagnation and low growth as a result of the economic pressure of meeting heavy demand with limited resources.

The very nature of drug therapy—largely palliative rather than curative—and a society conditioned by lay media to assume miracle drug cures questioned the credibility of the industry. This was followed by consumerist activity, primarily one of suspicion of the medical-industrial complex, due to the consumers' choice isolation by law and the scientific fact of life that no drug is completely nontoxic nor will it not produce unwanted side effects in certain circumstances. These trends programmed society to accept a lower level of risk for drug therapy and forced governments to impose progressively more stringent controls over the innovative and marketing functions.

Technological Environment

Research and development rapidly assumed a large role in the industry since the extent and success of R&D activities largely determine the future pattern of corporate earnings and growth. Until the early 1950s competition was largely based on price; however, the large innovative advancements in the 1950s changed the competitive stance to the ability to innovate and rapidly commercialize new products.

The mid-1970s brought a number of fundamental changes to the technological environment. New product innovation fell rapidly as a result of a complex series of constraints:

• A slowdown in advances in biological science which has failed to keep pace with those in medical chemistry and the lack of knowledge of the fundamental disease process and of the mechanics of action of existing drugs.

• Increasing regulatory requirements have forced many potentially valuable drugs from further development since the risks, although unknown, were assumed to be great. Similarly the public preoccupation with safety has changed the direction of private research toward drugs with acute, short-term usage, which offer less hazard and lower development cost than those for chronic and longterm degenerative diseases.

• Innovative costs have risen due to both increasing government control and the continued high levels of inflation. In the 1950s a new drug entity cost approximately $1.5 million to develop. By 1975 this was in the area of $30 million and by 1980 will be in the $40 million range. The inherently high risk factor of drug R&D and the inputs of large sums of cash and time, highly specialized manpower, and the use of costly advanced technology have weakened the ability of companies to fund innovative R&D activities.

Commercial Environment

The commercial activities of the pharmaceutical industry have come under wide attack primarily as a result of the changing economic conditions and social pressures on the political environment.

• Pricing has become possibly the main issue, with criticism resting on the supposition that unnecessarily high profits are being made through excessively high prices, thus profiteering on the weakness of human sickness as well as economic based criticism by the publicly funded healthcare systems. An outgrowth of this concern has been a welter of pricing controls on a national level with attention being paid to both finished prices in other countries as well as the transfer price of raw materials.

• Profits have received similar attention to that of prices since it is maintained that high profits are a direct result of excessive prices.

• Patents and trademarks have both been cited as granting monopoly situations for the holders and as such hinder free competition and offering to holders the opportunity to maintain high prices. This situation gave rise to the movement towards compulsory licenses, pirate drugs, and parallel importation in many countries.

• Promotion has been heavily censured for the techniques used which are assumed to have led to overprescribing and overconsumption and misleading claims. However, the main bone of contention has been in markets where public healthcare systems exist and it is presumed that the public is paying for the promotion of drugs and that this promotion is designed to increase drug expenditure at a time of economic pressure.

• Competitive activities of the pharmaceutical industry have been criticized on the theoretic issues of purchase choice, price identification, freedom of market entry, numerical competitive product alternatives, and the independent activities by all firms. These criticisms overlook the fact that the pharmaceutical industry is not a model of perfect competition due to the science-based nature of the industry with its high level of inno vation of highly differentiated products.

The Future Environment

Given the intensity, volatility, and direction of trends in the social, political, economic, technological, and commercial environments, the pharmaceutical industry will be operating in a new and hazardous world in the future.

Management will no longer be faced with the past tasks which centered around discovering, financing, producing, and marketing ethical drugs under relatively laissez faire conditions, but with a set of societal variables in a highly controlled environment largely determined by government acting on behalf of society. Each facet of the operating environment has a different set of conditions and implications for the pharmaceutical industry. Due to the synergistic nature of many factors, the individual environments are frequently interactive and interdependent.

Political Prospects

The healthcare market will become increasingly funded and controlled by the state throughout the industrialized countries. As such the existence of a private industry in an essentially public market will continue to be questioned due to the industry's high visibility. Demand will continue to outpace the ability to finance open-ended health care and governments will be forced to reevaluate the role and objectives of public healthcare systems. This will inevitably result in a major restructuring and rationalization of healthcare delivery with a heavy emphasis on increasing the operating efficiency which will, due to economic constraints, result in cuts in many tertiary and some secondary modes of healthcare delivery. It is unlikely that new services will be operated unless they are of a temporary nature and have overriding national implications such as mass vaccination programs. In the rationalization process, drug distribution systems may be acquired in the more socially oriented countries while indigenous production sources for a variety of nationalistic and protectionistic reasons may be fully or partly acquired or be forced to concentrate. Full nationalization, however, is most unlikely.

National and supranational controls of business will follow social perceptions of corporate abuse and the power of political interest groups and will result in both quantitative and qualitative increases in legislation covering all facets of business activity. The industrialized countries are moving toward a planned society. Governments in all countries are absorbing or directly influencing a greater share of GNP and, therefore, there is a growing temptation to interfere with and control the private sector of the economy.

Social Prospects

The main focus for society in the industrialized countries will be the pursuit of quantitative increases in the quality of life where political activity is influenced by the values and expectations of society, particularly in the areas of perceived need and responsibility.

It is unlikely that the pharmaceutical industry will be able to close the gap in values with society, however. The impact will vary from country to country. Similarly, the pharmaceutical industry will in all probability continue to underestimate purposeful and intelligent opposition in the short run; although in the mid-term there will be gradual increases in anticipation of, and sensitivity to, local social requirements. Consumerism will remain a progressive force, however, there will be some restraint of consumer sovereignty in the areas of complex scientific evaluation, and particularly in drug regulation.

There will be some voluntary moves to avoid criticism of the perceived disequilibrium of drug development. These moves will be limited by economic conditons and the governments of industrialized countries will fund most of these programs.

Indigenous intercompany cooperation in Europe will become widespread due to state direction of private sector research and marketing activity, for economic, social and political reasons, and will be a mix of voluntary and enforced cooperation.

Regulatory pressures will continue to be focused on society's perceptions of risk acceptance, and regulatory controls will be a mix of technical criteria and post-marketing surveillance. There will be eventual harmonization of drug regulatory requirements in Europe due to the EEC, but this will not advance on an international level outside Europe.

Product liability will become almost universal in the industrialized countries and will be a combination of enforced and voluntary adoption and a mix of individual and collective industry responsibility depending on the industry's response and local legal and political requirements.

Economic Prospects

The universal demand for health care will continue to outpace the ability of governments to fund supply. Open-ended supply will be curtailed and there will be an upper limit of 7 percent to 8 percent of GNP imposed on healthcare costs through economic necessity.

Cost constraint will force "best-buy" policies on healthcare systems and a greater number of formalized controls on prices and profits will be imposed. However, the economic importance of innovative drug therapy will be recognized in the more pragmatic countries and entrepreneurial rewards will be available if greater socioeconomic benefits can be demonstrated.

Formalized controls will also be imposed on physicians' prescribing habits and on promotional activities and access to price/profit criteria will become widespread.

Operating costs of the industry will move in line with general economic conditions. However, it will become increasingly difficult to fully recover cost increases due to price controls. This will intensify the liquidity problems of the smaller companies. Continued lower profitability will reduce R&D funding among smaller companies while larger companies will increase R&D to ensure survival.

The attraction of risk capital for all but the most financially secure companies may become a problem.

Technological Prospects

The technological plateau will continue well into the 1980s and new product innovation will remain at between 60 and 70 new chemical entities per annum. These products with a few notable exceptions will tend to be marginal improvements over existing therapy due to both technological problems and the need to avoid regulatory conflict.

Major innovation will be concentrated among the largest companies in the industrialized countries and fringe research will disappear as a result of economic constraint. Smaller companies will concentrate on "me-too" research as a result of increasing risk, high costs, and longer product payout periods although intercompany research nationally and transnationally will become widespread to assure access to new products.

Research activity will become concentrated in the epidemiologically more important disease states, particularly those of short-term acute nature to meet commercial criteria and regulatory problems. Government funding will increase in the area of the less epidemiologically important disease states and in tropical medicine.

Further innovation aimed at developing existing compounds and new delivery systems will depend on the socioeconomic importance attached to these developments by the pricing systems of healthcare organizations.

Commercial Prospects

The structure of the industry will change rapidly into large units with widespread merger and acquisition by larger companies of small and medium-sized companies which face liquidity problems as a result of price, profit, and promotional constraints and low levels of innovative output. To avoid political conflict these moves will largely be between indigenous companies except in the United States in view of stringent antitrust legislation.

Transnational acquisition will decline except among German and Japanese companies and by medium-sized companies seeking geographic diversification. Protectionism and nationalism will be the main deterrents of transnational acquisition.

The industry profile will change rapidly into a two-tier structure of specialist innovative supply and broad line generic supply, suiting the conditions in both industrialized and cost conscious segments in all markets. Small- to medium-sized companies will be forced to opt for one or other market segments.

A gradual change away from the traditional new product emphasis will occur toward a strong marketing profile devolving decision making to the marketplace with more focus on price competition and new promotional techniques.

Price will become more transparent and will be increasingly compared to other similar countries with rapid harmonization at all levels by voluntary and enforced measures.

Despite the extension of patent and trademark rights in the industrialized countries, compulsory license provisions will exist due to the widely held conviction that these contribute to monopoly and high prices.

Diversification outside the industry for those companies with access to adequate cash will become widespread as companies seek to minimize the impact of government controls. With the socioeconomic implications, few companies will seek to enter the pharmaceutical industry except by major acquisition.

The United States will lose its premier position in overall sales and innovation to West Germany by the early 1980s.

Implications for the Industry

Current trends imply a threat to the existence of many small- to medium-sized companies and the traditional ways in which the pharmaceutical industry has conducted its activities. However, these trends also imply considerable opportunity for those companies who are prepared to take the risk to invest and to influence change for the future.

The limits on commercial activity largely dictated by society and enforced by government, the cost consciousness of public healthcare systems and the short-term low growth of technological gain will change both the structure of the industry and the methods of supply and of market needs.

The large number of medical conditions where there are currently few and ineffective methods of control.

Theodore J. Gordon

President, The Futures Group, Glastonburg, Connecticut

SOME CRISES THAT WILL DETERMINE THE WORLD OF 1994

Twenty years, the time from now to 1994, is a very short interval when measured on a scale that dates the beginnings of civilization at ten thousand years ago. Two decades is an extension of two-tenths of one percent—only two more millimeters on the end of the meter stick. But perhaps because of our presence within it, because we experience change rather than only remember it, this next twenty years seems to be a crucial time, a time when diverse trends resonate, a time of climax, a time of the changing of revered values, a time when new capabilities and inhibitions change people and nations—their self-images and their myths. Twenty years is a generation; those in charge of institutions everywhere will retire, and those just entering will take charge. Within this twenty year period, two billion more people will be born and the world's invested capital will double. The amount of information recorded and transmitted may increase a hundredfold.

Indeed, from the standpoint of *possible change*, the next two decades seem fecund and profound. If we, in 1994, compared our lives then to our Olives now, we would, I think, find that the changes which seemed important came not only from science and technology but from the waxing and waning of institutions responding to external pressures and internal decay, from policies of governments and the values and actions of groups of people, but also from the unexpected action of the system which, through design or accident, links all of these agents of change together. These

Theodore J. Gordon, "Some Crises That Will Determine the World of 1994," *The Futurist*, June 1974, pp. 115–121.

unexpected system responses can be crises. We would, in describing our 1994 lives, be inclined to discuss not only new medical advances and laser fusion, not only welfare programs and the newest forms of mystic religion, but also the crises of the moment. Who, for example, in describing our time to a visitor from the past, would fail to include the energy crisis in his first list of descriptors of the present? Crises are unexpected consequences of the functioning of the complex and seemingly chaotic system which links agents of change together. Without focusing on potential crises, as depressing as that might be, we will know little of the potential world of 1994 and, more importantly, little of the immediate need for creative and decisive policy-making.

It's one thing to suggest that recognizing key future crises can form an interesting forecasting model; it's quite another to develop a metric for selecting a subset of issues to address. John Platt in his essay "What We Must Do," (included in his book *Perception and Change*, University of Michigan Press, Ann Arbor, 1970), suggested measures of crisis intensity, including the number of people likely to be affected, the degree of the effect, and the time until the effect is realized. In Platt's scaling, a grade 1 crisis represents total annihilation; a grade 2 crisis, great destruction or physical, biological, or political change; a grade 3 crisis, almost unbearable world tension, and so on.

Recent work in technology assessment has added other criteria to Platt's list. One might include "relative confidence" or certainty in the degree of effect of the crisis. For example, a potential crisis which is very uncertain and yet which could have a tremendous effect might be accorded a very high priority. The list might also include "reversibility," that is, the ability for any policy to reverse the consequences of the crisis. An irreversible crisis is, of course, much worse than a reversible one. Finally, "responsibility" could be an important priority-ordering criterion: If the responsibility for curing a crisis lies clearly within some existing institution's mission, the deleterious effects of the crisis might be mitigated. Alternatively, if the crisis falls in the province of more than one institution, jurisdictional disputes may inhibit clear-cut and decisive action.

Thus the dimensions by which the severity of a future crisis might be judged include:

1. Number of people affected
2. Degree of effect
3. Probability of timing of the impact
4. Reversibility
5. Responsibility

Some Important World Crises

	CRITERIA					
CRISIS	Number of People Affected	Severity of the Effect	Probability	Reversibility of the Course of Development	Responsibility	Confidence in Judgment
Nuclear war	Very Large	Very Great	Very Low	Possible	Diffuse	Moderate
Severe food shortages	Very Large	Very Great	High	Possible	Diffuse	High
Deterioration of the biosphere	Very Large	Moderate-Great	Moderate	Difficult	Diffuse	Low
Imbalances in the distribution of wealth	Very Large	Great	Very High	Very Difficult	None	Moderate
Material and energy shortages	Large	Moderate-Great	Very High	Very Difficult	None	High

6. Confidence in judgments

[Note: These criteria are clearly not of equal weight.] A most important crisis would be one in which a large number of people are likely to be severely affected, almost immediately, in an irreversible way, with no institutions clearly having responsibility for detecting or curing the problem. This situation would obtain at either of two levels of confidence; great certainty in the judgments, or great uncertainty.

What then are some of the issues which meet these criteria and should be addressed in defining the world of 1994? While I am sure others can extend this list considerably, my nominations for the top five are shown in the accompanying chart. How we resolve these potential world crises, it seems to me, will define, in large measure, the context of our lives in 1994.

NUCLEAR WAR

There are under the oceans now and in silos in the United States, Russia, France, and England, nuclear armed missiles aimed at important targets. The balance-of-terror strategy seems to have worked; nuclear war, despite its world-killing potential, is not much on the minds of most people. The initial phases of SALT have gone well, and there is a spirit of détente in the world which has not been paralleled since World War II.

Yet there are indications that the balance of terror could become less stable. In the early days of nuclear war gaming, there were three generally recognized routes by which a large scale war might emerge: inadvertence, escalation of an on-going conflict, or preemptory strike. Have the dangers of any of these mechanisms been diminished?

Inadvertence—that is, an error of electronics or detection—is still conceivable and becomes more probable as increasingly complex systems proliferate. American nuclear weapons, including missiles and atomic mines, are now stored at a large number of European sites for use by the U.S. armed forces as well as U.S. allies. Some weapons, such as Honest John and Pershing missiles, are on "quick reaction alert." Nuclear weapons currently carried in Polaris AC3 submarines are equipped with MIRVs (multiple independently targeted reentry vehicles). The French military forces have nuclear delivery capability in the form of IRBMs implaced in hardened silos, as well as Mirage aircraft. R&D funds have been requested for the development of maneuverable ICBM warheads, very high speed rocket-carrying submarines, and low altitude cruise missiles. Soviet weaponry is also apparently going through another round of development, featuring multiple separately targeted warheads and, possibly, anti-submarine flying boats weighing 500 tons with a 7000-mile non-stop range.

Could the route to nuclear war be escalation of an on-going conflict? Perhaps. Under difficult circumstances, with different leaders, with a different level of public support, and with a set of issues at stake which are perceived as a matter of survival, is it too difficult to imagine a nation currently possessing nuclear weapons, using them on the battlefield? We are not so far advanced as to exclude positively the atavistic use of such weapons for self-protection. To imply that the use of nuclear weapons is impossible in an on-going conflict would be to imply that the nature of man, as reflected in his military institutions, has changed in only thirty years.

Is a first-strike use of nuclear weapons conceivable? Secretary of Defense James Schlesinger recently disclosed that the country's nuclear doctrine had changed significantly. The balance-of-terror strategy, known more precisely as mutual assured destruction ("You can't launch an attack because even if you do I will have enough power left to destroy you."), is apparently being changed to permit a more measured response; for example, to destroy a submarine base at Murmansk in exchange for a hypothetical initial Russian obliteration of the U.S. base at Groton, Connecticut. The new measured-response policy has the effect of multiplying the number of buttons available to be pushed. To critics, at least, the new policy represents "a dangerous escalation, since it changes the rules of the nuclear game; by making nuclear war more flexible it becomes more thinkable, and therefore more possible." (See *Time* magazine, Feb. 11, 1974).

The situation is further complicated by the fact that there are many trends in progress today which suggest that animosity among nations may increase. For example, certain materials will be in very short supply and it appears that many nations may choose to use their ownership of these raw materials in a monopolistic way. Food may be scarce. The gap between developed and developing countries may increase in several dimensions, including affluence, average age, per capita food and education. Furthermore, the number of nations with nuclear capabilities seems certain to rise.

All of these considerations notwithstanding, **it still seems relatively unlikely that the world will engage in large-scale nuclear warfare in the next twenty years. Why? Because the balance of terror will still be at work. To attack or defend, using nuclear weapons, invites nuclear extinction. SALT is a unique occurrence; it has already led to the banning of certain kinds of weapons and seems likely to result in additional agreements which will have salutary and stabilizing consequences. Yet total nuclear disarmament seems unattainable.**

[The specific forecasts that the author makes in this article are presented in bold face type.]

SEVERE FOOD SHORTAGES_____

There are several trends which, taken together, suggest that large-scale food shortages may exist in the world in the very near future. From the mid-thirties to the late forties, almost all regions of the world exported grain; only Western Europe was an importer. That situation has now changed drastically. Only the United States, Canada, Australia, and New Zealand export grain; all other regions import grain. In 1972, more than 75% of grain exports came from the United States, about 15% from Canada, and the remainder from Australia and New Zealand. As Lester Brown of the Overseas Development Council points out, this places the world grain supply in a very precarious position. Any external event which can have the effect of diminishing grain exports from the United States and Canada will diminish grain imports elsewhere in the world. Among such events might be a climatic disturbance, or even a consumer revolt against higher prices in the United States. Nowhere in the world does there exist a world grain reserve which could "take up the slack" in the event of disappointing harvests in North America. Ten years ago the United States had great grain surpluses. Farmers were paid to keep land out of cultivation and large-scale food programs, such as Food for Peace, were implemented. This is no longer the case; all that we produce we either use domestically or export (See "Global Food Insecurity" by Lester R. Brown in the April issue of *THE FUTURIST*.)

The increasing price of fuels and the shortage of energy in general has exacerbated the situation. Agriculture in the United States is energy-intensive. Energy supplies are used to run tractors, to dry grain, to produce fertilizer, and to power irrigation systems. The price of increasing the per acre productivity of grain has been increasing energy intensity: for corn, the ratio of calories-out to calories-in was 3:7 in 1945; by 1970 the ratio was 2:82. (See "Food Production and the Energy Crisis" by David Pimentel et al. in *Energy: Today's Choices, Tomorrow's Opportunities*, edited by Anton B. Schmalz, World Future Society, Washington, 1974).

The increasing price of fuels and fertilizer inevitably has a greater effect on developing countries than on the developed countries, because they can ill afford the increased costs of input materials.

The use of new hybrid grain varieties in Japan, India, the Philippines, Mexico, and elsewhere has resulted in greatly increased grain productivity. But these new varieties have increased the energy intensity of agriculture in countries in which they are employed. It follows, therefore, that as energy shortages become more severe and costs increase, the outcome of the "green revolution" becomes less certain. As Pimentel and his co-authors noted, "green revolution agriculture . . . uses high energy crop production technology, especially with respect to fertilizers and pesticides. While one may not doubt the sincerity of the U.S. experts to share its agricultural technology so that the rest of the world can eat and live as it does, one must be realistic about the resources available to accomplish this mission. In the United States we are currently using an equivalent of 80 gallons of gasoline to produce an acre of corn. With fuel shortages and high prices to come, we wonder if many developing nations will be able to afford the technology of U.S. agriculture."

A third trend which must be recognized in this area is the rate of increase in world population. U.N. figures place the growth rate of world population at about 2.2% per year. At that rate, by 1994 world population will have reached about 6 billion, compared to the present world population level of about 3.9 billion. This implies that world output of food will have to increase by a similar amount simply to maintain the status quo. It remains to be seen whether or not developing countries can continue to increase their production of food at similar rates. In many places agricultural expansion is plagued by problems associated with soil erosion, irrigation, and drainage. Fertilizers, insecticides, and pesticides, which are presently expensive and polluting, will be required to a greater extent as agriculture in those countries becomes more intensive. Many countries which need assistance may not accept foods made available because of conflicting cultural constraints. Within many countries, the agricultural infrastructure is as yet inadequately developed to permit the evolution of the more intensive agriculture required in the years ahead.

Food is likely to become a central issue in the next two decades. Within the United States the question will be how high a price are we willing to pay for our food in order to support hungry people abroad? Will we be willing to eat meat, knowing that an animal takes in seven times the protein it provides, when people elsewhere are starving?

Tropical agriculture will be developed. New industries will emerge. One will seek to develop agricultural technologies appropriate to the Third World countries. Such enterprise has been frustrated in the past because the countries which most need food can least afford to pay for it. In the years ahead, world organizations will be formed to encourage the development of such multinational agricultural firms. They will be paid not by the receiving country necessarily, but from a world capital pool. In a concerted and well-planned program, the developed countries will export not only grain, but also the information and implements necessary to increase the production of food raised elsewhere in the world. A world granary will be established.

Within the developed countries, food manufacturers will move heavily into the manufacture of fabricated foods, including meat analogues and meat extenders. These foods will utilize soy or other protein sources and, through appropriate textural manipulation and flavor additives, will simulate more familiar foods.

A host of new food technologies will be pursued, including:

- New strains of bacteria for fixing nitrogen in the soil.
- Animal hotels for efficient raising of cows and pigs.
- Oyster farming in the thermal effluent of nuclear plants.
- Twinning drugs to produce more than one calf per cow per year.

DETERIORATION OF THE BIOSPHERE

Wastes grow as population, affluence and production grow. As has been eloquently pointed out by many ecologists, powerful economic and demographic trends are in progress in the world today which, if extended far into the future, could threaten the integrity of the life-supporting qualities of our environment. The discovery of trace metals and chlorinated hydrocarbon pesticides in fish, the eutrophication of some rivers and streams, and the increasing presence of carbon dioxide in the atmosphere, are current examples of the deterioration of the environment which have given impetus to the "ecological ethic." There has been much rhetoric and emotion over this crisis. By 1994 we may look back and wonder what all the fuss was about. We may see that anit-pollution technology has been able to reverse localized pollution. Life has come back to bodies of water once thought dead. Precipitators, cooling towers, sulfur removal techniques, catalytic converters for automotive exhausts: these devices can be and have been effective. Yet they are costly; therefore, inevitably they will come late to developing countries. In retrospect we may find that we were worried about the less significant aspects of pollution; that forces were at work as a result of the growth of world industrialism and population which made many of our efforts inconsequential. We may learn, for example, that our attempts to control automobile emissions were ultimately as ineffective as applying a bandaid to a broken arm.

It is possible that the biosphere is being degraded, compromised in its ability to support life. The ecology is so complex that it is difficult to assess just where we are on the curve, but there are symptoms of an emerging crisis.

Soil Erosion

As population levels increase, the amount of land under cultivation increases and the quality of agricultural land diminishes. Farmers plow valleys and then move to the hillsides, thereby creating soil erosion problems which lead to floods and droughts. The earth's surface supplies man with only a thin layer of topsoil for use in food production. As man and nature intervene and remove the land's year-round natural cover of grass or forest, the soil is eroded by wind and water. Soil is continually being washed into the sea and lifted into the atmosphere. At the present time, the remaining topsoil is being eroded faster than new topsoil can be formed.

Particulate Matter in the Atmosphere

The loss of topsoil is not the only consequence of erosion. Scientists have noted an increasing level of particulate matter in the atmosphere which could affect world climate by increasing the earth's albedo, the fraction of sunlight that is reflected away from our planet. The burning of hydrocarbons on all continents and wind erosion in the poorer countries contribute to this particulate accumulation. Today, the poorer countries are not able to amend this situation. If it were concluded that greater and greater levels of particulate matter in the atmosphere are altering the world's climate, it would be necessary for the richer countries to provide aid in terms of capital and technical assistance, for such a situation is a potential threat to all people and to all forms of life on the planet. While increased reflectivity of the earth due to particulate matter in the atmosphere tends to drop temperatures, the increasing levels of carbon dioxide provide a greenhouse effect and tend to raise temperatures. Thus, two forms of atmospheric pollution are in delicate balance.

Alteration of Climatic Patterns

During the past fifty years the Northern Hemisphere has been in a very unusual warm period, resulting in a favorable growing climate. At present, however, the climate appears to be cooling and glaciers expanding. Since 1950 the growing season in Britain has decreased by two weeks. However, the cooling of the earth is expected to prove favorable for the United States. According to some meteorologists, the western plains and the high plateaus will become wetter, with a climate comparable to that of approximately a few hundred years ago which was sufficient to sustain high prairie grass. The northeast region of the United States may continue to warm up, with the result that growing seasons will be better.

Any human undertaking which affects the ice layer of the polar regions of the northern and southern hemispheres could change the level of the oceans, resulting in marked changes in sea-land boundaries and climates contingent on those boundaries.

Irrigation Side Effects

Irrigation has contributed to world food production by permitting cultivation in the areas which normally would be unusable or only marginally productive. Along with its benefits, irrigation has contributed some noxious side effects. These include the raising of the water table by the diversion of river water onto the land, and increased soil salinity, caused by the water evaporating through the soil. This phenomenon was demonstrated recently in West Pakistan. For a century, the water from the Indus had irrigated the plain. In 1961, President Ayub asked President Kennedy for assistance, because West Pakistan was losing 60,000 acres of fertile cropland per year through waterlogging and salinity, at a time when its population was growing at a rate of 2.5% a year. A U.S. team recommended a system of tube wells to lower the water table by tapping ground water for intensive irrigation. While discharging this water onto the surface, the irrigation water also served to wash the soil's salt downward. This program is proving a success, and some of the damaged land of Pakistan is being reclaimed.

Demand for Water

Man needs water not only for direct consumption but for food and industrial production as well. These needs have resulted in an exponential growth rate for water consumption. Some ecologists warn that the United States has a potential water deficit of about 30% by the year 2020.

The exponential growth rate for water consumption means that the year 2000 will bring an end to freely available water. Present alternatives include the purification of used water and its recycling, as well as the desalination of ocean water. It is expected that water recycling will be in effect by the end of this century. At present, water salvage in industry helps reduce the pollution of streams. Plants such as Kaiser Fontana Steel save, recover, and reclaim water for use. The Kaiser plant uses 1400 gallons of water per ton of steel; by comparison, the average for the steel industry is 65,000 gallons per ton of steel.

What can we expect? The greatly extended use of artificial environments for agriculture, the manufacture of synthetic soil, massive land reclamation projects, polar ice cap and atmospheric monitoring programs, worldwide population laws and standards, increasing prices for water, and a growing consciousness of ecology, and the interconnectedness of the environment and growing organisms.

IMBALANCES IN THE DISTRIBUTION OF WEALTH_____

Both the developed countries and the developing countries have been getting richer in terms of annual income. This is a happy situation (and incidentally it is also true within the United States: both the poor and the non-poor are getting richer). But in the world as a whole, the rate of increase in annual GNP and GNP/capita is greater in the developed countries than in the developing countries, hence the gap in income is growing. And the gap is

Classifying World Problems

Grade	Estimated Crisis Intensity (number affected times degree of effect)		Estimated Time to Crisis (if no major effort at anticipatory solution)		
			1–5 Years	5–20 Years	20–50 Years
1.	10^{10}	Total Annihilation	Nuclear or RCBW Escalation	Nuclear or RCBW Escalation	(Solved or dead)
2.	10^9	Great Destruction or Change (Physical, Biological, or Political)	(too soon)	Famines Eco-balance Development Failures Local Wars Rich-Poor Gap	Economic Structure and Political Theory Population and Eco-balance Patterns of Living Universal Education Communications-Integration Management of World Integrative Philosophy
3.	10^8	Widespread Almost Unbearable Tension	Administration Management Need for Participation Group and Race Conflict Poverty-Rising Expectations Environmental Degradation	Poverty Pollution Race Wars Political Rigidity Strong Dictatorships	?
4.	10^7	Large-Scale Distress	Transportation Diseases Loss of old cultures	Housing Education Independence of Big Powers Communications Gap	?
5.	10^6	Tension Producing Responsive Change	Regional Organization Water Supplies	?	?

Classifying World Problems (continued)

Grade	Estimated Crisis Intensity (number affected times degree of effect)	Estimated Time to Crisis (if no major effort at anticipatory solution)		
		1–5 Years	5–20 Years	20–50 Years
6.	Other Problems—Important, but Adequately Researched	Technical Development Design Intelligent Monetary Design		
7.	Exaggerated Dangers and Hopes			Eugenics Melting of Ice Caps
8.	Non-Crisis Problems Being "Overstudied"	Man in Space Most Basic Science		

appreciable. Eighty percent of the world's people live in countries which generate only about 15% of the world's annual product. By 1994, assuming present trends continue, the 85% of the population of the world living in the poorer countries will generate only about 12% of the world's annual product.

In an attempt to change this situation, the United Nations began "The Decade of Development" in 1960. However, its strategies were only partially successful, and the development rate of the poorer countries remained relatively low.

Wealth is not equivalent to income. Wealth can be measured in terms of aggregated capital or natural endowment, and represents the potential for future income. While aggregated capital clearly is concentrated in the developed countries, natural resources are more evenly distributed. As the Middle East situation demonstrated, when a few nations control a resource which is in high demand they can readily exert monopolistic power (this gives rise to the next crisis on this list). Hence, as certain materials grow short, the definition of which countries are "have" and which are "have not" nations will change.

Unfortunately, if groups of nations exercise monopolistic pressures, others may be hurt severely. For example, while the oil situation confronts the developed nations with uncertainty about their balance of payments and economic stability, the underdeveloped countries may be on the verge of disaster. Treasury Secretary George Shultz recently stated that the under-developed countries are victims of a "horrible chain in which the lack of fuel goes to a lack of fertilizer, goes to lack of food, . . . which goes to starvation." India, for example, is experiencing tremendous hardship. The price of kerosene, its principal cooking fuel, recently rose 60%. Such an increase primarily affects the poor.

The *New York Times* recently summarized the situation:

> *Some developing countries such as Ecuador, Venezuela, and Indonesia will benefit from increased oil revenues but the 70 or so countries who must import petroleum face a threefold problem. They have to pay more for their oil; the possibility of cutbacks in the industrialized world means possibly reduced sales of their own exports of such commodities as coffee, sugar, and copper; they fear that industrial countries, facing their own balance of payments problems, will cut back on foreign aid. (Feb. 17, 1974)*

As for the developed countries, Japan has been affected severely because it imports all its oil, 42 percent from the Arab nations. It is expected that Japan's oil import costs will double, $16–18 billion, creating a trade deficit of about $4 billion. The Organization for Economic Cooperation and Development estimates that the balance of payments deficit of its 24 members will total between $35–40 billion. Britain's deficit alone is expected to be on the order of $6 billion. In anticipation of its impending deficit, France has already made known its plans for a $1.5 billion loan from the International Monetary Fund, the largest such loan ever transacted. Inflation is expected to increase rapidly all over the world.

Conservative estimates, based on the new oil prices which have been in effect since January 1, indicate that the six principal Arab oil producers will have earnings of $48 billion for their 1974 oil exports. A sizeable portion of this is expected to be placed in Western government securities and Western banks. Developed countries such as France, Britain, Japan, and West Germany are rushing to sell the Arab countries the necessary equipment, engineering, and technology. Monopoly still works.

Now, and increasingly in the next few years, the energy crisis will serve as a "reality test" for the people who advocate limiting growth. As they advance their arguments, a further difficulty arising from the unequal distribution of wealth will become more obvious. To limit growth across the world by fiat or national determination would tend to freeze the status quo, and this condition would not be acceptable to developing countries. Instead, achieving a world in which growth is limited probably means that the developed countries will have to limit their growth while developing countries grow—a very unlikely situation. Clearly, it will not be a matter of either growing or not growing, but rather in what way to channel growth. The termination of growth would lock impoverished countries into their present unsatisfactory conditions; yet, rapid exponential growth cannot, in a closed system, continue very long. The dilemma can be resolved through planned growth, but accomplishing this will require institutions and modes of international cooperation not yet invented.

Concern about and attempts to equalize income distribution among people within the United States and in other developed countries will certainly increase in the next twenty years. In the United States, the number of people still in poverty has continually diminished, if poverty is defined in terms of living standards rather than in relative terms of having less than others. The prospect is for still less poverty. We have had suggestions for a guaranteed income or negative income tax, the government acting as an employer of last resort, vastly increased inheritance taxes, and so forth. In the years to come, we will have to face up to this basic issue: Just what income is a person entitled to receive simply by virtue of his existence, rather than his accomplishments, or his intelligence?

What are some specific forecasts for the next twenty years? Neo-Malthusians will point to continuing shortages as a "reality test" for limits to growth concepts; whether or not our growth should be limited will become a central intellectual debate in the United States. The role of multinational corporations will be even more carefully scrutinized. New kinds of recessions may occur in many developed countries: Unemployment rates may rise while prices remain high. As affluence increases in the developing countries, possibly as a result of their capitalizing on their indigenous resources, birth rates will fall and the gap between nations will begin to narrow perceptibly. The spirit of nationalism will grow throughout the world, and the spread of communications and mobility will promote rising expectations in the developing countries. Industrialization will still be seen as the route to affluence.

MATERIAL SHORTAGES

Shortages of raw materials in the world can be real or artificial; that is, they can occur as a result of depletion or of manipulation. With respect to depletion, it does not appear that within the next twenty years any major raw material will be exhausted, but as supply diminishes, less economically favorable reserves will have to be tapped, substitutes developed, and prices will rise. *The Limits to Growth* by Donella Meadows et al. (Potomac

Associates, Washington, D.C. 1972), using projected rates of consumption for many non-renewable natural resources and five times known current reserves, gives the expected time to depletion of such materials as:

Aluminum	—55 years
Copper	—48 years
Gold	—29 years
Mercury	—41 years
Silver	—42 years
Zinc	—50 years

The countries controlling materials which are likely to be depleted in a relatively few years could well move to protect their resources and maximize their return; in other words, they might exert monopolistic pressures on consuming nations. The United States, while having abundant mineral raw materials, depends heavily on foreign sources for many minerals. It imports essentially all of the platinum, mica, chromium, strontium, cobalt, tantalum, aluminum ores, manganese, fluorine, titanium, and asbestos which it consumes. If world prices rise, currently marginal indigenous deposits would be exploited.

Of course, fuels are in short supply today. Will we be able to solve our energy problems by 1994? The question is exceedingly important, since without adequate energy we may have to limit our growth, like it or not. The relationship between energy scarcity and the economy is very complex. Simulation models have not yet indicated how much shortage, even under the best intentioned allocation policy, would trigger recession or depression. Prior studies which assumed that a linear relationship existed between GNP and energy consumption indicated that a 4% overall energy growth and a 7% electricity growth, would be necessary to "fuel" the economic growth expected in the next two decades. The extent to which we can cut back without causing unacceptable economic distortions is not clear. It does not appear that new technology can provide much help during the 1980s. Clearly we will be placing great emphasis on coal and nuclear energy sources in the near future. Natural gas is already scarce with shortages almost certain to increase. Even with increased importation of natural and liquefied gas, and production of synthetic gas from other hydrocarbon sources, total gas consumption is likely to remain only about constant.

The United States is rich in coal, an energy source that will be a major asset in meeting demand. The production of coal could be approximately doubled during the next 15 to 20 years, but, there are real limits on coal production and utilization, including: availability of manpower; environmental considerations, particularly those associated with strip-mining and the sulfur content of coal; and mine workers' safety and health. Conventional nuclear power, which furnishes a relatively small portion of our total energy today, will have to provide about 13% of our energy by 1985. By then, more energy will be supplied from the fission of uranium than from natural gas.

More exotic technologies, such as solar energy, geothermal power, and fusion, will require research and pilot plant operation before they can be counted on to produce appreciable amounts of power. At best, solar and geothermal may begin to make a substantial contribution in the 1990s; fusion power will probably not be a significant source before the mid to late 1990s, or perhaps even after the turn of the century.

Recognizing the potential for "materials blackmail," the United States will move to improve its strategic stockpile in certain areas, arrange for long-term bilateral agreements with supplying countries, and pursue the research work necessary to develop synthetic and substitute materials in critical applications. More importantly perhaps, the U.S. Government will intervene in dealings between corporations and foreign governments in order to ensure that "national interests" are protected. Within corporations, and for the consumer, shortages of certain materials may become a way of life. Large corporations dependent upon many raw materials from many different sources will routinely develop back-up plans to maintain their product lines. The pressure of shortages is all in the inflationary direction. With respect to energy, Project Independence will be pushed. Conservation will probably result in savings of 10–15% over previously anticipated levels of consumption. The relative use of nuclear energy for electricity generation will grow rapidly, and new industries attuned to the energy realities of the 1980s and 1990s will emerge: uranium enrichment, mass-produced reactors, and the production of fuels from electricity.

SIMULTANEOUSLY OPERATING FORCES IN FUTURE _____

In conclusion, we can anticipate the following forces operating more or less simultaneously in the next 20 years: (1) A continuing détente based on balanced fire-power, upset frequently by new weapons; (2) food shortages in many countries; (3) pollution; (4) growing disparity between the developed and developing nations; (5) monopolistic activities by some nations with regard to materials they control; and (6) energy shortages. What cannot be estimated is how these forces will change the economies and social structures of nations, nor how they will be reflected in the minds of leaders and would-be leaders of political forces yet unborn.

When we make it to 1994, we will undoubtedly remember other crises as well, but the ones mentioned here almost certainly will have to be faced. They cannot be avoided. Each in its own right presents enormous and unique difficulties; together, they form an unholy fabric which challenges our credulity. They interact and overlap; curing one intensifies another. Viewing them in juxtaposition leads one to ask if our system has finally become too complex to work.

Anticipating crises, understanding their nature to the degree possible, and moving to implement policies which mitigate them, seem to me an important thrust for the policy sciences in the next two decades. We need, following the suggestion of John Platt, a metric for crises, and following the suggestion of Harold Linstone, a system of crisis discounting akin to cash flow discounting, which lets us concentrate on the most important affairs first.

The world society of the next century will be shaped by these crises and our attempts at their solution. That future society will be described in terms of its values, its wealth, its people. But it will also be described in terms of our legacy: Will we leave then nuclear war, an inadequate food supply system, a world that cannot support life well? Will our legacy be a system in which poverty is an inescapable condition? Will we have left them insufficient materials to build with? These are questions that we may have begun to answer by 1994.

George T. Coker, Jr.

Shell Development Company, Houston, Texas

ALTERNATE FUTURES FOR THE CORPORATION

If we only knew the future of the corporation, we would know the future of the free world because society's future is linked to the corporation's future. As we begin this discussion, let us make sure we are on common ground. Corporations are those publicly owned stockholder institutions exemplifying the free enterprise system rather than those in which government is a significant stockholder, e.g. universities, hospitals, TVA, etc. Further these remarks must be prefaced with a disclaimer. Although the Shell Development Co., my employer, provided me the opportunity to present this paper, I alone am responsible for its contents.

Unfortunately, I cannot predict the future, for if I could, I would be living on my own south sea island rather than speaking to you today. But, I feel as qualified as any to speculate about the future of the corporation. My 25 year career with Shell Oil has given me a unique opportunity to work closely with the management of many industrial concerns throughout this country. The thoughts and remarks I share with you are drawn largely from thse experiences coupled with those arising from my activities as creator and coordinator of Project Forethought.

For those unfamiliar with this project let us pause for a moment to acquaint you with this unique project. Project Forethought was the outgrowth of my personal activities as Education Chairman of the Bay Area Corporate Planners Association, who as cohosts of the 1975 San Francisco

George T. Coker, Jr., "Alternate Futures for the Corporation," paper presented at the 1978 Annual Meeting of the Academy of Management's Symposium, "Enterprise 2000," August 1978, San Francisco, California.

517

Conference of the International Affiliation of Planning Societies, undertook a futures opinion poll with the memberships of each planning society invited to participate. The some 400 participants in this three round futures poll were all involved in corporate planning. The results were presented at the conference and subsequently summarized in the September 1975 issue of the Planning Executives Institute's magazine. Since then, the participants expressed interest in undertaking similar activities and therefore in response to this interest, in 1977, a series of futures polls were undertaken of the corporate planners that comprise this informal Forethought Network. Therefore the data base used for this paper comes from not only my own personal experiences but also from the invaluable information obtained from the various Project Forethought polls.

Many of my colleagues in the futures field believe that technological forecasting is the key to looking at the future. Implicit in this approach is the assumption, "whatever is possible will be." Following this logic leads one to ask what will be the next US SST venture. While technological forecasting is relatively easy and straightforward, unfortunately because of the SST syndrome, it provides little useful information about the future. In my opinion, although more difficult, speculation about the future must be based on stakeholders needs and desires. People sometimes ignore their needs to fulfill their desires. Therefore, perhaps the best way to approach this question of the future of the corporation is to try and identify the stakeholders and from speculation about their future needs and desires, generate some images of the future of the corporation.

In looking at the future avoid the trap of simple trend extrapolation over the next five to tend years. Rather focus attention some 25 or 50 years hence and generate images from stakeholder needs and desires in this time frame. Once a number of plausible images become clear, we can work backwards in time and thereby gain some insight as to what must happen today and tomorrow for a particular future to evolve. Also information can be gained about the long term impact of today's decisions.

This paper will attempt to identify the significant future needs and desires of the major stockholders in the corporation and these will be used to offer for your consideration several alternative futures of the corporation.

STAKEHOLDERS

While undoubtedly an oversimplification of a complex subject, the major stakeholders in the future corporation would appear to be society, management, employees, and stockholders. Corporations are chartered by society, run by management using employees' brains and brawn and stockholders' money. As shown in Figure 1, while society's needs and desires are impacted in many ways, government is the major vehicle through which society acts. Often, however, government's actions do not accurately reflect the real needs or desires of society but rather those of government itself, and therefore as shown in this slide, government and its subdivisions must be added to the list of major stakeholders.

STAKEHOLDER CHARACTERIZATION_____

With the major stakeholders in the corporation identified, perhaps it would be useful to digress a moment and briefly review the history of the corporation. Why was it created? Some 200 years ago society went through a significant transformation now referred to as the Industrial Revolution. The driving forces were new technology coupled with emerging new goals and values of society all directed toward increasing the output of goods. This production and consumption of goods resulted for the first time in history a steady increase in wealth and living standards, all by peaceful means. The secret was productivity made possible by new technology. With productivity as the means and more goods as the end the only missing piece was institutionalizing the process in some renewable system of organization. Thus was born the corporation.

Thus a major factor in the future of the corporation will be the changing goals, needs, and values of society, particularly those of the key stakeholders. In attempting to speculate on future goals, needs, and values of the stakeholders one begins with the realization that they are all human and therefore must share some common goals, needs, and values. This suggests beginning with Maslow's well-known hierarchy of human needs listed in Figure 2.

Many attempts have been made to translate and expand these broad generalities into specifics. Perhaps the best approach is based on Mitchell's, of SRI, concept of "Life Ways." According to him, "A life ways differs from the expression of life style in being focused on the core drives of an individual. A persons way of life is defined by the complex of inner motivating, guiding, meangiving values and feelings. Style of life in contrast describes the outward manner of living—how the inner drives are exhibited." Mitchell's Life Ways are divided into the six categories shown in Figure 3: Changers, Makers, Preservers, Takers, Seekers, or Escapers. The elements used to develop these six Life Ways are the six listed in Figure 4 plus Maslow's hierarchy of human needs. To appreciate the differences between these six Life Ways, Figure 5 tabulates the hallmark of each and suggests several goals for each. While it must be recognized that often not only do individuals exhibit some characteristics of more than one Life Way but also groups will of course be composed of some distribution of all six Life Ways. However for the purpose of this discussion it often will be necessary to classify some major stakeholders on the basis of a single Life Way.

STAKEHOLDER'S FUTURE NEEDS AND DESIRES

Now that the major stakeholders have been identified and a means suggested to characterize them, the next step in the process is to speculate about each's future needs and desires looking for points of potential conflict and reinforcement.

Government. Because of its increasing influence over the corporation's future, perhaps the stakeholder to consider first is the government. As indicated in Figure 6, government has to be subdivided into three groups: elected officials, staffers, and bureaucrats. While the number of government workers at the state and local levels far outnumber those of the Federal government, we will ignore state and local because of time limitations and also the Federal government's actions will have a more pronounced impact on the corporation. This is not to suggest, however, that for a detailed study that state and loal governments should be ignored. Consider, for example, Oregon's container laws and the no growth laws of some California cities. Also, as previously mentioned, within each group there exists people representing each of the six Life Ways, but for this discussion the perceived "average" is assumed.

The elected politician is typically a Maker. His main objective of course is re-election and visible achievement is the key. He needs to accomplish things, to be recognized and along the way he seeks and grasps power. One of the principles suggested previously was that in theory the elected officials pass laws for this country that reflect the needs and desires of our society. Realistically that is not necessarily the most expeditious route to assure re-election. They have yet to come to grips with problems of energy, unemployment, stagflation, trade balances, dropping stock prices, etc. . . . Perhaps a more realistic key to re-election is to pass laws that give the have nots a bigger piece of the pie and by all means slow down the inevitable and necessary changes in the life style of their constituents. An example of this attitude toward life style changes is government's inability to pass a meaningful energy plan, something they have worked on since the OPEC embargo. Why? Because any meaningful legislation will necessitate life style changes, certainly not the best route to re-election.

Also, special interest groups must be respected and given special consideration.

Another thought to understand the politician is his continual search to cover up government's past sins of fiscal irresponsibilities. He will look for help (laws) from corporations. Recent examples are increased social security taxes, both on the individual and corporation, but there was quite a movement within Congress to make corporations' contributions larger than the individuals'. One must speculate that the politician will find another means for the corporation to assist in income redistribution and relief from his fiscal problems. One choice suggests ever-increasing inflation. Could we see a U.S. version of the 1920's in Germany?

Perhaps one of the most powerful groups in government is the Congressional Staffers. They are difficult to classify as to Life Ways but one might suspect that most are either Makers or Changers. Power and influence are their goals. The route to success is to make the powerful elected officials dependent on you. This means develop expertise in those areas of interest to the powerful. This implies knowing the inclinations and needs of the boss. As a side thought, the Staffers' education by the corporation is probably the best hope for developing understanding by the elected officials.

Counterbalancing the politicians and staffers who tend to be Makers are the bureaucrats. Although undoubtedly, one could find bureaucrats representing all six Life Ways, in my opinion, most must be classified as Takers, sharing the general characteristics of Takers such as "me first," "job security." Indications of the validity of characterizing the bureaucrats as a group of Takers are increasing unionization of government employees, and certainly the majority's strong desire for maintaining the status quo. Let's not take on any new venture unless it creates a new bureaucracy and provides more job opportunities.

Stockholders. Although because of changes in the capitalistic system the stockholder is still a stakeholder in the entire system, his role has been greatly diminished. The stockholder, at least in theory, is the owner of the enterprise or corporation because he has put up the equity capital and thereby taken a risk. If this were really the situation, then he probably comes from all six Life Ways and his goals are simply stated in Figure 7. But the way corporations are organized and managed today, only a minor portion of corporate capital is raised through the sale of equity capital. A more significant portion of capital comes through self financing by the success of the enterprise itself. In fact, in recent years, more than 60% of the capital investment of the nation's 1,000 largest manufacturing firms was financed internally, thus, on a practical basis, under complete control of the management. The investment of this capital will undoubtedly reflect the needs and desires of the management.

Although highly unlikely, it has been argued by the famed economist Milton Friedman that under a free enterprise system, one would have to outlaw, or at least discourage self financing because under the pure theory of market capitalism, a firm risks a stockholder's capital and then pays back any profits in the form of dividends to its legal owners, the stockholders. And if the corporation seeks to risk that money again, it should ask those stockholders to reinvest that money rather than withhold it from them and reinvest it by managerial decision. Also, it must be recognized that individuals are rarely the investors in corporations today given the pattern of stock ownership, most of which is through mutual funds, and in such cases the individual stockholder is often an in and out person with little continuing interest in the fate of the enterprise. Thus, in realities of today's world, we find that corporate ownership is largely a legal fiction and if so, then one ought to adopt a more realistic attitude toward it. One can treat stockholders not as "owners" but as legitimate claimers to some fixed share of the corporation's profits and nothing more. Therefore, one would anticipate that their impact on the future of the corporation will be quite minimal except as they reflect society's desires in general and as they participate in other non-corporate institutions or within the political process.

Management. There are many levels of management and obviously any attempt to characterize management as a single entity with common needs and desires (Life Ways) would be futile. Therefore, in the context of this discussion, management is limited to those who make major decisions affecting the corporations. Even with this limitation differences in Life Ways are noted.

Lower and middle management are classified as employees and as such will be assumed to be a single group with their future needs and desires reflecting in general those of society.

Figure 8 suggests that among corporate management will be found Changers, Makers, as well as Preservers. In my opinion the Life Ways of management of an individual corporation tend to cycle. Initially a Changer with a vision is the manager of the enterprise. Some might call it entrepreneurial management. Henry Ford and his Model T is a classic example of this. Picture today, a young Henry Ford in a large multinational corporation pleading his case for commitment of corporate, human and capital resources necessary to fulfill his vision of average working people owning an automobile. The statements in Figure 9 might summarize management's comments. Changers in management are today few and far between—Dr. Land and his instamatic cameras might qualify. Also perhaps management of some of the young electronic industries might be Changers. But as this spirit of the "founding father" leaves the corporation, the Makers will tend to rise to the top of the corporation. As might be expected, as long as the corporation is considered to be growing faster than real GNP, management will likely be dominated by Makers. As a Maker, he will seek visible achievement, power, status, accomplishment, recognition, prosperity, etc.

As the corporation reaches that stage when it is no longer considered a growth company and its future is linked to GNP, the Preservers tend to take hold of the management reins. His goals are obviously "hang on and survive", but he would also like and tries to have all the privileges and images of his predecessors, the Changers and Makers. Unfortunately, as a Preserver he finds it difficult to break with tradition and much of his activities center on saying "no, let's maintain the status quo. We can't plan that far in the future," etc., etc. . . . . Obviously witin a given industry one will find examples of management representing the three Life Ways. Also, in general, industries themselves tend to be classifiable into one of these three Life Ways.

Society. By now it should be realized that society's goals, needs and values will ultimately determine the future of the corporation. Obviously there will be detours caused by self-seeking politicians or bureaucrats but in the long run society's needs and values will be imposed on the corporation. Several examples of this process come to mind.

President John Kennedy was able to capture the imagination of the American public which society accepted as a goal with his statement, "We shall place a man on the moon within this decade." With this, a societal goal, the necessary resources were committed and it was accomplished. Others in our society led by the defense industry said the U.S. must have its own commercial SST. To this end, Boeing undertook a large R&D effort, as did other segments of the aviation industry. The U.S. SST was to be far superior to the then fast emerging Concorde. Reviewing the history of these two SST ventures reinforces the premise that what society wants it will get. It got the

Concorde because the French and British politicians were successful in convincing their constituents but the U.S. SST was lost largely because of the environmentalists' impact on changing societal desires. Another example that comes to mind and one in which the outcome is still in doubt is nuclear power. Companies such as General Electric and Westinghouse have invested literally billions of stockholder dollars to satisfy a well identified societal need for more non fossil fuel generated power. Yet there is frustration at all levels and we may never see nuclear power make a significant contribution to the energy needs of this country. As an interesting sidelight, Japan's conversion to nuclear power leads the world's.

Within each society some percentage of the people will be classifiable in each of the six different Life Ways. The problem then becomes one of trying to determine the distribution of Changers, Makers, Preservers, Takers, Seekers, and Escapers. Many elected officials rely heavily on the Takers as their power base and means of re-election. Escapers really don't participate in the process which leaves only five Life Way groups with which to deal in trying to understand societal goals, needs, desires, and values. There are many ways to try to deal with this problem in order to speculate how they may influence the future of the corporation. In fact, this is the basis for much of the activity in the futures field.

One such source of information is based on a project in which I am involved. As indicated in the Introduction, Project Forethought and the Forethought Network is an ongoing futures opinion poll of people employed in corporate planning activities. This polling started in 1974 and the first series of polls indicated that both quality of life will be a major societal concern and also there will be increasing government intervention in all phases of business.

Recently the Forethought Network was activated to explore their latest opinions on societal trends. This latest work entitled "Survey '77," was based on a list of 36 societal concerns prepared by UNESCO. Each participant was asked to indicate whether the concern would be about the same, increase, or decrease during three different time frames. The results of this previously unpublished work may provide some clues to future societal needs and desires. These will then be integrated with the previously identified needs and desires of the major corporation stakeholders. With this as a data base, several alternate futures of the corporation will be offered for your contemplation.

Perhaps the best way to summarize the results of Survey '77 is to study Figure 10 which identifies the concern trends in the three different time frames; also the percentage of the panel voting the direction of the trend is indicated. Based on a detailed analysis of these data, the main point that stands out is society will demand more security: losses against income, health, etc. Also it seems clear that there will be increasing pressure for redistribution of the wealth and a further closing of the rich-poor gap. Also people anticipate receiving more leisure time and they are going to place a higher value and command on the use of time presumably either at work or leisure.

These results from Survey '77 are supported by a recently published Harris poll prepared for and reported by the Congressional Clearing House on the Future. The basic conclusion from this poll was, "Basically our people are far more concerned with the quality of life and far less with the unlimited acquisition of more physical goods and products. These radical findings by any measure mean the age of materialism as we have known it is going to be radically altered." This statement is a good starting point for our speculation about the future of the corporation. Figure 11 illustrates the changes taking place. As earlier suggested the production of goods is precisely what the corporation was created to do. Yet even today society is more concerned with the quality of life.

ALTERNATE FUTURES FOR THE CORPORATION_____

It seems inevitable that we can no longer avoid the purpose of this paper which was to speculate about the future of the corporation. To do this a data base was derived by trying to understand the needs and desires of the major stakeholders in the corporation. To start one might consider the extremes shown in Figure 12; these have been simply put by the famed economist Milton Friedman and Louis Lundborg, past Board Chairman of Bank of America. To quote Friedman, "In a free enterprise private property system, a corporate executive is an employee of the owners of the business. He has direct responsibility to his employers. That responsibility is to conduct the business in accordance with their desires which generally will be to make as much money as possible while conforming to the basic rules of the society, both those embodied in law and in ethical custom."

Lundborg in his recent book *Future Without Shock*, suggests that a corporation receives a franchise from society and thus does have certain societal responsibilities. It is his belief in order to earn and maintain this franchise the corporation is expected to do the right things at at least three levels:

1. At the first and most basic level to produce and deliver its product or service at a quality and at a price that the market will find acceptable.
2. Then to carry on its own operations in a way that is fair to its employees, customers, and suppliers and is not damaging in any way to the environment in which it operates.
3. And finally to be aware of the problems of the total community and of the total society and to do its share towards solving them.

Bell suggests the two diverse positions shown in Figure 11 to be an economizing mode at one extreme and a sociologizing mode at the other. He summarizes the two diverse positions conceding that corporations unlike universities, government agencies, or a large hospital, are competitive and have to be profitable. The profits moreover are often the major support through taxes of the other three. Even if we set up a continuum with economizing at one end of the scale in which all aspects of the organization are singlemindedly reduced to becoming the means to the goals of production and profit, and sociologizing at the other end in which all workers are guaranteed lifetime jobs and satisfaction of the work force becomes the primary levy on resources that we must recognize. In the last thirty years the company has been moving steadily toward the sociologizing end of the scale. How far this will go is really the answer to the question of the corporation's future.

In the remaining few moments, let me offer for your consideration the five different alternate futures for the corporation tabulated in the last slide. This is not to suggest that any of these is a forecast, but rather they illustrate possibilities. In truth, the future will probably contain elements from each of the alternates.

Business as Usual. The first and most obvious and the one most people assume will happen because a syndrome among many managers is, the "business as usual" future. Much long range corporate planning is based on the assumption that in the future business will be as usual only things will be a little bit better for us because we are smarter than our competitor. Sure, there will be increasing government intervention, but it will be fought and many of our points will be won. Also as long as the rules don't put us at a competitive disadvantage we can survive and prosper. Real GNP will continue to rise and demand for goods and service will continue to increase. These few words summarize the business as usual alternate future and most could expand this future complete with the traditional trend extrapolations beyond the year 2,000. Today's multi-national corporations will grow larger and operate tomorrow much as they do today.

Some food for thought for the business as usual trend extrapolators. Go back 25 years and consider the slide rule business in the 1970's. Think of the post-war baby boom in college and each with his own slide rule . . . Electronic slide rules for under ten 1978 dollars. . . . Business as usual?

Socialism.   Much of the world's population already lives under socialism in one form or another. It certainly provides a straight forward way to redistribute wealth and satisfy societal desires for security. . . . Could the United Kingdom be a model for our futre?

Pseudo Socialism.   This is the logical conclusion of the ever-increasing role government has been playing in corporate life. The impact on the corporations of government agencies such as OSHA, EEO and EPA are all familiar stories. Corporations have and continue to fight these agencies and cite their performance as reasons for less government. Yet curiously when the corporations get into trouble their ambivalence toward government interference begins to show because they look to "Big Brother" to protect them from the unfair competition from the Japanese TV sets, auto imports, and most recently, the steel industry. Thus it seems likely with this kind of attitude building among the Preservers and Makers in the corporations that they will be appealing to government more and more for help. Also the politicians in their desire to satisfy the Takers; namely, their constituents, they will look toward business to finance these in the form of tax reforms or increased taxes. Who is better able to hire the minority, the unemployable, and train them, etc. The Energy Crisis is another classic example where a pseudo socialism approach could easily be taken. The vast majority of both proven oil reserves as well as future reserves lie under government land. Also it is necessary for us to import from foreign governments at least 50% of our petroleum products. Thus it is fair to say that probably as much as two thirds of our oil supplies could quickly come under government ownership and control. Such plans have already been suggested in Congress and there is every reason to believe that those pressures will continue where the Federal government will either purchase the foreign oil or will completely control all of the domestically produced oil on Federal land. With the control of the raw material necessary to make the oil industry run, the government can control the industry. Another example of pseudo socialism.

Super Free Enterprise.   Although unlikely, if Friedman's concepts are followed to their logical conclusion: the employees become the stockholders. There have been some cases both here and abroad of total worker/ownership of companies and from all reports they could be quite successful. In this case all of the profits of the corporation would be returned to the stockholders; i.e., the workers, and they would make the determinations as to future capital risks. Contrast this with today, where management really controls the bulk of the profits of the corporation and uses them for re-investment as they see fit.

National Free Enterprise. Corporate Japan is the model from which this alternate is drawn. The success of Japanese industry is largely attributed to the Ministry of International Trade and Industry (MITI). Its function for industrialization was to provide government as a vehicle for industry's protection, promotion and guidance. The example of MITI's role in the steel industry illustrates the approach to a National Free Enterprise. The Bessemer process developed in the mid 1800's for the mass production of steel was the foundation on which the rapid expansion of railways, steel ships, and the production of various types of industrial machinery was based. This was perhaps one of the more important events in the Industrial revolution of the Western world. However in Japan in the mid 19th century, newly formed private companies did not have the capability of developing the iron and steel industry on their own. Thus was established a steel mill owned and run by MITI. Thereafter their iron and steel industry came to be run entirely by private companies. After World War II, MITI stepped in again to provide the iron and steel industry with financing, raw materials and other resources so it could recover as quickly as possible from its complete devastation. Now steel made in Japan can be purchased in Detroit for less than that made in Pittsburgh.

SUMMARY

A re-look at Figure 11 raises the question of how fast and by what means do we move toward the ultimate sociologizing mode in which the corporation is run entirely for the benefit of society.

SELECTED SOURCE MATERIAL

1. Mitchell, Arnold, "Consumer Life Ways, 1975–1985," Center for the Study of Social Policy, Stanford Research Institute.
2. Gordon, Theodore, et al., "A Forecast of the Interaction Between Business and Society in the Next Five Years," R-21 Institute for the Future.

3. Steiner, george, "Strategic Managerial Planning," PEI Research Series.
4. Little, Dennis, et al., "Some Trends Likely to Affect American Society in the Next Several Decades," WP-16, Institute for the Future.
5. Anon., "What Next," Congressional Clearinghouse on the Future, Vol. 2, No. 6.
6. Kami, M. J., "Planning and Planners in the Age of Discontinuity," Address at Planning Conference, May, 1975, San Francisco.
7. Theobald, Robert, *Beyond Repair*, New Republic Book Company, 1976, Washington, DC.
8. _____, *Habit and Habitat*, Prentice-Hall, 1972.
9. _____, *An Alternate Future for the World*, Swallow Press, 1972.
10. Bell, Daniel, *The Coming of the Post-Industrial Society*, Basic Book, Inc., 1973.
11. Lundborg, L., *Future Without Shock*, W. W. Norton & Co., 1974.
12. Drucker, Peter, *Management*, Harper & Row, 1974.
13. _____, *The Age of Discontinuity*, Harper & Row, 1969.
14. McDonald, John, *The Game of Business*, Doubleday, 1975.
15. Coker, G. T., Miller, D. C., "Project Forethought—World Corporate Planners Confront the Future," Managerial Planning, PEI, October 1975.
16. Coker, G. T., "Project Forethought—Survey 1977," Address 1977 Planning Executives Institute International Meeting, Louisville, Kentucky.
17. _____, "Project Forethought—Survey 1977 Update," Address at PEI 23rd Corporate Planning Conference, September 1977, Houston, Texas.
18. Gappert, G., "Post Affluence," *Futurist*, 1974, Vol. 8, No. 5.
19. Kahn, H., *Things to Come*, MacMillan Co., 1972.
20. Wardell, N., "The Corporation," *Daedalus*, Winter 1978.

	National	State & Local
• Government		
Elected Officials	3,	
Congressional/White House Staffer's	537	525,000
Bureaucrats	13,000	?
	2.7 MM	11.5 MM
• Stockholders		
Individuals		
Groups — Funds (Mutuals, institutions, pensions, etc.)		
• Management		
• Employees		
• Suppliers	Society	
• Consumers		

FIGURE 1   Corporate Major Stakeholders

- Survival
- Security
- Acceptance
- Mastery
- Achievement
- Self-fulfillment
- Unfolding

FIGURE 2 Maslow's Hierarchy of Human Needs

- Changers
- Makers
- Preservers
- Takers
- Seekers
- Escapers

FIGURE 3 Life Way Classifications

- Maslow's Hierarchy of Human Needs
- Life Goals
- Sources of Meaning
- Sources of Truth
- Belief Systems
- Morality Categories
- Time Orientations

FIGURE 4 Elements Comprising Life Ways

	Hallmark	Goals
Changers	Out of Phase	Change System Excitement Recognition
Makers	Visible Achievement	Accomplishment Prosperity Power Recognition
Preservers	Reverence for Tradition	Status Quo Salvation Recognition
Takers	Me First	Security Pleasure Friendship
Seekers	Inner Search	Serenity Wisdom Accomplishment
Escapers	Flight from Reality	Happiness Freedom Pleasure

FIGURE 5   Life Ways Descriptors

Government

- Elected officials — Re-election

    Income redistribution
    Reaction to special interest groups
    Slow changes in life styles
    Cover-up fiscal irresponsibilities

- Congressional Staffers — Power and Influence

    Develop expertise
    Know inclinations and needs of boss
    Develop dependency

- Bureaucrats — Survive and Advance

    Support those with power and influence
    Increase staff

FIGURE 6   Future Needs and Desires

· Better Return on Investment

· Less Risk

FIGURE 7   Stockholders

Changers   — Fulfill a Vision

Makers   — Power and Recognition

Preservers — Survival with Recognition

FIGURE 8   Management Needs and Desires

Marketing Factors

1. Average consumer income too low to afford motor car
2. Those interested in car want different models and colors
3. Gasoline too expensive to make operation economical
4. An expensive network of sales rooms will be needed
5. Price will be high because volume potential small
6. Too many people have horses and buggies and would not want to change

Systems Factors

1. Available roads will not handle car
2. No garages to repair car
3. Tire life too short
4. Available metal will not stand road shock
   at 15–20 mph
5. Too few places to buy gasoline
6. Many cities have legal restrictions on motor car use

FIGURE 9   Model T Marketing Analysis

1977-1982

Income Protection (69%)
Educational Investment (66%)
Wealth Redistribution (52%)

A ←

Population Growth Rate (75%)
Quality of Manpower Services (75%)
Employment Mobility (74%)

B ↑

Rich-Poor Gap (33%)
State and Distribution of Housing (23%)
Population Growth Rate (22%)

C →

1982-1991

Income Protection (67%)
State of Health (64%)
Availability of Health Services (64%)

Population Distribution (68%)
Population Growth Rate (64%)
Quality of Manpower Services (64%)

Characteristics/Treatment of Offenders (46%)
Rich-Poor Gap (42%)
Family Stability and Cohesion (26%)

1991-2002

State of Health (56%)
Availability of Health Services (48%)
Value on Time (47%)

State and Distribution of Housing (69%)
Quality of Manpower Services (66%)
Adequacy of Housing Supply (65%)

Population Growth Rate (44%
Family Stability and Cohesion (38%)
Characteristics/Treatment of Offenders (38%)

FIGURE 10   Survey 1977 Concern Trends

More Goods and Services _____ ? _____ Quality of Life

Profit   Societal Responsibility   Solve Social Problems

Economizing   _____ ? _____   Sociologizing

Production and Profit   Life Time Jobs

                                                      Work Satisfaction

                                                      Social Problems

FIGURE 11   Societal and Corporate Goals

- Business as Usual
- Socialism
- Psuedo Socialism
- Super Free Enterprise
- National Free Enterprise

FIGURE 12   Alternative Corporation Futures

YORK UNIVERSITY
BOOKSTORES

C22155240001

D0024125202

R155X>$13.50